THE MOST TRUSTED NAME IN TRAVEL

Frommer's®

NEW YORK CITY 2027

12th Edition

By Pauline Frommer

FrommerMedia LLC

Frommer's New York City 2027, 12th Edition

Published by
FrommerMedia LLC

ISBN 978-1-62887-679-6 (paper), 978-1-62887-680-2 (e-book)

Editorial Director: Pauline Frommer
Editor: Melinda Quintero
Production Editor: Kelly Dobbs Henthorne
Cartographer: Andy Dolan
Photo Editor: Topaz Le Tourneau
Indexer: Kelly Dobbs Henthorne
Compositor: Lissa Auciello-Brogan
Cover Design: Dave Riedy

Front cover: Little Island public park with view of the World Trade Center.
Title page: Sunset over the Statue of Liberty.

For information on our other products or services, see www.frommers.com.

FrommerMedia LLC also publishes its books in a variety of electronic formats. Some content that appears in print may not be available in electronic formats.

Manufactured in Malaysia

5 4 3 2 1

HOW TO CONTACT US

In researching this book, we discovered many wonderful places—hotels, restaurants, shops, and more. We're sure you'll find others. Please tell us about them, so we can share the information with your fellow travelers in upcoming editions. If you were disappointed with a recommendation, we'd love to know that, too. Please write to: Support@FrommerMedia.com

FROMMER'S HEART RATINGS SYSTEM

Every hotel, restaurant and attraction listed in this guide has been ranked for quality and value. Here's what the hearts mean:

♥ Recommended
♥♥ Highly Recommended
♥♥♥ A must! Don't miss!

AN IMPORTANT NOTE

The world is a dynamic place. Hotels change ownership, restaurants hike their prices, museums alter their opening hours, and buses and trains change their routings. And all of this can occur in the several months after our authors have visited, inspected, and written about these hotels, restaurants, museums, and transportation services. Though we have made valiant efforts to keep all our information fresh and up-to-date, some few changes can inevitably occur in the periods before a revised edition of this guidebook is published. So please bear with us if a tiny number of the details in this book have changed. Please also note that we have no responsibility or liability for any inaccuracy or errors or omissions, or for inconvenience, loss, damage, or expenses suffered by anyone as a result of assertions in this guide.

CONTENTS

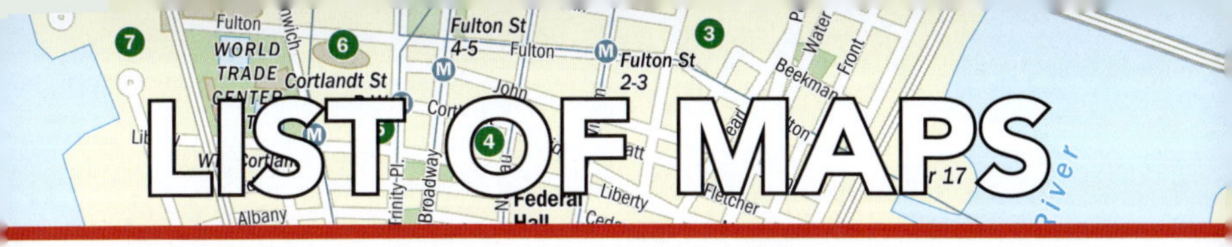
Fulton
WORLD TRADE
Cortlandt St
Fulton St
4-5
Fulton
Fulton St
2-3
John
Beekman
Water
Front
Trinity Pl.
Broadway
Liberty
Fletcher
Albany
River

LIST OF MAPS

ABOUT THE AUTHOR

Pauline Frommer is proud to be following in the footsteps of her father, the late Arthur Frommer. She is President of FrommerMedia LLC, the company he founded. The company publishes the Frommer's guidebooks, now in their 69th year. Pauline was also the original editor of Frommers.com, one of the first travel sites on the web. It, too, is part of FrommerMedia and receives more than 10 million page views per month. Pauline is the author of countless articles, and a number of award-winning guidebooks, including *Frommer's New York City Day by Day* and the upcoming *Frommer's New England*. She penned an internationally syndicated column on travel for King Features for more than a decade. In addition to writing, editing, and publishing, Pauline was the host of a nationally syndicated radio show on travel for more than 20 years and created travel segments for CNN's Headline News for 5 years. She currently hosts the Frommer's Travel Show Podcast, named one of the 13 best for travel by the *New York Times*. Pauline is married to Columbia University professor Mahlon Stewart, and the mother of two very well-traveled daughters.

Pauline dedicates this guide to the lovely people who shared a meal, a drink, or an attraction visit with her this year, making research that much more fun. They include Roberta Brodfeld, Mahlon Stewart, Veronica Stewart-Frommer, Beatrix Stewart-Frommer, Joel Fram, Adrien Glover, Kevin Cristaldi, Sumana and Raghu Rangachar, Lael Lowenstein, Gary Morris, Laura Nolan, Joel Ostrow, and Brent Heiggelke. I must also thank the stalwart, talented team at Frommers.com for keeping the online fires burning: Jason Cochran, Zac Thompson, and Bob Bosch, in particular. Onward ho!

THE BEST OF THE BIG APPLE

1

There's simply no place in the United States as brimming with opportunities as New York City. Those of us who live here open our doors to incredible options each and every day: the chance to experience the best and newest in the worlds of art, theater, dance, and music; the ability to feast on expertly prepared foods from all over the world; the belief that we can make our voices heard in this news media capital; and the opportunity to meet today's movers and shakers. The ambitious come here because they know that if they want to achieve a certain level of prominence, New York is the place to do it. (Are you humming "If I can make it there, I'll make it anywhere . . ." right now?)

There's a factual basis to this New Yorker's pride. Because of the density and diversity of our population; our long history as a center of commerce and ideas; our access to the United Nations, Wall Street, and the opinion makers of Madison Avenue; and endless other resources, there's simply more *more* here than in other places. And if that claim seems extreme, well, you'll just have to regard boastfulness as another unavoidable characteristic of "the Big Apple." What would we New Yorkers be without our big mouths?

In visiting New York, you, too, are opening yourself up to a world of wonderful opportunities. Yet that's what can make New York so intimidating to visitors: There are just so many darn choices. In this chapter, I've sorted through a book's worth of options, selecting some favorites to help you hit the city's highlights.

THE MOST unforgettable NEW YORK CITY EXPERIENCES

- **Seeing the City from on High:** It doesn't really matter if you do so from the **Empire State Building** (p. 203), **Summit One Vanderbilt** (p. 210), the **Edge at Hudson Yards** (p. 190), or one of the many other venues where one can get a bird's-eye view. What's really important is that you get a feeling for the immensity of the city, with Manhattan's wonderfully orderly grid system of streets (which plays off the hubbub on the streets themselves), and the dizzying variety of building types (many of which can't be adequately seen from the sidewalk). Try to get somewhere high early in your trip—there's no better way to orient yourself.

- **Walking the Brooklyn Bridge:** The bridge, too, offers glorious views of the city. But that's not the only reason you stroll here: Walking the span allows you to see this marvel of engineering up close. (It was the longest suspension bridge in the world when it was built in 1883.) See p. 164.
- **Tasting a Cuisine You've Never Tried Before:** Because one out of every four New Yorkers was born in a different country, the restaurant options here span the globe. That means you can taste foods in Gotham that you'd usually have to go to the other side of the planet to try—from Kosovar kebabs to lamb over hand-pulled noodles from the Uyghur region of China, from Burmese curries and Vietnamese pastries to South African stews, roast Bajan goat, and many, many more. See chapter 4.
- **Touring Ellis Island:** You'll see the **Statue of Liberty** (p. 172) first (also a thrill) and then spend several hours in the place so many of our ancestors passed through to settle in the "New World." Hearing the tales of what went on here is a tremendously moving experience. See p. 165.
- **Picnic in a Park:** On a sunny day, **Central Park** (p. 246), **Domino Park** (p. 255), **Brooklyn Bridge Park** (p. 254), and **Prospect Park** (p. 259) become a sea of sociability. Families, singles, seniors—everyone gathers in these green spaces to celebrate life. Join them, perhaps with some deli delights from **Zabar's** (p. 321), and you become an honorary New Yorker.
- **Going to a Big, Splashy Broadway Musical:** When they're done right—and they're not always—few experiences are as life-affirming (no, truly!) as

At the Edge observation deck in Hudson Yards (p. 190), glass walls afford lofty panoramic views of the city and beyond.

The walkway across the Brooklyn Bridge (p. 164) is justly popular, giving walkers stunning views up and down the East River plus a close-up look at the bridge's massive Gothic brownstone towers.

seeing ridiculously talented people sing and dance their hearts out in a show that makes you laugh, cry, and think about your own life story. See chapter 8.

- **Staying Out Late:** The city changes after dusk. All the people who were rushing by you during the day slow down and take to the city's bars, restaurants, and clubs to socialize. Even if you're not normally a nightlife person, try it while in NYC. If you're outgoing, you may be rewarded with some great conversations (despite its reputation, this is actually one of the friendliest cities on the planet); and if you're shy, well, the eavesdropping can be fascinating, too. See chapters 4 and 8.

THE best FREE NEW YORK ACTIVITIES

- **Visit a Museum for Free (or Nearly Free): P.S. 1** (p. 243), **The Museum at FIT** (p. 185), **The Museum of the American Indian** (p. 168), and the **American Folk Art Museum** (p. 223) are always free and always worth your time. A number of other top institutions allow free entry, or pay-what-you-wish, at certain times of the week. Fridays are free at the **New York Historical** (p. 228, 5–8pm), the **Morgan Library** (p. 207, 5–7pm), and at the **Whitney** (p. 183, 7–10pm). At the **Guggenheim** (p. 222), pay-what-you-wish hours are Tuesdays and Sundays from 4 to 5:30pm. Wednesdays are free all day at the **Museum of the City of New York** (p. 221) and between 1:30 and 5:30pm at the **Frick** (p. 213). Every day it's open, the **Cooper Hewitt** (p. 212) lets those who come after 5pm pay what they wish.

The **9/11 Museum** (p. 160) gives out some free tickets on Monday mornings on a first-come, first served basis. See chapter 5 for more.

- **Attend a TV Taping:** You'll get a behind-the-scenes peek at how Jimmy Fallon, Drew Barrymore, the *SNL* cast, and the other NYC-based TV stars work their magic. And you won't pay a cent more than you do to watch TV in your own home (less, in fact, if you pay for cable or streaming services)! See p. 352 for full details.
- **Take a Tour with a Big Apple Greeter:** Volunteers who love their hometown and love showing it to outsiders lead these unique tours. You'll need to sign up well in advance, but when you do, you'll be assigned a local with similar interests to yours who can show you the neighborhood of your choice. Possibly the best tours in the city and absolutely free. See p. 38.
- **Gallery-Hopping:** Wandering through NYC's galleries—the biggest concentration in the world—is an intellectually rich experience, as you explore the current zeitgeist of the art world, as expressed by hundreds of would-be Picassos. On some nights, you'll do it with a free glass of vino. The greatest concentrations of galleries are in Chelsea (p. 186), or you can combine a visit to the Sotheby's auction house with the museums of the Upper East Side (p. 178).
- **Ride the Staten Island Ferry:** The Staten Island Ferry is used daily by thousands of commuters. Ride it for a great view of the Statue of Liberty, Ellis Island, New York Harbor, and the lower Manhattan skyline. You can't beat the price: free. See p. 171.

Dip into the international art marketplace by browsing Sotheby's (p. 223). It is always free to visit.

Each season in New York brings its own kind of magic—here frosted trees sparkle above The Pond in Central Park. See p. 246 for yearly highlights.

- **Walk. Everywhere:** New York City is one of the world's greatest walking cities. Since most of Manhattan is planned on the grid system, it's hard to get lost in that borough (except below 4th St., where getting lost is part of the fun). Avenues go north and south; streets go east and west. You can actually walk the entire length of Manhattan—a walk that, done briskly, takes about 6 hours. That's a 13½-mile hike, by the way!

THE best WAYS TO SEE NEW YORK CITY LIKE A LOCAL

- **Do a Date Night at the Metropolitan Museum:** Friday and Saturday nights are when New Yorkers take over this storied museum. Wine, cocktails, and snacks are served in the Met's cafes; live music is performed in the galleries; and special tours and lectures are offered. It's very romantic and far less crowded than during the day. See p. 219.
- **Ride the Roosevelt Island Tram:** It may just be a 4-minute ride, but the views are spectacular, and you'll head to an island very few outsiders ever visit, home to the moving **FDR Four Freedoms Park.** See p. 206.
- **Get from Here to There by Citi Bike:** The city's bike-sharing program has shown locals just how much fun it is to get around on two wheels. Join them! The program is affordable, and thanks to all the new bike lanes in the city, getting around by bike is easier and safer than ever. See p. 387.

With many new bike lanes and easily accessible Citi Bike bike sharing (p. 387), it's easier than ever to explore the city on two wheels.

- **Do Brunch:** After dashing around all week, there's nothing we like better on the weekend than chowing down on avocado toast with poached eggs, in a restaurant with friends, and arguing about the week's news. See chapter 4.
- **Stand on Line for Shakespeare in the Park:** Shakespeare performed by stars, under the stars, in Central Park—for free! Even though you can put your name into an online lottery for tickets, every summer thousands of New Yorkers make a day out of waiting on line (and chatting, picnicking, and people-watching) for the tickets to be distributed. While you won't find a real New Yorker at Times Square on New Year's Eve, you will find lots of them on a summer's day waiting for the Bard. See p. 344.

Poke around the stalls at the four-day-a-week Union Square Greenmarket (p. 261) to get an idea of how Manhattanites go about their daily routines.

- **Browse the Greenmarket:** Union Square's farmers market has to be one of the best of its kind in the United States, especially on Saturdays, when it's jammed with vendors. You'll meet the farmers and get to sample all sorts of treats—from jams to artisanal wines to honey from a hive on a Brooklyn rooftop—when you wander through this bustling market. See p. 261.

THE best FAMILY EXPERIENCES

- **Central Park:** With its carousel, two zoos, two seasonal ice-skating rinks and pools, playgrounds, and ball fields, Central Park is a children's wonderland. See p. 246.
- **Bronx Zoo:** This sprawling wildlife park is one of the great zoos in the world, and you don't have to be a kid to love it. See p. 232.
- **Coney Island:** It's far grittier than Disney World, but for many that's a plus. Come here to taste the vintage pleasures of what was once New York City's favorite summer playground, including the landmarked Wonder Wheel and Cyclone roller coaster. Nearby is the **New York Aquarium** (p. 239), MCU Park (home of the minor league baseball team Brooklyn Cyclones), Nathan's Famous hot dogs, and, of course, the beach! See p. 236.
- **Climbing to the Crown of the Statue of Liberty:** You need to plan well ahead to get one of the limited tickets for this experience. But it's worth the effort because what's cooler than a boat ride, followed by a vertical hike up a twisting staircase, with the reward of a spectacular view? Kids over 6 will love this one. See p. 173.

At the heart of the Rockefeller Center complex, the iconic gilded statue of Prometheus presides over Rockefeller Plaza.

In summer in Central Park, storytelling sessions take place weekly at this beloved statue of Hans Christian Anderson next to the Conservatory Water boat pond (p. 251).

- **Museum of the Moving Image:** Make your own photo flipbook, dub your voice over Julie Andrews's in a clip from *Mary Poppins,* or play classic video games from the 1980s together. This highly interactive museum—dedicated to the craft of making movies, TV shows, and video games—is a blast for people of all ages. See p. 242.
- **Rockefeller Center:** Home to three highly interactive toy stores (Lego, Nintendo, and F.A.O. Schwartz), the FDNY Fire Zone (with hands-on activities to teach fire safety), an observation deck, and a famous ice-skating/roller-skating rink, this majestic city-within-a-city is a surprisingly tot-friendly scene. That's especially true in December, when the dazzling Christmas tree is up and the Rockettes are kicking up their heels at Radio City Music Hall. See p. 197.

THE best OFFBEAT NEW YORK EXPERIENCES

- **Ride the International Express:** The no. 7 train is known as the "International Express." Take it through the borough of Queens (where it runs aboveground for most of its length), and you will pass one ethnic neighborhood after another, from Indian to Thai, from Peruvian to Colombian, from Chinese to Korean. See p. 241.
- **Head to a Russian Nightclub:** At **Tatiana** (p. 369) or one of Brighton Beach's other supper clubs, you get a multicourse feast and a show in Russian featuring acrobats, showgirls, and lots and lots of feathers. It's a wacky way to spend the evening.

- **Attend a Learned Lecture . . . in a Bar:** Hottest new nightlife trend? Heady talks by real experts (on physics, anthropology, political science in more) held in bars. No joke: They sell out weeks in advance (p. 352).
- **Costume Yourself and Go Dancing:** Head to the **House of Yes** (p. 371) where most of the nights are theme nights, meaning you become part of the cast of the nightly show (those with the best outfits get tickets for free drinks on the way in).
- **Spend an Evening in a Historic Cemetery:** Green-Wood Cemetery (p. 237) has a more jam-packed evening schedule than many of the city's clubs, as locals flock to concerts in the catacombs, "Death Cafes," night-time art exhibits, and more.
- **Join the Artsy Crowd at a Gallery Opening:** When an exhibit premiers at a NYC art gallery, not only is everyone allowed to come to the party, you'll often get a free glass of wine to sip as you wander around looking at the paintings and sculptures. And since NYC has more galleries than any other city on earth, these shindigs happen regularly. See p. 342.

NEW YORK'S best MUSEUMS

- **Best All-Around Museum: The Metropolitan Museum of Art.** It's a case of more is more; the largest museum in the Americas is also the finest museum-going experience in New York. How could it not be, with the variety of treasures this fabled institution holds—from an actual ancient Egyptian temple to murals from a Pompeian villa to masterworks by Rembrandt, Vermeer, van Gogh, and on and on? See p. 219.
- **Best Museum for Understanding Today's World:** The **American Museum of Natural History**'s Gilder Center for Science, Education, and Technology takes a clear-eyed, compelling look at the interconnectedness of the world's ecosystems and the effects climate change is having on our planet. See p. 224.
- **Best History Museum: The Tenement Museum.** Usually, historic sites tell the tales of the rich and powerful. This tiny museum recalls a more moving story: that of immigrants who made their first "New World" homes in this actual tenement. Visiting here is an emotionally powerful experience. See p. 180.
- **Best New York Museum About New York: The Museum of the**

In every gallery at the vast Metropolitan Museum of Art (p. 219), you may stumble upon unexpected treasures.

At the Museum of the City of New York, exhibits of colonial artifacts show how early settlers persisted on this rock-bound New World island, ensuring its future as a dynamic hub of commerce.

City of New York. This savvy museum uses the lens of biography to tell the story of the city and its vibrant people. Through artifacts, state-of-the-art interactive panels, and a gangbuster half-hour-long film, you'll meet the men and women, famous and obscure, who shaped the city into the vital force it is today. See p. 221.

- **Best Museum for Hipsters: The Whitney.** This iconic home of American art has a party vibe, thanks to its location (right next to the High Line, NYC's coolest park); its hours (later than the others on weekends); and its in-your-face exhibits, which don't shy away from the raunchy or the political. See p. 183.
- **Best Home Posing as a Museum: The Louis Armstrong House Museum.** This unassuming house in Queens was Satchmo's home for almost 30 years, and it's been preserved almost exactly as it was when he died in 1971. See p. 240.
- **Best Bite-Sized Art Museum: The Frick.** The Frick is home to an unrivaled collection that focuses on quality over quantity, making visitors feel that they've discovered a secret art haven. See p. 213.

THE best NEW YORK CITY BUILDINGS

- **Best Skyscraper: The Chrysler Building.** Its sleek hood-ornament spire is as jaunty as ever, a heartening site to behold. Alas, the Chrysler has no observation deck, but this Art Deco masterpiece can be viewed from outside

When asked, most New Yorkers would name the Art Deco spire of the Chrysler Building (p. 202) as their favorite Manhattan skyscraper, seen here above Grand Central Terminal.

or from nearby observation decks, such as the Empire State Building's. See p. 202.

- **Best Historic Building: Grand Central Terminal.** A Beaux Arts gem, this iconic railroad station, built in 1913, was restored in the 1990s to its original brilliance. I recommend taking a building tour here. See p. 205.
- **Most Impressive Place of Worship: Cathedral of St. John the Divine.** Construction began on the world's largest Gothic cathedral in 1892—and it's still going. This is one structure that benefits from being a work in progress. See p. 226.
- **Most Fun Building to "Decipher": The Museum of the American Indian.** Every sculpture on this building, including four by Daniel Chester French (creator of the Lincoln Monument in Washington, D.C.), has a story to tell. See p. 168 to learn what those stories are.
- **Best for Contemporary Architecture Fans: The Oculus Transportation Hub.** Created by Spanish "starchitect" Santiago Calatrava, the Oculus is meant to look like—and kinda does—a hand releasing a dove. Pop inside for a selfie against a ribbed ceiling that's higher than any cathedral's. See p. 24 for more.

THE best NEW YORK CITY PARKS

- **Central Park:** One of the world's great urban refuges, Central Park has inspired city parks across the United States and abroad. It remains a center of calm and tranquility on this clamorous island. See p. 246.
- **Prospect Park:** The *other* masterwork by Frederick Law Olmsted and Calvert Vaux (designers of Central Park), Brooklyn's great green space offers a delightful exercise in compare and contrast. See p. 259.
- **The High Line:** Located in the Meatpacking District of Manhattan, this quirky, handsome park was once an elevated track for freight trains. It's immensely popular and a good object lesson in how New York City is constantly reinventing itself. See p. 257.
- **Little Island:** Set atop tulip-shaped piers, this floating island has superb views of lower Manhattan, an amphitheater that hosts genuinely intriguing performances in summer, and several different gardens for lounging. One of the city's newest must sees. See p. 258.

The High Line (p. 257), a park built on a former elevated railroad track, snakes between apartments and warehouses for 1½ miles.

- **Domino Park:** Set on the grounds of what was once the largest sugar refinery on the planet, the park artfully incorporates many of the industrial artifacts that were left behind. It also offers sweeping views of Manhattan, lots of activities for young and old, and a really great collection of eateries and drinkeries for those who want to linger. See p. 255.

THE best NEIGHBORHOODS TO STROLL IN NEW YORK CITY

- **Greenwich Village:** With its historic winding streets, cozy restaurants, and eccentric characters, Greenwich Village lives up to its reputation. See p. 289.
- **Chinatown:** You don't so much stroll here as elbow your way through crowds, peer in the windows of herbal medicine stores and jewelry marts, and fend off counterfeit-bag sellers. But if I've made this sound like a drag, I've done my job poorly; despite its teeming streets, Chinatown is fascinating to explore. See p. 36.
- **Brooklyn Heights:** This was the very first designated historic district in New York City, and you'll understand why when you stroll through its blocks of pristine 19th-century row houses, brownstones, and mansions.

Just across the East River from Manhattan, the landmarked neighborhood of Brooklyn Heights features block after block of pristine town houses.

Plus, there is no better view of Manhattan and New York Harbor than from the Heights' famous promenade. See p. 41.

- **Brighton Beach and Coney Island:** Explore the all-Slavic, seedy but fascinating Brighton Beach first, with its stores selling Russian nesting dolls, elaborate samovars, and all sorts of Russian and Ukrainian food items. (***Note:*** All the residents of this neighborhood have been horrified by Putin's war in Ukraine, no matter what their background. So don't avoid the Russian businesses here; there's a reason their owners left Russia). Then hit the boardwalk and walk half a mile to the classic, if definitely gritty, fun fest that is Coney Island. See p. 41.
- **The Upper East Side:** Madison Avenue from the upper 60s to the mid-80s is still one of the best window-shopping stretches on the planet. When you get tired of staring at overpriced baubles, you can duck into the side streets between Fifth Avenue and Madison for an array of historic town houses just as dazzling. See p. 40.
- **Harlem:** Harlem encompasses a large area where historic homes, lovingly preserved, abound. I think you'll be impressed by the architectural beauty, but beyond that, by the local spirit, which you'll experience in the area's restaurants, bars, churches, and stores. See walking tour, p. 280.
- **Williamsburg:** Brooklyn's hipster haven is a delight to stroll, less for the architecture (this was originally a very industrial area), and more for the astounding diversity of its shops, bars, and dining spots. See p. 41.

THE best FOOD

- **Best Cheap Eats:** Most New Yorkers would agree that pizza is Gotham's top cheap meal (especially considering that many pizzerias have charming settings and serve wine, beer, and/or cocktails). The difficulty comes in choosing which place is best . . . so I won't. Instead, for a steal of a meal try **DiFara Pizza** (classic New York), **Una Pizza Napoletana** (Neapolitan), or **Scarr's Pizza** (the beef pepperoni is exceptional). See p. 120 for descriptions of them all.
- **Best Splurge:** This is a tough one, but I'll have to go with the delicious tasting menu at **Aska** (p. 144). Its nouveau Scandinavian fare features many items that were foraged right outside the city and aren't usually considered edible (I'm looking at you, lichen). Service is unhurried and extremely warm, and tables are set a civilized distance apart. A truly grown-up and exciting culinary adventure.
- **Most Romantic Restaurant:** With its 1950s era decor and menu (checked table cloths, inlaid wood walls, floating Alaska!) dining at **Le Veau d'Or** (p. 138) is the best type of time travel. The pampering staff make sure this is a perfect place for proposals and couples' nights.
- **Most Family-Friendly Restaurant for Those with Kids over the Age of 8:** Let the kids cook for once. At **Shabu Tatsu** (p. 104) they can swish-cook their meats and vegetables in boiling water (set in the middle of the table) until they've created a savory noodle soup. Tons of fun.

The experience of cooking a meal right at the table makes a dinner at Shabu Tatsu (p. 104) a fun outing for families.

- **Most Family-Friendly Restaurant for Those with Kids Under 8: Serendipity 3** (p. 141) is an old-fashioned ice cream parlor, with a number of savory dishes. Kids love it, even if they don't get the nostalgia.
- **Best Pre-Broadway Show Restaurant:** For a cheap, quick, and mighty tasty feed try **Los Tacos No. 1** (p. 128). For a celebratory meal, head to **Le Bernardin** (p. 124). And if you want to feel like part of the city's theater community (and maybe spot a celebrity, or two), go to **Joe Allen** (p. 126).
- **Best Place to Go with a Group:** A dim sum brunch at **Jing Fong** (p. 94) is always a crowd-pleaser. Tables are large and round, so everyone can join the conversation, and with a group you get to try more of the delicacies being wheeled by, as all dishes are shareable.
- **Best Place to Go for Dancing and Dining: Sammy's Romanian** (p. 95) is a hoot: a steakhouse that channels your neighbor's bar mitzvah, down to a droll guy at the piano cracking jokes and urging diners to get up and dance the hora (everyone does).
- **Most Glamorous Gotham Dining Experience:** Rockefeller Center's **Le Rock** (p. 129), with its cathedral height ceilings and Art Deco finesse, is Gotham's finest "impress your date" venue.

From wide slices overhanging paper plates to delicate wood-fired pies topped with foraged herbs, New York City has a pizza for every taste and occasion.

- **Best Meal with a View:** Brooklyn's **Laser Wolf** (p. 133), has jaw-dropping across-the-river views of Manhattan. Multiple appetizers are included in the cost of an entree, for a meal that would feel special on the ground floor.
- **Best Places to Share Food:** At Middle Eastern restaurants **Eyval** (p. 149) and **Shukette** (p. 120), going in a group helps you avoid FOMO: meals consist of small share plates, and more diners allow for more variety.
- **Best Old-School NYC Dining:** We have two recommendations, both of which, bizarrely, opened in the past 6 years. **S&P** (p. 133) offers a luncheonette experience so classic, it feels lifted from an Edward Hopper painting. And the food is fab! On the other end of the price scale, **Gage & Tollner** (p. 144) with its suited waiters and a landmarked Victorian interior, would be still recognizable to Mae West, Fanny Brice, Diamond Jim Brady, and the other big names who ate here in its original heyday. It's a splendidly evocative time capsule, just reopened in 2021.

The Art Deco bar at the glamorous French restaurant Le Rock (p. 129).

THE best CULTURE & NIGHTLIFE IN NEW YORK

- **Best for Classic Concerts: The New York Philharmonic.** Regular performances by the top soloists in the world, in a hall with exquisite acoustics, make the NY Phil a must for classical music buffs. See p. 339.
- **Best Children's Theater: The New Victory Theater.** Savvy programmers bring in top children's productions from around the globe, from circus shows to plays and dance to performance art. See p. 336.
- **Best Jazz Club: The Village Vanguard.** It's the real thing. All of the greats have performed here, and because of the Vanguard's savvy bookers, this is where the current generation's stars (often up-and-coming) play, too. See p. 350.
- **Best Gay Bar: The Monster.** Sure, the overall scene is hotter in Hell's Kitchen than it is in the Village nowadays. But men have rediscovered this classic Village bar in the last few years and are flocking to its weekend tea dances and second-floor piano bar. See p. 374.
- **Best Comedy Club: Caveat.** Not your typical stand-up club, Caveat builds most of its shows around such heady topics as bioengineering, public

policy, and art history, bringing in hilarious performers (often moonlighting scientists and other wonks) to explain complex concepts in the funniest ways imaginable or to lead audience participation games on these topics. A good time! See p. 351.

- **Best Off-Broadway Theater: The Public Theater.** *Hamilton* started life at this storied playhouse. Need I say more? See p. 337.
- **Best Cocktail Bar: Broken Shaker.** This one's a close race, because the bartenders at this joint are friends with the mixologists of Death and Company, Apotheke, PDT, Mace, and Employees Only, and they all swap recipes. But I'm going out on a limb to say that the cocktails at this Flatiron District rooftop bar are both the most balanced and the most inventive. See p. 358.

The New York Philharmonic presents performances in Lincoln Center and on Central Park's Great Lawn during the summer.

- **Best Speakeasy: PDT.** Hidden behind a secret panel in the phone booth of an East Village hot dog stand, PDT (it stands for Please Don't Tell) serves some of the most expertly and creatively mixed cocktails in the city, in a hidden space that feels oh-so-exclusive. See p. 360.
- **Best Dive Bar: Dublin House.** Need a shot of whiskey at 10am in a place where no one will bat an eye? Head to this old-fashioned Irish pub that started life as a speakeasy in the 1920s (and doesn't look like it's been redecorated since the 1960s). See p. 366.
- **Best Hotel Bar: Bemelmans Bar in the Carlyle.** It's not a cheap experience, but enjoying an excellent jazz trio, Manhattan in hand, in this hoity-toity Upper East Side watering hole is one of those experiences that seems taken right from an episode of *Mad Men*. Classic. See p. 366.

One of the city's toniest drinking spots is Bemelmans Bar (p. 366), in the Carlyle hotel.

SUGGESTED ITINERARIES & NEIGHBORHOODS

2

How fast time flies on a visit to New York! With so many world-famous sights, the job of organizing a day of touring can be a daunting task. That's why I've placed this chapter early in the book. In it, I suggest several workable ways to organize your time. Each one hits many of the "bucket list" sights (and some of the lesser-known ones). And each one, I hope, will lead to an enjoyable New York vacation. Along the way, I'll also explain how NYC is laid out and what you'll find in the various neighborhoods, so that if you decide to skip these suggested itineraries, you'll be able to create a logical itinerary based on your own interests.

ICONIC NYC IN 1 DAY

If you have just 1 day in New York, you have my condolences. The first thing you'll want to do is slam your shoe into your rear end for allowing far too little time to experience the city. When you're done with that, try the following itinerary. ***Start:*** *34th Street and Fifth Avenue.*

---

1 The Empire State Building

Start your day with a King Kong's–eye view of the city. It will help you immensely to understand the layout and is a heckuva lot of fun (pre-purchase one of the first timed tickets of the day). See p. 203.

Walk uptown on Fifth Avenue, until you get to:

2 New York Public Library

You'll recognize this building by the lion sculptures guarding its gates. Step inside to see the grand interior and the free film about the library's collections; usually one or two free exhibits will be on display, drawn from the library's vast collections. See p. 208 for more.

The Statue of Liberty (p. 172) raises her torch above her own island in New York Harbor.

Iconic New York in 1, 2, or 3 Days
Iconic NYC in 1 Day
1 The Empire State Building
2 New York Public Library
3 Rockefeller Center
4 Grand Central Terminal
5 Oyster Bar
6 The Metropolitan Museum
7 Times Square
Iconic NYC in 2 Days
1 Statue of Liberty and Ellis Island
2 Wall Street
3 Kesté Pizza e Vino
4 The Oculus
5 9/11 Memorial and Museum
6 Washington Square Park
Iconic NYC in 3 Days
1 The Dakota
2 Central Park
3 American Museum of Natural History
4 Cathedral of St. John the Divine
5 Lincoln Center
"Take a Break" stop
0 1/2 mi
0 0.5 km
COLUMBIA UNIVERSITY
W. 110th St.
HARLEM
CENTRAL PARK
Amsterdam Ave.
Columbus Ave.
W. 96th St.
E. 96th St.
W. 86th St.
E. 86th St.
UPPER WEST SIDE
Central Park West
W. 79th St.
E. 79th St.
UPPER EAST SIDE
W. 72nd St.
Strawberry Fields
E. 72nd St.
Broadway
The Dairy
Madison Ave.
Park Ave.
Lexington Ave.
5th Ave.
W. 57th St
E. 57th St.
QUEENS
Radio City Music Hall
MIDTOWN EAST
E. 50th St.
St. Patrick's Cathedral
MIDTOWN WEST
TIMES SQUARE
Chrysler Building
W. 42nd St.
E. 42nd St.
HUDSON YARDS
MURRAY HILL
8th Ave.
W. 34th St
E. 34th St
GARMENT DISTRICT
Ave. of the Americas (6th Ave.)
GRAMERCY PARK
W. 23rd St.
E. 23rd St
7th Ave.
CHELSEA
FLATIRON DISTRICT
Union Square
East River
Hudson River
W. 14th St.
E. 14th St.
MEATPACKING DISTRICT
EAST VILLAGE
NEW JERSEY
GREENWICH VILLAGE
NOHO
Hudson St.
W. Houston St.
E. Houston St.
SOHO
NOLITA
LOWER EAST SIDE
Delancey St.
Canal St.
LITTLE ITALY
TRIBECA
CHINATOWN
Fulton St.
Federal Hall
New York Stock Exchange
U.S. Custom House
Battery Park
Castle Clinton Nat'l Monument
BROOKLYN
(See inset map at left)
FINANCIAL DISTRICT
Battery Park
Castle Clinton Nat'l Monument
Hudson River
East River
ELLIS ISLAND
Statue of Liberty
LIBERTY ISLAND
GOVERNORS ISLAND

Continue walking uptown until you get to 48th Street, home to:

3 Rockefeller Center

Scores of complexes across the United States house a mix of offices and arts buildings, but none have the visual wallop of Rockefeller Center. That's partly because of the harmony and grandeur of the Art Deco skyscrapers and partly because there's always so much to see and do here. You may just have time to stroll around, or, if you could, skate in the rink (ice skating in winter, roller skating in summer—skates are available for rent). I'd also recommend the tour of **Radio City Music Hall.** Since you've just come from the Empire State Building, it doesn't make sense to go to the **Top of the Rock,** the observation deck of the RCA Building in Rockefeller Center (but do so if you skipped stop #1). See p. 197 for Rockefeller Center details.

Radio City Music Hall (p. 200) is just one of several only-in-New York sights in Rockefeller Center, the "city within a city."

If you have time, stroll uptown on Fifth Avenue for primo window-shopping. Otherwise, hop a bus, or walk back downtown to 42nd and Fifth Avenue, then east until you get to:

4 Grand Central Terminal

Before stepping into the station, take a look east toward Lexington Avenue, and up, up, up you'll see the famed scalloped spire of the **Chrysler Building.** Then enter the terminal, one of the most justifiably famous train stations in the world. If you're there at 11am, take the tour for insights into the building's architecture and decor. See p. 202 for more.

5 Grand Central Terminal for Lunch

Head downstairs to the classic **Oyster Bar** (p. 132) if you're ready for lunch (take a peek even if you're not—it's a lovely space). If you're not a seafood fan, you have other good food court options at Grand Central.

In the station are the 4, 5, and 6 subway trains. Grab the 5 or 6 (they're the express trains) and head uptown to 86th Street. When you exit, walk west toward Central Park and then downtown until you come to:

6 The Metropolitan Museum

Since this is the largest museum in this hemisphere, and a wondrous one at that, you're going to spend the rest of the afternoon here. See p. 219.

Return to the subway station and take a downtown train back to 42nd Street, where you'll hop the S train to:

7 Times Square

Try to get your first glimpse of this famed square after the sun has set, when all the lights are glittering. Otherwise, it looks a bit, well, tawdry. But when it's aglow and the crowds are pulsing, it can feel like the most exciting place on the planet. Hopefully, you've gotten theater tickets in advance, the perfect capper for a day on the town. See p. 201. Depending on the timing of the show, you can eat early (see p. 123 for choices) or eat later, at the classic post-show eatery **Joe Allen** (p. 126, where the actors themselves often come after their shows).

ICONIC NYC IN 2 DAYS

Spend your first day on the whirlwind tour above; on the second day, head downtown to see where the city began, along with Lady Liberty and downtown's most sobering, but popular, sight: Ground Zero. ***Start:*** *Subway: 1 to South Ferry or 4 or 5 to Bowling Green.*

1 Statue of Liberty & Ellis Island

Whether or not you'll get to tour both depends on how early you can get to the ferry terminal and how large the crowds are. If you've scored advance tickets to go up to the crown or the museum, that's a good reason

SOME THINGS not to do IN NYC

Despite what you may have heard, the following experiences are best avoided:

New Year's Eve in Times Square: You won't find any New Yorkers in this crowd. They know better than to show up hours before the ball drops (there's no set time, but revelers have been known to show up at 6am) and stand around all day long in a massive crowd of people, with few eating options nearby and even fewer bathroom facilities. Did I mention they don't allow open champagne or other alcoholic drinks EVER on the streets of New York (and definitely not in Times Square that night)? 'Nuf said.

Chain Restaurants: Yes, we have them. But why would you eat at a place you can find in your hometown when right next door to these chains are restaurants lovingly created by some of the most talented chefs in the nation? And I'm not just speaking of haute cuisine! We have some of the most wonderful cheap eats, too, so don't resort to Mickey D's. You're missing a great opportunity if you do. See chapter 4.

Driving: Most New Yorkers don't own cars. They know that the traffic is impossible, finding affordable parking even more so, and one can get anywhere, much more quickly, on the subway, by loaner bike, or by walking. So don't drive yourself crazy by bringing your own car to Gotham. If you must get around in a private car, hail a cab or get an Uber (p. 379). Getting around that way will be cheaper than paying for parking or anteing up the new congestion fees charged for driving in midtown and downtown.

to get off at Liberty Island. But if the stars aren't aligned or you miss the first ferry of the day, take in the view of Lady Liberty from the ferry (without disembarking) so you can spend the bulk of your time at Ellis Island, the famed portal to the "New World" for millions of immigrants. See p. 172 and p. 165.

2 Wall Street

Return to Manhattan and walk uptown to the Financial District. Along the way you'll see structures such as **Castle Clinton National Monument** in Battery Park—it's what's left of a fort built in 1808 to defend New York Harbor against the British—and the impressive **U.S. Customs House,** which houses the **Museum of the American Indian** (p. 168). Once on Wall Street, stop for a photo-op at the **Federal Hall National Memorial** (p. 277), where George Washington took the oath of office as our first president (his statue is in front), and the **New York Stock Exchange,** across the street. Unfortunately, the Exchange is no longer open for tours. We have a complete, self-guided tour of this area on p. 266, but if you're planning on doing the 9/11 Museum (see below) you will not have enough time for our 2-hour tour.

Walk uptown and toward the river to the corner of Fulton and Anne St. There you'll find:

3 Kesté Pizza e Vino

This little restaurant serves some of the best pizza in NYC—and that's saying a LOT. You should be able to walk in during the daylight hours without a reservation. Very good gluten-free pies are available if you can't stomach the classic Neapolitan pizza served here. See p. 120.

Walk inland on Fulton until you get to:

4 The Oculus

Pop in to see this architectural marvel, designed by Santiago Calatrava to resemble a bird in flight. It's filled with shops and subway lines; if you're not in a buying mood, simply take a quick look from the top level.

Exit the way you came in and walk around the structure, following the signs to:

5 9/11 Memorial & Museum

Be sure to get advance tickets, as the line for day-of-entry admission to the museum can be long (and that's on top of the 20 min. it takes to get through security). Still, the opportunity to pay your respects to those who perished, and to see this moving museum and memorial, is not to be missed. Expect to spend at least 3 hours here. See p. 160.

Exit the site and head east toward Broadway and Fulton Street, to the Fulton Street subway stop. There, you'll hop a 4 or 5 train to 14th Street/Union Square, where you'll get off and walk downtown 7 blocks to:

6 Washington Square Park

As the sun starts to set, head to this carnival of a park, where street musicians are always performing and crowds of Villagers and NYU students gather. Spend some time relaxing here before heading somewhere in the vicinity for a terrific dinner. You have many options: The restaurants downtown and those a short subway ride away in Brooklyn are the best in the city. See chapter 4 for suggestions.

ICONIC NYC IN 3 DAYS

If you've followed the first 2 days' suggested itineraries, you've experienced a slice of the best of Manhattan, but there's still plenty to see (more than can be done in just 3 days, sadly). Note that this day should only be attempted if the weather is nice. If not, head inside to one or two of the city's great museums. ***Start:*** *Subway B or C to 72nd Street.*

1 The Dakota

The day begins in front of this 1884 French Renaissance–style apartment building (corner of 72nd St. and Central Park West). Besides being used for several films, the Dakota is in many ways a shrine for visitors, as this is where musician John Lennon lived (and where his widow Yoko Ono still lives) and where he was shot and killed in 1980. After seeing the building, head across the street to Central Park and **Strawberry Fields,** named in honor of the former Beatle; fans often gather to leave flowers, play music, and commune together. See p. 252.

Strawberry Fields, near the 72nd entrance to Central Park on the Upper West Side, still attracts Beatles fans who leave flowers and memorials for John Lennon.

2 Central Park

Wander deeper into the park. If you keep walking straight from Strawberry Fields, you'll hit the park's grand promenade area and boat pond. Another option is to take one of the Central Park Conservancy's terrific tours; head toward **The Dairy** (p. 251) if that's your plan. For more on what else to see in the park—which will easily occupy the rest of your morning (unless the weather is uncooperative)—see p. 246.

Make your way back to the west side of the park and exit at 81st Street. Walk west to Columbus Avenue and walk downtown 1 block to:

3 American Museum of Natural History

This is one of the country's greatest science museums. I highly recommend the tours led by well-trained docents of the museum's highlights.

Classical music, opera, ballet, theater, film—the Lincoln Center (p. 339) performing arts complex has it all, and it's a great way to end your sightseeing day.

If you'd rather go it alone, enter through the new Gilder Center (an architectural marvel), see the awe-inspiring insect exhibit and then head to Fossils Hall, which has the world's largest dinosaur collection. By the way, the museum has recently improved its food offerings (especially at the Restaurant at the Gilder Center), so make the most of your time by simply lunching here. See p. 224 for more.

Exit the museum and walk west to Amsterdam Avenue to catch an uptown M11 bus. Get off at 110th Street.

4 Cathedral of St. John the Divine

On the east side of Amsterdam Avenue is the world's largest Gothic cathedral and a sight that's overlooked by too many tourists. Construction began in 1892, but because the builders are using medieval techniques, it's still unfinished. Tours are offered of the spectacular interior, or you can see it on your own (p. 226).

Walk to the subway at 116th Street and Broadway and take the 1 train down to 66th Street, which will put you right in front of:

5 Lincoln Center

Attending a performance at this iconic arts complex is always a grand experience, whether you're going to the opera, seeing ballet, listening to a symphony, or heading slightly downtown to Columbus Circle for Jazz at Lincoln Center. See p. 339 for your many options here. You should have time to grab dinner at either **Tatiana** (p. 134, right in Lincoln Center) or another Upper West Side restaurant (p. 134) before the show.

THE HIGHLIGHTS OF BROOKLYN IN A DAY

Until what Brooklyn residents call "the great mistake of 1898," this borough was its own city. If it were to break off from NYC, it would be the fourth largest city in the United States, with some 2.6 million residents. This is a long way of saying: You're not going to be able to see it all in 1 day. But the following itinerary will give you a taste of a few of its top sights and experiences. ***Note:*** This itinerary is best done Wednesday through Sunday, when both the Brooklyn Museum and Brooklyn Botanic Garden are open. ***Start:*** *Subway 2 or 3 to Grand Army Plaza.*

1 Tom's Restaurant

If anyone tries to tell you that New Yorkers aren't patriotic, take them to Tom's, which sports more American flags per square inch than most places in the country. It also serves up a now-rare New York treat: egg creams (like a milkshake, but fizzy and less sweet). Pair one of those, or a coffee, with their famous lemon poppy pancakes and you'll be well-fueled for a busy day. See p. 154.

Head toward St. John's Place on Washington Avenue and then continue another 2 blocks, crossing Eastern Parkway to:

2 Brooklyn Botanic Garden

A scenic way to start your explorations, the BBG is among the most important public gardens in the United States. Home to one of the first Japanese gardens in this hemisphere, it also features a Shakespeare

The Japanese pond in the Brooklyn Botanic Garden exudes a Zen-like serenity.

garden (plants commemorated in the Bard's works), a section devoted to native flora, and an eco-conscious visitor's center with a "living roof" that's seeded with dozens of species. Depending on the season, the gardens open at either 8am or 10am (p. 233), so plan accordingly.

Exit where you entered and follow the signs to:

3 Brooklyn Museum

If NYC didn't have the Metropolitan, *this* would be considered the city's most important museum. It has masterworks from almost every era of human history, and an Egyptian department that's considered finer than the Met's. Spend the rest of the morning and early afternoon taking in the wonders here; grab lunch at one of the museum's darn good eateries. See p. 234 for more.

Jump on the 2 or 3 train in the direction of Manhattan, but get off at Atlantic Ave./Barclays Center, and change in that station to the G train going toward Queens, getting off at Metropolitan Avenue. Walk toward the elevated highway, go under it, and follow Metropolitan Avenue until you hit Bedford Avenue. Turn left and stroll 2 blocks to:

4 Grand Street & Domino Park

Turn right on Grand. You'll find a delightful mix of shops, bars, and restaurants on most every street in Williamsburg, but on Grand Street they're entirely local, one-of-a-kind enterprises of the type that reward lingering and/or browsing. As you slowly walk toward the Hudson River and Domino Park (turn right when you get to Grand), be sure to pop into some of the fantastic stores that line Grand and its side streets. These include a good dozen vintage clothing stores, tea shops, homewares stores, and handmade jewelry ateliers. Then take some time to explore the fabulous **Domino Park** (p. 255).

5 A Brooklyn Dinner

You have a wealth of choices for where to have a spectacular dinner, though you'll stand a better chance of getting a table if you make advance reservations. Easiest would be to stay in Williamsburg and head to either **Aska** (p. 144), **Lilia Restaurant** (p. 149), **Eyval** (p. 149), or **Roberta's** (p. 121), which has a branch right at the park. Or you might make your way to downtown Brooklyn for a meal in the fabulous time machine known as **Gage & Tollner** (p. 144).

NYC FOR FAMILIES

The key to enjoying NYC with kids is to take it easy and choose a hotel outside of the overcrowded Times Square area. Many youngsters find the incessant bustle of midtown, and the city in general, tiring (as do adults!). So, choose a hotel in a more residential area (the Upper West Side is a good choice). Also, build a lot of free time into your itinerary, especially if the kids are under the age of 8. Here's what this mom recommends for a 3-day visit.

Day 1: Boats, a Big Statue & Another Boat

What kid doesn't love a boat ride? You'll start day 1 on the very first ferry of the day heading across the Hudson River to visit the **Statue of Liberty** (p. 172). Get advance tickets, so you can climb up to either the pedestal or, even better, the crown (the latter is a narrow, winding staircase that most kids will find to be a great adventure). If your young ones are over the age of 8, continue to **Ellis Island** (p. 165); it was the point of entry for millions of immigrants, and older children will find the stories of how they were processed, with some turned away, both fascinating and moving. Once back on the isle of Manhattan, hop the 4, 5 or 6 subway train to Canal Street for lunch in Chinatown. Then hop the nearest subway to 42nd Street (any trains going uptown will stop there) and switch to the M42 bus going west to the **Intrepid Sea, Air & Space Museum** (p. 192). Set on a 40,000-ton aircraft carrier, it has all kinds of fun flight simulators, as well as an actual space shuttle, a submarine (for kids over the age of 6 only), and lots more neat hardware and gizmos to view.

Day 2: Museum & a Show

You may need to do this itinerary on day 1 or 3, as matinees are only on Wednesdays, Saturdays, and Sundays. But before you get to the theatrical part of your day, head to the **American Museum of Natural History** (p. 224), one of the finest science museums in the country. A terrific planetarium show, the massive dinosaur exhibit, and the huge whale that hangs from the ceiling of one gallery enthrall most children, as does the new Gilder Center with its highly interactive exhibits on bugs, ecosystems, and more. Eat lunch here before heading downtown to see the matinee of either a Broadway show (p. 330; there will be a few that are child appropriate) or a very fine kids' show at the **New Victory Theater** (p. 336). After the show, explore all the sights of Times Square. Most kids will love **Eye Candy NY,** a trick or treating experience at One Times Square, which can be paired with a trip to the observation deck there (p. 169). Your kiddos may notice the costumed characters in Times Square—be ready to tip the actors if you take a photo with them.

The Northwest Coast Hall in the American Museum of Natural History (p. 224) displays historic carvings by Indigenous nations up and down the coast.

Day 3: Park & Zoo

If you're visiting in winter, rent skates for a spin around Wollman Rink (p. 253), near the southeast corner of Central Park.

When the sun is up, **Central Park** is open, so if you have an early-rising tot, grab a bagel and explore the park over breakfast. With its playgrounds and boating ponds (both for rentable toy boats and rideable row boats), this should account for the entire morning and will make a nice change from all the sightseeing you've been doing. See p. 246 for more on visiting the park. Right before lunchtime, head out of the park on the east side at either 79th or 86th street and walk to **Lexington Candy Shop** (p. 140) to give your kids a taste of what a really old-fashioned diner is like. Then either hop a subway or walk to 99th street and Madison Avenue to catch the BXM11 express bus for a speedy 20-minute ride to the **Bronx Zoo** (p. 232). Spend the afternoon at the greatest zoo in the United States and consider heading to the nearby Italian-American enclave of Arthur Avenue for dinner afterwards (you'll need to take an Uber or taxi, as the subway stop is too far away). ***Note:*** If the weather is bad, do this itinerary on another day.

A WEEKEND FOR ROMANTICS

Friday: A Stroll, Brunch, Shopping & a Cabaret

Sleep in—you're on vacation! Then catch a subway to the Brooklyn side of the **Brooklyn Bridge** (p. 164). Saunter over it to Lower Manhattan, taking in the views. You can then either plunge into a self-guided walking tour of NYC's most historic neighborhood (see our Historic Lower Manhattan tour, p. 266), or if you're hungry, make a key decision: Do you want a classic dim sum brunch in Chinatown (p. 36) or a glam meal at the oh-so-French **Balthazar** (p. 100)? Head to one or the other and then spend the afternoon shopping (or window-shopping) in SoHo, Nolita, or the Lower East Side (p. 299 for a list of the city's best shopping streets). After dark, head uptown for an only-in-New-York cabaret performance with dinner at the swank **Feinstein's/54 Below** (p. 350) or **Café Carlyle** (p. 350)—your choice will depend on who is performing.

Saturday: Picnic in the Park, a Matinee & a Museum

Head to **Zabar's** (p. 321) to purchase the ingredients for brunch in Central Park (go to p. 246 to pick a spot). Then sightsee in the park for a few hours

The Kwoma ceiling from Papua New Guinea presides over the Arts of Oceania gallery in the Met (p. 219).

before heading to a **Broadway matinee** (p. 332). After the show, hop the S subway to Grand Central and the 4, 5, or 6 uptown for an evening visit to the **Metropolitan Museum** (p. 219)—open Friday and Saturday nights until 9pm. Then head across the park to **Tatiana** (p. 134) for a glam late dinner at Lincoln Center, in one of the city's most acclaimed restaurants.

Sunday: Gospel, Brunch & a Step Back in Time

Attend a **gospel service in Harlem** (p. 231) and then head to *Top Chef Masters* champion Marcus Samuelson's **Red Rooster** (p. 141) or classic soul food joint **Melba's** (p. 143) for lunch. For your last few hours in the city, head uptown even farther to the exquisite **Cloisters** (p. 228), which features art and artifacts from the Middle Ages in a setting that seems airlifted from Europe.

CITY LAYOUT

Lots of people travel to New York, plop themselves down into Times Square, and never go anywhere else. They seem to fear venturing into neighborhoods that exist for purposes other than tourism.

In this aerial shot, notice Broadway cutting its own diagonal path across Manhattan's street grid, emphasized here by the Flatiron Building at 23rd St. and 5th Ave (with the Washington Square arch visible less than a mile away).

You don't have to be among them. By devoting just a few minutes to learning the basic geography of New York and its distinctive neighborhoods, you can immensely enhance your enjoyment of this multifaceted city. And once you absorb the highly logical organization of New York's transportation system, you'll find that you can zip from place to place with minimal fuss.

The Grid Plan of Manhattan

The city is composed of five boroughs on four different pieces of land, only one of which is on the North American continent! When people talk about "New York City," however, most are referring to the borough of Manhattan, which is a narrow island between New Jersey and Long Island, bordered by the Hudson and East rivers.

Finding your way around Manhattan is easier than in almost any other city because of the careful plan that was adopted for laying out the city's avenues and streets. In the areas above 14th Street, the city fathers imposed a strict grid upon Manhattan, leveling hills and tearing down existing homes to create straight, evenly spaced thoroughfares in all but a few places. The grid consists of numbered streets and avenues that cross each other at right angles. If you can count up to 100, you can get around this surprisingly compact island.

Streets in Manhattan are numbered and run from east to west. So, if you're on 23rd Street and want to get to 42nd Street, you simply go 19 blocks north. To get from 80th Street to 75th Street, walk 5 blocks south. **The avenues of Manhattan run north to south,** with some bearing numbers and others names (which does complicate the picture, but only a bit). The numbering goes from east to west, with First Avenue being close to the East River and Twelfth Avenue on the far west side of the island near the Hudson River. Interspersed between these numbered avenues on the east side are several named avenues, including Park (the uptown name for Fourth Ave.), Lexington, and Madison. On the west side above 59th Street, Eighth, Ninth, and Tenth avenues turn into Central Park West, Columbus Avenue, and Amsterdam Avenue, respectively.

The exceptions to the grid rule (all found below 14th St.) are the Financial District, Chinatown, Little Italy, the Lower East Side, Greenwich Village, SoHo, and TriBeCa. These southern parts of Manhattan were the first to be settled and, therefore, follow a haphazard non-system of streets and alleys that curve and twist, sometimes doubling back on themselves (most famously in Greenwich Village, where W. 4th St. goes rogue, angling north to cross W. 10th, 11th, 12th, and 13th streets.). Because most of these southern-section streets bear names rather than numbers (Delancey St., Wall St., Church St.), orienting yourself can be tricky. It's important to have a map at the ready and ask for directions when necessary. Even native New Yorkers can get lost down there. As well, **Broadway** is a bit loopy. It follows the path created by Native Americans well before there was a New Amsterdam, so uptown and in midtown it's on the west side, and then it goes east at 23rd Street.

New York City Neighborhoods in Brief

It never fails to amaze. I'm strolling along a pleasant street of small brownstones; I come to the corner, and suddenly, the landscape morphs. I'm a small ant in a canyon of skyscrapers, or else I'm a visitor to India, surrounded by cumin-scented restaurants and men with melodic accents beckoning me into their curry joints. New York is a city of multiple personalities, and they can shift on a dime, within the space of 1 block going from elegant to seedy, from industrial to chic, from international to down-home American.

It's this quicksilver quality, this constant metamorphosis, that endows even a short stroll in New York with real excitement. I urge you to spend at least part of your vacation simply ambling around, window-shopping, eavesdropping on passing conversations, and exploring places beyond the heavily touristed areas.

Here's what you'll find in the various—and strikingly different—neighborhoods of New York City.

DOWNTOWN

The Financial District

Best for: *Museums, historic sites, architecture, and access to Ellis Island, the Statue of Liberty, and the Brooklyn Bridge*

What you won't find: *Highly populated streets after nightfall, theaters*

Neighborhood boundaries: *Everything south of Chambers St.*

This is where New York City—then New Amsterdam—was born. The area packs the same historic punch as colonial sections of Boston and Philadelphia. It was here, at Fraunces Tavern, that the Sons of Liberty gathered to plot the overthrow of the British. It was on Wall Street that George Washington took the oath of office as America's first president. It was at Castle Clinton and then Ellis Island that millions of immigrants flooded the city in the 19th and 20th centuries to get their first glimpse of a "promised land." The great financial movers and shakers also stalked the area (and continue to do so today), and a visit to these "canyons of greed" at the beginning of the day or at 5pm, when finance folks in suits and trader's smocks pour onto the streets, is an exciting sight. As recent history has overshadowed other sights, for many visitors this has simply become the place to pay respects at the **9/11 Memorial and Museum.** Interestingly, many former office buildings have transformed into apartments in the past decade, meaning there's far more life on the streets outside of business hours today than there used to be.

The Lunar New Year parade (p. 389) winds its way through historic Chinatown in an annual community festival.

Manhattan Neighborhoods
0 1/2 mi
0 0.5 km
HARLEM (110th St. and north)
W. 79th St.
Metropolitan Museum of Art
YORKVILLE
E. 78th St.
American Museum of Natural History
Columbus Ave.
Henry Hudson Pkwy.
W. 72nd St.
Frick Collection
E. 72nd St.
ASTORIA
UPPER WEST SIDE
Central Park West
CENTRAL PARK
UPPER EAST SIDE
ROOSEVELT ISLAND
21st St.
West End Ave.
Amsterdam Ave.
Lincoln Center
Central Park Zoo
Madison Ave.
Lexington Ave.
3rd Ave.
2nd Ave.
1st Ave.
Columbus Circle
Central Park So.
W. 57th St
Carnegie Hall
5th Ave.
Park Ave.
E. 57th St.
Queensboro (59th St.) Bridge
MIDTOWN WEST
Radio City Music Hall
St. Patrick's Cathedral
MIDTOWN EAST
E. 50th St.
LONG ISLAND CITY
Intrepid Sea, Air & Space Museum
Rockefeller Center
QUEENS
11th Ave.
10th Ave.
9th Ave.
8th Ave.
7th Ave.
Grand Central Station
United Nations
TIMES SQUARE
W. 42nd St.
E. 42nd St.
Long Island Expwy.
Port Authority Bus Terminal
N.Y. Public Library
E. 40th St.
FDR Dr.
Queens-Midtown Tunnel
Lincoln Tunnel
Jacob Javits Convention Ctr.
MURRAY HILL
Macy's
W. 34th St
E. 34th St
Ave. of the Americas (6th Ave.)
HUDSON YARDS
GARMENT DISTRICT
Penn Station
Empire State Bldg.
East River
GREENPOINT
Broadway
GRAMERCY PARK
High Line Park
Madison Square Park
E. 23rd St
W. 23rd St.
West Side Expwy.
CHELSEA
Flatiron Bldg.
FLATIRON DISTRICT
MANHATTAN
Little Island
W. 14th St.
Union Square Park
E. 14th St.
EAST VILLAGE
Whitney Museum of American Art
Greenwich Ave.
Tompkins Square Park
Ave. D
MEATPACKING DISTRICT
Washington Square Park
4th Ave.
Ave A
Ave. B
Ave. C
East River Park
Hudson River
GREENWICH VILLAGE
NOHO
E. 1st St.
E. Houston St.
W. Houston St.
Hudson St.
SOHO
NOLITA
Mott St.
LOWER EAST SIDE
Delancey St.
Tenement Museum
Williamsburg Bridge
Canal St.
LITTLE ITALY
Bowery
E. Broadway
Holland Tunnel
TRIBECA
FDR Dr.
CHINATOWN
W. Broadway
Church St.
Manhattan Bridge
Park Row
DUMBO
Brooklyn Bridge
9/11 Memorial and Museum
FINANCIAL DISTRICT
South Street Seaport
NEW JERSEY
Wall St.
New York Stock Exchange
BROOKLYN HEIGHTS
Flatbush Ave.
BROOKLYN
Battery Park
Brooklyn-Battery Tunnel

Chinatown (& Little Italy)

Best for: *Affordable dining and shopping*

What you won't find: *Top museums, streets without gridlock, theaters, much nightlife*

Neighborhood boundaries: *Chinatown is roughly bordered by Broome St. to the north, Allen St. to the east, Worth St. to the south, and Lafayette St. to the west.*

At points, Chinatown takes on aspects of Shanghai or Beijing: the dense crowds on the streets, the awnings with Chinese characters, the sound of Chinese conversation everywhere. It's a fun, truly transporting area to visit and one that's been voraciously swallowing up other neighborhoods—Little Italy, the Jewish Lower East Side—for the past few decades. In fact, except for 2 blocks of Mulberry Street (from Canal to Broome), strung with colored lights, Little Italy has ceased to exist and is really only a tourist-trapping shadow of its former self. There are a handful of worthwhile places to shop for Italian food, eat gelato, or get Italian coffee, but very few real Italian Americans are around anymore. For great, cheap eats (and shopping), stick with Asian restaurants and marts, for the most part.

TriBeCa, Nolita & SoHo

Best for: *Dining, bars, celebrity sightings, architecture, art galleries (the second highest density after Chelsea), shopping*

What you won't find: *Museums*

Neighborhood boundaries: *It's all in the names.* ***SoHo*** *means "south of Houston Street." This fashionable neighborhood extends down to Canal St., between Sixth Ave. to the west and Lafayette St. (1 block east of Broadway) to the east.* ***Nolita*** *means "**no**rth of **L**ittle **Ita**ly," referring to Mott St., Mulberry St., and Elizabeth St. north of Kenmare St.* ***TriBeCa*** *is the **Tri**angle **Be**low **Ca**nal St., consisting of all the blocks south of Canal St. and north of Chambers St., between Broadway and the Hudson River.*

Now that we've gotten *that* out of the way, we're left with the harder task of figuring out why the ultra-rich are so attracted to this area of former factories and tenements. They certainly wouldn't have wanted to work or live here back in the 19th and early 20th centuries, but these formerly industrial areas draw a lot of boldfaced names today. And with these *arrivistes* has come a welcome wagon of hot restaurants, boutiques, spas, and boîtes. Which means simply wandering these often-cobblestoned streets, by the cast-iron buildings (SoHo has the most of any area in the world), can be a hoot.

The Lower East Side & East Village

Best for: *Dining, bars, dance and music clubs, innovative theaters, shops run by local designers, cheeky art galleries*

What you won't find: *Many hotels, museums (with the exception of the very fine Tenement Museum, the International Center of Photography, and the New Museum of Contemporary Art)*

Neighborhood boundaries: *Between Houston and Canal sts. east of the Bowery*

For millions, these areas were once the portal to the United States. In fact, the buildings you see on the Lower East Side were built expressly to house the teeming masses of immigrants who flooded into New York between roughly 1840 and 1930. At the turn of the last century, this was the most densely populated area in the world, with a dozen people to an apartment and pushcarts jamming the streets. While some remnants of that life remain in the old-world fabric and luggage stores along **Orchard Street,** these areas are mostly known today for bars, lounges, art galleries, and music clubs. It's in these two neighborhoods that you're most likely to find young designers opening their own tiny stores and protégés of the town's great chefs trying out their own first restaurants. I may be prejudiced because I live in the East Village, but I find it one of the most vibrant areas of Manhattan, though many blocks have lost their gritty edges thanks to ever-rising real estate prices.

Greenwich Village

Best for: *Strolling, dining, historic sites, lovely architecture, specialty food shops, theater, live music clubs, celebrity sightings*

What you won't find: *Museums, many hotels*

Neighborhood boundaries: *From Broadway west to the Hudson River, bordered by Houston St. to the south and 14th St. to the north*

Greenwich Village has always been where the city's outsiders and oddballs have found a haven. In Dutch Colonial times, it was farmland set outside the walls of the city. At the turn of the 20th century, the area was a bohemian enclave where artists of all sorts (Mark Twain, Edgar Allan Poe, Eugene O'Neill, and Winslow Homer, to name a few) could find cheap lodging and companionship. In the 1950s, it was at the center of the Beat movement; in the '60s and '70s, the area around Christopher Street became the hub of a burgeoning gay rights movement (in the '80s, it was a hotbed of AIDS-related activism).

Today, high real estate prices have dulled the Village's edge, and you're more likely to see dads with strollers than long-haired poets walking these streets. And that dad might be Anderson Cooper or Alec Baldwin, two of the many celebs who now call the tree-shaded brownstones of the Village home sweet home. But the charms of the area are still intact, as is the illusion that you've entered another city altogether. Very few buildings in the neighborhood reach 10 stories, and small shops elbow out chain stores. It's a wonderful place to simply come and get lost. See our walking tour (p. 289).

The Meatpacking District & Chelsea

Best for: *Art galleries, nightlife, shopping, the High Line, gay bars, bars*

What you won't find: *Theaters, museums (other than the Whitney)*

Neighborhood boundaries: *Chelsea lies roughly west of Sixth Ave. from 14th St. to 30th St.; the Meatpacking District extends south to 12th St. west of Greenwich Ave.*

Manhattan's Chelsea neighborhood is today what SoHo was 20 years ago, and what Greenwich Village was 30 years ago, meaning that if you want to go art gallery hopping, this is where to head. The so-called Meatpacking District, named for the slaughterhouses that once filled the area west of Greenwich Avenue, has become an extremely popular nightlife destination (and a shopping mini-mecca for high-end

A fanciful artificial island rising over the Hudson River, Little Island has quickly become a popular warm weather hangout spot.

Free New York City Tours

If you'd like to tour a specific neighborhood with an expert guide, contact **Big Apple Greeter** (bigapplegreeter.org; ✆ **212/669-8159**). For 25 years this non-profit group has been pairing volunteers with visitors for free and highly personal looks at the city. The guides are not expected to be able to spout history or talk in detail about the architecture of the places you'll be visiting. Instead, they introduce tourists to the city they know and love deeply, taking them to areas that few outsiders see. The 4-hour tours are for individuals and couples (the largest group they accept is five people) and are hugely popular, so book 4 weeks in advance of arrival (or more), because many would-be participants are turned away.

European stores). It's NYC's adult Disneyland, filled with late-night clubs, bars, and restaurants that are unhindered by the city's zoning laws (since there are no schools or churches in this part of town). Three final reasons to come here: the fab **Whitney Museum** (p. 183); the **High Line park,** a shining example of urban reclamation (p. 257); and **Little Island** (p. 258), a custom-built pleasure isle in the Hudson.

The Flatiron District, Union Square & Gramercy Park

Best for: *Dining, hotels, historic sites, architecture, off-Broadway theater, shopping, bars*

What you won't find: *Museums*

Neighborhood boundaries: *The* ***Flatiron District*** *runs south from 23rd St. to 14th St., between Broadway and Sixth Ave.;* ***Union Square*** *is the hub of the district from 14th St. to 18th St.; the* ***Gramercy Park*** *neighborhood lies between 16th and 23rd sts., from Park Ave. S to Second Ave.*

As you meander through these three bustling, adjoining (and overlapping) areas, you're likely to see brown street signs proclaiming LADIES MILE. It was on this stretch, mostly on Broadway and Park Avenue South, that the first wave of department stores transformed the lives of New Yorkers in the 1850s. Instead of hopping from a dry-goods shop for fabric to a milliner for hats to a cobbler for shoes, women from all over the city came here to outfit themselves and their homes in stores that had everything they needed under one roof. Notice the large plate-glass windows on many facades, another department store innovation. Above, the windows are much smaller and point to a second element of the "Ladies Mile": brothels. When the stores closed for the day, the establishments upstairs opened. And where there's prostitution, theater often follows. The area around Union Square was New York's first show district and has become an important off-Broadway theater district again in recent years. The dining scene is also hot here.

For the best strolling, head directly to the **Gramercy Park** area, named for the only private park in the city (the keys go to those apartment owners whose windows overlook the park). Around the park, a number of beautifully preserved historic homes and clubs include the wisteria-clad home of former Mayor James Harper (4 Gramercy Park S), the Players Club (16 Gramercy Park S; its members included Edwin Booth and Mark Twain), and the National Arts Club (15 Gramercy Park S, a hangout for Woodrow Wilson and Theodore Dreiser).

MIDTOWN

Hudson Yards

Best for: *Shopping, dining, and performance art*

What you won't find: *Museums, hotels (with a few exceptions), real NYC street life*

Neighborhood boundaries: *From 30th to 35th sts. and Tenth Ave. to the river*

Gotham's newest neighborhood looks more like Dallas than New York City, due to its gleaming centerpiece mall and the proportions and placement of its skyscrapers. Still, a few attractions make it worth a visit,

Harlem, with its distinctive brownstones, has been at the center of African-American community in NYC since the 1920s.

foremost among them **The Shed** (p. 344), a spectacular new arts center.

Times Square & Midtown West

Best for: *Theaters and entertainment of all sorts, the Museum of Modern Art, Rockefeller Center, Macy's*

What you won't find: *Serenity*

Neighborhood boundaries: *From 35th St. to 59th St. west from Fifth Ave. to the Hudson River*

Midtown West, a vast area, encompasses several famous places: Madison Square Garden, the Garment District, Rockefeller Center, the Theater District, and Times Square. It's the area most people think of when they think of New York, and the reason why so many visitors say with a smirk, "Well, it's a nice place to visit, but I couldn't ever live there." And because they're basing their judgments on crowded, loud, pushy midtown, they're absolutely right: It's unlivable . . . which is why so few New Yorkers actually live in this area. In certain parts of midtown there's no residential housing whatsoever, and it's only the tourists who attempt to get a good night's sleep in this bustling neighborhood.

Midtown East & Murray Hill

Best for: *Great architecture, shopping (and window-shopping), historic sites, the United Nations, the Empire State Building*

What you won't find: *Museums, nightlife (again, with some exceptions)*

Neighborhood boundaries: *East from Fifth Ave. to the East River, north from 34th St. to 57th St.*

In the 1950s, Madison, Park, and Lexington avenues started to sprout skyscrapers and were soon rivaling the Wall Street area for office space. That's primarily what you'll find here: people in suits, looming glass towers, and lots of traffic. Among all that are some spectacular architectural sights like **Grand Central Station** (p. 205), **St. Patrick's Cathedral** (p. 210), the **Chrysler Building** (p. 202), and the **Seagram Building** (52nd and Park Ave.). Go closer to the East River and the area becomes largely residential, with little to recommend it to visitors beyond Bloomingdale's and the **United Nations** (p. 211). A tremendously popular stretch of Fifth Avenue, from 57th Street down to the

Empire State Building at 34th Street, offers some of the best window-shopping on the planet.

UPTOWN

Upper East Side

Best for: *Museums, architecture, window-shopping, Central Park*

What you won't find: *Fine dining (although I list some exceptions to that), theater, music clubs*

Neighborhood boundaries: *Starts at 59th St. and encompasses the area east of Central Park*

10021 is the richest zip code in the world, and it belongs to the Upper East Side; in particular, the swank swath of pavement that runs from 61st to 80th streets. Also known as "The Gold Coast" and "Millionaire's Mile," this is the stomping grounds for New York's high society: the Prada-clad women and old-money men who sit on the boards of the neighborhood museums, go to cocktail parties, and endow scholarships for kicks. Their mansions and marble-faced town houses make for nifty sightseeing for those interested in architecture, and the shops along **Madison Avenue** offer a peek into the extravagant fashions adopted by the 1% and the top designers who serve them.

Museums also play a key role on the Upper East Side; there's a greater concentration of top-flight museums here than anywhere else in the country, with the exception of the Mall in Washington, D.C. You'll want to spend at least 1 day exploring **Museum Mile**—the **Metropolitan** (p. 222), **Guggenheim** (p. 219), **Cooper Hewitt** (p. 212), and more are all in the area.

Upper West Side

Best for: *Museums (the American Museum of Natural History and the New York Historical), Central Park, kid-friendly restaurants, classical music and dance at Lincoln Center and elsewhere*

What you won't find: *Great shopping (with some exceptions), edge*

Neighborhood boundaries: *Starts at 59th St. and encompasses everything west of Central Park*

In some ways, the Upper West Side has the most suburban vibe of any of Manhattan's neighborhoods. National chain stores line the major thoroughfares, and the sidewalks swarm with strollers. It's a popular area for families thanks to its proximity to Central Park, the American Museum of Natural History, and the Children's Museum of Manhattan. It's still an extremely pleasant place to visit with good, if chain-oriented, shopping; a handful of top-notch museums; New York's famous performing arts hub, Lincoln Center; and, of course, access to the glories of Central Park.

Harlem

Best for: *Dining, bars, clubs, historic sites*

What you won't find: *Theaters, museums (except for the Museo del Barrio and the Studio Museum)*

Neighborhood boundaries: ***Harlem proper*** *stretches from river to river, beginning at 125th St. on the west side, 96th St. on the east side, and 110th St. north of Central Park. East of Fifth Ave.,* ***Spanish Harlem (El Barrio)*** *runs between E. 100th and E. 125th sts.*

Perhaps the most rapidly transforming neighborhood in the city, Harlem is safer and cleaner than it's been in decades . . . but may be losing some of its intrinsic character. A largely African-American neighborhood since the 1920s—and home to some of the greatest Black writers, politicians, and artists of the 20th century—the neighborhood now draws an increasing number of non-Black residents, lured here by lower real estate prices and the beauty of a brownstone-lined community. My recommendation: Visit here soon before the authentic soul and Caribbean joints disappear, the gospel churches lose their swing, and the rhythm of the streets changes its beat. There's much to see, including dozens of well-preserved Beaux Arts brownstones, the Apollo Theater, the newly reopened Studio Museum, and a hopping bar scene. See walking tour, p. 280.

THE OUTER BOROUGHS

Brooklyn

Best for: *Museums, parks, lovely architecture, innovative galleries, dining, the city's hottest club and bar scene, great views of Manhattan*

What you won't find: *You find pretty much all the same types of attractions in Brooklyn as you will in Manhattan. It deserves a visit!*

With 2.7 million residents (according to the last census), Brooklyn is the most populous borough of the city, and at 71 square miles, it's also the largest. It's very difficult to pin down Brooklyn's personality, as it's just too darn big to be summarized in a nutshell.

The two most affluent neighborhoods are **Brooklyn Heights,** which is right off the Brooklyn Bridge, boasting spectacular views of Manhattan; and **Park Slope,** the area bordering the westside of **Prospect Park,** Frederick Law Olmsted's *other* great work of landscape architecture (after Central Park). Both are stellar strolling areas, filled with lovely Beaux Arts brownstone buildings (Brooklyn Heights was the first neighborhood in the city to be landmarked). Not long ago, the *New York Times* discovered that apartments in these neighborhoods, for the first time, were selling for more than apartments in most areas of Manhattan.

The borough's artists tend to live in Bushwick, Red Hook, Greenpoint, Gowanus, Williamsburg (though many are getting priced out here), and a few holdouts still in DUMBO (the area "Down Under the Manhattan Bridge Overpass"). You can pop by all for afternoons of gallery- or artist-studio-hopping. **Williamsburg** has a split personality. Part of it houses one of the largest Hasidic Jewish communities in the world. Walk the streets peopled by this sect and you may feel as if you've stepped back into an old country shtetl (an illusion only somewhat ruined by the incongruous but ever-present cellphones). The other half is hipster heaven, a neighborhood of art galleries, bustling boîtes, and soigné boutiques. Rumor has it that men who move to this part of Billyburg must sign a pledge to grow a beard within 3 months of signing their lease.

Eastern Europe also makes an appearance in **Brighton Beach,** which has the largest expat Ukrainian and Russian community in the world. It's not the friendliest area, but fascinating to visit nonetheless, with stores selling endless rows of nesting dolls and Lenin T-shirts, and small-scale nightclubs that out-glitz and out-crass Vegas. Just up the shore from Brighton Beach, famed **Coney Island** (p. 236) still holds an amusement park, though one with less panache than in its heyday.

Among the touristic highlights of the borough are the views from the **Brooklyn**

As Williamsburg, Brooklyn, has morphed into a hipster haven, cafe life has blossomed.

Heights promenade and the new **Domino Park** (p. 255); **Peter Luger** (p. 147), an iconic steakhouse in Williamsburg; shows at the **Brooklyn Academy of Music** (p. 342); and in **Park Slope,** a constellation of sights including the **Brooklyn Museum** (p. 234), the **Brooklyn Botanical Gardens** (p. 233), and **Prospect Park** (p. 259).

The Bronx

Best for: *Baseball, Italian restaurants, zoos, and gardens*

What you won't find: *Museums, nightlife, other types of noteworthy food, hotels, theaters*

I may be condemned for this assessment, but to my mind there are only four reasons a tourist should even think of going to the Bronx: **Yankee Stadium** (p. 375), the **Bronx Zoo** (p. 232), the **New York Botanical Garden** (p. 233), and the Italian restaurants and stores of **Arthur Avenue** (p. 153). If you have no interest in any of these sights or facilities, you can skip this giant borough without too much regret.

Queens

Best for: *Museums, ethnic dining, affordable hotels*

What you won't find: *Theaters, great shopping, top architecture*

Archie Bunker no longer lives in Queens. In fact, the grouchy, bigoted xenophobe at the center of the famed 1970s sitcom *All in the Family* probably wouldn't recognize the borough today. In just the past 50 years it's gone from being a somewhat insulated community of Irish and Italian Americans to the most international community in the United States. A single afternoon in Queens can make a visitor feel like a globe-trotter, which gives Queens a special appeal, despite the dreary, industrial look of much of it. Whether you're downing samosas or shopping for saris in very Indian **Jackson Heights,** breaking plates at a Greek restaurant in **Astoria,** or buying miracle water and tacos at a Mexican *botanica* in **Corona,** there's much to taste, smell, and experience.

Museums are another big draw, and the borough now rivals Brooklyn for its cultural attractions, boasting four great ones: the **Museum of the Moving Image** (p. 242), **P.S. 1 Museum of Contemporary Art** (p. 243), **Isamu Noguchi Galleries** (p. 240), and the **Louis Armstrong House** (p. 240). In recent years, the neighborhood of **Ridgewood** has become a hipster haunt, with many hopping bars, dance clubs, and, to a lesser extent, creative restaurants.

Staten Island

Best for: *Views of Manhattan from the ferry, outlet shopping*

What you won't find: *Notable museums, nightlife, hotels, theaters, interesting architecture*

And I'll again be blunt: Except for the fun and free ferry ride here, plus a visit to either the outlet malls or the Lighthouse Museum near the ferry terminal, there's little reason for tourists to visit. Yes, there are a handful of cultural and historic sites, but none that are more compelling than those in the other boroughs. And a mall is a mall is a mall is a mall . . .

WHERE TO STAY

3

Time now for a change of mood. In a book that celebrates the joy of travel, it's necessary briefly to deal with a far less pleasant topic: the ridiculously overpriced accommodations of New York. By and large, hotels in Gotham charge more than hotels anywhere else in the United States (an average of $363 per night) for rooms that often aren't nearly as spacious or full of amenities.

Why? Hotels have long been pricey in Gotham, but in recent years the perfect storm hit, driving rates to absurd new heights.

First off, in 2023 Local Law 18 went into effect, making it virtually impossible to operate a short-term rental in New York City. Under the new law, it is illegal to rent an entire unit for fewer than 30 days (except under special, hard-to-obtain licenses). Overnight, the number of Airbnbs in the city plummeted from 50,000 to just 7,000 (the remaining ones are for renting rooms within larger apartments, where the owner lives with the visitors). Alas, the city has not responded by building many new hotels. Instead, a number that closed during the pandemic have remained closed or have become shelters for immigrants and unhoused New Yorkers. That has allowed the remaining hotels to charge what the market will bear, which means huge swings in price between low season and high, for the same damn rooms.

In response, I've reworked this chapter to include far more suggestions for lodgings in New Jersey and those parts of the city that remain affordable (see p. 83).

I've also emphasized hotels that could exist in only the Big Apple. They will give you a more authentic experience than staying in a place chosen randomly over the internet, I promise, and if you come at the right time of the year, they'll be affordable. If not, a commute that isn't too onerous (again, I promise) may be the way to accomplish your NYC vacay.

PRACTICAL MATTERS: THE HOTEL SCENE

In the following listings, I'll give you an idea of the kind of deals that may be available at particular hotels. But there's no way of

At Hosteling International's New York property, on the Upper West Side, guests can mingle in the community kitchen, cafe, games room, and a roomy outdoor patio.

knowing what the offers will be when you're booking, so also consider these general tips:

- **Choose your season carefully.** Room rates can vary dramatically—by hundreds of dollars in most cases—depending on what time of year you visit. Winter, from January 4 through mid-March, is best for bargains, with summer (especially July–Aug) second best. Fall is the busiest and most expensive season, especially Christmastime, New Year's, and the weekend of the NYC marathon—expect to pay top dollar then.

  Bizarrely enough, when the city fills up, lesser-quality hotels will often charge prices that are equal to or even higher than what the luxury hotels are asking. So, it's important to NEVER try to assess the quality of a hotel by the price it's asking. Instead, read the reviews carefully and compare the prices you're being quoted to make sure you're not getting taken.
- **Go uptown, downtown, to an outer borough, or Jersey City.** The advantages of a midtown location are overrated, especially when saving money is your object. The subway can whisk you anywhere you want to go in minutes; even if you stay on the Upper West Side, you can be at the ferry launch for the Statue of Liberty in about a half-hour. You'll not only get the best value for your money by staying outside the Times Square area, in the residential neighborhoods where real New Yorkers live, you'll also have a better overall experience: You won't constantly be fighting crowds; you'll have more higher-quality restaurants nearby; and you'll see what life in the city is really like. Lodgings in New Jersey and Queens offer particularly good savings, and all the ones I've included are easily accessible via public transportation.

- **Shop online.** There are so many ways to save online and through apps, I've devoted an entire box to the topic. See p. 46.
- **Choose a chain.** I list few chains in this guide as I feel that they tend to lack the character and the local feel that most independently run hotels have. And it's that feel, I believe, that is so much a part of the travel experience. But with prices at historic highs, it's more important than ever to get a deal. Chains can be a good option, particularly if you have reward points or can access some type of corporate discount. And every single major chain has hotels in the city, so go where you have the most points. ***Note:*** We start each geographic section below with a description of why or why you might not want to stay in the area under discussion, which will help should you go the chain route.
- **Budget for taxes.** They can increase the cost of a room in the city by 20%. Happily, in 2026 Mayor Mamdani put in place a rule that resort fees, and other junk fees, had to be included in the nightly rate on all search engines. So that ugly surprise is now a thing of the past.
- **Make a reservation you can cancel.** As the date of the stay approaches, hotels start to play "chicken" with one another, dropping the price a bit one day to try to lure customers away from a nearby competitor. So, search again the week you're traveling and then within 48 hours of arrival. This strategy takes vigilance and persistence, but since your credit card won't usually be charged until 24 hours before check-in, little risk is involved, and it's paying off more often than ever before, thanks to current conditions. In fact, you'll usually get a better deal on a last-minute booking than on those bookings that drop the price if you lock in a stay early.

Alternative Accommodations

- **Consider private B&B accommodations.** Alas, it is illegal to rent vacation apartments in New York City for fewer than 30 days. In December 2021,

WHAT YOU'LL really PAY

You'll notice that the rates listed in this chapter are more than a little bit odd. A typical hotel listing will state that rates start at $199 per night but can go up to $699—for the same room category. That's not a typo. Unfortunately, getting a bed in this city is a bit like playing roulette: You never know what number will come up. It's all based on occupancy rates. And in high season, that means hotels charge whatever they feel they can get away with.

I've calculated the rates in this chapter by looking at what online hotel booking engines are offering in deep winter (when prices are at their nadir) and in fall (when they peak) and then showing you the range, from low to high. But the sad truth is **rates can change at any time,** meaning you may find even higher rates than those listed in this guide. I've tried to list the averages, for high and low season, for these hotels, but nothing's average here. Alas, that's the nature of NYC, the city that not only never sleeps, it makes visitors pay through the nose if they try to.

TURNING TO THE internet or apps FOR A HOTEL DISCOUNT

Before going online, it's important that you know what "flavor" of discount you're seeking. Currently, there are several types of online reductions:

1. **Extreme discounts on sites where you bid for lodgings without knowing which hotel you'll get.** You'll find these on such sites as **Priceline.com** and **Hotwire.com,** and they can be money-savers, particularly if you're booking within a week of travel (that's when the hotels resort to deep discounts to get beds filled). As these companies use only major chains, you can rest assured that you won't be put up in a dump. For Priceline, you can install the browser extension **Hotel Canary** for free on your computer, and it will tell you the name of the hotel Priceline is trying to hide from you. There's not as easy a hack for Hotwire, but if you search on Frommers.com you'll find a four-step method we figured out for correctly guessing which hotel you're being shown.
2. **Consider joining Room Steals, Travel + Leisure's Go, or one of the travel clubs associated with many professional organizations.** These clubs have access to the "fire sales" of the hotel industry: room rates that are slashed to a level that hotels would never want to surface on a Google search. These clubs work best for frequent travelers, as there are initial membership fees. All these entities unlock wholesale prices that consistently shave 25% off the nightly rate at hotels, more for really pricey ones.
3. **Use the right hotel search engine.** They're not all equal, as we at Frommers.com learned in 2026 after putting the top 20 sites to the test in 20 cities (including NYC) around the globe. We discovered that **Trivago** and **Google/Hotels** both listed the lowest rates for hotels in the city center 20 out of 20 times—the best record, by far, of all the sites we tested.
4. **Last-minute discounts.** Booking last minute can be a great savings strategy, as prices sometimes drop in the week and days before travel as hoteliers scramble to fill their rooms. But you won't necessarily find the best savings through companies that claim to specialize in last-minute bookings. Instead, use the sites recommended above.

It's a lot of surfing, I know, but in the hothouse world of Big Apple hotel pricing, this sort of diligence can pay off.

the mayor's office also started requiring owners who rent for fewer than 30 days to register with the city, and companies that list unregistered apartments are now being fined. So, although **Airbnb, Vrbo, Wimdu.com,** and others list apartment rentals around the city, they are now almost always for rooms within apartments where the owner lives with you, which may raise privacy concerns. If you do decide to rent a room in an apartment with the owner in residence, think of it as a private B&B (though often breakfast is not included). This type of stay is usually much cheaper than a hotel room; it allows you to meet a friendly local; and it will most likely place you in a residential neighborhood where you live like a local, rather than a visitor.

- **Stay at a guesthouse affiliated with a religious order.** Around Manhattan are a few specialty lodgings operated by churches and other organizations. In some cases, they're open to all; in others you must be a veteran or member to stay there, but they all are clean, friendly, well-located hotels, offering private rooms for as little as $125/night for a single, rarely more than $170 for a double with private bathroom. In the case of the religious hotels, there's no required attendance at services, although at some, unmarried couples are not allowed to share the same room. Here are three I heartily recommend:

  The House of the Redeemer, 7 E. 95th St. off Fifth Ave. (houseoftheredeemer.org; ✆ **212/289-0339;** subway: 6 to 96th St.). Open to all, run by the Episcopal Church. Simple rooms but in a former mansion. No alcohol is allowed on guest floors.

  The Leo House, 332 W. 23rd St., btw. Eighth and Ninth aves. (leohousenyc.com; ✆ **800/732-2438** or 212/929-1010; subway: E or C to 23rd St.). Open to all, run by the Catholic Church.

  Menno House, 15 Rutherford Place, btw. 15th and 16th sts. (mennohouse.org; ✆ **212/677-1611;** subway: L to First Ave.). Run by the Mennonite Church and mostly for volunteers and students. Three nice rooms are set aside for transient visitors.

- **Look into hostels.** Open to people of all ages as well as families, the following hostels have a mix of dorm accommodations and private rooms. Rates range between $43 and $76 per person at these facilities, varying by date and type of room. Private doubles start at $120. Here are NYC's best-maintained (and most amenity-laden) hostels:

  Hosteling International New York, 891 Amsterdam Ave., at the corner of 103rd St. (hinewyork.org; ✆ **212/932-2300;** subway: 1 to 103rd St., or 1, 2, or 3 to 96th St.)

  The Local NYC, 13-02 44th Ave., Long Island City, Queens (thelocalny.com; ✆ **347/738-5251;** subway: E, M, 7 to Court Sq.)

  Q4 Hotel/Hostel, 29-09 Queens Plaza North, Long Island City, Queens (q4hotel.com; ✆ **718/706-7700;** subway: E, M, N, R, or 7 to Queensboro Plaza)

  West Side YMCA, 5 W. 63rd St. off Central Park West (ymcanyc.org; ✆ **212/912-2600;** subway: 1, A, B, C, D to Columbus Circle)

Price Categories

I list double room rates only. Please assume that suites will be pricier, and those few hotels that offer single rooms will do so for less than the rate listed in this guide.

Inexpensive: $205 and under
Moderate: $206–$400
Expensive: $401 and up

THE FINANCIAL DISTRICT

In this part of downtown, you are far away from the bustle of midtown. And while FiDi, as it's called, has become more residential in the past decade, parts of it will feel deserted on weekends and in the evenings. Some enjoy the after-dark serenity, while others find it a bit spooky.

Best for: Visitors doing business in the Financial District during the week and people who like things quiet (as quiet as they get in Manhattan) at night.

Drawbacks: It's a fairly long cab/subway/bus ride to many attractions.

Expensive

The Beekman Hotel, A Thompson Hotel ♥♥♥ This dazzler restores one of the city's first skyscrapers, built in 1881. Over the swellegant bar is a soaring nine-story atrium, with a pyramidal glass skylight; next to it are two restaurants, both from celeb restaurateurs: *Top Chef* judge Tom Colicchio (guests also get room service from Colicchio) and French master Daniel Boulud. Rooms are carved out of former offices, so each has a different shape and size, but all share quietly elegant furnishings with dashes of whimsy—a chinoiserie lamp in the shape of a dog here, a royal blue area rug there, perhaps a velvet couch. Set at the top of the Financial District, it's within walking distance of both Chinatown and the 9/11 Memorial and Museum (p. 160).

123 Nassau St. (at Beekman St.). hyatt.com. ✆ **212/233-2300.** 286 units. Doubles $498–$864. Subway: 4, 5, 6, R to Brooklyn Bridge/City Hall; 2, 3 to Park Pl.; A, C to Fulton St. **Amenities:** Bar; restaurant; room service; 2-story gym; free Wi-Fi.

In a restored 1881 skyscraper, the Financial District's Beekman Hotel nods to Victorian elegance in its lobby bar, set under a soaring atrium.

50 Bowery **10**
Arlo SoHo **15**
Artezen **5**
The Beekman Hotel, a Thompson Hotel **6**
Crosby Street Hotel **12**
The Jane **17**
Leon Hotel **9**
Mimosa Hotel **8**
Mint House at 70 Pine **4**
Nine Orchard **7**
NobleDEN **11**
Now Now Noho **14**
Placemakr Wall Street **2**
Untitled at 3 Freeman Alley **13**
The Wall Street Hotel **3**
The Wall Street Inn **1**
Washington Square Hotel **16**

Downtown Accommodations

The Wall Street Hotel ♥♥♥

Set where the very first indoor New York Stock Exchange stood, The Wall Street is an unusually pampering place to stay. On-site is a restaurant helmed by one of the best chef/owners working in Gotham today, John Fraser; 24-hour room service comes from this accomplished kitchen. And every wonderfully spacious room comes with such swank touches as Frette linens, cashmere blankets, and a fully stocked bar cart. Some suites have electric fireplaces that not only look like glowing embers, they fill the room with a humidifying mist and either emit a crackling sound or stay quiet (the guest's choice). On the design front, the hotel honors the area's history (the lobby murals showing downtown NYC through the ages are stunning) as well as the owner's Australian heritage, featuring very fine Aboriginal art from the owner's collection and lots of mother-of-pearl ornaments (the family made its fortune in the pearl trade).

The Lounge on Pearl at the Wall Street Hotel.

88 Wall St. (at Water St.). thewallsthotel.com. ✆ **212/688-9255.** 180 units. $527–$729 double. Subway: 2, 3 4, 5 to Wall St. **Amenities:** 2 bars; restaurant; coffee shop; room service; fitness room; mobile office (printers, scanners, and more delivered to guest rooms as needed); loaner bikes and scooters; free Wi-Fi.

Expensive/Moderate

Mint House at 70 Pine ♥♥ Hyperactive kids in tow? Looking for the perfect place for a family reunion? Mint checks a lot of boxes that no other place in the city does. Not only does it offer half a dozen activities free to its guests (bowling! a golf simulator! a fancy screening room! a two-story gym!), even its smallest rooms are larger than many NYC apartments, and all have kitchens, though in the smaller rooms they're fairly basic. Larger units have pullout couches and multiple bedrooms so that you can stack up the guests, and some have full-size dining room tables and washer/dryers. All of this is hidden within a glam Art Deco–era skyscraper, which has a full grocery store on-site. (The staff will stock your kitchen for you, charging only the cost of the groceries.) I had to deduct one heart for the spongy Casper mattresses—some will like them; I don't—and the spooky, luridly colored portraits that stare down at guests from every room (the gent showing me around admitted that a lot of guests cover the art with sheets!).

70 Pine St. (btw. Pearl & William sts.). minthouse.com. ✆ **855/972-9090.** 165 units. $166–$425 studio. Subway: 2, 3 to Williams St. **Amenities:** Gym (w/classes); 4 restaurants; food court; 2 bars; kitchens in rooms; grocery; co-working spaces; bowling alley; Pilates studio; golf simulator; screening room; business center; free Wi-Fi.

A tidy alcove bed and well-equipped kitchenette at Placemakr Wall Street.

Placemakr Wall Street ♥♥ Another family-friendly option, Placemakr is part of a small chain that's trying to walk the line between rental apartments and hotel rooms. That means its units have darn good cooking facilities and they get creative about making enough room for multiple guests to sleep and live. In all guest rooms Murphy beds can be pulled down from the wall above the couch, turning a sitting area into a sleeping area. Others also have queen-size "alcove beds" tucked into one quadrant of the digs. Since the windows are large and the furnishings cutely Scandinavian (lots of blond woods and wall pegs), the effect is cheery rather than desperate. Amenities like free communal laundry machines, a lovely sundeck with hot tub and loungers, and a big gym add to Placemakr's appeal. ***Note:*** This is one of the few places in the city where units can sleep up to 8. (They offer sizes from studios to 4-bedroom apartments.)

110 Wall St. (btw. Front & South sts.). placemakr.com. ✆ **646/568-4700.** 120 units. $144–$654 studio. Subway: 2, 3 to Wall St. **Amenities:** Cafe; gym; kitchens in rooms; co-working spaces; sun deck; free laundry; free Wi-Fi.

Moderate/Inexpensive

Rooms at the Artezen are comfy and clean, though the decor screams early '90s.

Artezen ♥♥ With a dated design sensibility—sparkly wallpaper and pleather headboards in the guest rooms, and an odd wall fountain in the lobby—Artezen doesn't get our highest marks for its looks. Not that it's ugly, but its decor feels like a throwback to the '90s despite the fact that it's relatively new. No, what we really like about Artezen is the staff—they genuinely care and seem to truly enjoy their jobs. That translates to a spotless hotel, a warm greeting whenever you hit the lobby, and deeply researched help when a visitor asks a question. The Artezen is also quite well located, within walking distance of the Statue of Liberty ferry and the 9/11 memorial, and across from subway stations with pretty much all the major lines, meaning you can zip to wherever you're going in the city in minutes.

24 John St. (btw. Broadway & Nassau St.). artezenhotel.com. ✆ **212/566-5511.** 89 units. $142–$409 double. Subway: 2, 3, 4, 5, J, Z to Fulton St. **Amenities:** Use of nearby gym; free Wi-Fi.

The Wall Street Inn ♥♥ Gracious. That's the first word that comes to mind when one walks into this frilled little inn, a place so old-fashioned it still has a payphone nook in the lobby (though it now just holds a house phone); only colonial style art adorns its walls. But the staff are cheery and helpful, the rooms decent-size (those ending in 01 are smallest) and quiet (except those overlooking the raucous outdoor party on Stone Street in warm weather months; see p. 274). As for the beds: They only *look* lumpy because real feathers are used in the comforters. Pre-pandemic, prices used to drop drastically here on weekends; we're no longer seeing that pattern, but know that you can save by booking direct (an action that will also get you a free room upgrade, and a waiving of extra-person fees on triple and quadruple rooms).

9 S. William St. (at Broad St.). thewallstreetinn.com. ✆ **800/747-1500** or 212/747-1500. 46 units. $117–$346 double; continental breakfast included. Subway: 2, 3 to Wall St.; 4, 5 to Bowling Green. **Amenities:** Babysitting; exercise room w/sauna and steam; communal guest kitchen w/microwave; free Wi-Fi.

THE LOWER EAST SIDE, CHINATOWN, NOHO & NOLITA

All four neighborhoods offer New York neighborhood living with lots of street life.

Best for: A taste of life Downtown with a capital "D." The Lower East Side, in particular, boasts some of the city's most vibrant clubs and hippest restaurants.

Drawbacks: These neighborhoods are a little off the beaten path in terms of sightseeing, and the LES takes more time to get to via public transportation.

Expensive

Nine Orchard ♥♥♥ When the Jarmulowsky Bank opened on this spot in 1912, the New York Architectural Digest described its cathedral-like central space as a "shrine to American Capitalism." That description certainly applies today. Not only is the lobby of this reclaimed historic building one of the most majestic spaces in Manhattan, but also every element of this lodging is curated to a T for its well-heeled guests. State-of-the-art sound systems are built into the walls of each room, which guests can easily connect to from their own devices; if the guests don't know which melody will suit the mood, they can tune into one of the hotels four private "radio" stations, spun by DJ Stretch Armstrong, who has a talent for finding music that's soothing but never dull. An art curator placed individual works in each room and a design team meticulously crafted new furniture using vintage methods and shapes, with rich, nubby fabrics adding a pop of modernity. Somehow the effect in the

The magnificent lobby bar of the Nine Orchard hotel, once a grand bank.

guest rooms is of a classic Edward Hopper painting, but for happy people, rather than ones filled with existential dread. Star chef Ignacio Matteo is in charge of palate pampering, which means that food and drink (in the hotel's two bars and two restaurants) is startlingly pricey, but topnotch. If you have the funds, this hotel, set in the Lower East Side's most happening nightlife and dining area, will be an exciting place to stay.

9 Orchard St. (off Canal St.). nineorchard.com. ✆ **212/804-9900.** 116 units. $529–$754 double. Subway: B, D to Grand; F to East Broadway. **Amenities:** 2 restaurants; 2 bars; room service; fitness room; free Wi-Fi.

Expensive/Moderate

NobleDEN ♥♥ Mostly Europeans book this sleek hotel, which sits on the porous border between Chinatown and Little Italy. My guess is they're drawn in by the clean Scandinavian-style design (lots of neutral colors offset by pops of primary colors, hidden drawers that double your storage space, angular lamps, and two-room bathrooms). I like the king units best, as they have floor-to-ceiling windows that open to a Juliet balcony overlooking the action on Grand Street below. But the rooms with queen beds, the cheapest on property, are a bit quieter as they face a courtyard rather than the street (that being said, Grand Street isn't particularly busy at night, just during the day). ***One note:*** The beds, though high-quality, are firmer than many Americans are used to (perhaps because the hotel's owner is Malaysian and that's the style there).

196 Grand St. (btw. Mulberry & Mott sts.). nobleden.com. ✆ **212/390-8988.** 54 units. $128–$553 double. Subway: B, D to Grand St.; N, Q, R, 6 to Canal St. **Amenities:** Restaurant; free use of nearby gym; free Wi-Fi.

Moderate/Inexpensive

50 Bowery ♥♥ When the foundations for this new hotel were excavated, its Chinatown site turned into an unexpected archeological dig. Artifacts from the 17th to the early 19th century were found, harkening back to the taverns, gambling dens, and vaudeville and movie theaters that once stood here. And you can still see all those objects: 50 Bowery partnered with the Museum of Chinese in America (p. 182) to create a permanent gallery on the hotel's second floor about the history and culture of Chinatown. That respect for the neighborhood is evident throughout the hotel: Large, splashy paintings by Beijing graffiti artist Dake Wong adorn the hallways, guest-room walls have a subtle blue-and-white pattern (evoking traditional chinaware), and archival photos of Chinatown hang everywhere. No interest in Asian culture? You can still enjoy your stay in wonderfully spacious rooms with floor-to-ceiling windows, rain showerheads, and modish decor. On-site amenities include a very good gym and a year-round rooftop bar with 360-degree views.

50 Bowery (near Canal St.). jdvhotels.com. ✆ **212/508-8000.** 229 units. $179–$364. Subway: 1, 2, 3, 4, 5, 6, N, Q, R to Canal St. Pets stay free. **Amenities:** Restaurant; rooftop bar; room service; music club; fitness room; free Wi-Fi.

Leon Hotel ♥♥ "When people call, I tell them this isn't a rinky dink Chinatown hotel, despite the location," the front desk clerk proudly told me on my last visit to the Hotel Leon. "We got luxury here!" While I wouldn't go quite that far, it's undeniable that the Leon has more niceties than its peers, both in this neighborhood (yup, it's Chinatown) and price range. Rooms, though beige, beige, beige in decor, are high ceilinged and roomy, with the kind of comfortable mattresses, good closets (or spacious armoires) and well-designed bathrooms that one usually only gets in hotels one price tier up. Other extras include cushioned window seats (for curling up and gazing at the Freedom Tower or the Manhattan Bridge), safes, and Keurig coffee machines. The Leon is an especially smart choice for families, thanks to its massive two-room suites that can easily sleep six in their three queen-sized beds.

125 Canal St. (at the entrance to the Manhattan Bridge.). leonhotelnyc.com. ✆ **212/390-8833.** 55 units. $84–$213 double. Subway: B, D to Grand St. or J, Z, N, Q or 6 to Canal St. **Amenities:** Free Wi-Fi.

Mimosa Hotel ♥♥ The staff gets top marks at the Mimosa. No, they don't greet guests with a mimosa cocktail on arrival, but really do go all out to make guests feel supported and welcome. The rooms are spic and span if forgettable looking, with sleepable beds and double-paned windows that do a surprisingly good job of keeping out the noise of the above-ground subway that passes by on the bridge across the street. (It sounds like a moving thunder storm out on the street, but barely registers inside the hotel.) You'll be bunking deep in Manhattan's Chinatown here, but near to the Lower East Side, and a good number of subway lines.

79 Division St. (near East Broadway). hotelmimosany.com. ✆ **212/343-4243.** $84–$212 double. Subway: F to East Broadway or B, D to Grand St. **Amenities:** Free Wi-Fi.

Now Now Noho ♥ Now Now is the U.S. equivalent of a Japanese capsule hotel . . . but with slightly less privacy, because the ceiling of each guest "cabin" is open, with slats across it to stop guests from climbing into each other's rooms. That means talking on your phone in your room is forbidden, and each unit comes equipped with eye masks, because if your neighbor has a light on, it will filter into your room. Also, bathrooms are shared: one toilet room and one shower room, for every 18 guests (additional facilities are in the basement, along with lockers for large luggage). Still, rooms are well-maintained and spiffy, if tiny at 27 sq. ft., with fine linens, luxe mattresses, loaner bathrobes, and wireless charging docks. Only one guest is allowed per room. The neighborhood is groovy, but we only recommend a stay here if it's the cheapest available sleep (otherwise: you can do better). ***Note:*** Two floors are for women and non-binary people only.

338 Bowery (btw. Great Jones and Bond sts.). staynownow.com. No phone. $98–$282 single with shared bath. Subway: 6 to Bleecker St. or B, D, F, M to Broadway/Lafayette. **Amenities:** Free Wi-Fi.

Untitled at 3 Freeman Alley ♥♥ Set at the end of a graffitied alley, with a tattoo shop right off the lobby and a kiosk of rental guitars, this hotel gives its guests massive street cred. Though the rooms are small (this used to be a homeless mission), they're handsomely wood trimmed. The highest ones have dazzling views, but they can get noise from the rooftop bar in the warmer months. The location is steps from some of the city's best restos and nightlife. ***Tip:*** Cheapest rooms here are the "mini-studios" but at just 125 sq. ft., they only have room for full-size beds, so are best for singles or very close couples. Bunkbed rooms are available for families.

3 Freeman Alley (off Rivington St., nr Bowery). untitledat3freeman.com. No phone. 200 units. $181–$366 mini-studio; continental breakfast included. Subway: F to Second Ave. **Amenities:** Rooftop bar; tattoo parlor; guitar rentals; free Wi-Fi.

SOHO

Despite SoHo's streets of chain stores (mostly the major boulevards), the area still has great charm, due to its proliferation of cast-iron buildings. In terms of hotels, the neighborhood is strictly high-end.

Best for: A stay in the SoHo area offers close proximity to Chinatown, top shopping, and some very fine restaurants.

Drawbacks: You won't find much in the way of budget/value accommodations in the neighborhood. Also, because of the downtown arts scene, SoHo has two high seasons: May/June and the fall months. So, you'll find fewer deals here than in other areas during those times.

Expensive

Crosby Street Hotel ♥♥♥ As much gallery as hotel, the Crosby Street is true eye-candy. Designed by co-owner Kit Kemp, every room and public area features quirky, often funny, and always compelling works of sculpture and painting. This includes the guest rooms, each of which has a different look from the next (mine was all done in black-and-white, but others are saturated with colors, perhaps taking on the ambience of a garden, or the vibrant color palette of Morocco). Floor-to-ceiling warehouse-style windows light up the rooms, and the deluxe bathrooms feature such niceties as heated towel racks and bidets. None of this comes cheap, but with an on-site movie theater, fabulous location, and very good restaurant, the Crosby Hotel is perfect for a special-occasion stay.

79 Crosby St. (btw. Prince & Spring sts.). crosbystreethotel.com. ✆ **212/226-6400.** 86 units. $1,365–$2,250 double. Subway: N, R to Prince St. **Amenities:** Restaurant; bar; fitness center; room service; screening room; free Wi-Fi.

The art-crammed lobby of SoHo's gallery-like Crosby Street Hotel.

Moderate/Inexpensive

Arlo SoHo ♥♥ "Our rooms are so small that we try to give guests somewhere else to go," the check-in clerk admitted when I asked him about the lobby sign announcing poker leagues, trivia nights, and wine tastings. He wasn't exaggerating: Many of the Arlo's rooms look like they could notch into a small corner of an IKEA showroom floor (some start at just 150 sq. ft., including the bathroom). Not that the quality of the furnishings is IKEA level: Space-saving fold-down desks are made of handsome walnut, bath products are luxe, and the beds, wedged into an alcove with floor-to-ceiling windows, are as fluffy as you'd get at the Plaza (and look almost like an art installation, the wooden frame on the walls around them announcing "Bed!"). For non-intimate twosomes, there are bunk-bed rooms; couples who don't wish to crawl over one another to get into and out of bed should request a queen room (there's JUST enough space to walk around the beds in those). And as for those heavily used public spaces, they're downright glamorous, with a bar, rooftop, and lobby set up like very well-appointed living rooms.

231 Hudson St. (btw. Canal & Dominick sts.). arlohotels.com. ✆ **212/342-7000.** 96 units. $172–$395 double. Subway: 1 to Canal St. **Amenities:** Restaurant; bar; rooftop bar; free loaner bikes; 24-hr. on-site store; free Wi-Fi.

THE VILLAGE

Greenwich Village, despite the influx of big-name stores, still has that romantic appeal with its winding, narrow streets, brownstones, and intimate dining spots.

Best for: People who love to explore classic/historic old neighborhoods; close to shops, restaurants, bars, and clubs.

Drawbacks: Can be noisy and crowded, particularly on weekends. While it's got its residential streets, this downtown area is where New York (and the surrounding area) goes to party.

Expensive/Inexpensive

Washington Square Hotel ♥ This hotel has always had a top location, right off graceful Washington Square Park, and has a decor to match, filled with Art Deco paintings, murals, and photos that pay homage to the many stars who have stayed here over the years. Built in 1904, it served as a second home for many top vaudeville and Broadway performers until the 1950s, when it devolved into a rather seedy apartment hotel housing a number of struggling artists including Joan Baez, Bob Dylan, Barbra Streisand, and Phyllis Diller. Legend has it that the Mamas and the Papas wrote "California Dreamin'" at the Washington Square. The rooms, though small, are smartly designed with cushy duvets, oversize 1940s photos of movie stars, and space-saving features (such as the wall-mounted TV) that make the rooms appear *slightly* bigger than they actually are.

103 Waverly Place (btw. Fifth & Sixth aves.). wshotel.com. ✆ **800/222-0418** or 212/777-9515. 160 units. $161–$430 double; continental breakfast included. Subway: A, B, C, D, E, F to 4th St. (use 3rd St. exit). **Amenities:** Restaurant; exercise room; free Wi-Fi.

Rooms at The Jane are extremely compact. Still, it's one of the most affordable places to stay in Manhattan, and in a lovely neighborhood.

Inexpensive

The Jane ♥ In 1912, when the survivors of the Titanic were brought back to New York by the *SS Carpathian*, many stayed that first night at this hotel. It seems appropriate, therefore, that most of The Jane's rooms have the look of a ship's cabin (or perhaps a railway sleeping car)—highly compact with a shelf above the bed for luggage. Let me go a bit further in explaining what I mean by "compact": These, and those of Now Now (p. 55), may well be the smallest rooms in NYC (which says a lot). When I was standing in one recently, I spread out my arms and came within about 5 inches of touching both walls at once. So, this ain't the place for claustrophobes. Rooms for two have bunk beds, making the space seem even smaller. Back when The Jane first opened in 2008, these dollhouse-size digs had every luxury (fine bedding, iPod docking stations, flatscreen TVs) and access to a high-end coffee shop and scenester bar. Alas, in 2025 a private club took over the glamorous public areas, and now guests at The Jane enter through a basement lobby. Rooms are clean but no longer have any luxe touches—the fine linens are gone and the mattresses are squeaky and hard. Still, for those willing to share a bathroom (all the rooms that once had ensuite baths are gone), this will be one of the cheapest sleeps in the city. And the Greenwich Village neighborhood The Jane inhabits is a tree-lined beaut.

114 Jane St. (at West St.). thejanenyc.com. ✆ **212/924-6700.** 150 units. $139–$199 double w/shared bath. Subway: A, C, E to 14th St. **Amenities:** Free Wi-Fi.

CHELSEA/HUDSON YARDS

A center for both contemporary art and nightlife, Chelsea is home to the High Line park, Hudson Yards, and many galleries and restaurants, and it's an easy walk to Herald Square.

Best for: People who want to be close to the action but not in the center of it; a good range of accommodations from high-end to moderate.

Drawbacks: Can be noisy at night along the main drags (especially the avenues and 23rd St.).

Expensive

Faena New York ♥♥ Real estate developer Alan Faena had a dream. No, not to eradicate world hunger. Faena wanted to grow roses on the beach (I kid you not). Eventually he was able to achieve his goal, and as a result, all of his hotels (two in Miami, one in Buenos Aires, and now one in NYC) have a rose theme. Rooms and hallways have pops of deep red, the hand-painted murals in the public areas feature the flower, and all guest rooms get a vase of fresh roses daily. These are just the start of the luxe touches here, which include beds that are at once soft as a snowflake while supportive of the back, multiple ways to light your room without ever leaving said bed, smart TVs hidden behind mirrors, and floor-to-ceiling windows with fun views of the High Line and Hudson River from many. The basement spa has an elaborate gym, 3 full-sized swimming pools (salt, warm, and cold), a hammam, and treatment rooms. There's also a restaurant and a bar with live music come

If you like gold and roses, the Faena New York is the hotel for you.

Midtown Accommodations

1 Hotel Central Park 9
3 West Club 11
The Carlton Arms Hotel 22
Casablanca Hotel 7
Chelsea Inn 25
Civilian NYC 8
Faena New York 1
Freehand New York City 23
Henn na Hotel New York 4
Hotel St. James 14
The Kixby 18
The Langham 19
The Leo House 2
Little Charlie Hotel 15
MADE Hotel 21
Menno House 24
Pendry Manhattan West 3
The Pestana CR7 Times Square 5
The Pod 39 16
The Pod 51 12
The Pod Times Square 6
The Refinery 17
U Hotel Fifth Avenue 20
The Waldorf Astoria 13
The Whitby Hotel 10

UPPER EAST SIDE
PARK
Center Dr.
East Dr.
South
Fifth Ave.
Madison Ave.
E. 64th St.
E. 63rd St.
E. 62nd St.
E. 61st St.
E. 60th St.
E. 59th St.
E. 58th St.
E. 57th St.
E. 56th St.
E. 55th St.
E. 54th St.
E. 53rd St.
E. 52nd St.
E. 51st St.
E. 50th St.
E. 49th St.
E. 48th St.
E. 47th St.
E. 46th St.
E. 45th St.
E. 44th St.
E. 43rd St.
E. 42nd St.
E. 41st St.
E. 40th St.
E. 39th St.
E. 38th St.
E 37th St.
E 36th St.
E. 35th St.
E. 34th St.
E. 33rd St.
E. 32nd St.
E. 31st St.
E. 30th St.
E. 29th St.
E. 28th St.
E. 27th St.
E. 26th St.
E. 25th St.
E. 24th St.
E. 23rd St.
E. 22nd St.
E. 21st St.
E. 20th St.
E. 19th St.
E. 18th St.
E. 17th St.
E. 16th St.
E. 15th St.
E. 14th St.
W. 32nd St.
Lexington Av/ 63 St F-Q
Roosevelt Island Tram
5 Av/59 St E-N-R-W
59 St 4-5-6
Lexington Av/ 59 St N-R-W
Queensboro (59th St.) Bridge
ROOSEVELT ISLAND
Sutton Pl.
Sutton Pl. South
57 St F
Lexington Av/ 53 St E-M
5 Av/53 St E-M
51 St 6
ROCKEFELLER CENTER
St. Patrick's Cathedral
47-50 Sts Rockefeller Ctr B-D-F-M
MIDTOWN EAST
Third Ave.
Beekman Place
Mitchell Place
First Ave.
United Nations
Lexington Ave.
Park Ave.
Vanderbilt Ave.
Madison Ave.
Fifth Ave.
(Ave. of the Americas)
Sixth Ave.
Second Ave.
Grand Central Terminal
East River
42 St Bryant Pk B-D-F-M
5 Av 7
Grand Central 42 St S-4-5-6-7-Metro North
Queens-Midtown Tunnel
Bryant Park
New York Public Library
MURRAY HILL
Upper Manhattan
Uptown
Midtown
Downtown
34 St Herald Square B-D-F-M-N-Q-R-W
Macy's
Empire State Bldg.
33 St 6
Broadway
Park Ave. S.
Franklin Delano Roosevelt (FDR) Dr.
28 St R-W
28 St 6
Sixth Ave. (Ave. of the Americas)
Madison Square Park
23 St R-W
23 St 6
23 St F-M
Asser Levy Pl.
Ave. C
Gramercy Park
GRAMERCY PARK
FLATIRON DISTRICT
14 St-Union Square L-N-Q-R-W-4-5-6
Irving Pl.
3 Av L
N.D. Perlman Pl.
1 Av L
14 St F-M
6 Av L
Subway stop
0 1/4 mi
0 0.25 km
9
10
11
12
13
14
15
16
17
18
19
20
21
22
23
24
25

FAMILY-FRIENDLY hotels

Lugging the kids to New York City can be a daunting experience. Finding a hotel that makes that experience a bit less overwhelming (whether in the accommodations themselves or via amenities) can be a huge help. Here are some of the city's best accommodations for families:

1 Hotel Central Park (Midtown West; p. 39) Your kids can pretend they're camping out, with loaner sleeping bags and games. Plus, Central Park is just steps away.

Freehand (Gramercy Park area; p. 38) Rooms with two bunk beds sleeping four are often on sale at this fashion-forward hotel that's also quite child-friendly, with a game room and eating options all day long.

Henry Norman Hotel (Greenpoint, Brooklyn; p. 40) Kitchens to feed hangry kids, in genuinely spacious and gracious suites. Plus, the staff here are gifted at making children feel like VIPs.

Hotel Beacon (Upper West Side; p. 40) In-room kitchenette, on-site laundromat, and spacious rooms in a kid-friendly neighborhood—what more do you want?

Mint House at 70 Pine (Financial District; p. 34) With one, two, three, and even four-bedroom apartment-style units, there's room for the *entire* family here. Plus, no one will get bored, thanks to half a dozen free activities that come with the nightly rate (bowling anyone?).

Pod 39 (Midtown East; p. 39) Bunk-bed rooms plus ping pong and pool tables in the lobby. Can you say kiddie heaven (and at an affordable rate)?

evening. I just wish the decor here was a bit less florid—it's impressively daubed with gold leaf, but overall the effect is garish rather than refined.

500 W. 18th St. (btw. 10th and 11th aves). faena.com. ✆ **212/545-8100.** $944–$1,432 double. Subway: L to Eighth Ave. **Amenities:** Restaurant; bar; room service; 24-hr. gym; spa; 3 pools; free Wi-Fi.

Pendry Manhattan West ♥♥♥ If Frank Lloyd Wright were to come miraculously back to life and start designing once more, this is the hotel he would have built. It takes its cues from nature, just as Wright's projects did: The soaring skyscraper's glass facade undulates like waves on a pond, and the interior is all white oak and sunlight, streaming through the floor-to-ceiling windows. What feels miraculous to this long-time New Yorker is that a hotel this sophisticated was built in an area that less than a decade ago was one of the most rundown and bleak parts of town. Nearby Hudson Yards changed all that, creating an audience for the Pendry's five exceptional bars and restaurants. Among the many perks: guest rooms that start at a generous 320 sq. ft.; beds draped in Fili D'Oro linens; all-marble bathrooms stocked with MiN bath products. For those who like to sweat, there's a state-of-the-art gym with Pelotons (suite guests can even request a Peloton to be delivered to their rooms for a private workout). In addition, the hotel's "Cadillac Ride or Drive" program allows guests to request a free car with chauffeur for jaunts around the city, or a loaner car if they want to drive themselves anywhere in the tri-state area.

438 W. 33rd St. (btw. Ninth & Tenth aves.). pendry.com. ✆ **212/933-7000.** 164 units. $875–$1,193 double. Subway: 7 to 34th St./Hudson Yards. **Amenities:** 5 restaurants and bars; room service; 24-hr. gym; business center; free Wi-Fi.

Moderate/Inexpensive

Chelsea Inn ♥ Straddling the border between Chelsea and Union Square, the Chelsea Inn keeps its prices (usually) low because many rooms share a bathroom (never more than two rooms to a toilet; you'll have a shower and sink in your room). Recent upgrading replaced grungy carpets and mismatched grandma's-house-style furnishings with billowy duvets on the beds, shiny wood floors, and exposed brick walls (showing the bones of this 1800s town house). A nice touch: All rooms have small fridges and microwaves. Bad news: street noise, loud plumbing, and prices that are sometimes the equivalent of places with private loos (book elsewhere when that's the case).

46 W. 17th St. (near Fifth Ave.). chelseainn.com. ✆ **800/640-6469** or 212/645-8989. $92–$299 double w/shared bathroom (more for rooms w/private bathroom); continental breakfast included. Subway: Q, N, R, L, 4, 5, 6 to Union Sq. **Amenities:** Small fridges and microwaves in rooms; free Wi-Fi.

UNION SQUARE, FLATIRON DISTRICT & GRAMERCY PARK

Farmers markets, top-notch restaurants, an active street life, and pockets of charming brownstones and historic buildings—what's not to like about this tri-partite district? I think it's probably the best place in the city to base yourself, partially because Union Square is one of the most useful hubs in the subway system, hosting a crosstown train (the L), several that angle from east to west (the N, Q, and R), and the green line that runs up the east side (4, 5, and 6).

Best for: People who like a centrally located neighborhood that's not dominated by skyscrapers, but still has great shopping, theater, and dining.

Drawbacks: Not the cheapest group of neighborhoods in Manhattan, plus no museums or major tourist sights are here.

Expensive/Moderate

MADE Hotel ♥♥ The bed is the keystone of a hotel room—and the beds at MADE are extraordinary for two reasons. First, the mattress, from a brand you've likely never encountered (Leesa Sapira), a dreamy hybrid that's half memory foam and half coils—the memory foam contours to the body while the coils circulate air so sleepers won't get too hot. Second, the bed is swathed in gazillion-thread-count sheets, as well as (a key design element) colorful South African "mudflap" cloths (no, they've never touched mud) at the bottom of the bed and woven into the bedframe slats, giving the room a

Beds in the MADE Hotel are done up with distinctive woven South African cloth.

glamping/safari vibe. Another striking touch: a wooden wall-grid system of shelves, desktop, and hangers. Amenities in the rest of the hotel are equal selling points—a very good gym, a view-blessed rooftop bar, a lobby coffee bar, and a tapas restaurant.

42 W. 29th St. (btw. Broadway & Sixth Ave.). madehotels.com. ✆ **212/213-4429.** 72 units. $237–$521 double. Subway: R, W to 28th St. **Amenities:** Restaurant; room service; cafe; 2 bars; fitness room; free Wi-Fi.

Freehand New York City ♥♥♥

Attention solo travelers: This is your hotel pick. With its unusually high number of small single rooms (each with private bathroom), you can score a room here with one cot-size (but very comfortable) bed for $66 to $80 less than the cheapest double rooms, except in the depths of low season when prices are closer. (These discounts are usually only on the hotel's own website, so go there if you're traveling alone.) What makes this offer even more extraordinary is how sweet the digs are—not only these rooms, but also the hotel's larger rooms. (Quad rooms with two bunk beds are also often on sale.) They have a '70s hippie vibe—earth tones, groovy wall murals, ceramic lamps, Native American–style throws. Public

Even the stairway at the Freehand New York City is crowded with artwork.

areas are equally fun, crammed with artwork by students and alumni of NY's Bard College. This artistic leitmotif has its roots in the history of this 90-year-old building, formerly the George Washington Hotel: Poet W. H. Auden crashed here, as did novelist Christopher Isherwood, punk rocker Dee Dee Ramone, and painter Keith Haring.

23 Lexington Ave. (at 23rd St.). freehandhotels.com. ✆ **212/475-1920.** 350 units. $142–$424 double. Subway: 6 to 23rd St. **Amenities:** 2 restaurants; 2 bars, including the Broken Shaker (p. 358); fitness center; game room; gift shop; free Wi-Fi.

Inexpensive

The Carlton Arms Hotel ♥♥ If you get worried when you notice that your room is listing a bit to the right, or if you expect a maid to change your sheets daily, then this ain't the hotel for you. But if you're the type who wants to try something really different, and who finds the idea of being cocooned in art interesting, then choose this 165-year-old hotel with the soul of William Blake. Over the years, the Carlton Arms has invited artists to paint murals and create unusual environments in the guest rooms, which many have done with wild glee. There's the Egyptian Hallway, with mummy portraits of staff members; a "Steampunk" room with pseudo-scientific diagrams on the walls and a chandelier; and the Goth Room, where gender-bending portraits leer down at the queen-size bed. The now-famous Banksy added murals to the stairwell. Rooms include super-cheap singles as well as affordable triples and quads; share a bathroom (an option in about a third of the rooms), and you'll save $10 to $30 a night. ***Note:*** There is no elevator and rooms don't have phones or TVs.

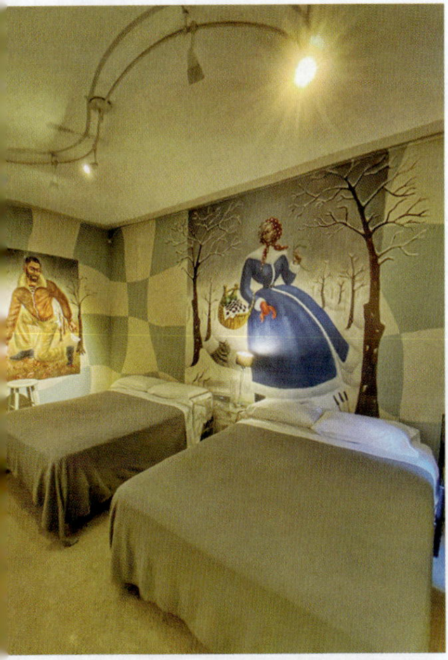

Every room in the Carlton Arms has unique art, like these murals by Magnus Irvin.

160 E. 25th St. (at Third Ave.). carltonarms.com. ✆ **212/679-0680.** 54 units. $137–$172 double. Subway: N, R, 6 to 28th St. **Amenities:** Free Wi-Fi.

TIMES SQUARE & MIDTOWN WEST

Times Square might be the heart of Manhattan, but it's also the city's most congested neighborhood (if you can really call it a neighborhood). Corporate

At 1 Hotel Central Park (p. 67), luxury and sustainability go hand in hand. Some suites include skyscraper and Central Park views.

Midtown West is centrally located, but as a result, high in demand for both business and leisure travelers. Hotels here almost always fill up fast, and thus prices tend to be substantially higher than most other areas.

Best for: People who want to be in the center of "the city that never sleeps," steps from Broadway theaters.

Drawbacks: Staying here puts you among tourists rather than locals and keeps you from experiencing more of the "real" New York. That certainly goes for food, which tends to be centered on multinational chains, though there are a few local gems. It's also the most frenetic, exhausting, loud neighborhood in the city (so not great for sleeping).

Expensive

1 Hotel Central Park ♥♥♥ I don't know if I've ever fallen in love with a hotel's smell before (usually, just the opposite happens, thanks to those chemical perfumes some pump into the air). But 1 Hotel smells like a field of herbs, heavy on the dill—it's delightful, and apropos for this nature-loving hotel with its ivy-bearded facade. The hotel uses sustainable practices throughout, taking a number of steps to moderate its carbon footprint, with all interiors crafted from reclaimed materials, including the ample guest rooms, which look airlifted from some tech billionaire's mountain cabin. I'm talking lots of wide, artfully weathered boards for the floors and walls, a glass box of a shower (drapes can be drawn around it by the modest), and live plants growing here and there. Oh, and the mattresses are stuffed with hemp and infused with green tea (inhale deeply). Their "Seedlings" program for kids loans sleeping bags and games so youngsters can pretend to "camp" in the rooms. Best natural touch? Some rooms have corner views of Central Park (it's a block from the hotel).

1414 Ave. of the Americas (at 58th St.). 1hotels.com. ✆ **212/703-2001.** $450–$1,103 double. Subway: N, R, W to Fifth Ave. or F to 57th St. **Amenities:** Restaurant; bar; business center; loaner iPads; gym; lobby farmstand (fresh produce for purchase); room service; free Wi-Fi.

The Whitby Hotel ♥♥♥ If filmmaker Wes Anderson had been allowed to design a hotel, but then Tom Hanks were charged with running it, you'd get the Whitby. Its decor (actually created by co-owner Kit Kemp) is a witty, charming, oh-so-chic mishmash—an antique chair here, a riotously colorful wallpaper there, a corner with 20 different hanging lamps just beyond. Everywhere there are whimsical contemporary and modern art pieces. The new building was custom-built for comfort—rooms are capacious, with floor-to-ceiling casement windows (and sometimes balconies), luxe BeautyRest mattresses, and bidet-laden marble bathrooms. A debonair restaurant, movie theater, and gym are also on the premises. As for the staff, they are the salt of the earth, a crew chosen for their kindliness and attention to detail. The hotel,

There's nothing cookie-cutter about the colorful, eclectic decor of the Whitby Hotel.

a sister property of the Crosby Street Hotel (p. 56), is the top midtown pick for fans of contemporary design. Just 2 blocks from Central Park.

18 W. 56th St. (btw. Fifth & Sixth aves.). firmdalehotels.com. ✆ **888/559-5508** or 212/586-5656. 86 units. $895–$1,495 double. Subway: F to 57th St. or N, R, W to Fifth Ave. **Amenities:** Restaurant; bar; room service; movie theater; gym; honor bar; library; free Wi-Fi.

Expensive/Moderate

Casablanca Hotel ♥♥ Yes, this hotel is an homage to that famous movie. So, the breakfast room, which doubles as a wine-and-cheese lounge in the evenings (and offers free treats all day), is called **Rick's Café.** Some nights there's free piano music ("Play it again, Sam!"). Rooms (small, but what else is new in New York?) are equipped with rattan furniture, ceiling fans, and wooden blinds for that 1940s hideaway-in-Morocco atmosphere. The building offers two outdoor areas, a rooftop deck, and a second-floor courtyard, so you can enjoy the sunshine without having to deal with the maddening crowds of Times Square (just down the block). Did I mention that most of the staff seem to have as sweet a temperament as Ingrid Bergman? (Translation: Service is top-notch.)

147 W. 43rd St. (just E of Broadway). casablancahotel.com. ✆ **888/922-7225** or 212/869-1212. 48 units. $299–$496 double; continental breakfast included. Subway: N, R, 1, 2, 3 to 42nd St./Times Sq. **Amenities:** Access to nearby gym; all-day cappuccino; nightly wine and cheese reception; room service; free Wi-Fi.

With its retro Moroccan decor, the Casablanca Hotel offers a welcome refuge just steps from Times Square.

The Refinery ♥♥ The Refinery has a sophisticated, celebratory vibe, thanks to the jazz soundtrack that echoes through the lobby (recorded during the day, at night live in the handsome lobby bar); the view-rich rooftop bar/restaurant; and the clever ways it pays homage to the manufacturing roots of this 1912 Garment Center building. A former hat factory, the Refinery places Singer sewing machine tables as desks in the guest rooms, while an installation behind the front desk features old millinery tools. Rooms come in a range of sizes, starting at a respectable 250 sq. ft., but feel bigger than they are thanks to 12-ft.-high ceilings and large windows. Original abstract artwork, oak hardwood floors, and custom furniture up the design ante. Bathrooms feature marble mosaic floors, polished brass fixtures, and rainfall showers. All in all, this is a nice place to stay, though it charges more than its worth in high season.

63 W. 38th St. (btw. Fifth & Sixth aves.). refineryhotelnewyork.com. ✆ **646/664-0310.** 197 units. $284–$751 double. Subway: N, Q, R, B, D to 34th St. **Amenities:** Restaurant; bar; seasonal roof bar/restaurant; room service; fitness room; free Wi-Fi.

Expensive/Inexpensive

Important note: Midtown hotel prices swing more widely between high and low season than any other area of the city. While I like all of the hotels listed in this section, not a one of them is worth what it's charging in the fall months (or when prices go above $400). You'll find hotels in other areas charging less at those times, for more space, and more amenities.

3 West Club ♥♥♥ Built by the Women's National Republican Club in the 1930s, this landmarked, 11-story hotel is open to all comers but feels like a private club. It has not one but two ballrooms where many weddings take place; a wood paneled library; and a weekday pub/restaurant (somewhat hidden upstairs). Guest rooms are defiantly old school: large by NYC standards, with fine prints hanging on Wedgewood blue walls, curvaceous real antique furnishings, and heavy brocade curtains. Most overlook Rockefeller Center, which is right across the street. Surprisingly, prices are relatively reasonable most of the year, perhaps because there's no fitness center or breakfast here. It's darn near impossible to get more centrally located digs.

3 West 51st St. (btw. Fifth and Sixth aves.). 3westclub.com. ✆ **212/582-5454.** 30 units. $145–$357 double. Subway: E, F to Fifth Ave/53rd St. **Amenities:** Restaurant; bar; free Wi-Fi.

Civilian NYC ♥♥ If you're in town specifically to see Broadway shows, make this your base. I say that not only because Civilian is just a 2- to 3-minute walk from most of the city's major playhouses, but also because the hotel itself is theater geek nirvana, taking "backstage" as its theme. The walls are hung with photos of the goings-on in the wings from famous productions; drawn velvet curtains frame the beds for a proscenium-like effect; and a cocktail lounge displays model sets, props, and costume pieces from recent Broadway musicals and plays. The hotel has a partnership with the American Theater Wing, which lends it memorabilia on a rotating basis in return for the hotel giving guests a gentle nudge to donate to this storied non-profit organization. Rooms are, alas, the size of the Great White Way's tiny dressing rooms, but they're decorated by style star David Rockwell, so they're quite pleasant. ***Tip:*** Make your reservation directly, and they'll match any price you find online and throw in free daily passes to a swish gym down the block (a $35 value).

305 W. 48th St. (btw. Eighth & Ninth aves.). civilianhotel.com. ✆ **646/692-8012.** 180 units. $129–$418 double. Subway: C, E to 50th St. Pets accepted (up to 100 lbs.) **Amenities:** Restaurant; 2 bars (one rooftop); free Wi-Fi.

Civilian NYC plays up its theater connections by dramatically displaying memorabilia in the Broadway Blue Room lounge.

Henn na Hotel New York ♥♥ The very first U.S. hotel from this tech-obsessed Japanese chain has some pretty nifty gadgets and gizmos. The fun

A serene guest room at the Kixby Hotel.

starts in the lobby, where a life-size animatronic dinosaur greets guests with lots of grunting and low roars. Upstairs, going to the bathroom is also an adventure, thanks to Toto interactive toilets that heat up and, um, clean users with jets of water. Those who upgrade to either an executive king room or a suite get both a temperature-controlled mattress and an L. G. Styler closet, which will press your trousers, steam your dresses, and disinfect clothing—all at the push of two or three buttons! Rooms are large for Gotham, and each gets a bathtub—a requirement in Japan. But beyond these perks, the place is almost monastically spare in its design: No art adorns the walls; no scent is allowed anywhere (a blessing, I think); and the decor is all monochrome, which some will find restful, others dreary.

235 W. 35th St. (near Eighth Ave.). hennnahotelny.com. ✆ **212/729-4366.** 92 units. $152–$599 double. Subway: A, C, E to 34th St. **Amenities:** Restaurant; access to nearby gym; free Wi-Fi.

The Kixby ♥♥ Erected as a hotel in 1901, this property has had many names and owners over the years. Since the 1990s it's been a family-run operation, first as the Hotel Metro, and then, when the son took over, as the Kixby. He, yes, kicked the operation up a notch, installing Peloton bikes in the small gym, painting guest rooms a soothing shade of slate blue, and upgrading to good quality pillowtop mattresses. Off the lobby is burger joint **Black Tap,** known for its over-the-top milkshakes; it also supplies breakfast to guests (additional cost). Many of the staff have been here for decades; they offer gracious, expert service and take obvious pride in the place.

45 W. 35th St. (btw. Sixth & Fifth aves.). kixby.com. ✆ **800/356-3870.** $233–$469 Subway: B, D, N, R, W to 34th St. **Amenities:** Restaurant; bar; gym; free Wi-Fi.

With its midtown views and sports-themed details, the Pestana CR7 Times Square delivers good value to an international mix of guests.

The Pestana CR7 Times Square ♥♥ Just how international is the NYC hotel scene? This midtown property is themed for (and partly owned by) Portuguese soccer star Cristiano Ronaldo—and that's proved a definite lure to the largely European clientele who come here. Even if you're not into *fútbol,* the sporty touches are good fun: lobby lights that take their inspiration from soccer balls, elevator-facing walls that resemble AstroTurf, carpeting patterned with Ronaldo's signature, and little plastic goalies on guest-room walls to be used as coat hangers. And it's not just soccer being celebrated: Handsome sports photos adorn all the rooms, paying homage to a number of different sports. As for the rooms—they'd be tiny in any other American city, but here they're a hair larger than normal, with high-quality mattresses.

338 W. 39th St. (near Eighth Ave.). pestanacr7.com. ✆ **833/341-2401.** 175 units. $134–$415 double. Subway: A, C, E to 42nd St. Pets accepted. **Amenities:** Restaurant; gym w/Peloton; business center; free Wi-Fi.

Moderate/Inexpensive

Hotel St. James ♥ My award for most improved hotel goes to this Times Square stalwart. The St. James spent the pandemic, and the years since, renovating and cleaning, and it shows. The hotel hasn't become fashionable or plush—furnishings are still all mass-produced—but its nightly rates remain lower than neighboring properties . . . most of the time. Expect spotless and highly functional guest quarters, with a tad more elbow room than usual, closets, private bathrooms, and blackout shades.

109 W. 45th St. (btw. Sixth & Seventh aves.). hotelstjames.net. ✆ **212/221-1600.** $141–$329 double (when booked on the St. James website; more on third-party sites). Subway: 1, 2, 3, N, Q, R, S to Times Square. **Amenities:** Free Wi-Fi.

MIDTOWN EAST & MURRAY HILL

This is *Mad Men* territory, where the barons of advertising and big business work. As a result, you'll find some of the grandest hotels—and also the most expensive.

Best for: People who like to stay in a more residential area, with a wide variety of (more high-end) accommodations.

Drawbacks: There's not a lot of variety in the dining options, and most attractions are farther west or farther uptown or downtown.

Expensive

The Langham ♥♥ Half hotel, half apartment building, this ultra-exclusive skyscraper is expert at coddling its guests. What that means is free shoeshines when guests arrive (can't have dusty tootsies in a place this fancy), a town car available at all hours, complimentary minibar, and rooms that feel like they're the dimensions of a squash court (the smallest start at 700 sq. ft.). Bathrooms feature soaking tubs and TVs hidden behind the mirrors. On-site is a celeb-helmed restaurant (Ai Fiori from Michael White) and a massive spa and gym. Those who ante up for suites get even more luxury, including full state-of-the-art kitchens (in the larger ones) and espresso machines. While the immediate neighborhood of the hotel is rather grungy, it's just a few short blocks from Bryant Park and the Empire State Building.

400 Fifth Ave. (btw. 36th & 37th sts.). langhamhotels.com. ✆ **212/695-4005.** 214 units. $625–$912 double. Subway: B, D, F, M, N, R, Q to 34th St. **Amenities:** Restaurant; bar; fitness center; room service; spa; salon; complimentary pressing service upon arrival; free Wi-Fi.

Modern furnishings and luxe amenities give the large rooms and suites at The Langham an air of exclusivity.

The Waldorf Astoria ♥♥ The Waldorf's guest rooms are generously proportioned now, after an 8-year-long renovation (completed in 2025) reduced the number from 1,400 to just 375, and upped the average size to 575 sq. ft. Rooms have such luxuries as Frette sheets, Aesop bath products, espresso machines, and full bathtubs (in 70% of the rooms). But there are hotel guest rooms in the city with more style (these are a bit generic looking) and more amenities for sure. What the competition doesn't have, and why staying here is such a treat, is the Waldorf Astoria's extraordinary history. I mean: That's Cole Porter's piano in the Peacock Alley bar, brought down here from what was his apartment upstairs (from 1939 to 1964, some of the composer's most fruitful years). That piano was also used by Frank Sinatra, who lived in that same apartment after Porter. (Look closely and you can see marks on the piano top from the pitchers of margaritas Porter ordered up from the lobby bar.) You also come here to dine on Waldorf salads, and throw back Rob Roy cocktails, in the place where both were invented. You stay because the Waldorf still *looks* much like it did in 1931—most of the interior public spaces are landmarked—when this iteration of the hotel opened as the largest and tallest one on the planet. And when you close your eyes to sleep, you just may have Presidential dreams: Every U.S. President from Hoover to Obama bunked here at one time or another. So, book, or just walk through, the Waldorf Astoria, so you too can become part of history.

301 Park Ave. (btw. 49th and 50th sts.). waldorfastorianewyork.com. ✆ **212/355-3000.** $935–$2,395 double. Subway: 6, E, F to Lexington Ave./53rd St. **Amenities:** 3 restaurants; bar; 24-hour room service; spa; massive fitness room (with classes); espresso machines in rooms; free Wi-Fi.

Moderate/Inexpensive

Little Charlie Hotel ♥♥ Nobody on staff knows why this hotel has its moniker, but I'll hazard some guesses. Rooms are little—not the smallest I've seen in NYC, but out of towners will still be shocked by their compactness. And there's something in the unpretentious, everyman quality of the nickname that sums up the vibe here. Guest rooms are very clean and feature blond wood furnishings, peacock blue mini fridges, shaggy throw blankets, and padded headboards that look vaguely Scandinavian enough to be of the moment, but could never be considered chic (can't imagine a chic Charlie either). Prices here are usually lower than you'll find for digs that are further west (but in return you'll have a longer walk to the subway and midtown attractions). ***Tip:*** Solo travelers can snag twin bedded rooms which are sometimes cheaper than the prices below.

837 Second Ave (at 45th St.). littlecharlie.com. ✆ **212/970-2837.** 12 units. $98–$375 double; continental breakfast included. Subway: 4, 5, 6, S, 7 to Grand Central Terminal. **Amenities:** Free Wi-Fi.

Inexpensive

U Hotel Fifth Avenue ♥ A sliver of a hotel in the shadow of the Empire State Building, the U has sliver-sized rooms, but they're unusually spiffy,

Art Deco elegance defines a stay at the Waldorf Astoria.

INVASION OF THE pods (hotels)

While many Gotham hotels have digs so small they could be considered "pods" rather than rooms (we're looking at you Now Now, p. 55, Arlo, p. 57, Jane, p. 58, and Riverside Tower p. 79) only one brand trumpets that fact in its name. Today, the **Pod Hotels** (thepodhotel.com) are a significant minichain, with four huge hotels—three in midtown and one in Brooklyn—all offering high style, and even high jinks, at low, low prices (as little as $70/night in low season). The hotels' designer has done a bang-up job of making savvy use of the space, building dressers into bed bases, attaching small TVs at each level of the bunk beds (yes, some doubles have bunk beds), and covering beds with sofa-like covers so they can be used as couches during the day. All this in rooms with a clean-lined Scandinavian look, with blond-wood-and-brushed-metal furnishings and fine modern prints on the walls. The very, very cheapest share bathrooms (at the 51st St. location only); all the rest have private loos. In addition, all properties have plenty of fun extras for guests, like free walking tours, rooftop bars, bustling on-site restaurants, and lobbies that double as lounges.

- **The Pod 51:** 230 E. 51st St., off Third Ave. (✆ **800/742-5945** or 212/355-0300)
- **The Pod 39:** 145 E. 39th St., off Lexington Ave. (✆ **855/763-5700** or 212/865-5700)
- **The Pod Times Square:** 400 W. 42nd St. at Ninth Ave. (✆ **844/763-7666**)
- **The Pod BK:** 247 Metropolitan Ave., Williamsburg, Brooklyn (✆ **844/763-7666**)

thanks to a relatively recent top-to-bottom renovation. Each has a marble bathroom, NYC art on the walls, and very comfy beds. Unfortunately, the rooms' A/C units jut into the room (they can't jut out because of landmarking laws), which can look awkward (and endanger knees). At the lowest prices you'll be sleeping in a full-size bed (all but very loving and slender couples, and solo travelers, should upgrade to a King or Queen room).

373 Fifth Ave. (at 35th St.). uhotelfifthavenue.com. ✆ **212/213-3388.** 117 units. $122–$201 double; breakfast included; discounts for stays of 3 nights or more. Subway: N, Q, R, B, D, F, M to Herald Sq. **Amenities:** Free Wi-Fi.

UPPER WEST SIDE

Families and chain stores are the chief residents of the Upper West Side, but it also has some significant sights (including Lincoln Center, Central Park, and the Museum of Natural History).

Best for: Visitors who want a more residential neighborhood, not as congested and noisy as midtown, and who are comfortable on the bus or subway; rooms are often larger and have a better value than in midtown.

Drawbacks: Midtown attractions are a bus/subway/taxi ride away, and downtown ones even more so.

Roomy one-bedroom suites at the Hotel Beacon are a great option for families.

Expensive/Moderate

Hotel Beacon ♥♥ With their olive-green or gold furnishings and plush leather headboards, rooms here are handsome in a "college town parent's hotel" sort of way. But what gives the Beacon two stars is its creature comforts: Each room comes with a fully usable kitchenette and a generous 340 sq. ft. or more, with a good-size marble bathroom and roomy closet. And because most standard rooms come with two double beds, they're ideal for families. Up one level are big one- and two-bedroom suites, each with a pullout sofa (families of five and six, take note). The two-bedroom suites have a second bathroom and are almost big enough for a softball team.

2130 Broadway (at 75th St.). beaconhotel.com. ✆ **800/572-4969** or 212/787-1100. 265 units. $289–$1,288 double. Subway: 1, 2, 3 to 72nd St. **Amenities:** Gym; kitchenettes; free Wi-Fi.

Hotel Belleclaire ♥♥ Built in 1903 as one of the first "skyscrapers" on the Upper West Side, the Belleclaire has housed such notables as Babe Ruth and Mark Twain. Its ambience is old-fashioned, both in its self-consciously "historic" lobby (the front desk looks like a library card catalog cabinet, for no apparent reason) and in the twisting, narrow hallways that lead from small guest room to even smaller guest room. The digs, however, are contemporary and comfortable, with hardwood floors, leather headboards on the beds, and geometric chandeliers. It has a great location (the subway is just 2 blocks away, Central Park is near), though lower-floor rooms that face Broadway can be loud.

250 W. 77th St. (at Broadway). hotelbelleclaire.com. ✆ **877/HOTEL-BC** [468-3522] or 212/362-7700. 189 units. $163–$603 double. Subway: 1 to 79th St. **Amenities:** Gym; coffee bar; free Wi-Fi.

Clever space-saving storage features make the most of the generously sized rooms at the Wallace.

The Wallace ♥♥♥ A lot of hotels claim to feel like a home away from home. But thanks to the staff's over-the-top kindliness, plus the fact that this was originally built as an apartment building, this one really delivers. All the rooms are quite spacious and there are a number of different suite configurations, with such niceties as good-sized fridges, marble counters, and large windows. They're also skillfully designed, with helpful space-saving measures—deep safes placed in bedside drawers, ironing boards and robes craftily tucked under the bed—so you don't lose valuable closet room. I'd call the design scheme "quietly contemporary": Think metallic wallpapers, net-like decorative curtains over the blackout curtains, and fine marble countertops.

242 W. 76th St. (just off Broadway). thewallace.com. ✆ **800/833-9622.** 115 units. $299–$439 double. Subway: 1 to 79th St. **Amenities:** Gym; bar; free Wi-Fi.

Expensive/Inexpensive

The Empire ♥ You're paying for location at the Empire, but frankly, that location is both a blessing and a curse. Yes, the hotel is right opposite Lincoln Center, but that puts it on one of the busiest strips in Manhattan, so the symphony you're likely to hear—all night—is that of car horns. Rooms vary greatly: Some have a feeling of real luxury, with Rothko-like paintings on the walls, handsome leather and dark-wood furnishings, and cushy beds; others are overdue for an update and feature rusted shower fixtures and chipped furnishings. Still, this is that rare NYC hotel to have a rooftop pool (it's small, but usable) and a fun sun-tanning deck with cabanas. Plus, the staff is helpful and friendly, meaning you could potentially switch to a better room at no extra cost if you get a lemon.

44 W. 63rd St. (btw. Broadway & Columbus Ave.). empirehotelnyc.com. ✆ **212/265-7400.** 420 units. $132–$422 double. Subway: 1 to 66th St.; A, B, C, D, 1 to 59th St./Columbus Circle. **Amenities:** Restaurant; 2 bars; fitness center; spa; pool; free Wi-Fi.

Inexpensive

Riverside Tower ♥♥ In previous editions of this guide, I called staying here "indoor camping" because rooms were halfway-house basic. A top-to-bottom renovation in 2024 changed all that, adding custom furnishings like lighting fixtures that would suit a 1920s-era cruise ship, slate-blue shiplap on the walls, and quality mattresses. What couldn't be fixed, however, were room sizes, which means the standard category rooms are among the smallest digs in the city, only able to accommodate full-size beds (not queens or kings) and very little else—there are no desks and you only get about a foot and a half, in most rooms, between the bed and the wall (they vary in shape and "suites" are larger, though not actual suites since they're just one room). Still, the Hudson River views are soothing, as is the pricing, and the location just off Riverside Park is unbeatable.

80 Riverside Dr. (at 80th St.). riversidetowerhotel.com. ✆ **212/877-5200.** 116 units. $114–$195 double. Subway: 1 to 79th St. **Amenities:** Coffee/tea bar in lobby; gym; free Wi-Fi.

UPPER EAST SIDE

Beautiful town houses, world-class museums, and the shops of Madison Avenue define the Upper East Side. It's a tony, quiet area to use as a base.

Best for: Visitors who like an upscale residential neighborhood, close to Central Park and Museum Mile, with luxury shopping and some fine dining.

Drawbacks: It can be one of the more expensive areas of town, if you stay and dine close to the parks and museums.

Expensive

The Surrey by Corinthia ♥♥ For those who want a resort-like experience, and can pay top dollar, the Surrey, with its state-of-the-art spa, on-site restaurant and lounge, and impressive fitness center, will likely fit the bill. Emerging from a several-year renovation in late 2024, its decor today is a little less quirky than before (the large painting of Kate Moss that used to dominate the lobby is gone), but it still is quite handsome, with contemporary Art Deco-ish touches like inlaid wooden walls, and a color palette of golds, tans, baby blues, and blush pink. Beds are swathed in Frette linens, which maids fluff up twice daily, and complimentary shoeshines keep guests looking spiffy. The hotel is a short stroll from Museum Mile and Central Park.

20 E. 76th St. (btw. Fifth & Madison aves.). corinthia.com. ✆ **800/662-6684.** 70 units. $975–$1,610 double. Subway: 6 to 77th St. **Amenities:** Restaurant; lounge/bar; fitness room; full-service spa; room service; in-house laundry/dry cleaning; free Wi-Fi.

Expensive/Moderate

voco–The Franklin New York ♥♥ Tiny but genteel rooms are for nightly rent here, with crystal chandeliers lighting raw-silk gray wallpaper,

The swanky lounge at The Surrey on the Upper East Side.

polished wood antiques, and Egyptian linen–swathed poufy beds with all their poufy pillows. Room rates include a generous continental breakfast and a wine-and-cheese reception each evening, both served in two stately lounges. The staff couldn't be a sweeter bunch and the location is within walking distance of Museum Mile.

164 E. 87th St. (btw. Lexington & Third aves.). franklinhotel.com. ✆ **212/369-1000.** 15 units. $212–$555 double; continental breakfast included. Subway: 4, 5, 6 to 86th St. Pets accepted. **Amenities:** Nightly wine-and-cheese reception; free shoeshines; free Wi-Fi.

BROOKLYN

Beyond the hotels profiled below, also be sure to check out Brooklyn's **Pod Hotel** (p. 76).

Best for: Visitors who have been to New York City before and want to concentrate on this fabulous borough's sights. Also, a smart pick for anyone coming to Gotham for nightlife, dining, or shopping.

Drawbacks: Some of the top Manhattan attractions will be a haul.

Expensive/Inexpensive

Henry Norman Hotel ♥♥♥ Like many places in Brooklyn, this property went from a 19th-century warehouse to become low-cost housing for artists, then a glossy biz venture, in this case in the hospitality industry. What's unusual here, at least if what the chatty receptionist told me is true, is that many of the original art works that dot the walls, in both public spaces and guest rooms, were done by tenants from the artist-garret days. Also uncommon: how large, light, airy, and handsome these rooms are, each with high ceilings, good beds, and hardwood floors. "Found objects" (like antique snowshoes) are interspersed on the walls with the paintings, giving the rooms a kooky charm. The suites are particularly good for families and small groups, as they're quite spacious, with pullout couches in the outer room and many with full kitchens. So why does this come priced at usually a good $50 less than what you'd pay at other NYC hotels of this caliber? It all comes down to the Henry Norman's location, which is in a hipster enclave, yes, but one that's a loooong 15-minute walk to the subway. ***Tip:*** The Henry Norman has a

Art-filled rooms at the Henry Norman Hotel, in Greenpoint, Brooklyn.

At the Hoxton, about half of the guest rooms get Manhattan skyline views while still being in the heart of Williamsburg hipness.

sister hotel called the **Franklin Guesthouse,** also in Greenpoint. Oddly it's a hair more expensive while being a hair less stylish. Still, it's a good second choice if this one is full (it's at the same website).

251 N. Henry St. (near Norman Ave.), Greenpoint. henrynormanhotel.com. ✆ **718/663-2100.** 52 units. $189–$444. 3-day minimum in some seasons. Subway: G to Nassau Ave. **Amenities:** Gym; neighborhood shuttle; business center; free Wi-Fi.

The Hoxton ♥♥♥ If you're looking for a stay in the heart of the Williamsburg scene, this should be your pick. The hotel is a design-forward beaut, set in a former water tower factory, and has three hopping bar/restaurants, including a rooftop one with Instagram-worthy views of the Manhattan skyline (see **Laser Wolf,** p. 146). About half of the hotel's guest rooms have the same heart-stopping views, through floor-to-ceiling windows (the others get a closer look at Williamsburg). Rooms are compact but cleverly set up to feel larger (the walls of glass help), with drawers under the bed, a thin rail to hang clothes, and very comfortable beds. Staff are unusually helpful—and unusually attractive.

97 Wythe Ave. (at N. 10th St.), Williamsburg. thehoxton.com. ✆ **718/215-7100.** 150 units. $166–$350 double; breakfast included. Subway: L to Bedford Ave. **Amenities:** 3 bar/restaurants; coffee shop; gym; free Wi-Fi.

Moderate/Inexpensive

Aura Hotel ♥ The Aura is in the heart of Hasidic Williamsburg with mezuzahs on the door frames, but other than that, it's its own bird: a clean, if somewhat worn place to stay with generously proportioned rooms that hold dated furnishings, minifridges, and microwaves. The location is a challenge:

a half-mile hike from the nearest subway, and not within walking distance of any tourist sights. Still, that's what keeps the prices here reasonable.

56 Franklin Ave (near Flushing Ave.), Williamsburg, Brooklyn. https://aurahotelbrooklyn.com. ✆ **718/676-1488.** 35 units. $105–$205 double. Subway: G, J, M to Flushing Ave. **Amenities:** Fridges and microwaves in rooms; free Wi-Fi.

Hotel 1080 ♥ If hotel rates weren't so insane, I might not be recommending this hotel. It's right under the elevated J subway line, so for two-thirds of the rooms, bunking here means sleepless nights. But those who are smart enough to grab a room facing the back of the building and away from the trains (those numbered 01, or on the 7th or 8th floors), this could be a fine place to stay. Caring staff keep rooms dust and dirt free, the beds are comfy (a little softer than the norm but not saggy), and there's even a bit of charm to the digs, thanks to the giant photos of that elevated train, which grace one wall of each guest room. Bedford-Stuyvesant is a rapidly gentrifying neighborhood, so some nice restaurants and bars are within walking distance, and hey, the subway is right there to whisk you to tourist sites quite rapidly.

1080 Broadway, at Pulaski St., Bedford-Stuyvesant. hotel1080.com. ✆ **718/715-4850.** $85–$251 double. Subway: J to Kosciuszko St. **Amenities:** Bar; free Wi-Fi.

The Lodge Red Hook ♥♥ You may notice something odd about your fellow guests when you bunk here: Many will dress like they're in the Bahamas, not NYC. That's because the lion's share of the Lodge's clientele are cruise passengers: This is the only decent hotel near the Brooklyn Cruise Terminal. That being said, this place is more than just "decent," with hardwood floors, sleep-promoting beds, and a hint of style, thanks to the adorable, framed Spanish prints on the walls. It's also pin-drop quiet because it's surrounded by warehouses. There's little street life, or Brooklyn flair, to the hotel's direct vicinity, but all that's within easy walking distance. What's not in easy walking distance, alas, is the subway (get ready for a 10-min. walk minimum). ***Tip:*** If you're planning on staying more than 4 nights, contact the hotel directly for deeper discounts than you'll find online.

17 Seabring St. (btw. Richards and Columbia sts.), Red Hook. lodgeredhook.com. ✆ **718/675-5200.** 81 units. $142–$337 double. Subway: F, G to Carroll St. or take a ferry to Red Hook. **Amenities:** Free Wi-Fi.

NEW JERSEY & QUEENS

I'm not a fan of commuting while on vacation, especially considering the maddening traffic into and out of Manhattan. And since most of what visitors come to New York City for is in Manhattan or Brooklyn, I've only chosen properties that are convenient to that famed isle and that hip borough—meaning hotels with access to speedy public transportation. That means you won't have to drive into Manhattan (and pay exorbitant parking rates or congestion fees) or spend an hour on a bus crawling from the far reaches of New Jersey into the city. To make it into this book, these properties also had to offer savings compared to what you'd pay for equivalent hotels in Manhattan or Brooklyn.

Best for: People who are comfortable with public transportation. New Jersey may be the pick for those driving into the metro area (parking is sometimes free) or those who want a short-term apartment rental (still legal in New Jersey but not NYC). Queens is a good option for foodies eager to sample restaurants serving cuisines from all corners of the globe (many of which are rarely served in the United States) or folks hoping to visit Queens attractions (see p. 240).

Drawbacks: You'll be taking a cab/train/bus/ferry ride twice daily and spending at least 40 minutes each day just getting to the sights.

New Jersey

Comfort Inn Edgewater ♥♥ Choose the right room, and it will have views of the NYC skyline (skyscrapers waaay in the distance, the apartment buildings of Washington Heights right across the river). That's what's most notable about this small motel, along with affable staff, and the fact that, on weekdays during rush hour, you can walk to the ferry to get into the city. (It's a lovely ride; at other times, you can take the public bus for 30-40 minutes or so.) Rooms are tidy, with good quality mattresses but forgettable decor (laminate floorboards or industrial carpets, lots of shades of brown and tan, white duvets). The area is residential, with not much of interest. In low season, rates here will match those in the city, so this is only a choice for high- and shoulder-season.

725 River Rd., Edgewater. choicehotels.com. ✆ **201/943-3131.** 110 units. $147–$288 double; breakfast included. **Amenities:** Gym; free parking; free Wi-Fi.

Days Hotel By Wyndham North Bergen ♥ Though it's in New Jersey, this hotel feels like it's in another country, perhaps India or Zimbabwe or Chile. That sense starts in the lobby with its shiny marble floors and

Sleek modern design adds to a pleasant stay at Element Harrison—Newark, which gets bonus points for being super close to the commuter train into Manhattan.

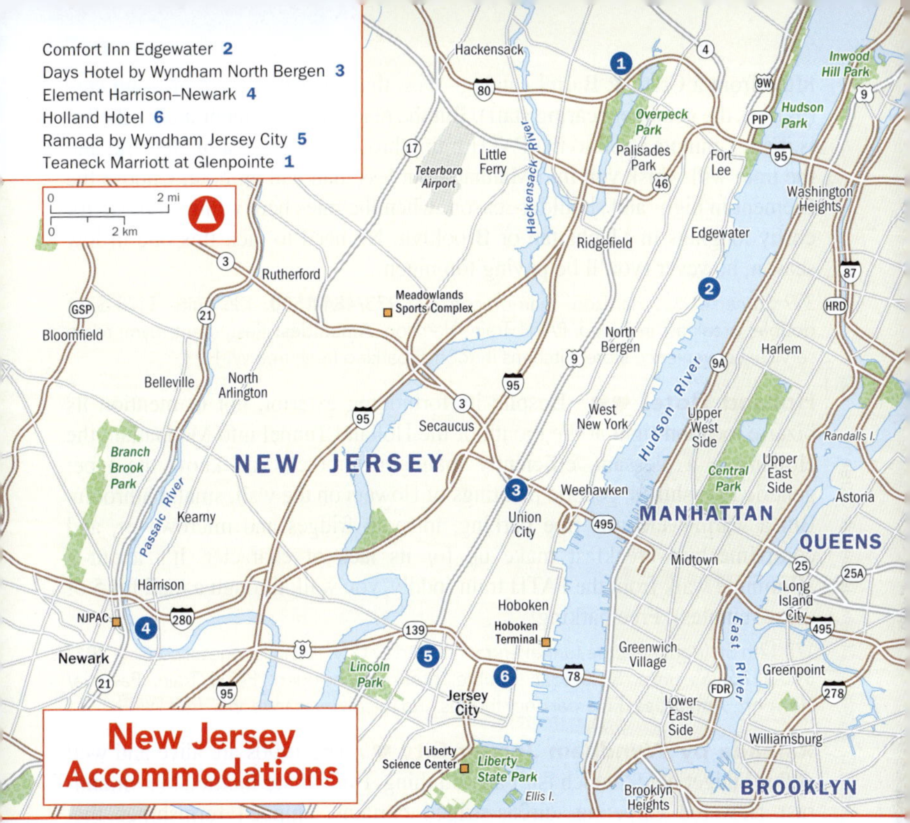

continues in the jewel-toned guest rooms, with their massive wall-mounted TV's set above an oddball amenity: a flat fake fireplace, with digital flames available at the flick of a remote. These aren't design choices I've seen in the tri-state area before, and they made me feel like I'd been transported farther away than Jersey. As for those guest rooms, they're spotlessly clean, but with small dings (like paint peeling from the face of a door, or scratches on the wood furniture). There is an outdoor pool, but it was out of order when we visited, so check in advance if that's of interest to you. Guests have two ways to get into NYC (beyond their own cars): either the public bus ($4/person) or a private shuttle ($10/person). Both have frequent service and take between 25 and 55 minutes to get you into Manhattan, depending on traffic. You'll want to get into the city, as the area directly around the hotel is nothing more than highway.

2600 Tonnelle Ave., North Bergen. wyndhamhotels.com. ✆ **201/866-0400.** 111 units. $115–$252 double; breakfast included. **Amenities:** Outdoor pool; gym; fridges and microwaves in some rooms; free parking; free Wi-Fi.

Element Harrison—Newark ♥♥♥ Apartment-style units, with truly useable kitchens (big fridges, stovetop cooking area, pots, pans, plates—the works), smartly designed work areas, and furnishings that look like they were lifted from a Crate & Barrel catalog—yes, that all makes for a pleasant stay (as does the genuinely caring staff). But the real reason Element makes the list is it's a 1-minute stroll to the PATH train, through a nice area of Newark, and the train will whisk you into Manhattan in less than half an hour. Choose the Element in high- and shoulder-season, when the rates here will beat those for cushy lodgings in Manhattan or Brooklyn. No need to pick this one in low season, however (you'll be paying too much).

399 Somerset St., Harrison. marriott.com. ✆ **973/484-1500.** 136 units. $178–$261 double; breakfast included. PATH Train: Harrison. **Amenities:** Restaurant; gym; room service; convenience store; kitchens in rooms; parking (fee); free Wi-Fi.

Holland Hotel ♥♥ Despite its forbidding exterior, not to mention its bizarre location right at the mouth of the Holland Tunnel into Manhattan, the Holland is a pleasant, efficiently maintained motel. You know the type: generic furnishings, generic paintings of flowers on the wall, small bathroom. But a warm welcome, free parking, in-room fridges and microwaves, and complimentary breakfast make up for its lack of character. It's about a 10-minute walk from the PATH train (oddly, you walk through a mall for 5 of those minutes). Free parking!

175 12th St. (right near the tunnel entrance), Jersey City. thehollandhotel.com. ✆ **201/590-2186.** 55 units. $120–$328 double; breakfast included. PATH Train: Pavonia/Newport. **Amenities**: Free parking; fridges and microwaves in rooms; free Wi-Fi.

Ramada by Wyndham Jersey City ♥ The 1990s are alive and well at this budget hotel, which isn't a good thing. I'm talking mottled brown-and-rust flowered carpeting, circus-striped curtains, chipped furnishings that clearly were in place before the turn of the last century, and hard mattresses. On the walls are prints of Belle Epoque Paris, which somehow make the rooms look even more shabby by comparison. So why did this even make it into the book? The staff here are doing the very best with what they have, especially the housekeepers, who ensure that sheets are spotless and dust is banished. Plus, the Ramada is an easy walk to the PATH train through a bustling commercial area and often has very low pricing compared to NYC. Think of this as indoor camping and you'll be fine.

65 Tonnele Ave., Jersey City. wyndhamhotels.com. ✆ **201/432-6100.** $116–$259 double; breakfast included. PATH train: Journal Square. **Amenities:** Gym; convenience store; free Newark Airport shuttle; small fridges and microwaves in rooms; free Wi-Fi.

Teaneck Marriott at Glenpointe ♥♥ Conventions are the *raison d'etre* for this hotel, which means amenities (and crowds) galore. These include a big bar, an Italian restaurant, room service, and, in the attached office building, free use of a massive local gym with an indoor pool, fitness classes, and every weight machine known to man. Best amenity? That would be the public bus that stops at the hotel and whisks guests into the city in less than 30 minutes. Rooms are oversized and handsome, with dedicated work areas, wall-sized photos of the Manhattan Bridge, and comfy beds. This is

Manhattan views add to the appeal of The Boro Hotel, just a few subways stops into Queens.

another "only if prices in NYC have skyrocketed" choice as the immediate vicinity is only highways.

100 Frank W. Burr Blvd, Teaneck. marriott.com. ✆ **201/831-0600.** $179–$240 double. **Amenities:** Restaurant; bar; room service; gym; free parking; gift shop; free Wi-Fi.

Queens

The Boro Hotel ♥♥ Most of the city's built-from-the-ground-up hotels borrow an ugly tactic from the airlines: They try to cram as many people into as little space as possible. Not the Boro. Here most of the rooms are a capacious (by local standards) 260 sq. ft. and up, that space made even larger-looking by floor-to-ceiling windows, some with views of the Manhattan skyline, some with balconies. The hotel is on trend in other ways, with its industrial-chic looks warmed by lots of wood (hardwood floors, barnlike planked walls) and white-duvet-swathed beds. It also has a living-room-style lobby with lots of borrowable books and magazines, plus a fancy coffee bar, a rooftop bar, room service, and a classy restaurant. The hotel's immediate neighborhood is very quiet (lots of one-family clapboard homes), but nearby are some trendy restaurants, and the subway's a 3-block walk.

32-28 27th St. (at 39th Ave.), Long Island City. borohotel.com. ✆ **718/433-1375.** 108 units. $138–$343 double. Subway: 7 to Queensboro Plaza, or N, W to 39th Ave. **Amenities:** Restaurant; coffee bar; room service; fitness room; free Wi-Fi.

WHERE TO EAT

4

Its competitors are Hong Kong and Paris, Brussels and San Francisco, Copenhagen and New Orleans. But I'll argue hard that none of these other great restaurant cities has quite the same number of serious, satisfying eateries as New York, nor its amazing variety of cuisines in every price range . . . and quirk. Would you believe there are restaurants that serve only grilled cheese sandwiches (all different types)—and flourish doing so?

How did the surprising volume and variety of NYC restaurants come about?

- New York has a larger and more varied immigrant population than any of the other foremost restaurant cities—and that means specialties on offer from every nook and corner of the planet.
- New York has top-notch cooking schools, the offices of international magazines and websites devoted to the art of cooking, and the headquarters of the Food Network.
- The pace of life here is more hectic and pressured than in other famous restaurant cities, creating a vast population with "no time to cook."

Mix all these reasons together, sauté them over the bright flame of the city's celebrity, and you have a mecca for foodies, a place where people obsess over the gratification of their tastebuds without anyone thinking it is odd. In China, one way of saying "hello" is to ask, "Have you eaten?" In Gotham, we say, "Where have you eaten—and do you need a reservation?"

PRACTICAL INFORMATION

Sad but true, sometimes a restaurant that's crowded one week will be closed by the next. That's particularly true in the New York City of today. So, although I fully re-researched this book in 2026 and have done my best to only recommend the eateries I think have staying power, I don't have psychic abilities. Do call in advance to make sure the place you're intending to dine is still in business. It likely will be, but better safe . . .

Reservations

Reservations are always a good idea in New York and a necessity for popular restaurants. Call or get online reservations *far* ahead for any special meal you don't want to miss. Most top places start taking reservations 30 days in advance; for the uber-popular joints you'll need to log onto their reservation service right after midnight on that day to score a meal. Some other strategies include involving your credit card company's concierge service (some partner with NYC restos); going with a larger group (reservations for 4 or 6 are often easier to grab than those for 2); or going online at 10am or noon the day you want to dine to check for openings, as that's when general managers tend to post changes, according to a recent *New York Times* article on snagging reservations. **OpenTable.com** or **Resy.com** are the two sites that book tables at the majority of the city's restaurants. If you can't get a reservation for the restaurant you wish to go to through Resy, it does allow you to get on the waitlist for it. To make sure you actually get *off* the waitlist, download the Resy app, so that it can ping you if a table opens up (email notifications take longer, meaning the reservation will likely be gone by the time you try to nab it). Alas, getting reservations at hot places has become a sport among finance bros, some of whom use AI-powered apps (costing $65/month) to snap them up before others do.

But if you didn't reserve well ahead, don't despair. Often, early or late hours—between 5 and 6pm or after 9:30pm—are available, especially on weeknights. And most restaurants have bar seating, for which one needs no reservation. Or go for lunch, which is usually much easier to book without advance notice. If you're staying at a hotel with a concierge, don't be afraid to use them—a well-connected concierge can often get you into hot spots.

In a perfect reproduction of a Parisian bar, Frenchette quietly reinvents classic French bistro food.

Foodie Food Courts

Sorry Auntie Anne, in New York City food courts are out of your league. Dedicated to non-chain, gourmet fare, their booths are being claimed by some of the city's most celebrated chefs. And the number of these multiple-venue eateries has exploded in just the last 4 or 5 years. So, I'm starting each neighborhood section with a shout-out to the best food courts in the area, with a quick run-down on their top specialties. ***Note:*** All have seating, and most serve alcohol along with the food.

Tipping

Tipping is easy in New York. The way to do it: Double the 8.75% sales tax and *voilà,* happy waitstaff. Don't forget to tip: Waiters make less than minimum wage and are taxed on what the government expects them to make in tips. So, when you stiff the server, they not only lose that extra bit of income, they still have to pay taxes on it. Also, leave $2 per item, no matter how small, for the checkroom attendant. You don't need to tip the host who escorts you to your table.

How to Order

The dividing line between appetizers and entrees has been purposefully blurred in Gotham, meaning it can be really hard to tell just how much food you're actually ordering. At many places, the size of the portions for what are supposedly appetizers and one-person entrees has expanded, along with their prices. Adding to the confusion is the sad fact that waiters will often advise patrons to order more food than they actually need. The best strategy is to under-order. For a couple, that might mean two appetizers and a split entree. You can always order more if you're still hungry.

Price Categories

Meal per person, not including drinks or tip:
Inexpensive: $30 and under
Moderate: $31–$45
Expensive: $46 and above

FINANCIAL DISTRICT & TRIBECA

Beyond the restaurants below, know that you can have a fine meal at some Financial District bars, specifically **Dead Rabbit** (p. 355), and, for pub-style grub in a lively atmosphere, the bars on Stone Street right off Hanover Square. Tables are set up on that cobblestoned lane (the oldest one in Manhattan; p. 274), and half a dozen taverns provide food and drink. Or head to pizza impresario **Kesté** (p. 120) at 66 Gold St. for superb 'za. For a meal up in the clouds, **Saga ♥♥,** 70 Pine St., 63rd floor (saga-nyc.com; tasting menu from $298/person), could be the pick for a very special occasion, though the meal tab here is as gasp-inducing as the views.

Lower Manhattan Restaurants
Banh by Lauren 15
Dead Rabbit 1
Eataly 5
Frenchette 8
Great New York Noodletown 12
Hudson Eats 7
Jing Fong 9
Kesté Pizza & Vino 3
Kiki's 13
Lei Wine 11
Mott Street Eatery 10
Saga 2
Smorgasburg 6
Sunn's 14
Xi'an Famous Foods 4
Subway station
0 1/4 mi
0 0.25 km
TRIBECA
LITTLE ITALY
LOWER EAST SIDE
CHINATOWN
FINANCIAL DISTRICT
Spring St 6
Canal St 1
Canal St A-C-E
Canal St N-Q-R-W
Canal St 4-6
Grand St B-D
Franklin St 1
Chambers St A-C
Chambers St 1-2-3
Chambers St J-M-Z
City Hall R-W
Brooklyn Bridge-City Hall 4-5-6
Park Pl 2-3
Fulton St 4-5
Fulton St 2-3
Cortlandt St R-W
WTC Cortlandt 1
Rector St R-W
Rector St 1
Wall St 4-5
Bowling Green 4-5
Whitehall St-South Ferry R-W
South Ferry 1
City Hall Park
Woolworth Building
One World Observatory
WORLD TRADE CENTER SITE
Trinity Church
Federal Hall
NY Stock Exchange
National Museum of the American Indian
Castle Clinton National Monument
Battery Park
Wagner Park
Rector Park
South Cove
Vietnam Veterans Plaza
Staten Island Ferry Terminal
Pier 17
East River
Brooklyn Bridge
Manhattan Bridge
West Side Hwy.
Spring
Dominick
Broome
Canal
Vestry
Laight
Hubert
Beach
N. Moore
Franklin
Harrison
Jay
Chambers
Warren
Murray
Park Pl.
Barclay
Vesey
Fulton
Liberty
Cedar
Albany
2nd Pl.
1st Pl.
Battery Pl.
Sixth Ave.
W. Broadway
Wooster
Greene
Mercer
Broadway
Crosby
Lafayette
Mott
Elizabeth
Bowery
Allen
Orchard
Grand
Howard
Hester
Lispenard
Walker
White
Leonard
Worth
Thomas
Duane
Reade
Cortlandt
Centre
Baxter
Mulberry
Bayard
Division
E Broadway
Henry
Madison
Catherine
Cherry
Water
St. James Pl.
South
Frankfort
Spruce
Beekman
Ann
Park Row
Gold
Pearl
Dover
Front
John
Maiden
Platt
Cliff
Fletcher
William
Nassau
Trinity Pl.
Church
Greenwich
Hudson
Greenwich St.
Wall St.
Pine
New
Beaver
Stone
Bridge
State
Whitehall
Broad

Many NYC Restaurants No Longer Have a Phone Number

Now that online services are taking reservations, many restaurants have gotten rid of their phones entirely. If you see a listing in this chapter without a phone number, it means you need to contact the restaurant through its website.

Financial District Food Courts

Eataly, 4 World Trade Center, Liberty St. at Church St., 4th floor (eataly.com). *Highlights:* You'll find sit-down restaurants here for the holy trinity of Italian food: pasta, pizza, and antipasta.

Hudson Eats, inside the Brookfield Place Mall, 250 Vesey St. (across from the 9/11 Memorial and Museum). *Highlights:* Brisket from **Mighty Quinn's Barbecue** and burgers or clam chowder from **PJ Clarkes.**

If you're downtown on a Friday during the warm weather months, the top option is to head to the massive food festival **Smorgasburg** (p. 144), in the plaza in front of the Oculus in the World Trade Center 11am to 7pm.

Expensive

Frenchette ♥♥ FRENCH The current wave of food trends has more Gallic flair than Marion Cotillard. After years in which all the hottest new restaurants were Japanese, Chinese, or Asian fusion, classic French cuisine is back at the fore, and nowhere better than at this canny bistro, winner in recent years of a James Beard Award for best new restaurant in the U.S. Its founders, Riad Nasr and Lee Hanson—long-time chefs at some of the city's best restaurants (including **Balthazar,** p. 100)—have sagely included such old favorites as *côte de boeuf* and oysters with mignonette among their offerings. But there are also experiments here: a creamy egg dish with snails, only "natural" (self-fermenting) wines on the liquor menu, and duck frites rather than the usual steak frites. It's a nice mix of options, all served in a setting that couldn't be more Parisian, with its parfait zinc bar, leather banquettes, and vintage sconce lighting. The founding duo is also behind **Le Rock** (p. 129) and **Le Veau D'Or** (p. 138), and **Wild Cherry** (not recommended).

241 W. Broadway (btw. Walker & White sts.). frenchettenyc.com. ✆ **212/334-3883.** Entrees $38–$64. Mon–Fri noon–10pm; Sat 11am–10pm; Sun 11am–9:30pm. Subway: 1 to Franklin St.

Inexpensive

Xi'an Famous Foods ♥♥ CHINESE If this restaurant were a laboratory—and it looks very much like one, with its sterile white-tiled walls and stools for chairs casually pulled up to counters built into the wall—the scientists working here would be studying just how much spice the human tongue can take before it explodes. This is a restaurant for chili heads, and its menu doesn't lie: "Spicy and tingly beef with hand-ripped noodles," the house specialty ($13.35), will make your entire body heat up. This is truly authentic Sichuan food, family recipes of a caliber rarely tasted in the United States. For

Authentic Sichuan food is known for its spiciness, and the cooks at Xi'an Famous Foods don't stint on the heat factor.

those who can't take the heat, the less fiery choices are nearly as delish. Brave the line to get in: It moves quickly.

8 Liberty Place (near Maiden Lane). xianfoods.com. ✆ **212/786-2068.** Entrees $5.75–$16.50. No reservations. Daily 11:30am–8:30pm. See website for other NYC branches. Subway: 2, 3, 4, 5 to Fulton St.

CHINATOWN & LITTLE ITALY

Chinatown Food Courts

Mott Street Eatery ♥♥, 98 Mott St. (btw. Canal & Hester sts.). Here's where the folks who live in Chinatown eat; the food is tremendously authentic and affordable. *Highlights:* Tofu desserts from **Yan Wo Dou Bun Inc.,** Taiwanese-style dumplings from **Sanmiwago,** roasted duck over rice from **89 Eatery.**

Inexpensive

Great New York Noodletown ♥♥ CHINESE It ain't much to look at—the lighting's too bright and the seats are crowded together—but there are few finer dining experiences to be had in this restaurant-crammed city. In fact, in the years I've been coming here, I've seen chefs from far pricier places, still in their chef's whites, eating here after their shifts were over. I couldn't see what they ordered, but I always go for the sauteed pea shoots (a delicate, very green taste sensation); the salt-baked shrimp (the seafood equivalent of potato chips, they're that light and crunchy); and some slices off one of the ducks or suckling pigs that hang in macabre style in the window. Portions are big, and service is quick, so under-ordering will keep the tab in line (you can always order more if needed).

28½ Bowery (at Bayard St.). greatnynoodletown.net. ✆ **212/349-0923.** Entrees $8.50–$22. No credit cards. No reservations. Daily 9am–10pm. Subway: N, R, 6 to Canal St.

There's usually a wait for tables at Great New York Noodletown, but because service is fast, you'll rarely stand outside for longer than 30 minutes.

Jing Fong ♥♥ DIM SUM The classic Chinatown meal is dim sum brunch or lunch. For those who've never tried it, dim sum is a meal made up of many small dishes, primarily different sorts of dumplings and buns, a tradition that started in the tea houses that lined China's Silk Road many centuries ago (scholars believe the custom began shortly after A.D. 300, when the long-held notion that tea should not be accompanied by food fell out of favor). And the top place for dim sum in Manhattan's Chinatown today is this cacophonous, always-jammed restaurant. The clientele is often entirely Chinese, and the dishes range from the expected (shrimp and pork dumplings and sticky rice wrapped in lotus leaf) to the un: chicken feet, stinky durian pastries. Since many of the servers don't speak English, you'll have to point at what interests you. If you make a mistake (hard to do, as it's all tasty), it's no big deal—most dishes cost just a few bucks.

202 Centre St. (at Hester St.). jingfongny.com. ✆ **212/964-5256.** Meals $18–$28/person on average. Daily 10:30am–9pm. Subway: 4,5, 6 to Canal St. Also on the Upper West Side at 380 Amsterdam Ave. (at 78th St.).

Kiki's ♥♥♥ GREEK A "sit down and linger" ambience, simple but delicious food, and reasonable pricing—that's a rare combo in Manhattan. It's the reason this sleeper is always packed, drawing an under-40 boho crowd who lounge in a warren of artfully distressed-looking rooms (rough wood tables, mottled gray walls, beamed ceilings), chowing down on such Greek classics as grilled octopus, savory spreads with pita, and roast meats or whole fish—the latter big enough for two, and a steal at $25 (including a side). ***Two notes:*** Don't be confused by the awning's Chinese characters (a leftover from the previous tenant) and don't leave if you see a line—it moves quickly, especially now that Kiki's has taken over another space across the street.

130 Division St. (at Orchard St.). kikisnyc.com. ✆ **646/882-7052.** Entrees $12–$46 (pricier dishes large enough for 2 or more). No reservations. Sun–Mon noon–11pm; Tues–Sat noon–midnight. Subway: F to E. Broadway; B, D to Grand St.

LOWER EAST SIDE

The Lower East Side has an unusually large number of hole-in-the-wall restaurants that are immensely appealing—cute-as-kittens decor, affordable

pricing, and food that's so good you wonder why the chef isn't working in a place that can serve 40 at a time, rather than just 15 or so. Of these, the best is **La Contenta** ♥♥, 102 Norfolk St., near Delancey (lacontentanyc.com; ✆ **212/432-4180;** Mon–Wed 4–11:30pm, Thurs–Sun 11am–11:30pm) for accomplished Mexican in a festive atmosphere.

Lower East Side Food Court

Essex Street Market ♥♥, 88 Essex St. (at Delancey). *Highlights:* Coffee at **Porto Rico Importing Co.,** Thai burgers at **Zaab Burger,** chicken mole burritos from **Puebla Mexican Food.** The star restaurant here is **Dhamaka** (p. 97).

Expensive

Sammy's Roumanian Steakhouse ♥♥ ROMANIAN At some point in their lives, nearly every New Yorker visits Sammy's, a nightly bar mitzvah masquerading as a steak joint. Now set in a storefront on the Lower East Side (the original location closed during the pandemic), its decor is unapologetically tacky, with photos of patrons cramming every wall. Completing the ambience is an aged fellow at an electric keyboard who regales the crowd with

well paired: 3 DINNER-WORTHY WINE BARS

And interestingly, these three serve Asian food paired with grape wines—an unusual combination. All are downtown, all are tiny, all are reasonably priced, and all are superb. Oh, and the wine selection at all three is well curated, with good options for natural wines as well as traditional ones.

Ha's Snack Bar ♥♥, 297 Broome St. (btw. Forsythe and Eldridge sts.; no website or phone number; subway: B, D to Grand St.). Creative Vietnamese/French fusion food is the draw here, and their treatment of snails—doused in fish sauce, tamarind, garlic, and lime, and sided by a hunk of baguette so that you can mop up every drop—is a dish I would walk over hot coals again to eat. Alas, sometimes getting a seat here feels like just that. Reservations are impossible to snag, so many diners line up for the hour before opening to vie for a place inside. I say "place" because about a fifth of the dining area is a tall table with no chairs, where people nosh standing up. Is it worth the hassle? Only you can decide.

Lei Wine ♥♥, 15-17 Doyers St. (off Pell St.; leiwine.nyc; subway: 4, 6, J, N, R to Canal St.). Set on the most evocative street in Chinatown, and founded by one of the partners at **King** (p. 109) and **Jupiter** (p. 129), Lei turns dishes served elsewhere in the 'hood on their heads. So a plate of chrysanthemum greens, which would normally be stir fried, is here served as a refreshing salad; a Uygher-style lamb stew with cat's ear pasta comes topped with a dry fudge of fresh chopped herbs a third of an inch thick; and celtuce, a lettuce used for its asparagus like stem, is fanned out in a geometric wedge, set atop a tart red wine vinaigrette, and stuck together with jellied kombu, for one of the most unusual but craveable dishes in the city.

Sunn's ♥♥♥, 139 Division St. (near Canal St.; sunnsnyc.com; subway: F to East Broadway). *Ban chan*, that array of small appetizer plates that's often an afterthought at Korean restaurants, are elevated here to high art. They might include candied anchovies (addictive!), creamy potato salad with slivers of Asian pear, or a cabbage kimchi that puts all other versions of that dish to shame. But that's just the beginning of the treats here. The menu changes, but it often includes: salads you eat with your hands so you can use crisp endive shoots to scoop up creamy tofu and tahini dressing; crab and chicken dumplings furry with dill and slathered in schmaltz (chicken fat) for richness; and soy caramelized brisket (*ssam*) you wrap in lettuce leaves and slather with tangy, peppery Korean BBQ sauce. The quality of the food here is miraculous, especially considering the kitchen is no wider or longer than most coffins.

Yiddish songs, selections from *Fiddler on the Roof*, and the hoariest Jewish jokes you've ever heard. Diners dance in the aisle (especially if they've ordered the house special drink: a bottle of vodka encased in a block of ice). The crusty, jokey waiters will try to push you into ordering too much food: Resist them. There's no reason whatsoever to order the $75 prix-fixe menu. The "large" steaks ($52) are a good two feet long and overhang the platter; on a recent visit, one order fed 6 people. You have to start with a helping of the chopped liver ($28), a heart attack in a bowl, which the server mixes tableside, combining the liver with fried onions, plain onions, and literally a cup and a half of *schmaltz* (for the uninitiated, that's liquefied chicken fat); one order is enough for 6 to 8 people. Bring a group, as there are few better places in the city for a blowout party.

112 Stanton Street (btw. Ludlow & Essex sts.). Entrees $33–$52. Sun and Wed–Thurs 4–11pm; Fri–Sat 4–11:30pm. Subway: F to Delancey St., B, D, Q to Grand St

Moderate

Dhamaka ♥♥♥ INDIAN In the year that it opened (2021), Dhamaka ended up on every major publication's list of the best new restaurants in the U.S. But that doesn't mean it's a fussy, expensive, tasting menu–type joint. Dhamaka is its own type of fine dining: Its decor is casually exuberant, its prices fair, and, most importantly, its food will make you rethink what you thought you knew about Indian food. That's partially because the dishes served here are taken not from India's urban centers, but from villages all over the subcontinent. Using these recipes, chef/owner Chintan Pandya offers a masterclass in the variety of ways spice can be delivered. Pandya also now has a celebrated Bengali restaurant in Park Slope, Brooklyn (**Masalawala;** masalawala.com), a West Village spot dedicated to the foods of Southern India (**Semma;** semma.nyc); an outpost known for goat dishes (**Adda Canteen**); and a fast-casual fried chicken place, **Rowdy Rooster** (p. 123). All are superb.

In the Essex Market, Dhamaka has expanded diners' notions of Indian food.

119 Delancey St. (at Essex St., in Essex Market). dhamaka.nyc. ✆ **212/204-8616.** Entrees $17–$42 (a few luxe dishes cost more). Tues–Fri 5–9pm; Sat–Sun 11:30am–2:30pm and 5–9pm. Subway: F, M, J, Z to Delancey St.

Kisa ♥♥ KOREAN Who knew Korean cab drivers had it so good? This corner spot pays homage to the quick service cafes across the Pacific that keep drivers, and other time-stressed workers, sufficiently fueled. So the decor, if you can call it that, is brown-upon-brown (except for a tiny black-and-white TV flickering in a corner) and simple in the extreme. And diners have a choice of just four entrees—bulgogi, spicy squid or pork, or bibimbap—each of which comes with a soothing broth, white rice, and 7 bowls of *ban chan* or side dishes, from fermented spicy cabbage (kimchi) to potato salad to fried chicken. It's all served in metal bowls upon a metal tray, following the theme. All in all, it's a feast and quite tasty, especially at just $36 for everything, a price which draws crowds of ebullient (mostly) young people. Humorous touch: at the end of the meal, diners can go up to an ancient-looking machine, press a button, and get a to-go paper cup of what seems to be Sanka coffee or Swiss Miss hot chocolate.

205 Allen St. (at Houston). kisaus.com. ✆ **646/866-8622.** Set meal $36. Mon–Thurs 5–10:30pm; Fri–Sun 11am–2:30pm and 5–10:30pm. Subway: F to Second Ave., J, Z to Bowery.

Rebel ♥♥ HAITIAN A nightly party is taking place at Rebel, complete with a DJ. So, if you're looking to have a quiet *tête-à-tête*, look elsewhere—this may well be one of the loudest restaurants in the city. But if you're in the mood to be bouncing in your seat to Afrobeats, Kompa, hip hop, and classic R&B, while dining on food that makes your tongue dance, make a reservation (Rebel is small and fills up with a loyal Haitian clientele). Top dishes include smoked herring egg rolls (really! they're delish); slow-braised-then-fried spicy pork; and jerk fish with traditional Haitian black mushroom rice. Don't be afraid to share—portions are large. Skip the desserts, which don't shine here.

29 Clinton St. (at Stanton St.). rebelrestaurantandbarnyc.com. ✆ **973/750-6262.** Entrees $16–$52. Sun and Tues–Thurs 5–10pm; Fri–Sat 5pm–10:30 (bar open until 2am). Subway: F, M, J, Z to Delancey/Essex St.

Russ & Daughters Cafe ♥♥ DELI After peddling smoked fish, caviar, and other "appetizings" for a full century out of their iconic Lower East Side shop (at 179 E. Houston St.), the family behind Russ & Daughters (yes, they're descendants of the founders) decided to go into the restaurant biz. And though it seems odd to say this about a company this old: They were an overnight success! Part of this has to do with lack of competition: If you want to taste the classic flavors that were once ubiquitous on the Lower East Side, this is the only sit-down option. But that wouldn't matter if they weren't doing deli right, which they are: bright pink borscht so flavorful it would make your bubbe kvell, the silkiest of smoked salmons lazily draped over a cream cheese–laden bialy, deviled eggs, pickled herring, beet salad, and an innovation—sinful halvah-flavored ice cream. Kudos to the designer who channeled the essence of the original counter joint for the decor here. Breakfast, brunch, and lunch only.

127 Orchard St. (btw. Delancey & Rivington sts.). russanddaughterscafe.com. ✆ **212/275-4881.** Entrees $22–$28. Mon–Thurs 8:30am–2:30pm; Fri–Sun 8:30am–3:30pm. Subway: F, M, J, Z to Delancey/Essex St.

A bagel platter comes with silky smoked salmon at Russ & Daughters Cafe.

Inexpensive

Ivan Ramen ♥♥ JAPANESE Ramen isn't an authentically Japanese food. Traditionally, Japanese noodle soups used seaweed, and sometimes chicken, as their base; only in the early 20th century did chefs start experimenting with the Chinese method of building broths with pork. So, it shouldn't be a surprise that the hottest ramen chef in Tokyo was, for many moons, not Japanese, but a dude from Long Island, NY. After perfecting his craft in Japan (and becoming a celebrity there), Ivan Orkin returned home and has been wowing diners ever since with both his classic ramens and the pork-a-palooza he calls "triple pork, triple garlic mazeman." The latter is just barely soup (more like noodles with sauce), but who cares when you've got chopped bacon, simmered pork belly, and *tonkatsu* (pork broth) generously seasoned with raw, roasted, and pickled garlic?

25 Clinton St. (at Stanton). ivanramen.com. ✆ **646/678-3859.** Ramen $20–$24. Daily noon–9pm. Subway: F to Delancey St.

Katz's Delicatessen ♥♥ DELICATESSEN One of the city's longest-running success stories, Katz has been in business since 1888. You may feel a sense of déjà vu as you enter, as this is where Meg Ryan, ahem, made a scene in *When Harry Met Sally,* and it looks just as it did in the flick: a cavernous, loud space with linoleum-topped tables, celebrity photos and testimonials plastering the walls, and curtains of hanging salami in the window. Though its menu is varied and long, only the uninitiated bypass the corned beef sandwich (the best in the city), a towering stack of meat cured for as long as 30 days, which gives it a richness and depth that you simply don't find with commercially prepared corned beef (which is "pressure injected" to cure in a mere 36 hours). ***Tip:*** Half sandwiches with either soup or salad are offered, and they're usually more than hearty enough for one person. ***Tip two:*** Katz's website has suggested dining times, as there's often a line around the block to get in. Try to eat in an off hour so you don't have to wait.

205 E. Houston St. (at Ludlow St.). katzsdelicatessen.com. ✆ **212/254-2246.** Sandwiches $17–$29. No reservations. Mon–Thurs 8am–11pm; Fri–Sun open 24 hrs. Subway: F to Second Ave.; F, M, J, Z to Delancey/Second Ave.

Shu Jiao Fuzhou Cuisine ♥♥ CHINESE Anyone who says you can't get a good and really cheap meal in NYC hasn't been to this budget wonder. Sure, the lighting is as bright as a hospital's and the decor about as stylish, but nobody is complaining when they're slurping down freshly made peanut noodles ($3.25—not a typo!) or sharing an enormous plate of tasty pork and chive dumplings (same price). In the early evenings, 20-somethings bring in their own bottles of wine and this no-frills spot becomes a party place.

295 Grand St. (at Eldridge St.). shujiaofuzhou.com. Entrees $3.25–$6.50. Daily 8am–8pm. Subway: F, M, J, Z to Delancey St.

SWEETS FOR THE sweet

Dessert is given a place of honor on the NYC restaurant scene, with venues ranging from beloved bakeries to all-dessert restaurants. Here are some of the best:

Banh by Lauren ♥♥, 42 Market St. (at Madison St.; banhbylauren.com; subway: F to East Broadway). French/Vietnamese pastries for folks who don't usually like dessert, these cakes and cookies are only lightly sweet, flavored (often) with pandam, a grassy, vanilla-ish plant.

Dominique Ansel ♥♥♥, 189 Spring St. (btw. Thompson & Sullivan sts.; dominiqueansel.com; ✆ **212/219-2773;** subway: C, E to Spring St.). Now that the craze for cronuts—the unholy union of a donut and a croissant—has passed, sugarholics can enjoy the better pastries at this oh-so-Gallic little bakery without waiting on line. Try "Paris–New York," which teams choux dough with peanut butter, rich chocolate, and caramel; or the wonderful cinnamon rye shortbread. Also at 17 E. 27th St.

Glace New York ♥♥, 1266 Madison Ave. (btw. 90th & 91st sts.; glaceny.com; ✆ **347/502-6445;** subway: 4, 5, 6 to 86th St.). Instagram-famous hot chocolate with a rim of roasted marshmallow and a slew of other toppings. The surprise? It tastes as delightful as it looks. Look also for Glace's food truck on 50th St. between Fifth and Sixth avenues in Rockefeller Center.

Lady M Cake Boutique ♥♥♥, 41 E. 78th St. (near Madison Ave.; ladym.com; ✆ **212/452-2222;** subway: 6 to 77th St.). The specialty here is crepe cakes, particularly green tea cakes, which are so well balanced they win over even non-sweet-lovers. The seating area is usually crowded; get your slices to go and have a picnic in Central Park. See website for other outlets in Manhattan.

Lady Wong ♥♥, 332 E. 9th St. (btw. First & Second aves; ladywong.com; ✆ **646/422-7189;** subway: L to First Ave.). Steamed Malaysian pastries known as *kuih* are the creamy, not-too-sweet treats to get here, many of them crafted from pandan, a fruit rarely seen outside Southeast Asia. They make a great gift, as beautiful to look at as they are to eat. Also at Urban Hawker (p. 123).

Levain Bakery ♥♥, 351 Amsterdam Ave. (btw. 76th & 77th sts.; levainbakery.com; ✆ **212/874-6080;** subway: 1 to 79th St.). A "cookie line camera" on Levain's website testifies to New Yorkers' rabid devotion to the chocolate chip cookies baked here since 1994. Massive, fluffy, and intensely chocolatey, they deserve the acclaim. See website for other outlets.

Lysée ♥♥♥, 44 E. 21st St. (near Park Ave. S.; lyseenyc.com; ✆ **646/678-3131;** subway: 6 to 23rd St.). Usually food this exquisite-looking falls short in the flavor department. Not at Lysée, a Korean pastry boutique where *tromp l'oeil* ears of corn are filled with corn mousse, and apple tarts fan out the fruit with mandala-like intricacy. The bottom-floor tearoom often

SOHO, NOLITA & NOHO

Brave the lines at **Prince Street Pizza** ♥♥, 27 Prince St., near Elizabeth St. (✆ **212/966-4100;** daily 11:30am–11pm), for crunchy squares of the best pepperoni pizza you'll likely ever try.

Expensive

Balthazar ♥♥ FRENCH Walt Disney's Imagineers couldn't do a better job than restaurateur Keith McNally has of re-creating the quintessential requires reservations; to-go pastries, cookies, and cakes are available upstairs.

Madison Fare ♥♥, 1225 Madison Ave. (btw. 88th and 89th sts.; madisonfare.com; ✆ **917/261-4662;** subway: 4, 5, 6 to 86th St.). Gelato? So 2022. Now the cool kids are lining up for frozen yogurt, and this upscale grocery store, near Museum Mile, makes the most tantalizingly tart stuff in the city. Toppings are upscale, from raw honey to pistachio butter.

Mary O's Irish Soda Bread Shop ♥♥, 93 E. 7th St. (near First Ave.; maryos.nyc; ✆ **212/505-5611;** subway: F to Second Ave.). During the pandemic, the Instagram sensation @HumansOfNY featured Mary O'Halloran, who took up selling scones to make ends meet after her pub was shuttered. Thanks to HoNY fans, her pub is now thriving again, as is this shop where you'll get a fresh-from-the-oven scone topped by Irish butter and homemade blackberry jam. Sounds simple, tastes delightful, but only open Thursday to Sunday 7am to noon.

Rice to Riches ♥♥♥, 37 Spring St. (btw. Mott & Mulberry sts.; ricetoriches.com; ✆ **212/274-0008;** subway: 6 to Spring St.). This delightful one-trick pony serves only rice pudding, tarted up with all sorts of exotic flavorings (and unfortunately cutesy names like "Sex, Drugs, and Rocky Road"). I have yet to discover a flavor that wasn't ambrosial.

Venieros ♥♥, 342 E. 11th St. (at First Ave.; venierospastry.com;

Levain's famous dark chocolate chip cookie.

✆ **212/674-7070;** subway: L to First Ave.). This beloved Italian bakery has been in business since 1894, with an attached cafe for those who'd like an aperitivo or coffee with their cannoli. The cannolis are legendary, but I'm a particular fan of their scrumptious pignoli cookies.

Win Son Bakery ♥♥♥, 23 Second Ave. (near First St.; winsonbrooklyn.com; ✆ **646/869-0150;** subway: F to Second Ave.). A Taiwanese operation whose pine nut sun cookie was rightly named by the *New York Times* as one of the best pastries in the city (the mochi donuts are also spectacular). The original outlet is in Brooklyn at 164 Graham Ave. with an attached restaurant we adore (p. 153).

Parisian brasserie. But not only does Balthazar look picture-perfect with its zinc bar, smoked mirrors, soaring ceiling, and serious, vest-wearing waiters, the food hits the mark as well. Open for breakfast, brunch, lunch, and dinner, it's the place to come for delectable pastries, perfectly executed French classics (like *steak au poivre* or *moules frites*), and tiptop cocktails. The whole concept should feel phony, but instead the effect is charming. By the way, there's no more interesting Instagram follow than owner McNally's account,

Chef Paul Carmichael celebrates Caribbean flavors at Kabawa.

where he often shares the backstage goings-on at Balthazar and his other restaurants.

80 Spring St. (btw. Broadway & Crosby St.). balthazarny.com. ✆ **212/965-1414.** Entrees $30–$47 (more for steak). Mon–Fri 8am–11am, 11:30am–4:30pm and 5pm–midnight; Sat–Sun 9am–4pm and 5pm–midnight. Subway: 6 to Spring St.; N, R to Prince St.

Kabawa ♥♥♥ CARIBBEAN The chefs wear tie-dyed aprons at Kabawa, the first clue that it's not business as usual at this high end, Momofuku joint. The celebrated restaurant group created this place specifically to showcase the talents of Chef Paul Carmichael. He hails from Barbados and is a talented proselytizer for the delights of Caribbean cuisine. To the muted sounds of reggae, ska, soca and salsa, diners cut into happily funky goat as tender as filet mignon, creamy raw shrimp with a welcome kapow of scotch bonnet pepper, or a rapturously complex fish stew (*blaff*) featuring cobia fish, among other dishes (the menu changes seasonally). Try to get a seat at the three-sided counter facing into the kitchen so you can watch the crew make its magic.

8 Extra Place (off East 1st St.). kabawa.com. 3 course tasting menu $145. Tues–Sat 5:30–10pm. Subway: 6 to Bleecker St, F to Second Ave.

Moderate

Thai Diner ♥♥ THAI Fun, kitschy decor belies the serious ambitions of the chef/owners, a married pair who met working at California's famed Per Se restaurant. Their version of Thai food is complex, toothsome, and often surprising, with many dishes the U.S. hasn't seen before; such standards as *massaman* curry and pad Thai are stripped of cloying sweetness and endowed with a punch of spice. This being a "diner," they also serve some American

Balthazar **13**
Carnitas Ramirez **32**
Che Li **20**
Dame **6**
Dominque Ansel Bakery **10**
Emily **5**
Hamburger America **7**
I Sodi **3**
Joe & Pat's **25**
Kabawa **17**
King **8**
Lady Wong **22**
L'Industrie Pizzeria **1**
Little Myanmar **31**
Lombardi's **15**
Lord's **11**
Mary O's Irish Soda Bread Shop **29**
Panna II **30**
Penny/Claud **19**
Prince Street Pizza **12**
Raku **9**
Rice to Riches **14**
Shabu Tatsu **23**
Smithereens **26**
Spice Brothers **27**
Superiority Burger **28**
Sushi Katsuei **4**
Thai Diner **16**
Venieros **24**
Veselka **21**
Via Carota **2**
Win Son Bakery **18**

SoHo, East Village & West Village Restaurants

Thai Diner combines classic American diner food with fresh takes on Thai cuisine, while the decor leans heavily on kitsch.

fare, and some fusion dishes, the best of which are the disco fries—classic strips of fried potato topped with a complex curry and cheese curds. It'll make you want to dance, I promise.

186 Mott St. (at Kenmare St.). thaidiner.com. ✆ **646/559-4140.** Entrees $15–$29. Mon–Weds 8:30am–10:30pm; Thurs–Fri 8:30am–11:30pm; Sat 10am–11:30pm; Sun 10am–10pm. Subway: N, Q, R, 6 to Canal St.

Inexpensive

Raku (see p. 130) is another excellent affordable meal in Soho.

Hamburger America ♥ AMERICAN YouTube burger guru George Motz is serving his signature Oklahoma fried-onion burgers at his first real restaurant, after famously serving them from a slide out a window in his home during the pandemic (over 30,000 in 2+ years, he claims). If you like your burgers crisp and very oniony—I don't, to be honest—you'll enjoy the experience of dining in this facsimile of a 1930's-era diner. He also serves a smash burger, several sandwiches, fries, and milk drinks. Most pleasing: the fair prices.

51 MacDougal St. (entrance on Houston). hamburgeramerica.com. Burgers $7.75. Sun–Thurs 11am–10pm; Fri–Sat 11am–11pm. Subway: 1 to Houston, C, E to Spring St.

THE EAST VILLAGE

Kids, and any folks who like to do their own cooking, love **Shabu Tatsu** ♥♥, 216 E. 10th St., off Second Ave. (shabutatsu.com; ✆ **212/477-2972;** Mon–Thurs 5–11pm, Fri–Sat noon–3pm and 5pm–1:30am, Sun noon–3pm and

5–11pm), where diners dip meats, noodles, and vegetables into a pot of boiling water before immersing them in scrumptious dipping sauces.

Expensive

Penny/Claud ♥♥♥ SEAFOOD/EUROPEAN Seafood restaurant Penny made every "best of" list in Gotham when it debuted in 2024, matching the record set by its downstairs sibling Claud, founded in 2022. Both are the work of Joshua Pinsky, a chef whose name will someday be as well recognized as Daniel Boulud or Eric Ripert, I have no doubt. Of the two, I prefer Penny, which elevates the fruits of the sea, both raw and cooked, to new heights. Though sometimes not literally: what's usually a "seafood tower" is here the "ice box" with marinated, poached, and raw clams, oysters, mussels, creamy poached shrimp, and raw fish laid in a box of ice with three delicious dipping sauces on the side. Other menu masterpieces include savory strips of roasted

EAT & learn: COOKING CLASSES

Though ideally you should be interested in cooking to take a class, the **Institute of Culinary Education ♥♥♥**, 225 Liberty St., at West St. (recreational.ice.edu; ✆ **212/847-0700**), has another trait that makes it fun for visitors: It's one of the easiest places to meet and actually get to know New Yorkers in the city. That's because since its inception, originally as the Peter Kump School in 1976, the emphasis here has been on "hands-on" classes. You won't be sitting in some dim lecture hall among a group of strangers. Instead, your class will be divided into small groups, and for 3 to 4 hours you'll cook or bake with your partners, poring over recipes, consulting with the teacher, and chatting away. The crowd is well mixed: young people in their 20s; professional types in their 30s, 40s, and 50s; and a smattering of retirees. At night classes, the ratio of men to women is pretty close to 50:50 (in the daytime, women predominate).

If you're serious about cooking, you won't find a better school in the city. The instruction here is highly practical, and it aims to teach as much about the principles of cooking as specific recipes. The classes in which I recently sat taught me how to choose fresh herbs; when it's important to buy expensive ingredients and when it won't matter; and the technique of putting my thumb and forefinger on the blade of a knife to stabilize it. The Institute offers over a thousand recreational classes a year, more than any other cooking school in the world. Class prices range from $150 to $300 for a good 4 hours of instruction, plus a feast at the end, often including wine.

Pastry cooking class at the Institute of Culinary Education.

mackerel topped with just-hot-enough peppers; a seafood "cassoulet"; and the best wedge salad in the city, topped by mimolette cheese and a delightfully tart vinaigrette. You eat all this at a long marble counter, while watching the beanie-hatted chefs at work. Really fun. Claud, down in the basement, is still serving accomplished European food, though it doesn't have the buzz Penny does, or the chef-front seating. But a meal at either will be memorable.

90 E. 10th St. (btw. Third & Fourth aves.). claudnyc.com. penny-nyc.com. Entrees $21–$88. Daily 5–10pm (Penny until 10:30pm). Subway: 6 to Astor Place.

Moderate

Che Li ♥♥♥ CHINESE St. Mark's Place has become one of the city's most authentically Asian scenes in the past few years, with karaoke parlors, snack shops, and stores from across that continent. It's an appropriate setting, therefore, for a restaurant that takes a deep dive into the Chinese region of Jiangnan, both its small towns and Shanghai. It's a subtle cuisine, one that (often) involves quickly frying the ingredient in question and then stewing it for a long period in a closed container, to get the best of all its natural flavors. That may mean crab braised in peach resin, for example, or a meaty fish head long-poached in a delectable sweet-and-salty broth. Other delights include picture-perfect dim sum, soy-shellacked smoked fish, and green-tea-infused shrimp. Some have a bit of heat, but nowhere near what you get with Sichuan cuisine. All this is served in a setting that charmingly evokes a traditional Chinese village, with hanging lanterns and wooden dividers between the tables.

Che Li serves the regional cuisine of Jiangnan in a setting that feels like a traditional village.

19 St. Mark's Place (btw. Second & Third aves.). che-li.com. ✆ **646/858-1866.** Entrees $15–$38 (up to $76 for Dungeness crab). Sun–Thurs 11:30am–10:30pm; Fri–Sat 11:30am–11pm. Subway: 6 to Lafayette; N, R to 8th St.

Smithereens ♥♥♥ SEAFOOD The team at this restaurant—alums of both Claud (above) and the Momofuku empire—are adept at sow's ear/silk purse transformations. They've taken what should be a dingy basement space and turned it into one of the coziest eateries in town, coloring the walls a moody Atlantic ocean blue-gray and placing tables just the right distance from one another. They're also making diners rethink such lowly items as beans (transformed into creamy, briny goodness with a topping of sea urchin, red shrimp, and squid), buckwheat pancakes (a delivery vessel for perfectly smoked fish), and celery (whipped into ice cream and floated in a celery

The quality cooking at Smithereens accentuates seafood with simple, elegant preparations.

soda—it's odd but delish). The drinks list, crafted by the young sommelier/co-owner, is heavy on unusual and marvelous German whites; there's also a savvy cocktail program (try the tasty "Ben Afflek"). ***One warning:*** If you don't like seafood, dine elsewhere, as there's not much else on the menu. The restaurant was named for a film about the East Village in its punk rock era.

414 E. 9th St. (btw. First Ave. & Ave. A). smithereensnyc.com. Entrees $19–$42. Tues–Sat 5:30pm–10pm. Subway: L to First Ave.

Inexpensive

Carnitas Ramirez ♥♥ MEXICAN Unrepentant carnivores: this is the taco shop for you. Every part of the pig is served here, from snout to tail, and all are simmered many hours into tasty, tender goodness before being mounded into $5 tacos. My favorite cut is the cheek, to which I add a dollar's worth of *chicharrón* crumbs for crunch, but it's all good. Two tacos is enough for a filling meal, one for a light one. ***Warning:*** The red salsa on the fixings bar (included in the cost) will sear your face off. For something a little less fiery, choose the green salsa with avocado.

210 E. 3rd St. (at Ave. B). carnitasramirez.com. Tacos $5. Wed–Thurs noon–9pm; Fri–Sat noon–10pm; Sun noon–6pm. Subway: F, J, M, Z to Delancey St.

It may look like your average taco shop, but Carnitas Ramirez wows with the deep flavors of its long-simmered pork fillings.

Little Myanmar ♥♥ BURMESE Just like a double espresso, the tea leaf salad at Little Myanmar will leave you buzzing. It's packed with caffeine, but also with a small mountain of textures and tastes, thanks to fermented leaves, crunchy dried shrimp, crispy soy beans, peanuts, green and red tomatoes, and a kapow of chili flakes. It's a marvelous introduction to a cuisine rarely found in the U.S., as are the curries, satays, pancakes, and other Burmese specialties on the menu. Alas, there's no real feeling of Asia in the decor here, which is simple in the extreme and cramped (the space is quite small). But since the servers are the lovely and attentive owners, most folks don't mind.

150 E. 2nd St. (at Avenue A). ✆ **917/475-1183**. Entrees $13–$22. Sun–Thurs 11am–9:30pm; Fri–Sat 11am–10:30pm. Subway: F to Second Ave.

Panna II ♥ INDIAN The *Village Voice* newspaper once called Panna II the "best unintentional art installation" in the city, which seems right. It's a wacky-looking place. Over the years, the owners have covered every possible inch of this small restaurant with Christmas lights, chili lights, hanging beach balls, Hawaiian leis, and other kitsch, packing it so tightly that those over 5'8" have to duck to get a seat. Once inside you dine on solidly tasty and very affordable Indian food. And if you're an Instagrammer, you'll be in heaven here. Fun, fun, fun!

93 First Ave. (upstairs, near 6th St.). pannatwo.com. ✆ **212/598-4610.** Entrees $10.95–$18.95. Daily noon–midnight. Cash only. Subway: 6 to Astor Place; F to Second Ave.

Spice Brothers ♥♥♥ MIDDLE EASTERN Not many shawarma-and-falafel-joints have this kind of pedigree, with an owner who learned his trade in the kitchen of star chef Daniel Boulud. But fine dining's loss is cheap eats' gain, with chef/owner Lior Lev Sercarz (and partner David Malbequi) serving up meal-sized sandwiches and platters for less than the cost of most appetizers in nearby restaurants. Yes, you have to go up to the counter to order, but nothing else here feels lowbrow—the room with its five tidy tables and blue mural is pleasant, and beer and wine is available. As you might have guessed from the name, what's special here is the way everything is spiced—but spiced doesn't always mean fiery. When Sercarz stopped working in restaurants he opened a business procuring seeds, bark, leaves, peppers, and roots from farmers around the world, and processing them into dry spice mixes which he sold to chefs like Eric Ripert and Michael Solomonov, along with the general public. Those spices are put to excellent use here in dishes like lamb *arayes*—cinamonny meatballs fried in a pita pocket, sided by creamy tahini and a mango pickle sauce called *amba*. The chicken shawarma is yellowed by turmeric, mellowed by cumin, and given a smoky punch by pimenton. There are also excellent and crispy felafel, chicken schnitzel, and more.

110 St. Marks Place (near Avenue A). spicebrothersny.com. Entrees $12–$18. Sun–Thurs 11:45–9:30pm; Fri–Sat 11:45–11pm. Subway: L to First Ave.

Superiority Burger ♥♥♥ VEGETARIAN Vegetarianism can be a blast! That's the message this hip diner trumpets loud, clear, and quirkily. Set in a space that was a beloved Ukranian diner for many decades, it has kept the

Vegetables play a starring role at Superiority Burger.

long counter but dimmed the lights and added a bar at the back. It also has filled the place with oddball ephemera from the neighborhood—a display of branded plastic bags and menus from long-time local businesses; placemats with ads for Alphabet City institutions that sell rubber stamps, vinyl records, and socks; and a soundtrack in the bathrooms featuring classic ads for long-gone services, like Dr. Zizmore's skin care. For native New Yorkers, all of these touches are catnip, though visitors will enjoy them, too. None of this would matter if the food wasn't good, and it is—spectacular, in fact. The menu dances from hit to hit, like an appetizer of vinegared beets in a pool of spicy cream cheese, topped by fried pretzels, to a focaccia sandwich with kale so rich in darkly vegetal flavor it must have been a prime rib in another life. The signature dish, an all-veggie burger crafted from 14 ingredients (the recipe has been posted online), is a wonder: Set on a perfectly griddled soft bun that's slathered with eggless mayo and topped with roasted mushroom and shredded cabbage, it may well be the most satisfying burger in Gotham. Desserts are primo, too.

119 Avenue A (btw. St. Mark's Place & 7th St.). superiorityburger.com. Entrees $15–$25. Mon–Wed 5–10:30pm, Thurs noon–10:30pm, Fri noon–11:30pm, Sat 11am–11:30pm, Sun 11am–9:30pm. Subway: L to First Ave.

Veselka ♥ UKRAINIAN A popular spot for East Village hipsters, families, businesspeople, and anybody who's ever had a deep need for cold borscht at 11pm. When Veselka debuted in 1954 the area was awash in Ukrainian diners, but most have since gone belly-up (or have upgraded to the point of assimilation), leaving this crowded, tall-windowed eatery the standard-bearer for pierogi, kielbasa, and other Eastern European fare. The matzoh ball soup will restore your faith in humanity.

144 Second Ave. (at 9th St.). veselka.com. ✆ **212/228-9682.** Entrees $14–$27. Open 24 hours. Subway: 6 to Astor Place. Also in Grand Central Terminal, Madison Square Garden, and Williamsburg, Brooklyn.

GREENWICH VILLAGE

Expensive

King ♥♥♥ EUROPEAN King looks like a typical, cozy Greenwich Village bistro from the outside, but the cooking being done here is, yes, fit for royalty (and I say that knowing this place is named for the street it is on). The menu changes daily to take advantage of what's most tantalizing at the green market, and though they do proteins with elan, it's the vegetable elements on the menu that really set King apart. Recently that meant one of the most satisfying salads in the city: a blood orange and red endive, its bitterness perfectly balanced by paper thin sheets of *ricotta salata*. And siding perfectly seared duck breast with prunes was celeriac pureed to the texture of a cloud and bracingly green braised chard. An excellent date place.

18 King St. (at Sixth Ave.). kingrestaurant.nyc. ✆ **917/825-1618.** Entrees: $42–$48. Daily 5–10pm; Fri–Sat also noon–3pm. Subway: 1, 2 to Houston, A, B, C, D, E, F to West 4th St.

Sushi Katsuei ♥♥ JAPANESE An omakase meal is a multicourse sushi tasting, one that usually requires a major investment of both money and time. Not at Sushi Katsuei. This generically Japanese looking, too brightly lit restaurant, with one counter and a scattering of tables, serves the real deal for "just" $65, a price that might sound high (heck, it's enough to put this in our "expensive" section) but is about a third of what more famous omakase restaurants in town charge. That covers one hand roll, and 9 nigiri (its $90 omakon menu adds 5 sashimi pieces to the mix). The ingredients are all world class: caviar, exquisite cuts of fish, silky soft scallops, and monk fish liver are all on the menu, as they'd be in the pricier places. The expert chefs know how to nudge flavors to their peak, with a scattering of pink salt here, a swipe of yuzu there. Sushi Katsuei keeps its prices low by serving everything relatively rapidly, meaning the meal lasts only 1 hour rather than 2 to 2½ (the common length of time for an omakase meal). ***Note:*** See "Sushi On Me" for another style of affordable omakase (p. 155).

357 Sixth Ave. (btw. 3rd and 4th sts.) sushikatsuei.com ✆ **646/789-4664.** Omakase menu $65. Mon–Sat 2–10pm. Subway: A, B, C, D, E, F to West 4th St. Also in Brooklyn at 210 7th Ave.

Moderate

Dame ♥♥ BRITISH Chef Ed Szymanski has a savant-like talent with fish, a protein he prepares every which way, from delicate crudos to grilled and sauced wonders. Best on the menu are the U.K. classics, like the perfect Pimm's Cup cocktail, *kedgeree* (a colonial-era throwback of curried rice with smoked fish), and fish and chips—miraculously crunchy fish alongside potatoes that are boiled and then twice fried so they're both

Dame draws crowds for U.K. classics, like crisped-to-perfection fish and chips.

creamy and crisp. But this is *not* a place for a romantic meal. The space is tiny, tables are jammed together, and the soundtrack is a thumping, loud mix of '80s and '90s disco hits, which can get annoying. For a less frenetic Brit meal, head to **Lord's ♥♥**, 506 LaGuardia Place (near Bleecker St.), the meat-centric off-shoot of Dame. It's as accomplished on the culinary front, but has significantly more room, making it a more relaxed dining experience.

87 MacDougal St. (btw. Bleecker & Houston). damenewyork.com. ✆ **929/367-7370.** Entrees $32–$38. Mon–Sat 5:30–10pm. Subway: A, B, C, D, E, F to W. 4th St.

Inexpensive

Via Carota ♥♥♥ ITALIAN Restaurant years are like dog years: hit 10, as Via Carota did in 2024, and you become a senior citizen. But somehow this ode to Italian cuisine still feels like a puppy. Diners line up nightly to get tables (very few reservations are given out), and among them will often be some celebs (Taylor Swift, for example), as this is still one of the Village's prime see-and-be-seen spots. Why the continued fuss? Rooms that look lifted from a trattoria in Siena and straightforward but spectacularly flavorful food from various regions of The Boot. Among the most celebrated dishes are *cacio e pepe* pasta (Tay Tay's fave), Sicilian-style meatballs with pine nuts and raisins, and a negroni so iconic they're now selling it bottled in liquor stores. If you want to guarantee a waitless-meal, show up at 11:30am for lunch, or attempt to snag one of the few reservations well in advance on Resy. We also highly recommend its Tuscan sister resto **I Sodi ♥♥♥**, 314 Bleecker St.

51 Grove St. (btw. Seventh Ave & Bleecker St.). viacarota.com. ✆ **212/255-1962**. Entrees $26–$32 (with one fish dish at $69). Daily 11am–11pm. Subway: 1 to Christopher St.

Lunch is a good option for getting a table at Via Carota; nighttime reservations can be hard to snag.

UNION SQUARE, FLATIRON DISTRICT & GRAMERCY PARK

In Madison Park visit the actual shack where **Shake Shack** (shakeshack.com; ✆ **212/889-6600;** burgers $5.55–$9.95; Mon–Fri 7:30am–11pm, Sat–Sun 8:30am–11pm) was founded in 2004.

Ace's Pizza **24**
All'Antico Vinaio **11**
Ben & Jack's Steakhouse **32**
Berimbau Brazilian Table **35**
Björk Café & Bistro **34**
Borgo **42**
Burger Joint **21**
Chelsea Market **2**
Çka Ka Qëllue **41**
Coppelia **1**
Coqodaq **47**
Cote **51**
Eataly **49**
Grand Central Oyster Bar and Restaurant **33**
Hav & Mar **4**
Hawksmoor **44**
The Hugh **30**
Ichiran Times Square **19**
Joe Allen **12**
Jupiter **25**
Kazu Nori **39**
Keens Steakhouse **37**
L'Ami Pierre **22**
Le Bernardin **20**
Le Relais de Venise L'Entrecôte **29**
Le Rock **26**
Len Len **45**
Los Tacos No. 1 **8**
LumLum **14**
Lysée **46**
Margon **9**
Mercado Little Spain **5**
Monkey Bar **28**
Moynihan Food Hall **6**
Naro **27**
Portale **52**
Poseidon Greek Bakery **13**
Poulette **16**
Raku **15**
Rowdy Rooster **38**
S&P **50**
Second Avenue Deli **40**
Shake Shack **48**
Shukette **3**
Sparks **31**
Tengri Tagh **7**
Tête d'Or **43**
Three Roosters **18**
Uncle Ray's **17**
Urban Hawker **23**
The View **10**
Yoon Haeundae Galbi **36**

Midtown Restaurants
UPPER EAST SIDE
MIDTOWN EAST
MURRAY HILL
GRAMERCY PARK
FLATIRON DISTRICT
PARK
ROCKEFELLER CENTER
St. Patrick's Cathedral
Grand Central Terminal
United Nations
Bryant Park
New York Public Library
Macy's
Empire State Bldg.
Madison Square Park
Gramercy Park
Union Square
Roosevelt Island Tram
Queensboro (59th St.) Bridge
ROOSEVELT ISLAND
East River
Queens-Midtown Tunnel
Franklin-Delano-Roosevelt (FDR) Dr.
Subway station
Upper Manhattan
Uptown
Midtown
Downtown
0 1/4 mi
0 0.25 km

Flatiron District Food Court

Eataly ♥ at 200 Fifth Ave. (btw. 23rd and 24th sts.; eataly.com). Eataly was founded here, but has since become a major chain and has seen a dip in the quality of its eateries. Still, the simple Italian food here is usually tasty.

Expensive

Borgo ♥♥♥ ITALIAN Borgo doesn't hit diners over the head with its brilliance. On first glance, its pressed-tin ceiling, globe lighting, white tablecloths, and wood trim look like what you'd see at hundreds of other NYC restaurants. But then you notice that the tables are a civilized distance apart, the art is quirky (some is by chef/owner Andrew Tarlow), and though the restaurant is loud enough to seem "buzzy" it's actually quite easy to hold a conversation here. The menu, too, seems just shy of cookie cutter. But when the food starts to arrive, you realize that Tarlow is crafting the platonic ideals of many dishes (like his masterfully creamy but toothsome risottos, and his perfectly crisp fried artichoke), and getting very creative with others (the fried delicata squash with honey chili coating tastes like a sophisticated version of the fried dough you'd get at a carnival). Cocktails, too, are next level, like the "Golden Bachelor," compiled from an orgeat syrup flavored with rose petals and pistachio nuts, plus toasted coconut milk, genever, white rum, and rose water. A meal to remember.

124 E. 27th St. (btw. Park Ave S. & Madison aves.). borgonyc.com. ✆ **646/360-2404.** Entrees $32–$72. Daily 11:30am–2:30pm and 5:15–10pm. Subway: 6 to 28th St.

Borgo serves a sophisticated Italian menu in a setting that checks all the boxes for a refined NYC dining experience.

An array of sauces and other accompaniments surround the perfectly grilled Korean-style meat at Cote.

Cote ♥♥♥ KOREAN Back in the 1970s, an Asian night on the town likely would have consisted of a trip to Benihana, where a chef would chop, chop, chop, and sizzle, sizzle, sizzle your meal in front of you in an elaborate show. Decades later, as Korean barbecue places opened up in New York City, diners were handed the cooking responsibilities, performed on a grill in the middle of the table. And now we have Cote, somewhere in the middle of those styles—that grill is still in the center of the table, but there's also a battalion of servers/chefs cooking, and hovering, so that every morsel of meat is turned over at just the right instant. It's less dramatic, but infinitely more coddling. And it would be too twee a display if the food weren't so splendid. Cote serves up beef that wouldn't be out of place at the city's top steakhouses (p. 125). Accompanying the meat are a panoply of smaller plates with chunky sauces, lettuce leaves, pickles, scallion salad, and more. If you order the "Butcher's Feast" (recommended for its array of fine cuts), you'll get a delicious helping of soft-serve ice cream, drizzled with high-quality caramel, at the end.

16 W. 22nd St. (off Fifth Ave.). cotenyc.com. ✆ **212/401-7906.** Entrees $32–$85; Butcher's Feast $78. Daily 5–11pm. Subway: R, W to 23rd St.

Moderate

Coqodaq ♥♥ KOREAN A smartly crafted set meal is a thing of beauty. At Coqodaq, the set meal, called "the Bucket List," comes out on very differently sized plates, with all sorts of accoutrements, for maximum drama. First course is a soothing chicken consommé; second course is the excellent "dry" fried chicken, accompanied by an adorable quartet of sauces in squeeze bottles, alongside *ban chan,* the classic Korean side dishes—in this case a massive heap of refreshing scallion salad and three plates of subtly pickled

THE hole TRUTH: NEW YORK'S BEST BAGELS

Not many things are more "New York" than a bagel, and New Yorkers are loyal to their favorite bagel stores. In fact, discussions about who makes the best bagel can lead to broken friendships. Following are the top contenders:

Absolute Bagels 2708 Broadway (btw. 107th and 108th streets; ✆ **212/932-2052;** subway: 1 to 110th St.). The egg bagels, hot out of the oven, melt in your mouth, and their whitefish salad is perfectly smoky, not overpowering.

Apollo Bagels 73 Greenwich Ave. (at Seventh Ave.; apollobagels.com; subway: 1, 2, 3, F to 14th St.). Montreal-style bagels (they're chewier), with generous portions of smoked salmon, high-quality cream cheese, and heaps of dill, inspire lines out the door daily. Also at 242 E. 10th St., and 133 N. 7th St. in Brooklyn.

Bo's Bagels 235 W. 116th St. (near Frederick Douglas Blvd.; bosbagels.com; subway: 2, 3 to 116th St.). Tradition rules for the prep of these Harlem bagels: after a 24-hour fermentation period, they're boiled and then baked. Along with the usual spreads, Bo's serves up a very popular bagel version of pigs in a blanket. Also at Broadway and 155th St.

Ess-a-Bagel 831 Third Ave. (btw. 50th & 51st streets; ess-a-bagel.com; ✆ **212/980-1010;** subway: E, F to Lexington/53rd St, 6 to 51st St.). When it comes to size, Ess-a-Bagel's are the best of the biggest: plump, chewy, and oh so satisfying. Also at First Ave and 19th St. and 32nd St. between Sixth & Seventh aves.

Kossar's Bialys 536 W. 30th St. (kossars.com; ✆ **877/4-BIALYS** [424-2597]; subway: 7 to 34th St./Hudson Yards). Bialys—flat, yeast rolls with savory fillings—are the star offerings here, but don't ignore Kossar's bagels. Also hand-rolled, they have a slightly crunchy exterior with a tender, moist middle. Sure, you came for the bialys, but you will leave with both. Three other outlets are in Chinatown, the Upper East Side and the Upper West Side (see website for addresses).

Liberty Bagels 260 W. 35th St. (near Eighth Ave.; libertybagels.com; subway: A, C, E to 34th St.). Hand-rolled and kettle-boiled the old-fashioned way, these were named the best bagels in Manhattan by a dude on TikTok who seems to have nothing better to do than try every bagel shop in the city. Now in 6 locations including Grand Central Terminal.

Modern Bread and Bagels 472 Columbus Ave. (at 83rd St.; modernbreadandbagel.com; subway: B, C to 81st St./American Museum of Natural History). Modern in this case means gluten-free and kosher, making these the bagels of choice for those with celiac disease and other types of gluten aversions. Also at 1427 Third Ave. (btw. 80th & 81st sts.), 630 Lexington Ave., and 139 W. 14th St. (btw. Sixth & Seventh aves.).

vegetables. Next you get glazed fried chicken (your choice of spicy or savory), then a palate-cleansing bowl of cold dressed noodles, and for dessert, a swirl of frozen yogurt with seasonal fruit. It's slightly too much food for one person, but they don't allow sharing, so if you're on a budget, consider ordering just some of the elements (it will come out to less money, and who needs that much chicken?). So why just two stars? For the nightclub-like setting, which gives a meal here definite buzz but inhibits deep conversation. Some people will love the ambiance, others will find it sensory overload. ***Tip:*** To get a reservation email reservations@coqodaq.com if your party is four or more, a more sure fire method than relying on Resy.

12 E. 22nd St. (btw. Broadway & Park Ave. S). coqodaq.com. Set meal $38. Mon–Fri noon–3pm and 5–11pm; Sat–Sun 5–11pm. Subway: N, R or 6 to 23rd St.

Len Len ♥♥ THAI Len Len gave me my first taste of durian. It's a fruit I've smelled in Asian markets—rotting flesh is an apt comparison—but at Len Len the culinary skills are so high that stench entirely vanishes. Here all you smell is the crab curry it's in, and that allows the custardy, vanilla-adjacent flavor of the fruit to shine through. It's just one of many champs on the menu, which includes a *yum* salad with silky raw salmon and just a hint of burn, and fried chicken wings with the crackliest of lime-kissed skins. The quality of the food is unexpected because Len Len presents itself as a party place, with late hours, a long bar, a poppy soundtrack (you can talk over it), and quirky decor that evokes a 1970's Thai shophouse (love the ramen packages presented here as art). But you'll dine well here whether or not you've danced up an appetite first.

40 E. 20th, off Park Ave. S. lenlen.nyc. Entrees $23–$36. Sun–Wed 5pm–midnight; Thurs–Sat 5pm–1am. Subway: 4, 5, 6, N, Q, R, W, L to Union Square.

Buzzy Len Len serves tasty Thai late into the evening.

Inexpensive

Kazu Nori ♥♥ JAPANESE Kazu Nori calls itself a "hand roll bar," an apt description. Guests sit at a counter and order sets of up to six rolls. The rice is comfortingly warm, the fish of high quality, and the prices surprisingly low. It's simple food in a simple atmosphere, but really delish (and they do serve alcohol). ***One warning:*** There's often a wait to get in, but the line moves quickly.

15 W. 28th St. (btw. Fifth Ave. & Broadway). handrollbar.com. Sets range $20–$38. Sun–Thurs 11:30am–11pm; Fri–Sat 11:30am–11:30pm. Subway: N, R to 28th St. Also at Hugh Food Court (p. 131), 205 Bleecker St., and University Place at 13th St.

S&P ♥♥♥ LUNCHEONETTE Since 1928, a beloved luncheonette has served hangry New Yorkers in this spot. Actually, make that five luncheonettes, all of which operated from behind the 40-ft.-long lunch counter that's at the center of this long, railway-car-shaped eatery. The latest iteration (named

S&P is a wonderful throwback to the days when New Yorkers took a meal most every day at the neighborhood luncheonette.

for the first) opened in 2022, but you'd never know it hasn't been here for decades. The workers wear the classic white paper hats with red detailing; faded celebrity photos are on the wall, along with ancient posters for "Hellman's Salad Week"; and the menu is a greatest hits of NYC breakfast and lunch fare, everything from egg and cheese on a roll, to tuna melts, Reubens, and egg creams. Owners Eric Finkelstein and Matt Ross have made sure every ingredient is just right, from the thin bacon piled atop purposefully sugary peanut butter (for that funky sandwich), to pastrami sourced from upstate New York. My favorite sammy is constructed from creamy chopped chicken liver pate, corned beef, Russian dressing, and rye (shh! don't tell your cardiologist). Prices are higher than they used to be (so what else is new?) but still well below what you'd pay at equivalent restaurants. (***Note:*** Most sandwiches here are overstuffed, thus big enough to share.) Fave touch: They don't give you a check at the end of your meal. Instead, diners go up to the register and tell the cashier what they ordered . . . and she trusts them to tell the truth! If that isn't old-fashioned goodness, I don't know what is.

174 Fifth Ave. (off 23rd St.). sandwich.place. ✆ **212/691-TUNA** [8862]. Entrees $13–$21 (many shareable). Mon–Fri 8am–5pm; Sat–Sun 9am–5pm. Subway: N, R to 23rd St.

CHELSEA & HUDSON YARDS

Chelsea & Hudson Yard's Food Courts

Chelsea Market ♥♥♥, 75 Ninth Ave. (btw. 15th & 16th sts.; chelseamarket.com) is the most fun food court in Manhattan. *Specialties:* Authentic, Tijuana-style tacos from **Los Tacos No. 1,** *halvah* (sesame candy) from **New York Seed + Mill,** and Israeli hummus from **Dizengoff.**

Mercado Little Spain ♥♥, in the basement of the Shops at Hudson Yards (entrance on 29th St. off Tenth Ave.; littlespain.com). All the fare is Spanish, and the paella may be the best of that dish in the city. Among the stations for takeaway food are several sit-down restaurants.

Moderate

Hav & Mar ♥♥♥ SCANDINAVIAN/ETHIOPIAN The first time I dined at Hav & Mar, a miracle occurred. No, it wasn't that I got a glimpse of chef/owner/food TV star Marcus Samuelsson, although that happened, too. It was that the waiter said to my husband and myself, totally unprompted: "Our entrees are all quite big. You should probably share one of those, and each get an appetizer." Why was that such an event? Because it makes Hav & Mar possibly the only restaurant in town where waiters aren't being trained to get their customers to *over order.* So, bravo for ethics! But the primary reason Hav & Mar gets my thumbs up is that the food, which follows Mr. Samuelsson's own journey (he grew up in both Ethiopia and Sweden before moving to the United States), is off-the-charts awesome. Dishes mix culinary traditions, so the "Swedopian" appetizer features silky salmon cured with berbere spices, and my favorite entree, the Addis York, is a plate with both classic southern-fried chicken and *doro wat,* a spicy Ethiopian chicken stew. Desserts and cocktails are delicious, too, and the spacious restaurant, decorated with curvaceous wood screens and painted black mermaids cavorting on the walls, is one of the buzziest scenes in this buzzy city.

Seafood starters at Hav & Mar.

245 Eleventh Ave. (at 26th St.). havandmar.com. ✆ **212/382-8041.** Entrees $35–$48 (with two shareable specialty dishes for $60 and $90). Sun–Mon 5–9pm; Tues–Sat 5–10pm. Subway: 7 to 34th St./Hudson Yards.

Portale ♥♥♥ ITALIAN Remember when Angelina and Brad split up? The divorce between chef Alfred Portale and the owners of Gotham Bar and Grill was *far* more shocking. Portale, widely considered one of the pioneers of contemporary American cuisine, had helmed the kitchen there for nearly 4 decades when he was booted out. In short order, he started his own place and has been thriving . . . while Gotham closed. Revenge has been a creative muse for Portale, who's cooking better than ever, using precise French techniques (reductions, gastrics, and more) to create some of the most intensely flavorful, opulent Italian food in the city. Pastas are the thing to get here, not just

THE pizza CAPITAL OF THE UNITED STATES

New York City not only has the best pizza in the country, it's now a showcase for regional pizza specialties from around the world. Here are our top picks, most of them sit-down eateries, with table service, alcoholic beverages, and pleasant-to-really-lovely decor.

CLASSIC NYC PIZZA (HAND-TOSSED, THIN CRUST)

Juliana's ♥♥, 19 Old Fulton St., Brooklyn (julianaspizza.com; ✆ **718/596-6700;** subway: A, C to High St.). Run by members of the famed pizza-making Grimaldi family, it even uses the original wood stove from the first Grimaldi's pizzeria. If there's a wait for a table, get a pie to go and dine in lovely Brooklyn Bridge Park nearby.

Lombardi's ♥, 32 Spring St. (btw. Mulberry & Mott sts. (firstpizza.com; ✆ **212/941-7994;** subway: N, Q, R, W to Prince St.). Claiming to be New York's first "licensed" pizzeria, Lombardi's opened in 1905 and still uses a coal oven and a generations-old Neapolitan family pizza recipe.

Mama's Too ♥♥♥, 2750 Broadway (at 106th. St; mamastoo.com; ✆ **212/510-7256;** subway: 1 to 103rd St.). Can we call this "New" New York pizza? This place puts the cheese on before the sauce, so the crust has a distinctive crackle, and the tomatoes shine more fiercely than usual. Mama's Too also experiments successfully with unusual toppings, like pear and gorgonzola, and a *cacio e pepe* Sicilian pie. Also at 323 Bleecker St.

Paulie Gee's ♥♥♥, 60 Greenpoint Ave., Brooklyn (pauliegee.com; ✆ **347/987-3747;** subway: G to Greenpoint Ave.). Designed to look like a classic 1970s slice joint, down to the checkerboard floors, here you can order one triangle at a time, allowing you to mix and match flavors, many of which are quite creative. The Hellboy, which uses hot honey, is a revelation. Vegan pizza also available

Prince Street Pizza ♥♥, 27 Prince St., near Elizabeth St. (princestreetpizzamenu.com; ✆ **212/966-4100;** subway: N, Q, R, W to Prince St.). The pepperoni masters. This is strictly a slice joint, with little seating, but the pizza—square here—is primo.

Scarr's Pizza ♥♥♥, 22 Orchard St., btw. Canal & Hester sts. (scarrspizza.com; ✆ **212/334-3481;** subway: F to East Broadway). Scarr Pimental, a Black Latino pizzaiolo, worked at some of the city's finest parlors before opening this joint. He mills his own flour in the basement, eschews pork (the pepperoni is beef here), and slathers on a sauce that packs a tomatoey punch.

CLASSIC NEAPOLITAN PIZZAS (ROUND, HAND-TOSSED, EXTREMELY PLIABLE THIN CRUST)

Kesté Pizza & Vino ♥♥♥, 77 Fulton St., enter from Gold St. (✆ **212/693-9030;** kestepizzeria.com; subway: A, C to Fulton St.). Pizzas created by an

because they'll keep the meal in the moderate range, but because they're truly outstanding.

126 W. 18th St. (btw. Sixth & Seventh aves.). portalerestaurant.com. ✆ **917/781-0255.** Pastas $28–$48. Sun–Thurs 5–9:30pm; Fri–Sat 5–10:30pm. Subway: 1 to 18th St.

Shukette ♥♥♥ MIDDLE EASTERN Diners experience an uncomfortable sensation when they come here: FOMO. Even if you're with a group, it's impossible to try all the stars on this long menu, and if you're sitting at the actual Neapolitan (Roberto Caporuscio) are topped by house-made mozzarella, with a perfectly balanced sauce and a whole raft of ingredients (40 options).

L'Industrie Pizzeria ♥♥, 104 Christopher St., near Bleecker (lindustriebk.com; subway: A, B, C, D, E, F to W. 4th St.). Started by Tuscan immigrants from Pistoia, L'Industrie imports all of its toppings from Italy. Order your slice with a mound of burrata cheese on top—it'll perfectly complement the funk of the long-fermented, perfectly blistered crust. Alas, the line here is too long, so go elsewhere if it's a madhouse. Also at 254 S. 2nd St. in Williamsburg, Brooklyn.

Roberta's ♥♥, 6 Grand St., at Domino Park, Brooklyn (robertaspizza.com; ✆ **718/417-1118;** subway: L to Bedford Ave.). Wood-fired ovens and quality ingredients give this pizza its special char. Also at several Manhattan food courts, and in Bushwick.

Una Pizza Napoletana ♥♥♥, 175 Orchard St., at Stanton St. (unapizza.com; ✆ **646/476-4457;** subway: F to Second Ave.). Naturally leavened dough left to rise unrefrigerated for 48 hours is the key to sublime pies—and one of the reasons they sometimes run out at the end of the night, so get an early reservation.

Zero Otto Nove Trattoria ♥♥, 2357 Arthur Ave., at 186th St., the Bronx (zeroottonove.com; ✆ **718/220-1027;** no subway within a mile). Ingredients are from Arthur Avenue neighbors and pies are cooked in a wood-burning brick oven—the result: pizza perfection. Good news: Zero Otto Nove now has a Manhattan outlet (15 W. 21st St.; subway: R, W to 23rd St.).

REGIONAL SPECIALTIES

Ace's Pizza ♥♥, underground at 30 Rockefeller Plaza in Rockefeller Center (acespizzaspot.com; subway: B, D, F, M to 47th–50th sts./Rockefeller Center). Detroit-style pies are fluffy and rectangular; Ace's are known for their perfectly charred crusts. (Also in Williamsburg, Brooklyn.)

Emily ♥♥, 35 Downing at Bedford St. (pizzalovesemily.com; subway: 1 to Houston). The other top choice for Detroit pizza, Emily is also TikTok-famous for its pretzel-bun burgers slathered in a delish hot pink secret sauce. Bonus points for its cute Greenwich Village setting.

Joe & Pat's ♥, 9168 First Ave., btw. 10th & 11th sts. (joeandpatsnyc.com; ✆ **212/677-4992;** subway: L to First Ave.). Cracker-crisp crust makes these Staten Island–style pies unique. Fans also love the vodka-sauce pies.

Speedy Romeo ♥, 376 Classon Ave., Brooklyn (speedyromeo.com; ✆ **646/542-1848;** subway: G to Classon Ave.). An extra yeasty crust means this St. Louis–style pizza ain't foldable. It also features a bechamel sauce in many incarnations, which can get drippy when you're holding slices.

chef's counter (recommended!) you'll keep second-guessing your order as you watch the parade of fascinating dishes being assembled. Chef/partner Ayesha Nurdjaja's version of Middle Eastern fare is far more inventive and opulent than one gets most places. So a small plate of roasted cauliflower is pushed into the wood-fired oven with sweet figs and a careful dusting of herbs and comes out tasting like the rich cousin of other cruciferous veggies. To drag through the dips (and they're all fab in their own ways) are four different

The busy chef's counter at Shukette.

house-made breads, each better than the next. There are also scintillating salads, tagines, perfectly charred lamb sausages, and more. The one thing you *must* order is *toum,* an assertive whipped garlic condiment that improves anything it's slathered on. ***Warning:*** It gets loud, thanks to the beat-heavy soundtrack.

230 Ninth Ave. (at 24th St.). shukettenyc.com. ✆ **212/243-1803.** Average meal cost $38. Mon–Sat 5–11pm; Sun 4–10pm. Subway: C, E to 23rd St.

Inexpensive

Coppelia ♥ LATIN AMERICAN The sign outside reads DINER, but the Caribbean colors inside (down to the teal faux shutters on the walls), and the salsa-and-samba soundtrack let you know this ain't your usual NYC greasy spoon. As does the menu, which ranges across the Caribbean and Latin America, offering up perfect renditions of such regional stars as Cuban roast pork with crispy chicharrónes, and Brazilian sweet-corn empanadas. Coppelia also offers breakfast items, day and night, and these, too, have a Latin flair. Best of all: Coppelia never closes, making this a rare late-night option.

207 W. 14th St. (near Seventh Ave.). ilovecoppelia.com. ✆ **212/858-5001.** Entrees $14–$35, most in the teens. Open 24/7. Subway: 1, 2, 3 to 14th St.

TIMES SQUARE, ROCKEFELLER CENTER & MIDTOWN WEST

If you're in the neighborhood around breakfast or lunch, head to **L'Ami Pierre ♥♥**, 149 W. 51st St., btw. Sixth & Seventh aves. (lamipierre.com; ✆ **917/639-399;** lunch items $7.50–$13; Mon–Fri 7am–7pm, Sat 10am–6pm), a very fine French bakery with seating, and savory as well as sweet options (it's associated with the ultra-gourmet **Le Bernardin,** p. 124, next door). Another lunch-worthy neighborhood bake shop, the 101-year-old **Poseidon Greek Bakery ♥♥**, 629 Ninth Ave, btw. 44th & 45th sts. (poseidonbakery.com; lunch items $6–$12; Tues–Sat 10am–6pm), makes fresh filo dough daily, meaning their spinach, cheese, and meat hand-pies are real treats (as are the *finikia*, a Greek honey cookie). Another lunch or early dinner take away option: **All'Antico Vinaio,** 729 Eighth Ave., between 45th and 46th streets (allanticovinaiousa.com), an offshoot of a famed Florentine sandwich shop. Its sandwiches are tasty but massive enough for three to share. See website for other locations throughout the city.

For chili heads: if you wanted to try the food at **Dhamaka** (p. 97), but couldn't get a reservation, head to their fab takeout fried chicken joint **Rowdy Rooster,** 140 W. 32nd St., between Sixth and Seventh avenues (rowdyrooster.com; daily 11am–11pm, Thurs–Sat until 1am). If you have a wimp with you, know that diners can pick from a range of spice levels, from blow-your-head-off to mild. Excellent chutneys allow customers to further customize their birds, available by the piece or in a sandwich ($14). Some seating.

Midtown West Food Courts

Moynihan Food Hall, in the Amtrak station, at 421 Eighth Ave. (moynihan foodhall.com). *Highlights:* Burgers from **Burger Joint** (p. 127), gut busting pastrami sammys from **Pastrami Queen** (p. 137), bagels from **H&H Bagels.**

Urban Hawker ♥♥♥, 135 W. 50th St. (urbanhawker.com). The first Singaporean-style market outside of Asia is staffed by actual vendors from Singapore, handpicked by that country's version of the late, great Anthony Bourdain, KF Seetoh (a friend of Bourdain's, Seetoh has a hugely popular food TV show in Asia). *Highlights:* **Hainan Jones** (addictive chicken and rice), **Mr. Fried Rice** (try version #1), and **Prawnaholic Collections** (for prawn noodle soup).

Expensive

Keens Steakhouse ♥♥♥ STEAK For a taste of Olde New York—and some of the best chops in the city (lamb chops, mutton chops, short ribs)—head to this iconic restaurant, established in 1885 and still going strong. The portions are humongous, so don't be afraid to share. Spend some time simply wandering around this museum-like eatery, with its collection of ceramic pipes on the ceiling (some of the regulars who had their own pipes here

Pipes cover the ceiling inside Keens Steakhouse, established 1885.

include Albert Einstein and Babe Ruth), its working fireplaces, memorabilia-laden walls, and plush leather banquettes.

72 W. 36th St. (at Sixth Ave.). keens.com. ✆ **212/947-3636.** Entrees $38–$89. Mon–Fri 11:45am–10:30pm; Sat 5–10:30pm; Sun 5–9:30pm. Subway: B, D, F, N, Q, R, M to 34th St./Herald Square.

Le Bernardin ♥♥♥ FRENCH/SEAFOOD When you dine at Le Bernardin you witness a delightfully formal bit of choreography. Every dish comes out in tandem with those of your fellow diners, and like magic, each one hits the table at exactly the same moment, a waiter poised at each diner's elbow. That synchronicity is a signal of respect, both for the eaters and for master chef Eric Ripert, who has appeared on every TV cooking show at this point (really!) and is still at the height of his powers. Yes, this will be a pricey meal, but it's one you'll remember long after you leave NYC. An iconic dining experience. La Liste named Le Bernardin the best restaurant in the U.S. in 2026.

155 W. 51st St. (btw. Sixth & Seventh aves.). le-bernardin.com. ✆ **212/554-1515.** Lunch $130 (3 courses), dinner $210 (4 courses), $325 tasting menu. Mon–Fri noon–2:30pm and 5–10:30pm (Fri until 11pm); Sat 5–11pm. Subway: B, D, E to Seventh Ave.; 1 to 50th St.

The View ♥ AMERICAN The name gives away why you come here for dinner: at this revolving restaurant, the views of the Times Square area are pretty darn spectacular. As for the food: it is better than it has to be, but isn't as exciting, or creative, as what you'll get at other NYC venues in the same price range. Still, the quality of the beef here is high, the veggies are fresh and cooked in a way that will please non-veggie fans (read: lots of butter), and the cocktails expertly mixed. And those views make this a fun place to come for a celebratory meal.

1535 Broadway (at the top of the Marriott Marquis Hotel). theviewnewyorkcity.com. Entrees $39–$74. Daily 4:30–10pm. Subway: 1, 2, 3, N, Q, R, W, S to Times Square.

THE prime cut: STEAKS! STEAKS!

Though NYC is no longer famous for its cheesecakes, or even its deli fare (with some exceptions; see p. 137), for red meat it still reigns supreme. The city brims with top-notch steak joints, where you'll pay top dollar for a perfectly aged rib-eye with a side of creamed spinach and crisped potatoes. The three classics—**Keens Steakhouse** ♥♥ in Midtown (p. 123), and, in Brooklyn, **Peter Luger Steakhouse** ♥♥ (p. 147) and **Gage & Tollner** ♥♥♥ (p. 144)—are still a very special experience, but these competitors give them a run for their money.

Ben & Jack's Steakhouse ♥ 219 E. 44th St. (benandjackssteakhouse.com; ✆ **212/682-5678;** subway: 4, 5, 6, 7, S to 42nd St./Grand Central). Opened by two former Peter Luger staffers, it shows—they learned their trade well.

Cote ♥♥♥ An upscale Korean resto with a new take on the center table grill. See p. 115.

Hawksmoor ♥♥ 109 E. 22nd St. (hawksmoornyc.com; ✆ **212/777-1840;** subway: 6 to 23rd St.). This British restaurant is beloved for its unusual-for-NYC method of charcoal grilling steaks. Many come on Sunday afternoon for their famous Sunday Roast (roast beef, Yorkshire pudding, and all the fixings for $48).

Le Relais de Venise L'Entrecôte ♥♥ 155 E. 54th St. (relaisdevenise.com; ✆ **212/201-4069;** subway: 6, E, F to Lexington Ave./53rd St.). A skirt steak with house sauce, green salad, and French fries for only $38? The price is kept low because they *only* offer that set meal. But since it's an offshoot of the Parisian classic, it's delish.

Sparks ♥♥♥ 210 E. 46th St. (sparkssteakhouse.com; ✆ **212/687-4855;** subway: 6, E, F to Lexington Ave./53rd St.). A former Mafia favorite (Gambino family member Paul "Big Paul" Castellano was killed here in 1985), its "ye olde steakhouse" decor still has that Cosa Nostra air, part of the fun of coming here. The other part (along with perfect hollandaise sauce and aged meats) is the wise-cracking waitstaff, who deliver the type of service that was once de rigueur in NYC, but alas, rarely exists anymore. Take a look at the wall of cigars before you head out; you can't legally smoke them inside, but they're still big sellers.

Tête d'Or ♥ 318 Park Ave. S (latetedorbydaniel.com; ✆ **212/597-9155;** subway: 6 to 23rd St.). Star chef Daniel Boulud's first steakhouse is aimed squarely at the finance crowd; there's even a cocktail named "New Money." It's a more bombastic affair than his other restaurants, with a loud classic rock soundtrack and French fries furry with parmesan and truffles. But the steaks are solid: expertly aged and seared to perfection.

Moderate

Berimbau Brazilian Table ♥♥

BRAZILIAN Meals here are a party, thanks to a boppy soundtrack, geometric Brazilian decor (it's Insta-worthy), and creative caipirinha menu. Berimbau's coconut-laced entrees, while new to most diners, are comforting rather than wildly spicy or challenging.

3 W. 36th St. (near Fifth Ave.). berimbaunyc.com. ✆ **212/401-0021.** Entrees $29–$42. Mon–Thurs 11:30am–3 and 4–10pm; Fri 11:30am–3 and 4–10:30pm; Sat 11:30am–4pm and 5–10:30pm; Sun 11:30am–4pm and 5–9:30pm. Subway: B, D, F, M, N, R to 34th St. Also in Greenwich Village at 43 Carmine St.

Pull up a chair at Berimbau Brazilian Table, where the menu's tropical flavors match the suave decor.

Joe Allen ♥♥ AMERICAN Joe Allen has always been a fun place to go after or before a Broadway show, because actors love it here, so your chances of a celebrity sighting are high. And the atmosphere—with its long bar, exposed brick walls, and posters from Broadway flops—screams Old New York. But in the last few years it's seen a substantial culinary improvement, meaning the quality of the food and drink now match the setting. Cocktails are expertly mixed, and hearty menu staples such as sautéed calf's liver, a grandmotherly meatloaf, and the southern-fried chicken sandwich, are knock-you-off-your-barstool delish.

326 W. 46th St. (btw. Eighth & Ninth aves.). joeallenrestaurant.com. ✆ **212/581-6464.** Entrees $24–$42. Tues 4:30–11:30pm; Thurs–Fri noon–11:30pm; Wed and Sat 11:30am–11:30pm; Sun 11:30am–10:30pm. Subway: C, E to 50th St.

Tengri Tagh ♥♥ UYGHUR The Uyghurs, an ethnic group from the western provinces of China, have very distinctive culinary traditions, borrowing from both Han Chinese cooking and the "Stans" of Central Asia. So diners here devour cumin-scented stir fries atop toothsome hand-pulled noodles, alongside plates of kebabs with pilaf. Because almost all Uyghurs are Muslim, no pork or alcohol is served. Instead, wonderfully flavorful, tender lamb is the centerpiece of many dishes. Tenghri Tagh is a very simple counter-service joint, but it's one of the best places to eat in the vicinity of Macy's and the Empire State Building—the cooks put great care into their cooking, and once your food is ready they will bring it to your table with a smile.

144 W. 37th St. (btw. Broadway & Seventh Ave.). tengritaghny.com. ✆ **646/964-5418.** Most dishes $17–$25. Sat–Sun and Tues–Thurs 11am–8pm. Subway: 1, 2, 3, B, D, F, N, R to 34th St./Herald Square.

Yoon Haeundae Galbi raises the level of tabletop barbecue in Koreatown.

Yoon Haeundae Galbi ♥♥ KOREAN Serving the best barbecue in Koreatown, YHG is the first American outpost of a beloved family restaurant from Korea's second largest city, Busan. Across the Pacific, this eatery became famous, beginning in 1964, for making short ribs, a notoriously chewy cut of meat when grilled, tender as a mother's love. They're the item to get here, too, and they come every which way: seared right on the domed stove embedded in your tabletop, or in dumplings, pancakes, stews, and soups. The secret to their deliciousness? It's the complex pattern that the chef slashes onto the meat, which breaks apart the sinews. You'll see it most easily on the grilled short ribs.

8 W. 36th St. (near Fifth Ave.). yoon-nyc.com. ✆ **212/244-5345.** Shared meal from $55 for 2. Mon–Thurs 11:45am–3pm and 5–11:30pm; Fri–Sat 11:45am–11:30pm; Sun 11:45am–10:30pm. Subway: B, D, F, N, Q, R to 34th St.

Inexpensive

Burger Joint ♥ AMERICAN A greasy spoon among silver spoons, Burger Joint is hidden behind a curtain in the lobby of the ultra-swank Thompson Hotel Central Park. Pull back that curtain and you enter a hidden diner that looks like it was yanked off some side street in Detroit. And it serves up the juiciest, most perfectly charred burgers in the western half of midtown—order them with "the works" (red onions, lettuce, tomato, pickles, mustard, and mayo) for not a cent extra.

In the Thompson Hotel Central Park, 118 W. 57th St. (btw. Sixth & Seventh aves.). burgerjointny.com. ✆ **212/245-5000.** Burgers $16. Daily 11am–11pm. Subway: B, N, Q, R to 57th St. Also in Moynihan Train Hall and Industry City.

Ichiran Times Square ♥♥ JAPANESE No distraction from the ramen is allowed at Ichiran. It's the only thing on the menu—no appetizers and no sides are offered. It will also be your sole focus because the restaurant is four rooms of counter seating only, and, in an introvert-pleasing move, panels separate each solo diner (pairs have no barrier between them, but there is a barrier to the strangers on either side of you, almost as if you were taking a test!). A woven curtain also separates diners from waitstaff; you don't speak

Servers deliver your steaming ramen to your personal cubby at Ichiran Times Square.

to them, just ring a buzzer and deliver a checked-off menu with your order. So, does the ramen deserve this sort of intense concentration? I'd say yes, especially if you like your noodles spicy—a dollop of house-made hot sauce is in each bowl, with customers checking off a menu box to determine how much heat. The location, right off Times Square, is also super-convenient for theatergoers. ***Two warnings:*** Sharing a bowl is strictly forbidden and there's often a line to get in, so budget time for waiting.

152 W. 49th St. (btw. Seventh & Sixth aves.). ichiranusa.com. Ramen $23 (more with added ingredients). Mon–Thurs 11am–10pm; Fri–Sun 11am–10:30pm. Subway: N, Q, R to 49th St.; 1 to 50th St. Also in Brooklyn and near Penn Station.

Los Tacos No. 1 ♥♥ MEXICAN One of the best 5-minute meals in Times Square can be had here. You'll walk up to a counter seemingly airlifted from a roadside in Tijuana, order either flour or corn handmade tortillas, and then watch as busy chefs fill them with chicken, cactus, pork, or beef, all of which is cooked right in front of you. Then you'll grab a space at the tile counter (no seats) and gulp it down. Totally authentic, totally unpretentious.

229 W. 43rd St. (btw. Seventh & Eighth aves.). lostacos1.com. Entrees $5–$12. Mon–Sat 11am–midnight; Sun 11am–10pm. Subway: A, C, E to 42nd St.; 1, 2, 3, S, L to Times Sq. See website for other NYC locations.

LumLum ♥♥ THAI LumLum—which appropriately means "yum yum" in Thai slang—is very much a family business. Opened by sisters Sommy and Mo Hensawang in 2023, it uses many of the same recipes their mother and grandmother cooked at the clan's beachfront restaurant in the Attutayah region of Thailand. So get ready for authentically spicy fare, and seafood dishes you likely won't find elsewhere in the U.S., like a creamy squid ink soup flavored with lime leaf, a lobster-like grilled river prawn

At Los Tacos No. 1, fresh tortillas are stuffed with hearty fillings like *pollo asado* (seen here) or *nopales* (cactus).

hungry FOR ROCKEFELLER CENTER

When the pandemic emptied Rockefeller Center of tourists, owner Tishman Speyer made the radical decision to try to fill the Rock with locals. Food would be the lure: The real estate company partnered with five of Gotham's most exciting star chefs to create new restaurants in spaces that once held only blah chain eateries. The result has utterly transformed The Rock, making it the city's hottest new dining destination.

But unlike the rest of Gotham, the restaurants here come alive during the daylight hours, not at night, perhaps because that's when crowds tend to be at Rockefeller Center. The result? It's often easier to get a dinner reservation than one for lunch.

Here's a rundown of the top dining choices at The Rock, in order of my preference. I'm also a fan of **Ace's Pizza** (p. 121).

Le Rock ♥♥♥ (45 Rockefeller Plaza, on 50th St.; lerocknyc.com; ✆ **332/258-8734**). Le Rock delivers in every way possible. It has the best location by far: a glam Art Deco space with two-story-high ceilings. The staff are pros, friendly in just the right degree, and able to accommodate time limits. And the French food here is ooh la la! There's not a miss on the menu, even, surprisingly, the vegan offerings (like an amazing cabbage Farsi) in what is often described as a surf-and-turf restaurant. The same team operates **Frenchette** (p. 92) and **Le Veau d'Or** (p. 138).

Jupiter ♥♥ (20 W. 50th St., skating rink level; jupiterrestaurant.nyc). The two popular rising chefs behind this enterprise (Jess Shadbolt and Clare de Boer) are noodle whisperers. Each pasta iteration here is accolade-worthy, whether it be rabbit-stuffed ravioli, spicy spaghetti with *bottarga* (roe), or a rustic cheese-filled *pansotti* with pumpkin and parmesan sauce. Because the restaurant is in the low-ceilinged basement level, it's not quite as handsome as the first two, but some seats have nice views of the skaters on the rink.

Naro ♥ (30 Rockefeller Plaza, skating rink level; naronyc.com). An offshoot of the Korean tasting-menu-only restaurant Atomix—one of the hardest reservations in NYC to snag, though I've always wondered why—Naro raises the same questions for me, especially after downing octopus with *granita* (flavored ice) and other odd nibbles here. Unique? Absolutely. Craveable? Not for me. Still, unlike Atomix, Naro does offer some a la carte options for folks who want to try husband-and-wife chefs Jung-hyun "JP" and Jeongeun "Ellia" Park's food; and its decor uses the lower-level setting to its advantage, creating a space that looks like the top restos that often inhabit tiny spaces across the Pacific.

Of these four, **Ace's** and **Jupiter** are the most affordable, with a number of meal options in the $30-or-less range (and well under that for Ace's); you'll need to double or triple that amount to dine at the other two. Go to rockefellercenter.com/dine for info on all the dining options here.

in a chili dressing, and crispy crab omelet over rice. The sisters also do well with meat eaters with a Thai take on beef tartare, and "Crying Tiger"—a plate of sliced grilled ribeye steak over piping hot garlic rice topped with a raw egg yolk (you swish it in for velvety goodness). The beachy ambiance—bamboo clad walls, hanging lights ensconced in woven straw, surfer music—makes this an appropriately festive place for a pre- or post-Broadway show meal.

404 West 49th St. (off Ninth Avenue). lumlumnyc.com. Entrees $22–$32 ($42 for shareable whole bronzino dishes). Sun–Thurs noon–10pm; Fri–Sat noon–11pm. Subway: C, E to 50th St.

poultry ROW

If you'd like a quick, very tasty sit-down meal in Hell's Kitchen, head to Ninth Avenue between 52nd and 53rd streets (subway: A, C, E to 50th St.). On the east side are three competing chicken joints, each serving marvelously moist, affordable chicken in dignified—if tiny—settings. At each you can get a hearty meal for less than $20.

- **Three Roosters** (threeroostersthai.com): Thai chicken with rice, served a number of ways. Star preparation: the Zab fried chicken which is citrusy, with just a hint of heat (you can make it spicier with their sauces). My fave of the restaurants, by a hair. ***Tip:*** Their "extra" chicken portion is just $6.95 and quite a good amount of food, though it doesn't come with sides.
- **Uncle Ray's** (uncleraysschickenrice.com; ✆ **646/992-4343**): Traditional and oh-so-comforting Singaporean chicken and rice, either poached or roasted; plates come with three sauces and a lovely soup.
- **Poulette** (pouletteny.com): French-style rotisserie chicken with a choice of sides, this outlet is part of an NYC mini-chain with other stores in the Financial District and across town on the East Side.

Margon ♥ CUBAN Though it's just steps from Times Square, tourists don't venture into this scruffy, low-ceilinged, basement-level diner. A shame, since it's serving some of the best-priced, tastiest grub in the area. And it does so with great heart: The ladies behind the counter greet everyone with a full-throated "What you like, *mi amor?*" and chit-chat away, cooing over the photos of their kids that Broadway stagehands, office workers, musicians, Cuban expats, and other regulars bring in. Then they heap the plates with colossal piles of rice and beans, sided by tender beef stew, shredded pork, fried plantains, and half a dozen other daily specials. The Cuban sandwiches are also *sabrosisimo.*

136 W. 46th St. (off Times Square). ordermargon.com. ✆ **212/354-5013.** Entrees $9–$16. Mon–Sat 7am–4:30pm. Subway: N, Q, R to 49th St.

Raku ♥♥ JAPANESE For a good two decades, NYC has been obsessed with ramen and for good reason: many of the top Japanese ramen chains have opened outposts here (we cover some in this chapter). But now there's a new noodle in town, and Raku's udon is creating line-out-the-door excitement. Udon is thicker than ramen, with a pleasing springy gumminess to it. Here it's served in a number of different preparations: in clear dashi broth with stacks of tempura, as part of a curry soup, in a tinglingly spicy thick udon broth, chilled with dipping sauce, and as a stir fry. You can customize your bowling-ball-sized portion with add-ons, from grated yam or daikon to mochi to slices of prime beef, along with a long list of worthwhile appetizers and desserts. ***One note:*** The line moves quite quickly, so don't get discouraged (they take few reservations). It will also give you a preview of the very Japanese experience to come: the last time I was on this line, I was the only one speaking English.

776 Ninth Ave. (btw. 50th & 51st sts.). rakunyc.com. Entrees $15–$32 (up to $38 for wagyu). Tues–Sun noon–9:30pm. Subway: C, E to 50th St. See website for 3 other locations.

MIDTOWN EAST & MURRAY HILL

Beyond what's recommended below, I have to give a shout out to **Monkey Bar ♥** in the Hotel Elysée, 60 E. 54th St. (btw. Park & Madison aves.; nycmonkeybar.com; ✆ **212/753-1066;** entrees $29–$150; daily 11:45am–2:30pm and 5–10:30pm, Sun & Mon until 10pm), simply for its Mad Men-era murals and red banquettes. The ambiance can't be beat, but the food quality can (the burgers are fine and reasonably priced, but the same can't be said for the rest of the menu).

Midtown East Food Courts

You'll dine under full-size trees and lots of twinkling hanging lights at **The Hugh ♥♥**, 157 E. 53rd St., near Lexington Ave (thehughnyc.com), choosing from an impressive range of cuisines, from West African fare to Israeli specialties to affordable and very fresh sushi rolls from **Kazu Nori** (p. 117).

Moderate

Çka Ka Qëllue ♥♥♥ ALBANIAN "Albanian is the world's oldest language," our handsome server told me, as we discussed the traditional folk

Step through the front door of Çka Ka Qëllue and you'll feel transported to Albania.

music that was accompanying dinner. Professor Google later told me that may or may not be true (at 6000+ years it's darn old but several others may be older), but no matter—his comment spoke to the deep pride in all things Albanian that the staff here carry. That sentiment is apparent from the moment you step into this unapologetically old-world restaurant, with its costumed waitstaff, wood-beamed ceilings, and exposed brick walls covered with Albanian ephemera (shelves of ancient farm implements, paintings of women in 19th-century wedding dresses, and actual antique wedding dresses framed and hung). I know this all sounds hokey, but it isn't: You'll feel teleported to the Balkans. It's an illusion furthered by the food, from the splendidly fresh cabbage salad, to baked-on-site pillows of bread sided by an array of dips, to the toothsome *mantia* (veal dumplings served with a tart yogurt sauce). Mains tend toward cream-based stews, and they, too, are transporting. For dessert you really must order the Trileçe, a layered sponge cake that's a cousin to Latin Tres Leches cake.

118 E. 31st St. (off Park Ave. South). ckakaqellue.com. ✆ **212/213-2082.** Entrees $20–$44 (most in the mid $20s). Sun–Thurs noon–10pm; Fri–Sat noon–11pm. Subway: 6 to 33rd St.

Grand Central Oyster Bar and Restaurant ♥ SEAFOOD Opened in 1913, this Gilded Age holdover in Grand Central Station has changed very little in the last century, and the architecture—a series of swooping tiled vaults

Generations of diners have devoured chowders, pan-roasts, and other shellfish classics in Grand Central Oyster Bar's tile-vaulted premises.

family-friendly **RESTAURANTS**

While it's always smart to call ahead to make sure a restaurant has kids' menus and highchairs, you can count on the following to be especially accommodating. And what kid doesn't love pizza? See p. 120 for that. Here are some other options:

Laser Wolf ♥♥♥ (p. 146) A special-occasion meal for families, most definitely, but the view will enchant wee ones (and their parents), and the abundant small plates included with each entree means everyone can find something they like.

Parm ♥ (p. 137) Classic Italian-American dishes in a room so bustling, no one will notice if your tyke kicks up a fuss.

S&P ♥♥♥ (p. 117) Perch your tots on a twirly stool, order them an egg cream and a sammy, and tell them about the good old days when old-fashioned luncheonettes like this one were the norm rather than the exception. Plus, the Harry Potter and Lego stores are just a block in either direction.

Serendipity 3 ♥ (p. 141) Kids adore this whimsical restaurant and ice-cream shop, which serves up a huge menu of American favorites, followed up by colossal ice-cream treats.

Shabu Tatsu ♥♥ (p. 104) Another cook-your-own-meal joint, which is great fun, but because boiling water is involved, this is a better choice for kids over age 7.

Shake Shack ♥♥ (p. 111) Burgers and shakes, consumed outdoors (perhaps in the playground that shares this park)—what could be more tyke-pleasing?

that always remind me of the grand crypts of some European cathedrals—still impresses. Don't bother going to the restaurant side; you want to be able to see the handwritten menu above the shelling station (on the right as you enter), where the best choices will be laid out. There will be fresh oysters and clams, flown in from all parts of North America; shellfish pan-roasts and stews; and chowders of all kinds (from $5). Ignore the paper menu entirely (for some reason, everything that comes out of the kitchen is overcooked and tepidly sauced); confine yourself to the list of foods that are prepared right at the bar, and you'll have a real old-fashioned feast.

Lower level, Grand Central Station (42nd St., btw. Vanderbilt & Lexington aves.). oysterbarny.com. ✆ **212/490-6650.** Entrees $17–$53, more for lobster and stone crab. Mon–Fri 11:30am–9:30pm. Subway: 4, 5, 6, 7, S to Grand Central Station.

Inexpensive

Björk Café & Bistro ♥♥ SCANDINAVIAN If the only Swedish meatballs you ever tasted were the rubbery ones at Ikea, you owe it to yourself to come to Björk. At the lobby restaurant of the Scandinavia House cultural center, these little orbs are more tender than the smiles Swedish *mormors* (grandmothers) give their grandchildren, and they're sided by tangy lingonberry jam and mashed potatoes—a hearty meal for just $16. Bjork also has *smörrebröd* (open-faced sandwiches) starting at $9, herring plates, potato waffles with all sorts of sexy toppings (gravlax, roe, cold water shrimp, and more), and a number of other Nordic specialties. ***Note:*** On days that the Scandinavia House has an evening event you may need a reservation to dine here, so do check the calendar before heading over (usually you can just walk in).

58 Park Ave. (btw. 37th & 38th sts.). bjorkcafe.com. ✆ **212/779-3587.** Entrees $9–$37. Tues–Sat 11am–8pm; Sun–Mon 11am–5pm. Subway: 4, 5, 6, S to Grand Central Station/42nd Street.

UPPER WEST SIDE

Some of the best pizza in the city is being served at **Mama's Too** (p. 120). It's one of our favorite Upper West Side noshes—but get ready for a line out the door.

The iconic restaurant **Tavern on the Green,** in Central Park at 67th St., just off Central Park W. (tavernonthegreen.com; ✆ **212/877-8684;** Mon–Thurs 11am—9pm, Fri 11am–10pm, Sat 9am–10pm, Sun 9am–9pm), serves so-so food nowadays, but eating in Central Park is a treat, and happily, all of the tables on the open-air terrace are reserved for walk-ins. If you'd like to take a picnic with you into the park, stop by **Charles Pan Fried Chicken ♥♥**, 144 W. 72nd St. (charlespanfriedchicken.com; ✆ **212/281-1800;** Sun–Thurs 11am–10pm, Fri–Sat 11am–11pm), a soul food mecca. Everything is tasty, since it's made to order, but that can mean a bit of a wait while the chicken fries.

Expensive

Tatiana ♥♥♥ AFRO-CARIBBEAN At Lincoln Center's Tatiana restaurant, the GOAT on the menu doesn't stand for Greatest Of All Time. It stands for, well, goat. As in the bleating ruminant that hasn't been a widely available source of protein in this neighborhood since about 1959, when the performing arts complex broke ground and displaced thousands of working-class New Yorkers, many of Puerto Rican heritage. (Stephen Spielberg wove that backstory into his film adaptation of *West Side Story*.) By serving goat in this rarified setting—heck, you can see the Chagall murals through the windows of the Metropolitan Opera House as you dine—chef/owner and *Top Chef* alum Kwame Onwuachi isn't just cooking up seriously tasty food, he's also planting a flag of sorts, returning this space to its roots. Prepared in a wonderfully crisp fried patty, the curried goat is served with a creamy, tangy sauce—as delicious as it is elegant—on a heavy black plate. And those patties aren't the only returned-to-the-hood tastes Onwuachi has in store: The entire menu riffs on Caribbean and African foods, such as braised oxtail stew, crispy okra, and head-on creole shrimp. Everything

At Lincon Center's Tatiana, chef Kwame Onwuachi and his team surprise diners with refined takes on Caribbean and African food.

Uptown & Harlem Restaurants
0 1/4 mi
0 0.25 km
M Subway station
HARLEM
Dr. Martin Luther King Jr. Blvd.
E. 124th St.
E. 122nd St.
Marcus Garvey Park
Broadway
Amsterdam Ave.
Morningside Park
Frederick Douglass Blvd.
St. Nicholas Ave.
Adam Clayton Powell Jr. Blvd.
Lenox Ave.
E. 118th St.
E. 116th St.
Lexington Ave.
3rd Ave.
Henry Hudson Pkwy.
BARNARD COLLEGE
COLUMBIA UNIVERSITY
W. 115th St.
W. 114th St.
W. 113th St.
W. 112th St.
W. 111th St.
EAST HARLEM
Cathedral of St. John the Divine
Cathedral Pkwy.
Central Park North
E. 110th St.
RIVERSIDE PARK
Riverside Dr.
W. 109th St.
W. 108th St.
W. 107th St.
W. 106th St.
W. 105th St.
W. 104th St.
Harlem Meer
Lasker Rink & Pool
E. 109th St.
E. 108th St.
E. 107th St.
E. 105th St.
Hudson River
CENTRAL PARK
Madison Ave.
Park Ave.
2nd Ave.
W. 100th St.
W. 99th St.
North Meadow
UPPER EAST SIDE
W. 97th St.
W. 96th St.
W. 95th St.
W. 94th St.
W. 93rd St.
W. 92nd St.
W. 91st St.
W. 90th St.
W. 89th St.
W. 88th St.
W. 87th St.
W. 86th St.
97th St. Transverse Rd.
Tennis Courts
Jacqueline Kennedy Onassis Reservoir
E. 96th St.
E. 95th St.
E. 94th St.
E. 93rd St.
E. 92nd St.
5th Ave.
Joan of Arc Park
West End Ave.
Central Park West
Guggenheim Museum
E. 88th St.
E. 87th St.
E. 86th St.
E. 85th St.
E. 84th St.
E. 83rd St.
86th St. Transverse Rd.
Great Lawn
Metropolitan Museum of Art
Children's Museum
Columbus Ave.
W. 81st St.
Delacorte Theater
Belvedere Lake
Obelisk
American Museum of Natural History
Belvedere Castle
79th St. Transverse Rd.
W. 77th St.
W. 76th St.
W. 75th St.
W. 74th St.
W. 73rd St.
W. 72nd St.
New York Historical Society
The Ramble
Conservatory Pond
The Lake
Boat House
E. 76th St.
E. 72nd St
Strawberry Fields
UPPER WEST SIDE
Sheep Meadow
Bandshell
The Mall
East Green
E. 68th St
E. 67th St
E. 66th St
E. 65th St
65th St. Transverse Rd.
W. 65th St
LINCOLN CENTER
Zoo
E. 63rd St
FORDHAM UNIVERSITY
The Pond
E. 60th St.
Columbus Circle
Central Park South
Grand Army Plaza
Bánh 12
Barney Greengrass 8
Bayon 26
Bohemian Spirit 25
Café Sbarsky 19
Charles Pan Fried Chicken 5
Cocina Consuelo 14
Flor de Mayo 7, 10
Glace New York 17
Jacob's Pickles 9
Kaia Wine Bar 16
Lady M Cake Boutique 21
Levain Bakery 6
Le Veau d'Or 28
Lexington Candy Shop 20
Madison Fare 18
Mama's Too 11
Melba's 13
Parm 3
Pastrami Queen 4, 22
Red Rooster Harlem 15
ROKC 14
Second Avenue Deli 24
Serendipity 3 27
Tatiana 1
Tavern on the Green 2
Xi'an Famous Foods 23

comes in massive portions, so most couples can get away with sharing one appetizer and one entree—useful to know since the appetizers mostly cost in the mid-$20s and the mains run $42 to $50 (the star dish, an African interpretation of on-the-bone pastrami, is a whopping $82—it's good, but I'm not sure it earns that hefty price tag). Don't be shy about wearing your special occasion duds: Tatiana has the same handsome brutalist elegance as the rest of the arts complex, serving as a fine backdrop for formal wear.

10 Lincoln Center Plaza (near 65th St.). tatiananyc.com. ✆ **212/875-5222.** $45–$82. Mon–Sat 5–10pm. Subway: 1 to 67th St.

Moderate

Jacob's Pickles ♥ SOUTHERN Pickles, pick-ups, and artisanal beers: Those are the holy trinity at this buzzy tavern. It's become THE place for the neighborhood's singles to scope one another out, and they do so over better-than-the-norm comfort food. I'm talking fried chicken atop huge and satisfyingly flaky biscuits; creamy grits with head-on shrimp; and, yes, jars of artisanal pickled foods of all sorts. As for the beer, some 20 taps gush unusual brews from around the Northeast, with a particular emphasis on sour beers. ***One warning:*** The noise level here is epic, so don't go here for a quiet tête-à-tête.

680 Columbus Ave. (btw. 93rd and 94th sts.). jacobspickles.com. ✆ **212/566-6630.** Entrees $21–$34. Mon–Fri 10am–midnight; Sat–Sun 9am–midnight. Subway: 1, B, C to 86th St. Also in Moynihan Train station.

Inexpensive

Bánh ♥♥ VIETNAMESE The offerings here go well beyond the *pho* and *banh mi* sandwiches that dominate the city's other Vietnamese joints. Sure, those are served, and heck, they do half a dozen well-executed versions of each, but what's exciting here are the specialties one rarely finds this side of the Pacific, like *Bánh Chưng Chiên,* mung beans and either pork or

Jacob's Pickles scores big for its Southern comfort food and craft brews with matching flavors.

THE NEW YORK deli NEWS

Alas, New York delicatessens are a dying breed. Here are the few that are left (and still worth recommending):

Barney Greengrass, the Sturgeon King ♥♥ 541 Amsterdam Ave. btw. 86th & 87th sts. (barneygreengrass.com; ✆ **212/724-4707;** subway: 1 to 86th St.). This unassuming, daytime-only Upper West Side deli is legendary for its high-quality salmon (sable, gravlax, Nova Scotia, kippered, lox, pastrami—you choose), whitefish, and sturgeon.

Katz's Delicatessen ♥♥ (p. 99). It's rightly famous for its corned beef and remains fabulously old-world despite its hipster-hot Lower East Side location.

Pastrami Queen ♥♥ 138 W. 72nd St. and 1125 Lexington Ave. (pastramiqueen.com; subway: A, B, C to 72nd St.). There's no seating at either of its outlets, but since both are within walking distance of Central Park, the Queen's excellent matzoh ball soup and namesake pastrami sandwich have graced many a picnic blanket over the years. There's also an outlet now in Moynihan Food Hall (p. 123).

Russ & Daughters ♥♥♥ (p. 98). Midtown, downtown, and Brooklyn outlets now open.

Second Avenue Deli ♥♥ 162 E. 33rd St. and 1442 First Ave. (2ndavedeli.com; subway: 6 to 33rd St.). The name lies: neither of the outlets of this deli is now on Second Ave. Still, you'll get some of the best corned beef in town here (if only meh pastrami), as well as *kishka* and challah French toast.

mushrooms wrapped in glutinous rice and deep fried (a snacky treat); barbecued ground pork wrapped in betel leaf; and *Bun Bò Bơ*, noodles topped with sizzling butter beef. The dining space is bright and cheery but small, so there's a wait many nights.

942 Amsterdam Ave. (btw. 106th & 107th sts.). banhny.com. Entrees $18–$25. Tues–Thurs 6–10pm; Fri–Sat noon–4pm and 6–10pm; Sun noon–4pm and 6–9pm. Subway: 1 to 103rd St. Offshoot **Bánh Anh Em** is at 99 Third Ave. (near 13th St.).

Flor de Mayo ♥ CUBAN/CHINESE When Cubans of Chinese heritage came to the city after the Cuban revolution, they brought this hybrid "Chino-Latino" cuisine with them. It's an interesting concept, but the Latino side of the menu is far better than the Chinese here—whether you order the chopped beef with yellow rice, the excellent avocado salad, or Dominican chicken with rice. Solid food and wonderfully affordable.

484 Amsterdam (btw. 83rd & 84th sts.). flordemayo.com. ✆ **212/663-5520** or 212/595-2525. Entrees $12–$34 (more for steak or lobster but this isn't a place for those two dishes). Mon–Fri noon–10:30pm; Sat–Sun noon–11pm. Subway: 1 to 86th St. Also at 2651 Broadway.

Parm ♥ ITALIAN There's Italian food and then there's Italian-American food. And for decades the latter version was looked down upon as being, well, a bit déclassé. No more. This proudly old-fashioned red-sauce joint does such a nifty job with the "canon" of Italian-American staples—chicken parmigiana, sausage and peppers, baked ziti—that you come away feeling you've experienced something brand-new (and very satisfying). And all in a checkered-tablecloth restaurant that will bring you back, in spirit, to 1950s NYC.

235 Columbus Ave. (btw. 70th & 71st sts.). parmitalian.com. ✆ **212/993-7189.** Entrees $12–$28. Daily 11am–10pm. Subway: 1, 2, 3, C, E to 72nd St. Also downtown at 250 Vesey Street, and 248 Mulberry St.

UPPER EAST SIDE

For a quick, affordable bite, head to **Xi'an Famous Foods** (328 E. 78th St., btw. First & Second aves.; p. 92).

Expensive

Le Veau d'Or ♥♥♥ FRENCH Remember that episode of *The Marvelous Mrs. Maisel* when she went to the fabulous French restaurant and had a blowout feast? Neither do I, but if that TV show *had* done that, they would have filmed it in this perfect early 1960s throwback, with its low ceilings, red-checkered tablecloths, inlaid wood walls, and a menu that harks back to when floating island desserts were the height of sophistication (they may be again soon, frankly, when other chefs have tasted the scrumptious version here). Reopened by the team behind **Frenchette** (p. 92) and **Le Rock** (p. 129), this culinary time capsule gives classic Gallic dishes the respect they deserve—like escargot, served not in the shell but in separate little cups where they can be sufficiently doused in a garlicky green sauce. At the other end of the color wheel, the duck breast with zippy cherry sauce is a smile on a plate. Meals are prix fixe only, but at $135 for five courses (an excellent salad, bread, and extra dessert are part of the deal) this is far from the priciest restaurant in the city, though it ain't cheap. A really fun addition to Gotham's dining scene.

A throwback retro setting is perfect for a French meal at Le Veau d'Or in the tony Upper East Side.

129 E. 60th St. (near Lexington Ave.). lvdnyc.com. ✆ **646/386-7608.** Prix-fixe dinner $135, $85 at lunch. Tues–Fri 11:30am–2pm and 5–9:30pm, Sat 5–9:30pm. Subway: 4, 5, 6 to 59th St., F, N, Q, R to Lexington.

Moderate

Bayon ♥♥ CAMBODIAN Named for a temple in Siem Reap, and filled with works of art from the homeland—a giant Buddha's head here, a painting of a ruin-filled jungle there—this quiet, welcoming restaurant does an excellent job introducing this lesser-known cuisine to Americans. It does so by featuring dishes with several culinary elements, like the *Prahok* crudité, which comes with bowls of 3 different curries, rice to cool the mild spice, and lettuce and sticks of raw vegetables to wrap around or dip in the curries. The giant *Banh Chao* crepe, crafted from rice flour and stuffed with chicken and shrimp, is another multi-taste extravaganza, as diners can use several sauces and green leaves (mint, lettuce) to customize each bite. The baked fish curry known as *Amok* is also a top choice, as is the shredded mango salad. The only thing we'd suggest skipping are the too-sugary desserts.

408 E. 64th St. (off First Ave). bayonnyc.com. ✆ **646/476-4709.** Entrees $22–$38. Mon and Wed–Thurs 4–10pm; Fri–Sat 2–10pm; Sun 3:30–9:30pm. Subway: F, N, Q, R to Lexington Ave./63rd St.

Bohemian Spirit ♥♥ CZECH Or should we make that "spirits"? Suds are king at this wonderfully friendly, tchotchke-laden Czech beer hall, where there are always three Eastern European draft beers on tap, along with pilsners, wines from that region, and a full liquor menu. Food is of the kind that effectively soaks up all that alcohol, by which I mean hearty/heavy meat-laden plates, like schnitzels and sausages. The Svíčková is the signature dish, and it's mighty tasty, a flatiron steak sided by bread dumplings and swimming in a sweet-and-sour cream sauce with an additional swirl of whipped cream on

The cozy, cluttered dining room at Bohemian Spirit.

top, as if it were a meat sundae. If you still have room for dessert (doubtful, unless you share entrees, which you should), the fruit dumplings are a delight.

345 E. 73rd St. (off Second Ave.). bohemianspiritrestaurant.com. ✆ **212/861-1038.** Entrees $28–$37. Sun–Mon 5–10pm; Tues–Sat 5–11pm. Subway: Q to 72nd St.

Café Sbarsky ♥♥ AUSTRIAN For breakfast, lunch, or dinner on or near Museum Mile, there's no place better than this transplanted Viennese cafe, set in a wood-paneled mansion designed by Carrere and Hastings (architects of the New York Public Library at 42nd St.; p. 208). Actually part of the Neue Galerie, a museum of Austrian and German art (p. 222), it serves all the Teutonic specialties, from bratwurst to goulash to creamy spaetzle, along with an assortment of lighter salads and sandwiches, all expertly executed. Save room for the delicious pastries and Viennese coffee, so strong it will grow hair on your tongue. ***Warning:*** Because this place has no peer, there's always a line to get in. Allot an extra 30 minutes to wait for a seat (they don't take reservations).

Inside the Neue Museum, 1048 Fifth Ave. (at 86th St.). neuegalerie.org. ✆ **212/288-0665.** Entrees $14–$43. Wed–Sun 9am–9pm; Mon 9am–6pm. Subway: 4, 5, 6 to 86th St.

Kaia Wine Bar ♥♥ SOUTH AFRICAN It's easy to walk by this brick-walled tavern without giving it a second glance. Don't. This is the city's one and only South African restaurant, and it does that country's specialties proud, serving a mighty tasty *bobotie* (a fruit-laden curried ground-beef casserole topped with egg custard), falling-off-the-bone tender tea-and-cranberry BBQ-glazed baby back ribs, and the king of African sandwiches, the Gatsby (curried chicken with pickles and peppadew peppers on a Portuguese roll), among other items. These are enhanced by a choice of 50 wines from the motherland, and a gently thrumming soundtrack of South African music. Kaia may also be one of the most unselfconsciously inclusive restaurants in the city, with locals of all backgrounds and races filling the tables and bar stools here, something that is sadly not always the norm in New York City.

1614 Third Ave (btw. 90th & 91st sts.). kaiawinebar.com. ✆ **212/722-0490.** Entrees $19–$43 (most in the mid $20s). Mon 9–6pm; Wed–Sun 9am–9pm. Subway: 6 to 96th St.

Inexpensive

Lexington Candy Shop ♥♥♥ AMERICAN One of the city's last classic luncheonettes, this Instagram-worthy eatery was founded in 1925 and is little changed since then. It's a true time machine, still run by the same family that founded it. Stop by for a bologna sandwich or a butter burger (yes, that would be a burger slathered with butter) accompanied by, what else, an egg cream.

1226 Lexington Ave. (at 83rd St.). lexingtoncandyshop.com. ✆ **212/288-0057.** Entrees $9–$24. Mon–Fri 7am–6pm; Sat 8am–6pm; Sun 8am–4pm. Subway: 4, 5, 6 to 86th St.

Serendipity 3 ♥ AMERICAN A good ol'-fashioned ice cream parlor complete with Tiffany-style lamps and a toy shop that you have to pass to get in and out (quite a feat when you have sugar-crazed kids in tow). The dish to order here (one tureen of it will easily satisfy two or three) is the deservedly famous Frrrozen Hot Chocolate, a slushy, utterly satisfying chocolate soup. You can get an idea of the magical effects of that treat if you rent the treacly John Cusack rom-com *Serendipity* (filmed here). It now has a Wonka-esque offshoot in the Times Square area (at 157 W. 47th Street) but we prefer the original.

225 E. 60th St. (btw. Second & Third aves.). serendipity3.com. ✆ **212/838-3531.** Entrees $12–$30; sweets and sundaes $7–$24 (most under $18). Mon–Wed 11am–midnight; Thurs–Sun 10am–midnight. Subway: N, R to Lexington Ave.; 4, 5, 6 to 59th St.

HARLEM

Beyond the restaurants suggested below, I like **ROKC** ♥♥, 3452 Broadway (rokcnyc.com) which serves up all types of ramen and raw oysters. Specialty cocktails put ROKC on the map, but the food is mighty fine, too.

Moderate

Red Rooster Harlem ♥ SCANDINAVIAN/SOUTHERN A destination restaurant with a celeb chef (Marcus Samuelsson, a former winner of *Top*

You'll find a wide-ranging menu and friendly atmosphere at Red Rooster.

Chef Masters), Red Rooster is the primary reason many well-heeled New Yorkers come to Harlem. But it's not as good a restaurant as his latest, Hav & Mar (p. 119). Yes, Red Rooster has a hopping bar, handsome decor, a wonderful atmosphere, and live music in the basement club. Most of the appetizers—which, like the rest of the menu, range from Southern classics to African fare to Scandinavian cuisine—are delish. But when it comes to the pricier main dishes, I'm inevitably disappointed, especially in the signature yard bird (fried chicken, very dry) and Helga's meatballs (too heavy). When I go, I make my meals entirely of appetizers. If you do the same, you'll enjoy it.

310 Lenox Ave. (btw. 125th & 126th sts.). redroosterharlem.com. ✆ **212/792-9001.** Entrees $26–$36 (lobster and steak are more). Mon–Thurs noon–9:30pm; Fri noon–10:30pm; Sat 11am–10:30pm; Sun 10am–9:30pm. Subway: 2, 3 to 125th St.

Moderate/Inexpensive

Cocina Consuelo ♥♥♥ MEXICAN For 15 hours every day, chef/owner Karina Garcia slow roasts birria, a beef stew from the Mexican state of Jalisco whose secret ingredient is bone marrow. When it comes time to plate the stew, she ups the umami factor by serving it atop a large bone, so that diners can scoop even more marrow into the stew. Let's just say that it's far richer than Bill Gates and it shows the level of care that goes into every dish at this tiny, folk art-laden eatery (the vibe here is Central Mexican village, in the best way possible). The food is accompanied by beers and wines all created in Mexico. They also serve an excellent breakfast.

130 Hamilton Place (at W. 142nd St.). cocinaconsuelonyc.com. ✆ **646/250-7172.** Entrees $18–$35. Wed–Sat 9am–2pm and 5–9:30pm; Sun 9am–4pm. Subway: 1, A, C, B, D to 145th St.

Eggnog in the batter is the secret to Melba's signature fried chicken and waffles.

Melba's ♥♥ AMERICAN REGIONAL Melba Wilson is Harlem royalty. The niece of Sylvia Woods, founder of the iconic soul food restaurant Sylvia's, Wilson learned her trade from her aunt and has had a thriving eatery of her own for over 20 years. She famously bested Bobby Flay on his TV show *Takedown,* taking *him* down with her chicken and waffles. (Secret ingredient? Eggnog in the batter . . . year round.) Frankly, we much prefer her restaurant to Sylvia's, which is now overrun by bus tours. Melba's is still a locals' joint, with paintings of Black celebrities and politicians brightening the brick walls and serving the best collard greens in the state. As for those chicken and waffles: they're still championship level. ***Tip:*** Melba's hot sauce is on the milder side of spicy but mighty flavorful. You can buy a bottle to go for $8, a nice souvenir.

300 W. 114th St. (at Frederick Douglass blvd). melbasrestaurant.com. ✆ **212/864-7777.** Entrees $18–$39. Mon–Wed 11am–10pm; Thurs–Fri 11am–11pm; Sat–Sun 10am–11pm. Subway: 2, 3 to 110th St.

THE OUTER BOROUGHS

Brooklyn

Pizza is big in Brooklyn. See "The Pizza Capital of the United States" on p. 120 for details on borough faves **Juliana's, Paulie Gee's Slice Shop,** and **Roberta's.** Mexican food is also quite popular in this borough, and in addition to the places highlighted below, I have to give a shout out to **Dolores ♥♥**, 397 Tompkins Ave. (doloresbk.com; daily 5–11pm), which is bringing top-notch Mexico City (Chilango) cuisine to Bedford-Stuyvesant (Bed-Stuy), a neighborhood that's rapidly gentrifying, but gets almost no tourism. If you're in this neighborhood though, do stop by. You'll also find a place near to my heart that pairs imaginative cocktails with equally creative, often Japanese-influenced food, called **Shalom Japan ♥♥**, 310 S. 4th St. at Rodney St. (shalomjapan nyc.com; ✆ **718/388-4012;** Tues–Sat 5–10pm, Sun 5–9pm, Sun noon–3pm and 5–9pm), where the signature dish is a carbapalooza: Ramen noodle soup with matzoh balls.

BROOKLYN FOOD COURTS

Dekalb Market Hall, basement of City Point Mall, 445 Albee Square W. (dekalbmarkethall.com; daily 7am–10pm), hosts the only offshoot of famed **Katz's Delicatessen** (p. 99), along with a number of food stands serving specialties you'll rarely see outside of Asia, like *jianbiang* (Shanghai crepes) and *Isan* chicken (Northern Thailand). It also has a bar, beer hall, and more standard offerings, all in a very festive setting.

Time Out Market, 55 Water St. (timeout.com; Sun–Thurs 8am–10pm, Fri–Sat 8am–11pm), is a multi-story, genuinely hip place to hang, especially when its rooftop bar is open (the market is between two bridges so the views are fab). Among the treats here are handrolls from Iron Chef Masaharu Morimoto, bagels from Ess-A-Bagel (p. 116), and very good falafel. The

Union Square version of the Time Out Market isn't nearly as fun (and not recommended).

Smorgasburg (smorgasburg.com; warmer months Sat–Sun 11am–6pm) is the largest outdoor food market in the United States and features 100 or so food vendors who take their stands outdoors to Marsha P. Johnson State Park in Williamsburg on Saturdays (enter at Kent St. and N. 7th St.) and to Prospect Park on Sundays (use Breeze Hill entrance, East Dr. at Lincoln Rd.). *Highlights:* You pick; I can't. With dozens of vendors, the variety of foods is staggering. On a recent visit, my group noshed on curried hot dogs with kimchi apple slaw; oysters with three mignonette sauces; fried eggplant with yogurt sauce; fab barbecue; and El Salvadorian *pupusas* (like tortillas).

EXPENSIVE

Aska ♥♥♥ NEW NORDIC As my dining companion on my last visit exclaimed, as we scraped our plates clean, "We just ate the forest!" Aska's chef Frederik Berselius takes ingredients that one doesn't think of as edible and creates dishes with flavors that are at once totally unique and seriously satisfying. That might mean fried lichen with caramelized cream and chanterelle mushrooms; ice cream made from birchwood; langoustine cooked in a burnt bundle of hay stalks and herbs; or a pig's blood pancake topped with fat-stuffed rose petals. The menu constantly changes, based on what can be foraged nearby or in season; the chatty servers and the kitchen staff (who also serve at table) launch into rapturous explanations about provenance and cooking chemistry.

47 S. 5th St. (near Wythe Ave.), Williamsburg. askanyc.com. ✆ **929/337-6792.** 12–14-course tasting menu $375. Wed–Sun 5–11pm. Subway: J, M, Z to Marcy Ave.

On the ever-changing menu at Aska, exquisite dishes are crafted from locally foraged ingredients.

Gage & Tollner ♥♥♥ STEAK No restaurant in New York City does as good a job at making special occasions special as Gage & Tollner. Which is part of its legacy. One of the United States' oldest oyster and chops joints, the original restaurant was opened in 1879 and was patronized over the years by such bon vivants as Mae West, Jimmy Durante, and "Diamond" Jim Brady. But in 2004, after 175 years in business, the original restaurant went bankrupt

and shuttered. Luckily, its magnificent Gilded Age interior, with its ornate cherry-framed mirrors, expansive bar, and brass fixtures, was landmarked in 1975 (it was one of New York's first interiors to get that designation). So when a young group of restauranteurs decided to revive the place in 2018, they could do so with a dollop of authenticity. The new Gage & Tollner opened in 2021, and beyond the decor, chef/co-owner Sohui Kim has taken culinary inspiration from the original, filling the menu with scintillating takes on such classic dishes as Parker House rolls, she-crab soup, Devils-On-Horseback (dates and smoked almonds wrapped in bacon), pork pot pie, baked Alaska,

The dry-aged rib-eye, a classic favorite at the revived Brooklyn chophouse Gage & Tollner.

and Brooklyn cheesecake (one of the best I've ever eaten). Start or end your evening upstairs at the wonderfully kitschy Sunken Harbor Bar.

372 Fulton St. (btw. Jay St. & Red Hook Lane), downtown Brooklyn. gageandtollner.com. ✆ **347/689-3677.** Entrees $33–$65; more for some steaks. Mon–Fri 5–10pm; Sat–Sun 11am–10pm. Subway: A, C, F, R to Jay St./Metro Tech; 4, 5 to Borough Hall.

Laser Wolf ♥♥♥ ISRAELI If we're lucky, sometime in the near future people across the U.S. will exclaim, when it's time for dinner, "Hey, let's go to a *shipudiya* tonight!" That's what folks in Israel do, because this type of eatery is as ubiquitous there as American diners are here. But more than that, feasting at one is just so darn fun. The meal starts with a generous (included) array of salads and spreads; at Laser Wolf, it's a large platter topped with 11 metal cups of different sorts of veggie treats, from mushroom salad with sour cherries and chard, to a comforting Yemenite potato salad, to baba ghanoush, pickles, and more. That is followed by meats, seafood, or vegetables seared over very hot charcoal (in this category, Laser Wolf's BBQ short rib is such a knockout, it often runs out early in the evening). Drinks are de rigueur, as is fun music. And at Laser Wolf, which was created by Philadelphia celeb chef Michael Solomonov, the culinary pleasure is heightened by the fact that you're dining on a rooftop with awe-inspiring views of the Hudson River and

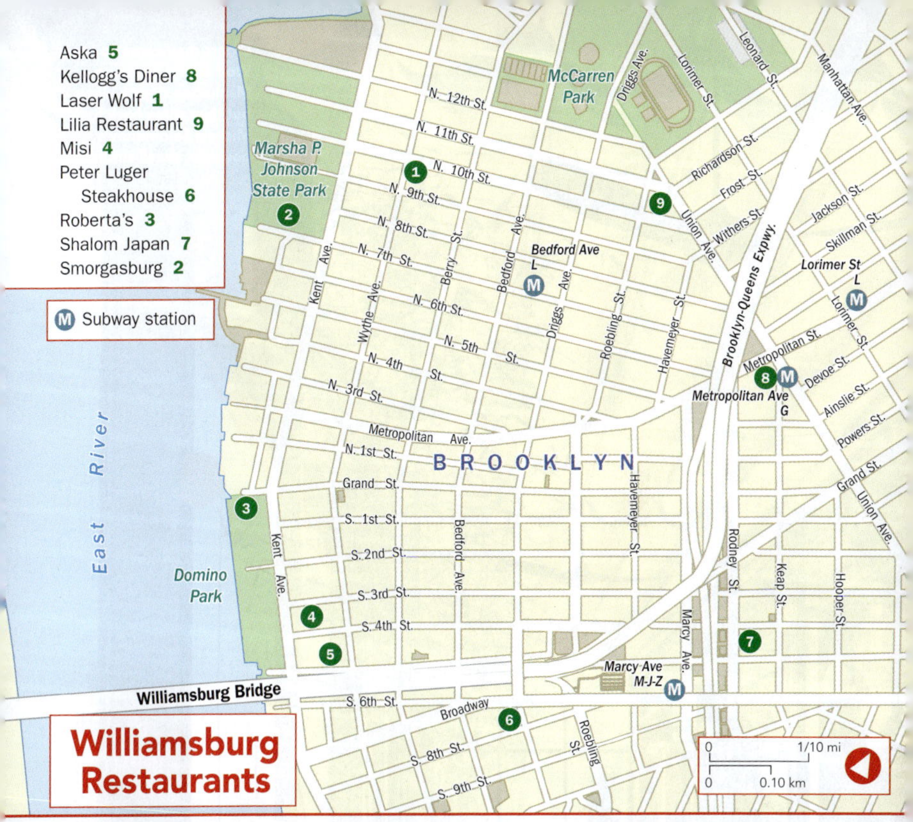

Manhattan skyline. ***Two notes:*** Don't be shy about sharing one entree between two people. I didn't and ended up bringing home enough leftovers for two full meals, thanks to the many included salads. And for the musical theater geeks: Yes, the restaurant *was* named after the butcher in *Fiddler on the Roof!*

97 Wythe Ave., at 10th St. (top floor of the Hoxton Hotel, p. 82), Williamsburg. laserwolfbrooklyn.com. 3-course meals $48–$59. ✆ **718/215-7150.** Mon–Wed 5–11pm; Thurs–Fri 5pm–1am; Sat noon–3pm and 5pm–1am; Sun noon–3pm and 5–11pm. Subway: L to Bedford Ave.

Peter Luger Steakhouse ♥♥ STEAK Grumpy waiters? Check. Sawdust on the floor? But of course! Beef so tender you can use a butter knife on it? Well, that's why people still come to this iconic steakhouse set in an unusually barren stretch of Williamsburg. It's still hard to beat a meal here, and that goes for everything from the beef to the lamb chops to the legendary creamed spinach. ***One important note:*** Credit cards aren't accepted, so be sure to bring wads of cash.

178 Broadway (at Driggs Ave.), Williamsburg. peterluger.com. ✆ **718/387-7400.** Entrees $55 and up. Daily 11:45am–9:30pm. Subway: J, M, Z to Marcy Ave.

Diners may come to Laser Wolf for its stunning Manhattan skyline views, but they come back for Michael Solomonov's bountiful Israeli cuisine.

MODERATE

Casa Ora ♥♥ VENEZUELAN Most of the city's Venezuelan eateries are cheap and cheerful counter-service joints serving the diaspora of Venezuelans living in NYC. Casa Ora, by contrast, is a glossy, fine-photography-filled sit-down restaurant with grander ambitions. Run by a mother/son duo—he's cooked at some of the best restaurants in New York City, she did so in Caracas in the early 1980s (when Venezuela was one of the wealthiest countries on earth)—the menu hops from internationally-known Venezuelan dishes like arepas and empanadas to elevated plates of their own devising, like monkfish wrapped in ripe plantain and smothered in cheese, caramelized coconut milk, and pepper sauce that's a sweet-and-sour enchantment. Venezuelan rum-based cocktails are nicely balanced and will have you dancing in your seat—or is that the kicky soundtrack of dance music (played at conversation-allowing levels)?

148 Meserole St. (off Ave of Puerto Rico), Bushwick. casaoranyc.com. ✆ **718/223-3116.** Entrees $24–$34. Mon–Thurs 5:30–11pm; Fri 5:30–midnight; Sat 11:30am–3pm and 5:30–midnight; Sun 11:30am–3pm and 5:30–10pm. Subway: L to Montrose.

Eyval ♥♥♥ CONTEMPORARY PERSIAN Saffron is a key ingredient in many Persian dishes. At Eyval, the spice stars in the restaurant's best cocktail, the Saffron Martini—a playful move in line with the eatery's name, which means "right on!" in Farsi. Eyval offers a hipster's take on traditional Iranian street foods, so although the menu revolves around yogurt-based spreads, kebabs, and long-simmered stews, each has a twist. The mushroom kebab, for example, isn't just veggies on a skewer. It's composed of curvaceous king trumpet mushrooms, grilled to a perfect char atop the wood-fired oven and then offset by tiny pickled beech mushrooms and an earthy lentil stew. And each of the classic strained yogurt dips known as *borani* features a seasonal North American vegetable at the center—perhaps fiddlehead ferns—with the bitterness of the veggies perfectly counterbalancing the creamy tang of the yogurt. The short-rib stew—a mix of falling-off-the-bone tender meat in a surprising sauce of pomegranates, pistachios, and North African barberries—also knocks it out of the park. The space is casually cool, with lots of white subway tiles upon which scenes from Iranian films are projected (with the sound off). If you want to know what today's Brooklyn is all about, dine here.

25 Bogart St., Bushwick. eyvalnyc.com. Shared plate meals $35–$45 per person. Tues–Sat 6–10pm; Sun 5-9:30pm. Subway: L to Morgan.

Lilia Restaurant ♥♥♥ ITALIAN *New York Magazine* called chef Missy Robbins a "pasta goddess"—an apt title. A darling of the New York culinary scene, she certainly knows her way around noodles, stuffing agnolotti with a honey-sweetened ricotta that's cut by tart strips of dried tomatoes or pairing crunchy broccoli and pistachio pesto with the softest of gnocchi. She's also a fish whiz, not afraid to be decadent, piling cured sardines over frozen curls of

Simple yet elevated cuisine—here mackerel on toast topped with fluffy dill and zest—by chef Missy Robbins at Lilia.

butter-topped toast and slathering wood-grilled scallops with walnut-studded yogurt. But what I most respect about this chef/owner is how she's giving a hand up to other women. Her austere dining room (in a high-ceilinged former garage) offers full views of the open kitchen, where you'll see that fully half of the line cooks are female—a rarity in this male-dominated industry. Robbins' empire includes another eatery called **Misi,** 329 Kent Ave. (misinewyork.com), which has the same extraordinary food, but in a more contemporary-looking dining space.

567 Union Ave. (at N. 10th St.), Williamsburg. lilianewyork.com. ✆ **718/576-3095.** Entrees $20–$43. Mon–Thurs 5–10pm; Fri–Sun 4–10pm. Subway: L to Bedford Ave.

Oxomoco ♥♥♥ MEXICAN Don't believe anyone who tells you NYC doesn't do Mexican food well. The city now rivals—dare I say it?—Los Angeles for the quality and variety of its south-of-the-border eats. And this may well be my favorite of the crew, both for its evocative setting—with high rough-hewn white walls and an abundance of hanging plants, it captures the spirit of Mexico's colonial cities—and its authentic fire-kissed Oaxacan cuisine. The spices will engulf your tongue, and the fabulous steak tartare comes with a sprinkling of fried grasshoppers. Especially recommended: lamb barbacoa and squash-blossom tacos, and masa-fried cauliflower in mole sauce. Be careful on the margaritas: They're potent and huuuuuge.

128 Greenpoint Ave, Greenpoint. oxomoconyc.com. ✆ **646/688-4180.** Entrees $24–$46 (with 3 luxury items for more). Mon–Fri noon–3pm and 5:30–10pm; Sat–Sun 11am–3pm and 5:30–10pm. Subway: G to Nassau Ave.

Sailor ♥♥♥ GOURMET AMERICAN April Bloomfield! She's the reason we're sending you to the wilds of Fort Greene, Brooklyn. A long-time star chef who found her previous restaurants destroyed by a #MeToo scandal (which involved her male business partners, and not Bloomfield directly—grr), Bloomfield is cooking at the top of her powers here, turning out a menu that's both quirky and comforting, in a very pleasant, woodsy, lightly-maritime-themed restaurant. It's hard to order wrong here, but I think you'll be particularly pleased if you go for the toast with green sauce (which tastes like spring even in the depths of winter); braised pork shoulder that comes in a *jus* so luscious it's hard to stop from licking the plate; and the Platonic Ideal of roast chicken (for two) sided by garlic-infused chard and parmesan potatoes. ***Note:*** Sailor is quite small so this is a hard reservation to nab, but they do hold aside the bar area seating for walk-ins.

228 DeKalb Ave., Fort Greene. sailor.nyc. Entrees $32–$42. Wed 5–10pm; Thurs–Fri 5–10:30pm; Sat–Sun 10am–2pm and 5–10:30pm. Subway: G to Clinton-Washington aves.

At the tiny Fort Greene restaurant Sailor, chef April Bloomfield is cooking at the top of her game.

Fried seafood sandwiches at Strange Delight are a straight-up dose of New Orleans comfort food.

Strange Delight ♥♥♥ NEW ORLEANS/SEAFOOD You won't hear jazz or zydeco playing from the speakers here, and there's not a Carnival mask or beaded necklace in sight. But somehow Strange Delight manages to channel the spirit of New Orleans like no other NYC restaurant. There's a laid-back conviviality to the service, with the kind of warmth you get in Crescent City. And though the white-on-white, subway-tiles-and-marble interior is all New York, the cramped confines recall NOLA's many hole-in-the-wall haunts as well. But foremost is the menu, a love letter to the seafood dishes of New Orleans, with a special focus on oysters. Those come fried, barbecued, raw (with mignonette sauce), caramelized in a live fire oven (with scrumptious toppings), or embedded in an oyster loaf that's crammed into a sandwich with pickles and iceberg lettuce, between the softest of milk bread slices. The huge sandwiches are a meal in themselves, so don't believe the waiter if you're advised to order two to three dishes per person. Also tops on the menu: tender blackened swordfish belly, a broccolini salad with nutritional yeast dressing, and a shrimp-and-crab remoulade. Strange Delight is located relatively close to two massive venues—the Brooklyn Academy of Music and the Barclays Center—so be sure to get advance reservations, especially on game days or when big concerts are scheduled. ***One warning:*** It's all surf, no turf here. If you don't like seafood, eat elsewhere.

63 Lafayette Ave. (at Fulton St.), Boerum Hill. strangedelight.nyc. Entrees $24–$40. Mon–Thurs 5–9:30pm; Fri–Sat 11:30am–3:30pm and 5–10:30pm; Sun 11:30am–3:30pm and 5–9:30pm. Subway: G to Fulton St., C to Lafayette Ave.

MODERATE/INEXPENSIVE

Win Son ♥♥♥ TAIWANESE You can remember this place as "winsome." It's not the name, I know, but a perfect description of the experience of dining here, from the sociable waitstaff to the setting (brick walls, groovy chandeliers, and paintings) to the menu, which is an excellent introduction to the delicious hodgepodge that is Taiwanese food. For those who don't know the culinary history, food on this island nation has a lot of different influences:

THE real LITTLE ITALY

You'll notice there are no listings for Manhattan's "Little Italy" in this book. That's because this once-vibrant neighborhood is a shadow of its original self, with few recommendable Italian restaurants. Smart foodies head instead to Arthur Avenue in the Bronx, an authentic Italian enclave that's been going strong since it was settled by Neapolitan immigrants in the late 1800s.

There are two ways to "do" Arthur Avenue. You can either "graze" it or have a real sit-down feast. For a simple snack, there are a variety of options. You might start with a half-dozen *bocconcini* (creamy, salty mozzarella balls) at **Casa Della Mozzarella,** 64 E. 187th St., (just off Arthur Ave.), and then gulp down some freshly opened oysters—either sweet West Coasters or briny East Coast varieties—from the ice-covered tables outside **Cosenza's Fish Market,** 2354 Arthur Ave. Wash the snacks down with the local brew at the **Bronx Beer Hall,** in the Arthur Avenue Market (2344 Arthur Ave., a covered market created by the legendary Mayor Fiorello LaGuardia; thebronxbeerhall.com). And then for dessert, nothing beats cannoli at **Madonia Bakery,** 2348 Arthur Ave. (madoniabakery.com), which has been filling the morning-baked shells fresh for each customer since 1916.

If you decide to go the full-scale restaurant route, you have a ton of options. I'm partial to **Roberto's,** 603 Crescent Ave. (just around the corner from Arthur Ave.; robertosbronx.com; ✆ **718/733-9503;** Tues–Thurs noon–2:30pm and 5–10pm, Fri noon–2:30pm and 5–11pm, Sat noon–2:30 and 4–11pm), because I'm wild for their house specialty: different types of pasta placed into tinfoil and then set over a grill, which gives the noodles a smoky and at points crispy taste. But **Trattoria Zero Otto Nove,** 2357 Arthur Ave. (zeroottonove.com; ✆ **718/220-1027;** Tues–Sat noon–2:30pm and 4:30–10pm, Sun 1–9pm), is also beloved by many. For still another old-school red-sauce alternative, head to **Enzo's,** 2339 Arthur Ave. (enzosofarthuravenue.com; ✆ **718/733-4455;** Mon–Sat 11:30am–10pm, Sun noon–9pm), which features grandmotherly service and classic Italian-American cooking.

To reach Arthur Avenue, take the B, D, or 4 subway to Fordham Road and walk from there (about 15 minutes) or a Metro-North Train to Fordham (Metro-North leaves from Grand Central Station).

Indigenous Cultures, Japanese invasions, and, in the 20th century, the migration of people from across mainland China when Mao came to power. I've never tasted anything here that I wouldn't order again, but some stand-outs are a no-insects-were-harmed "fly's head" (a stew of ground pork, wonderfully funky fermented black beans, garlic chives, and chili); *zha jiang mian* (a lamb and noodle dish, with the pleasant lip buzz of Szechuan peppers and a luscious mouth feel from yellow bean paste); and the "nutritious sandwich" (shrimp cake, crispy mortadella, and pickled pineapple on a squishy bun). Cocktails are also first-class and very original, especially the one with mushroom-infused liquor. ***Tip:*** Reservations are only taken for groups of six or more diners, so get here early to get a seat. The restaurant has an off-shoot bakery nearby and in Manhattan (p. 101) that is excellent.

159 Graham Ave. (at Montrose Ave.), Bushwick. winsonbrooklyn.com. Entrees $21–$33. Tues–Sat 5:30–11pm; Sun 5:30–10pm. Subway: L to Montrose Ave.

INEXPENSIVE

Kellogg's Diner ♥♥ TEX MEX/DINER Open 24 hours, this classic diner has long been the place the club kids come in the wee hours. But in 2024, new management added a Texas twang to the menu, so now it's possible to get real chili or a moist and spicy poblano meatloaf, alongside more typical diner fare like pancakes and burgers. Cocktails, wine, and beer are also on offer, and desserts are a specialty: the *New York Times* named Kellogg's Passion Fruit Tajín Icebox Pie one of the best dishes in the city.

518 Metropolitan Avenue (at Union Ave.), Williamsburg. kelloggsdinernyc.com. ✆ **718-782-4505.** Entrees $14–$26 (with a few pricier items). Open 24/7. Subway: G to Metropolitan Ave., L to Lorimer St.

Pierozek ♥♥ POLISH We're not the only source heaping praise on this pierogi master: it's also in the foodie bible Michelin Guide. The Polish dumplings here come in many varieties, from traditional (pork, cheese, or sauerkraut and mushroom) to ones that push the envelope, like a recent collab with pizza shop Paulie Gee's (p. 120) that stuffed these babies with Italian cured meats and tomato sauce and topped them with spicy honey. A mug of the excellent hot borscht is the obvious accompaniment, but if you want a harder beverage, you might try one of their infused vodka shots (they also have a full bar). It's not a fancy place—how could it be at these prices?—but the use of traditional Bolesławiec flatware elevates the meal, and the waitstaff are a genial crew.

592 Manhattan Ave. (btw. Driggs & Nassau), Greenpoint. pierozekbrooklyn.com. ✆ **718/576-3866**. Meal $13–$20. Mon–Sat noon–10pm; Sun noon–8pm. Subway: G to Nassau.

Tom's Restaurant ♥♥♥ BREAKFAST Pair a trip to the nearby Brooklyn Museum with a meal at the classic diner, Tom's. Just slide into one of the vinyl booths, marvel at how many American flags a place this small can hold (interspersed with all sorts of commemorative plates and other knick-knacks), and order up one of the best breakfasts in town. You can do so at any time because the overstuffed omelets, French toast, smoked sausage, and other morning fare are served all day long, as they should be. My favorite: the lemon ricotta pancakes, which taste like the best lemon poppy-seed muffin you've ever had, but fluffier. This is also *the* place to try NYC's fast-disappearing staple: the egg cream soda. And service is the friendliest in the borough.

782 Washington Ave. (at Sterling Place), Prospect Heights. tomsrestaurant.net ✆ **718/636-9736.** No reservations (lines on weekends). Entrees $7–$18. Daily 7am–10:30pm. Subway: 2, 3 to Grand Army Plaza. Also in Coney Island.

Queens

QUEENS FOOD COURTS

What Smorgasburg did for Brooklyn foodies, **The Queens Night Market ♥♥♥**, in the parking lot of the New York Hall of Science in Flushing Meadows Corona Park (queensnightmarket.com; mid-April–Oct Sat 6pm–midnight; subway: 7 to 111th St.), has done for this borough. In the 9 years this Taiwanese-style night market has been in existence, it has hosted over 2 million diners, and vendors from over 90 countries. And it's done so affordably: Food prices are capped at $5–$6 per plate. *Highlights:* Romanian chimney cakes, Sudanese salads, Tibetan dumplings, Salvadoran *pupusas.*

Year-round eats can be had at the **New World Mall ♥♥**, 136-20 Roosevelt Ave (Flushing; new worldmallny.com; ✆ **718/353-7327**), the largest indoor Asian food court in the Northeast, with some 26 stalls. *Highlights*: **Tien Fu's** drypot, the pork chop plate at **A Zhong Taiwanese Cuisine,** and **Chongqing Zaier's** spicy noodle soup.

EXPENSIVE

Sushi on Me ♥♥ JAPANESE Actually, it's the sake that's on the house at this gonzo party masquerading as an omakase restaurant. The chefs stand behind a long sushi bar in a frat house-esque basement space (neon signs, basic furnishings) and they keep the rice wine flowing in unlimited quantities during the course of your one-hour meal—no small feat, as they're also cracking jokes non-stop, DJing pop songs, and slicing up unusually dramatic sushi and sashimi dishes (15 courses!). The raw fish gets blowtorched, or served dabbed with a bubble of smoke, or set afloat in an intriguing sauce, or yes, wrapped around rice. It's all tasty and though it may not be the most refined sushi you could try in NYC, I can guarantee this will be the most festive meal of your trip.

71-26 Roosevelt Ave., Jackson Heights. ✆ **929/268-5691.** $99 per meal. Cash or Venmo only. Seatings at 5, 6:30, 8, and 9:30pm. Subway: 7 to 69th St. Also at 742 Driggs Ave, in Brooklyn.

MODERATE

Casa Enrique ♥♥ MEXICAN For 8 hours each day, the spices, chocolate, plantains, almonds, raisins, and sesame seeds that form the basis for Casa Enrique's *mole* bubble and blend on the stove, creating one of the most complex, rich, not-too-sweet iterations of this dish that Gotham has to offer. Not all end up trying it, however, as the temptations here are many, from the guajillo-pepper marinated ribs, to ceviche crafted from fluke caught in nearby Montauk, to the creamy enchiladas that chef/owner Cosme Aguilar recreates from his mother's recipe. Aguilar brings a sophisticated version of southern Mexican food to this gentrifying section of Queens (just one subway stop from Grand Central Station). His insistence on respect for this type of food also shows in the decor, which is minimalist in the extreme—white walls with no decorations, a stainless-steel bar, and painted white wood tables.

5-48 49th Ave. (near Vernon Blvd.). casaenriquelic.com. ✆ **347/448-6040.** Entrees $16–$42. Mon–Thurs 5–10:15pm; Fri 5–10:30pm; Sat 11am–10:30pm; Sun 11am–10:15pm. Subway: 7 to Vernon Blvd.

Cosme Aguilar's rich, complex mole sauce transforms the southern Mexican food at Casa Enrique.

Taverna Kyclades ♥♥ GREEK Nobody will be smashing plates, but other than that, eating here is a Zorba-rific experience, thanks to the all-Greek waitstaff and the seafood, simply prepared, that tastes like it jumped out of the bluest of seas and right onto your plate. Start with a tasting of spreads, make your way to the grilled octopus (Taverna's signature dish), and end with fresh fish sided by their famous lemon potatoes. The only downer? The Taverna doesn't take reservations, so come early or be prepared to wait.

3307 Ditmars Blvd. (at 33rd St.), Astoria. tavernakyclades.com. ✆ **718/545-8666.** Entrees $13–$35; more for larger shareable dishes. No reservations. Mon–Thurs noon–11pm; Fri–Sat noon–11:30pm; Sun noon–10:30pm. Subway: N, Q to Astoria/Ditmars.

EXPLORING NEW YORK CITY

5

Ask New Yorkers about their feelings for their city, and they will often respond, "There's just one New York." By that they mean: one city so full—of museums (more than 40 major ones); historical sites; world-famous institutions; parks; zoos; universities; lectures; concerts and recitals; theaters for opera, musicals, drama, and dance; architectural highlights; presidents' homes; and kooky galleries—that its diversions are limitless. If you had the speed and stamina of a Lionel Messi, you'd still be hard-pressed to cover all the attractions in months of touring.

Because your time is more limited than that, I'm confining my coverage in this chapter to two categories of sights: first, the city's "iconic" attractions, the places universally associated with Gotham—the headliners that make the city so massively popular. These include major museums (the Metropolitan Museum of Art and the Museum of Modern Art, just to name two); great historical and architectural sites (including Grand Central Terminal and the Brooklyn Bridge); and, in a category all its own, New York's most sobering site: the 9/11 Memorial and Museum.

Second are the less famous attractions that, if they were magically transported to almost any other city in America, would instantly become that city's top cultural draw, bringing acclaim, prestige, and millions of dollars in tourist revenue (no, I do not exaggerate). These attractions—such as the Tenement Museum, The Frick Collection, the Brooklyn Museum—can add immensely to a New York City visit. It's important occasionally to step off the tourist treadmill (Empire State Building, Times Square, Statue of Liberty) and try one of the so-called secondary sights. If you have the time, visit at least one of the places you might never have heard of before picking up this book.

How do you plan (and time) a satisfying itinerary? I've given you a slew of suggestions in chapter 2 of this book. This chapter contains individual sights grouped by area. I truly believe you'll enjoy your visit more if you don't run yourself ragged, dashing around different parts of the city each day. Instead, divide Manhattan into three sections (downtown, midtown, and uptown) and create a daily plan that keeps you in one of those areas for a full day, or in one of

The Big Apple has multiple iconic sights, like the Empire State Building, but look beyond these classics for even more first-class museums, parks, and architectural marvels.

our fabulous boroughs (again for the day). You'll see more that way, you'll have time to enjoy an unhurried meal, and you'll find the kinds of serendipitous sidewalk encounters that don't happen when you're stressed out by subway connections, hop-on bus pickup schedules, and attraction closing times.

NEW YORK CITY'S TOP SIGHTS

Because New York City has a larger population than 40 of the 50 states, it has enough curious, engaged locals to support more museums, and other types of attractions, than most cities. EVERY attraction listed in this chapter is visit-worthy. But because there are so many, I thought it would be helpful to include a list of the attractions that are unmissable. There are more below than can be visited in a week . . . so it's time to start planning your return trip.

DOWNTOWN

Financial District/New York Harbor

9/11 Memorial and Museum ♥♥♥ HISTORIC SITE/MUSEUM For well over 2 millennia, humans have been telling one another stories of the dangers of looking back at evil or death. Lot's wife turned to a pillar of salt because she dared glance over her shoulder into the maw of destruction. Orpheus lost his beloved forever for the same reason: He turned around before he'd reached the realm of light. And in a case of real life imitating iconic tales, on September 11, 2001, those people who were on the streets surrounding the Twin Towers when they fell had to run for their lives to escape the deadly debris cloud that pursued them with unrelenting fury. "Don't look back, just run," one bystander yells to another in one of the many moving videos at the 9/11 Memorial and Museum.

Visitors at the 9/11 Museum and Memorial in front of one of the steel beams that was part of the original World Trade Center.

For over a decade it looked as if the survivors, politicians, and others who had vowed to create this museum might not actually have the *ability* to look back at that world-changing September day. Bickering over every element of the design and contents of the museum caused endless delays and became newspaper fodder; controversies seemed to erupt daily over such issues as the high cost of entry to the museum, its portrayal of Islam, even the fact that it had a gift shop. Yet despite all this, the 9/11 Museum has emerged as what may be one of the most important history museums in the United States. Out of all the chaos and well-publicized postponements comes an institution that seamlessly blends design and content, transporting visitors back, in a very visceral way, to the day on which four separate, airplane-fueled attacks killed close to 3,000 people (the museum relates the stories not just of the Twin Towers but also of the Pentagon attack and Flight 93).

After a thorough security check (make sure you allot 20 min. minimum for that and the entry line), visitors descend down, down, down into this underground museum. It's a fitting metaphor not only for the escape route that Twin Towers survivors had to take when fleeing by stair (a remnant of the famous "survivors' stair" is to the right of the museum's staircase at one point) but also for the darkness the attacks plunged the United States into. At the bottom of the final staircase, to the left (oddly, as most visitors want to turn right) is the museum's beating heart: its history exhibition. A masterful mix of video, audio clips from survivors, wall text, and poignant artifacts—the burnt-edged papers that fluttered from the Towers, children's clothing recovered from Flight 93—the exhibit manages to bring to life the personal stories of

The Victims' Memorial Quilt is among many artifacts preserved at the 9/11 Memorial and Museum.

those who lived or died that day, while also explaining some of the forces that led to the attacks. A thought-provoking section explores the rise of Al Qaeda (you even see a brick from Bin Laden's Abbottabad compound). Lingering health issues that survivors and first responders still struggle with are discussed, as is the issue of who, beyond the attackers, should be held accountable. Museumgoers also see the famous Ground Zero cross (a severed chunk of metal beams that accidentally formed this Christian symbol), a squashed fire truck, and the Memorial Room, which tells the story and shows the face of every person who died on 9/11.

I, for one, am glad that the founders of the museum were finally able to look back and to do so in such a clear-eyed, multifaceted way. I don't know if the museum has one overarching point to make, but it offers revelations at every turn about our recent history and the many people who shaped it. And everywhere are boxes of tissues (refilled every hour, according to the guard I spoke with), as the museum is ultimately quite an emotional experience.

Surrounding the museum is the 8-acre **Memorial Plaza,** which features two reflecting pools and waterfalls, located in the 1-acre footprints of the individual towers. Each reflecting pool is surrounded by a brass parapet where the names of victims of both the 9/11 and February 1993 bombings are engraved and arranged in order according to where they worked, close to their co-workers or friends, or wherever their families thought they would best be located.

A Few Notes: A limited number of free tickets are given out on the website each Monday, starting at 7am (the number varies by season, and most will be gone by midmorning, after which admission can be purchased). Tours of the museum do sell out in advance, so if you plan to take one of those, book that and your ticket a few days ahead. (Frankly, I don't think taking the tour improves the museum experience.) The museum itself rarely sells out, but purchasing timed entry in advance lets you skip one line. "Early access" tours several times a week, starting at 8:15am, may be worthwhile for those with limited time in the city.

Entrances at intersections of Liberty and Greenwich sts., Liberty and West sts., or West and Fulton sts. 911memorial.org. ✆ **212/266-5211.** Museum admission $36; $30 seniors/youth ages 13–17/U.S. college students with ID; $25 U.S. veterans; $24 children 7–12; free for children 6 and under and for some on Mon (see above); additional cost for guided tour. Memorial park daily 8am–8pm; museum daily 9am–7pm (closed Tues in Jan, Feb, Nov, and the first two weeks of Mar and May); last entry 1½ hr. before museum closes. Subway: A, C, J, Z, 2, 3, 4, 5 to Fulton St.; 2, 3 to Park Place; E to World Trade Center; R to Rector St.

African Burial Ground ♥ MUSEUM/MEMORIAL Some 15,000 enslaved African people were buried in a Manhattan graveyard in the 17th and 18th centuries, but their final resting places were lost to memory until 1991 when construction workers stumbled upon human remains during renovations of a federal building. The site is now considered one of the most important archeological finds in the United States. In 2006, a handsome, symbol-laden

Downtown & Chelsea Attractions
9/11 Memorial and Museum 9
African Burial Ground 15
Artechouse 27
Brooklyn Bridge 14
Ellis Island National Museum of Immigration 2
Flatiron Building 30
International Center of Photography 20
Jackie Robinson Museum 16
Leslie-Lohman Museum 17
Merchant's House Museum 24
Museum at Eldridge St. 19
The Museum at FIT 29
Museum of Chinese in America 18
The Museum of Illusions 28
Museum of Jewish Heritage—A Living Memorial to the Holocaust 4
National Museum of the American Indian, George Gustav Heye Center 6
New Museum of Contemporary Art 22
Old St. Patrick's Cathedral 23
One World Observatory 10
St. Paul's Chapel 11
Skyscraper Museum 5
South Street Seaport Museum 13
Staten Island Ferry 3
Statue of Liberty 1
Stonewall National Monument 25
The Tenement Museum 21
Trinity Church 8
Wall Street & the New York Stock Exchange 7
Whitney Museum of American Art 26
The Woolworth Building 12
Subway station
0 1/4 mi
0 0.25 km
CHELSEA
GREENWICH VILLAGE
EAST VILLAGE
NOHO
SOHO
NOLITA
LITTLE ITALY
TRIBECA
CHINATOWN
FINANCIAL DISTRICT
High Line Park
Little Island
Washington Square
Tompkins Square Park
City Hall Park
Vietnam Veterans Plaza
South Gardens
Battery Park
Castle Clinton Natl. Mon.
Staten Island Ferry Terminal
Brooklyn Bridge
Manhattan Bridge
East River
(See inset at left)
0 1/2 mi
NEW JERSEY
NEW YORK
Hudson River
Liberty State Park
Ellis Island
Ellis Island Immigration Museum
Liberty Island
Castle Clinton Nat'l Monument Ferry tickets
Battery Park
Governors Island
East River

National Monument (operated by the National Parks Service) was dedicated by poet Maya Angelou and Mayor Michael Bloomberg. Inside the small museum nearby are smartly crafted exhibits about the lives of the city's enslaved African people, the laws surrounding slavery, and the history of the site. Ask the on-site ranger to play the excellent 20-minute introductory film when you arrive; it's only played on request. A visit to the African Burial Ground and museum should take no more than half an hour, but it's a worthy pilgrimage, uncovering, as it does, a part of American history that is too often buried just below the surface.

Memorial at corner of Duane and Elk sts., museum at 290 Broadway. nps.gov/afbg. ✆ **212/637-2019.** Free admission. Tues–Sat 10am–4pm. Subway: 4, 5, 6, R to City Hall; J to Chambers St.

Brooklyn Bridge ♥♥♥ ICON/ARCHITECTURE New York has a grand Gothic cathedral in St. Patrick's (p. 183), but for many New Yorkers, the city's true cathedral, the point at which earth and water join and thrust upwards toward the heavens, is the Brooklyn Bridge.

To fully appreciate its dazzle, you must **walk the bridge.** Start on the Manhattan side and walk first to one of the great Gothic towers that hold up the bridge's cables. It took 7 years and massive heartbreak to build these two structures. When architect (and immigrant) John A. Roebling was surveying

Big Onion Tours (p. 264) leads a group walk across the Brooklyn Bridge with its iconic Gothic-arched towers.

the area in 1869, just 2 weeks after the project had been approved, a ferry accidentally rammed into the place where he was standing, crushing his foot. He died of lockjaw 3 weeks later. His son Washington took over and created a method of sending pneumatic caissons—basically large, pressurized pine boxes into which compressed air was pumped to keep the water out—down to the riverbed. This allowed six workers at a time to descend and lay the foundation for these towers. Because they didn't have a good understanding of the effects of underwater pressure on the human body (known to scuba divers as "the bends"), many were killed or injured in the caissons, including Washington Roebling. In 1872, he had to be carried out of the chamber, partially paralyzed. He remained bedridden for the rest of his life, and his wife Martha took over directing the job, learning advanced mathematics in the process. Washington watched the progress of the bridge through binoculars from his apartment, and when the bridge was completed after 13 years, President Grover Cleveland, the governor, and the mayor all came to his home to personally thank him for his efforts.

Walk to the center of the bridge and take in the spectacular views of both Brooklyn and Manhattan. When the bridge was built, its span—1,595 ft.—was the longest leap across an open space of any on Earth, and the first bridge to connect Manhattan with any of the lands that surrounded it. Take a look up at the cables; these, too, were an innovation, the first steel cables to be used on a bridge (before then cables were iron). It took 2 years to string the cables back and forth before work could begin building the suspension bridge. The cables each contain 5,434 wires and weigh 870 tons. Take a moment at the Brooklyn side to read the plaque on the construction of the bridge.

When you depart the bridge, consider taking a stroll in either Brooklyn Bridge Park (p. 254) or brownstone-heavy Brooklyn Heights, the first neighborhood in the city to be landmarked.

To start in Manhattan, 4, 5, 6 to Brooklyn Bridge–City Hall. To start in Brooklyn, 2, 3 train to Clark St.; or 2, 3, 4, 5, N, R to Court St.–Borough Hall.

Ellis Island National Museum of Immigration ♥♥♥ HISTORIC SITE The epicenter of the largest migration in human history, Ellis Island was in near-continuous use from 1892 to 1954 as the point-of-entry processing center for the majority of immigrants (including my grandmother) who settled in the U.S. during those years. Over 12 million people passed through its halls, sometimes as many as 12,000 in a single day. The stories of these immigrants—what they were escaping, what they found once here, and what they experienced in their short time in the purgatory that was Ellis Island—are the core of the Ellis Island experience. Several years ago, Ellis Island widened its focus to embrace the *entire* history of immigration to America; it well deserves a repeat visit from those who toured it before then (more on that below). First-time visitors, however, will want to concentrate on the original exhibits, which remain the most emotionally resonant—for the simple reason that they're about Ellis Island itself. Learning about this endlessly fascinating place while walking through its hallowed halls is a powerful experience.

Start in the awe-inspiring second-floor **Grand Hall** (officially the **Registry Hall**), with its massive white-tile vaulted ceiling (created by the same firm that did the ceiling in Grand Central Terminal's Oyster Bar; p. 132), most likely larger than any church or temple these immigrants would have attended in their home villages. Behind the Grand Hall lies a warren of small rooms where immigrants were tested for mental competency, literacy, and communicable diseases. How these tests were done—and the fear they inspired—is chronicled in historical photos, wall text, and most poignantly at listening stations (or over the free audio-tour headphones) on which you hear actual immigrants share their memories of their time on the island. The top floor chronicles the history of the processing facility itself. These exhibits can be skipped if you're short on time, but don't miss the **Treasures from Home** exhibit, also on this floor, which features 2,000 of the possessions that were brought through Ellis. Somehow seeing the china dolls, the precious wedding photos, the native costumes, and the letters home brings the immigrant experience more vividly to life than any other part of the museum.

More than 12 million people passed through the Grand Hall at Ellis Island upon arrival in the United States.

For those coming on a repeat visit, on the ground floor are four new exhibitions of note. Two of them expand the story of immigration to America, to the era before Ellis Island opened **(Journeys: The Peopling of America)** and to the period after World War II through today **(The Journey: New Eras of Immigration).** Both are quite wall-text heavy, which may frustrate some visitors. If you have to choose between them, I'd pick "New Eras of Immigration," as it features affecting videos profiling recent immigrants, who have come to the U.S. in many different ways. It also tells a story that's rarely discussed in a balanced fashion: the myriad surprising ways in which immigration is reshaping today's America. The highlight of the

Clothing from immigrants' native countries is displayed in the Treasures from Home exhibit.

American Stories exhibit is a set of interactive monitors that allow visitors to take an actual, current citizenship test (I'm proud to say I got a perfect score). Another experience recommended for repeat visitors is the **Hard Hat Tour ♥♥**, which takes visitors through the unrenovated—and haunting—Ellis Island hospital. Some 10% of Ellis Island immigrants spent some time here, often only to be shipped back to Europe, their only crime being ill. The facility was closed for 60 years and it's falling apart—hence the need for hard hats. The only new items added are oversize archival photos of hospital residents that French artist JR mounted onto the crumbling walls, broken windows, and metal lockers—a moving tribute.

Also on the island is a cafeteria, along with the **American Family History Center,** which holds millions of records. Trained genealogists are on-site to help visitors navigate the computer search; a session costs $7.

As one of the 40% of all Americans who had a relative come through Ellis Island, I find it difficult to tour this museum without tearing up at some point. I have no doubt that visitors without such a direct connection will find the journey through Ellis one of the most moving experiences of their New York visit.

In New York Harbor; ferry departs from Battery Park. nps.gov/elis/index.htm or statuecitycruises.com. ✆ **212/363-3200** (general info) or 877/LADY-TIX (523-9849; ticket/ferry info). Free admission. Ferry ticket $26 adults, $23 seniors, $17 children 4–12; free for children 3 and under. Hard Hat Tour, including ferry ticket $81, ages 13 and up only. Included in CityPass (p. 176). Ferries depart Sept–May 9am–3:30pm (June–Aug until 5pm). Ferries also depart from Liberty State Park in New Jersey. For subway and ferry details, see Statue of Liberty, p. 172 (ferry stops at both sights).

Museum of Jewish Heritage—A Living Memorial to the Holocaust ♥♥ MUSEUM It used to be an emotionally draining experience to visit the Museum of Jewish Heritage, which deals in explicit fashion with the Holocaust. But thanks to a recent overhaul of its core exhibit, the museum today focuses far more on the personal stories of those whose lives were upended (or ended altogether) by the Holocaust, including hopeful

BOGO Season: "Must See Week"

If low hotel rates aren't enough of a lure to get you to Gotham in the frigid weeks of mid-January and early February, perhaps this buy-one-get-one-free deal will be. Sponsored by the city's official tourism board, **Must See Week** drastically cuts the cost for couples for all kinds of sightseeing and some nightlife. Included in the offer are a two-for-one-entry to the city's top museums (such as the Guggenheim, the Museum of the City of New York, and the Whitney); observation decks (One World Observatory and Top of the Rock); historic sights (the United Nations Tour, the USS Intrepid, the 9/11 Memorial and Museum); performance venues (Jazz at Lincoln Center, the Metropolitan Opera); and even the ice skating rink at Rockefeller Center. To see all of the deals, go to nyctourism.com/must-see-week. Despite the name, this promotion lasts nearly 3 weeks most years.

Schoolchildren examine elaborately decorated Indigenous clothing at the National Museum of the American Indian.

stories of those who survived, often against all odds. They do so with thousands of personal accounts, never-before-seen photos, compelling video interviews with survivors, and striking artifacts—a breadloaf-size suitcase that one family of four escaped to freedom with, or, more chilling, an annotated edition of *Mein Kampf* that belonged to Heinrich Himmler. The exhibit "The Danish Escape" is suitable for children 9 and up, as it tells the largely positive story of how the Danes saved much of their Jewish population. The core exhibit is best for those 13 and over.

36 Battery Place (at 1st Place), Battery Park City. mjhnyc.org. ✆ **646/437-4200.** Admission $18 adults, $12 seniors and students; free for children 12 and under; free admission Thurs 4pm to closing. Sun and Wed 10am–5pm; Thurs 10am–8pm; Fri 10am–3pm. Subway: 4, 5 to Bowling Green.

National Museum of the American Indian, George Gustav Heye Center ♥ MUSEUM Housed in the magnificent Customs House, designed by architect Cass Gilbert (for more on the edifice, see p. 270), this museum is a sister institution to the one in Washington, D.C., though it was founded a decade earlier in 1994. Both are now part of the Smithsonian (free to enter!) and have as a foundation some 1 million objects from Indigenous nations across the Americas, from the Inuit to the Inca. The ground floor is an interactive learning space for children called **imagiNATIONS Activity Center** (during the week it's often reserved for school groups). On the upper story are three exhibition spaces. **Native New York,** which tells the stories of the Indigenous Peoples who have lived in New York State since time immemorial, seems geared to those of elementary school age. Of more interest for adults is the **Infinity of Nations** galleries, which showcases exquisite Indigenous art and artifacts: baskets, blankets, masks, dresses, intricate stone and wood sculptures, beaded moccasins, jewelry, and paintings on hides showing initiation ceremonies, to name just a fraction of what you'll see here. The museum has two interpreters on staff who roam around answering questions—alas, they aren't always in this gallery, which is a real shame, as they are able to relate fascinating background for many of the objects. The final gallery area, the **Diker Pavilion for Native Arts and Cultures,** hosts changing exhibits, some of which, to be frank, have been quite dull recently. But heck: the museum's free, so if you're in the vicinity, pop inside, and be sure to go into the **gift store,** where you'll see the original tellers' windows from when this was a customs house.

1 Bowling Green (btw. State and Whitehall sts.). americanindian.si.edu. ✆ **212/514-3700.** Free admission. Daily 10am–5pm. Closed Christmas. Subway: 4, 5 to Bowling Green; R to Whitehall; 1 to South Ferry.

One World Observatory ♥♥ VIEW I'm going to say what no polite travel writer does: A big part of the allure of seeing the view from atop the Western Hemisphere's tallest building (at 1,776 ft.) is the knowledge that you may be tempting fate by doing so. The skyscraper was built as a nose thumb to the terrorists who had *twice* attacked the World Trade Center on this same acre of ground. That may be why (according to the scuttlebutt) the building's office space is still not fully rented. But the observation deck is popular because, along with the tremendous views, visitors can show their patriotism by ascending to this eagle's-eye perch. That point is brought home when you head into the part of the lobby that shows the tunnel developers dug into the bedrock—and kept purposefully rough-hewn, filling it with signs (in lights) about the durability of the rock foundations and the fact that the building contains 5.4 million cubic ft. of concrete "making this the strongest building ever constructed." Is this meant to reassure

One World Observatory sits at the apex of the Western Hemisphere's tallest building, One World Trade Center.

patrons or hype up the excitement? I'll leave that to the cynics among you to decide.

The Observatory also lures customers with some pretty whiz-bang features. Its elevators not only shoot passengers up 102 stories in an ear-popping 47 seconds (they're among the fastest elevators in the world), but also have walls that turn into video "windows," through which riders see a computer-generated visual history of the city, from meadowlands to the skyscrapers of today. (Be sure to look right to glimpse the Twin Towers, just a brief blip in this 500-year timeline.) There's also a fun multimedia presentation at the top, and a "tour guide" often stationed to answer questions about visible landmarks with the help of an interactive wheel of screens.

That being said, I think the designers made several key errors. Unlike the city's other observation decks, OWO has no outdoor areas, so the views are sealed behind glass, which is less exciting than feeling skyscraper-top winds whip your hair as you stare into the abyss. Plus, the powers that be now ask visitors to pay extra to look through a tablet at the view. Save your money! The tablet is loaded with not-very-exciting videos, plus text giving background information for only a handful of the buildings you'll see through the glass. Final disappointment? Though you can see 50 miles in all directions on a clear day you do so from the foot of Manhattan, meaning the buzzing, crowded streets of midtown are far in the distance. If you go to any of the other of the city's decks, you'll be in the middle of the action, which makes the views more dynamic (I think).

Some notes: On-site are a bar/restaurant (One Dine) and a souvenir store. As at the other observation decks in town, tickets are timed, which should mean minimal waits (so don't pay extra for VIP access).

1 World Trade (entrance on Vesey St. at West St.). oneworldobservatory.com. ✆ **844/696-1776.** Basic admission, with booking fee and tax, starts at $46.50 adults, $44.50 seniors, $40.50 children 6–12; free for children 5 and under. Note that base prices increase $5–$10 at sunset and on popular dates. Daily 9am–9pm (hours can change by season). Subway: E to World Trade Center; A, C to Chambers St.; N, R to Cortland St.; 4, 5 to Fulton St.

Skyscraper Museum ♥ MUSEUM Don't dismiss this small museum: It's far more interesting than one would expect. An architecturally innovative space in and of itself (notice how the shiny metals, ascending ramp, and mirrored surfaces gives the smallish room its own skyscraper aspect), the museum explores not only the structural feats behind these soaring structures, but also the economic forces that shaped them and their sociological impact.

39 Battery Place (Little West St. and 1st Place). skyscraper.org. ✆ **212/968-1961.** Free admission. Wed–Sat noon–6pm. Subway: 4, 5 to Bowling Green.

South Street Seaport Museum ♥ HISTORIC SITE New York is NEW YORK because it was once the most powerful maritime trading city on the planet. That legacy undergirded its importance to the nation and allowed it to accumulate prominence in other spheres. This little museum unpacks that

TICKET WEBSITES vs. booking direct

As with most things in life, cutting out the middleman will save you money. So, though it may *feel* convenient to book all your museum and attraction tickets through a single app—and there are several that allow visitors to book local attractions and tours this way—we suggest you don't.

Here's why. Say you decided to visit the Statue of Liberty or Ellis Island. You need to board a ferry to get to them, and the third-party apps that book that trip add on a booking fee. How much extra will vary by vendor, but why pay it at all? Statue City Cruises, the official concessionaire for the National Park Service has no booking fees whatsoever. It just sells you the damn ticket. You'll find the same holds true for other major sites around town, which is why we've included the websites for every one of them in this guide. Even worse, at the Statue of Liberty and Ellis Island many websites will sell you a tour of these sites despite the fact that *only rangers are allowed to give tours inside NY's NPS sites*. So, your tour could cost up to $80 per person and will keep you outside the main events (what's exciting at both are the sights inside!).

But what about those companies that sell "priority access" for a bit extra, allowing their customers to get on the "reserve line" rather than the regular one? When visitor numbers are down, as they are, say, in deep winter (the off season), VIP lines are totally unnecessary—there just won't be many folks on the regular line. But even in high season, gaming the line in this way can backfire. Many travelers are reporting in online chat groups that, with so many folks purchasing this VIP treatment, the "reserve line" moves just as slowly as the regular one.

We *do* recommend some sightseeing passes. See p. 176 for more on those.

history in two former warehouse spaces crammed with artifacts. How much you'll enjoy them depends on your natural appreciation for scrimshaw and boats in bottles. More compelling for most visitors, and included in admission, will be tours of two historic vessels moored off Pier 16. If you only have time for one (each takes about 30 minutes to see) make it the ***Lightship Ambrose*** which, though smaller, played an essential, and somewhat weird, role in protecting the harbor of the city. The museum also hosts sails of the harbor on other historic vessels when the weather is nice.

213 Water St., 12 Fulton St., and Pier 16. southstreetseaportmuseum.org. ✆ **212/748-8600.** Admission $18 adults, $15 seniors/students, $5 children ages 8 and under. Fri–Sun 11am–5pm. Subway: 2, 3, 4, 5 to Fulton St. (walk east, or downslope, on Fulton St. to Water St.).

Staten Island Ferry ♥♥ ICON/TRANSPORTATION Most visitors—and even some New Yorkers—don't know that the Staten Island Ferry makes its own daily excursion within Instagramable distance of the Statue of Liberty, Ellis Island, and Governor's Island. And riders pay absolutely nothing for the great views. You simply board the ship (be sure to wait for one of the older orange-and-green boats—newer ones don't have decks for viewing). As with the Circle Line (p. 262), sit on the right side (stay at the back of the ferry for the best view of the Manhattan skyline). Locals joke that this is the best "cheap date" in the city, so don't be shy about toting along a bottle of wine, some bread, and cheese. But be sure to dress warmly: In winter the outdoor decks can be frigid. One-way, the trip takes approximately a half-hour, after which you can either embark on the next ferry back, or take a 10-minute stroll to the **National Lighthouse Museum** ♥, 200 The Promenade at Lighthouse Point (lighthousemuseum.org; $7 admission; Tues–Sun 11am–4pm). It's housed in what was once (from 1862 on) the depot for the U.S. Lighthouse Service, a major center of production for the specialized gear lighthouses needed; all of the Fresnel lenses that came in from France were tested here before being sent to lighthouses around the United States. The museum has an excellent short video on lighthouse history in the United States, as well as exhibits about how the lenses work, lighthouses around the globe, and portraits of the people who undertook this (often) isolating career.

Departs from Whitehall Ferry Terminal, 4 South St. (at Whitehall St.). siferry.com. Free admission. Daily 24 hr.; Mon–Fri every 15 min. during rush hour, otherwise every 30 min. on the half-hour and hour. Subway: N, R to Whitehall St.; 4, 5 to Bowling Green; 1 to South Ferry (ride in first 5 cars of train).

Statue of Liberty ♥♥♥ ICON/MONUMENT The great harbor of New York and the grand lady who guards it are, after Ground Zero and the Empire State Building, the city's top must-visit attractions. You'll follow in the footsteps of the millions of immigrants and visitors who came here before you,

Liberty Island's on-site museum gives insight into the Statue of Liberty's history and how it was built. To enter the statue itself, you need advance reservations.

THE STATUE OF LIBERTY—in brief

French connection: Dreamed up at a dinner party of French intellectuals in 1865, the statue was first proposed as a 100th-birthday present from France to the United States (and as a not-so-subtle jab at France's then-authoritarian Second Empire). Fundraising woes kept it from being completed in time for that anniversary, but in 1881, after over a decade of begging for money (a lottery finally did the trick), sculptor Frédéric-Auguste Bartholdi was able to finish the massive work.

Battle for the base: Though the statue was completed in 1881, it took another 2 years for the Americans to keep their half of the bargain and create a pedestal for it. Newspaperman Joseph Pulitzer finally stepped in, and in a series of angry editorials condemning the wealthy for not contributing, he convinced thousands of lower-income Americans to send in what they could to get the job done. Thanks to their dimes and nickels, the pedestal was finally built (designed by Richard Morris Hunt), and the statue was dedicated on October 28, 1886.

Crafting the Lady: *Repousse*, a technique of hammering and shaping thin strips of copper, was used to create Lady Liberty. Though the statue is massive at over 151 ft. from base to torch, the "skin" of the piece is just 3⁄32 of an inch thick. It is thought that the ancient Colossus of Rhodes was built using this method.

Key to the symbolism: Every piece of the statue has meaning. The seven rays in the crown represent the seven seas of the world, and the 25 windows there give a nod to the 25 gemstones found on Earth. On the tablet Liberty is holding are inscribed the Roman numerals for July 4, 1776. And though it's difficult to see, Liberty is breaking shackles with her right foot.

their way lighted by the torch and the promise inscribed on the statue's base: that the "teeming masses yearning to breathe free" would find succor, freedom from persecution, and economic opportunity in this new land.

You will have a fine view of Lady Liberty from the shores of Battery Park, but planning ahead to take the ferry out to the island and visit the statue's interior rewards the effort. **This is the major New York site that you really do have to plan ahead for.** Please do understand that if you *don't* make advance reservations, you risk waiting up to an hour, or more, for room on the ferry. And you'll likely only get to visit the on-site museum, which is not as thrilling as seeing the view from the statue's pedestal or crown. Some 8,000 visitors get to enter the statue each day, but on many days, nearly 7,000 others show up and are turned away. So put down this book and make your reservation *now* for a date and time slot.

If it's available, book a visit to the **crown of the statue** (this can sell out weeks in advance). It's a thrilling, exhausting climb up a circular stairway, 146 steps to the crown of the statue. On the way up, you'll view the intricate metal work that French engineer Gustave Eiffel (of Eiffel Tower fame) created to anchor the statue; it acts like a spring, allowing the "skin" of the structure to adjust to different temperatures and sway up to 3 inches in 50-mph winds.

Those without monument tickets can still take a free ranger-led tour of the island, use the audio guide (also free), and visit the museum, which has a small but intriguing exhibit about the statue's history and the extraordinary engineering that went into creating it. Note that exhibits are not chronological: If one area is too crowded, move to the next and circle back when the crowds thin. You won't miss anything by doing so. The museum features a terrific film about Lady Liberty (try to stand in the center of the room to hear better), and the original torch, which was replaced in 1983 because its glass panels leaked, causing water damage to the statue. But the museum isn't reason itself to get off at Liberty Island. If your time is limited, the better option may be to simply stay on the ferry, which slows down as it nears the statue, giving those on board a good view of Lady Liberty in all of her surprisingly delicate beauty. Spend the time you'll save to go on to Ellis Island (p. 165), Liberty's sister monument, with no entrance quotas. I think Ellis is ultimately the more rewarding of the two . . . unless you can visit Lady Liberty's crown (which is really, really fun).

Warning: If you don't buy tickets in advance, the *only* place to buy them near the ferry is inside Castle Clinton (you'll see signs). A large number of tourists were scammed in 2026 by official-looking "vendors" selling tickets near the entrance to the ferry terminal. Don't buy from them!

Liberty Island, New York Harbor; ferry ticket booth at Castle Clinton in Battery Park. nps.gov/stli or statuecitycruises.com. ✆ **212/363-3200** (general info) or 877/523-9849 (ticket/ferry info). Free admission. Ferry ticket $26 adults, $23 seniors, $17 children 4–12; free for children 3 and under. Included in CityPass (p. 176). Ferries depart daily 9am–3:30pm (extended hours Memorial Day–Labor Day). Ferries also depart from Liberty State Park in New Jersey. Subway: 4, 5 to Bowling Green; 1 to South Ferry.

St. Paul's Chapel ♥ CHURCH/HISTORIC SITE Built in 1766, this is not only the oldest church in the city, it's the only public space in continuous use since the colonial era. The design of the church, with its Ionic columns and huge pediment, was based on St. Martin-in-the-Fields in London, though I think the overall effect of this church is not nearly as graceful. Still, St. Paul's is redolent with history: George Washington had a pew here (now marked by a plaque), and he came directly to the church after his inauguration at nearby Federal Hall (p. 277) to pray and give thanks. On 9/11, the church miraculously survived a rain of fiery metal when the Twin Towers collapsed, then served as a focal point for the volunteer effort that ensued, as hundreds of people came from all over the world to search for survivors and then human remains. Many slept at St. Paul's and took meals here (an onsite exhibit details this history).

209 Broadway (btw. Fulton and Vesey sts.). trinitywallstreet.org. Free admission. Daily 8:30am–6pm. Subway: A, C, 2, 3, 4, 5 to Fulton St.

Trinity Church ♥♥ CHURCH/HISTORIC SITE This is actually the third Trinity Church to stand on this site. The first version was destroyed in the fire set by fleeing colonists in 1776 to thwart British occupiers (the fire ended up

Intricate Gothic Revival details surround the altar at Trinity Church.

razing one-third of the structures in Manhattan). The second church building was poorly constructed, and its roof collapsed in a heavy snowstorm. But the third, consecrated in 1846, was a keeper and is considered by many to be one of the best, if not *the* best, Gothic Revival buildings in the United States. Designed by Richard Upjohn, the church building embodied in stone a theological movement that rocked the Anglican Church in the mid-1800s, harkening back to its Catholic roots with more elaborate decoration, ceremony, and hierarchy. So instead of creating a boxy, continuous space, like so many churches of the period (like nearby St. Paul's; see above), Upjohn used self-consciously medieval features to underscore the sacred nature of the space. Normally, in a Gothic cathedral, the chancel (the area behind the altar, reserved for the clergy and choir) is marked off by railings, but that idea was quite controversial in democratic New York, so Upjohn created a subtle solution, raising this area a few feet above the ground to give the feeling of an exalted place, without prominent barriers. Other Gothic features include lovely stained-glass windows, flying buttresses, and a towering 280-ft. spire, which was the tallest structure in the city until the stone towers supporting the Brooklyn Bridge were built. The doors, modeled after Ghiberti's famous bronze doors for the Baptistery of Florence, were designed by noted American architect Richard Morris Hunt (who also designed the base of the Statue of Liberty); the sculptures on them were done by Austrian immigrant Karl Bitter. You can see the latter's self-portrait in the knoblike head sticking out of the lower right-hand corner of the door; above him is Richard Upjohn and above that Richard Morris Hunt. Don't miss touring the graveyard, which holds the remains of many Revolutionary War–era New Yorkers. Among the notables are Captain James Lawrence, who uttered the famous command, "Don't give up the ship" in the War of 1812; he's buried in a tomb that looks like a ship, on the southern side of the church, surrounded by a fence made from captured British cannons. Behind Lawrence and to the right a bit is the most famous tomb here, that of Alexander Hamilton; beside Hamilton is the grave of steamboat designer Robert Fulton. Download the church's app for more info.

At Broadway and Wall St. trinitywallstreet.org. ✆ **212/602-0800.** Free admission. Daily 8:30am–6pm; graveyard until 4pm. Subway: 4, 5 to Wall St.

A MONEY- & TIME-SAVING tip

CityPass is New York's best sightseeing deal. Three versions are available, all of which can be useful, though you'll need to choose carefully between them, so you get enough oomph for your buy. Here are the details:

THE ORIGINAL: With this one, you pay one price ($154 or $129 for kids 6–17) for admission to five major attractions:

- The American Museum of Natural History (plus one ticketed special exhibition)
- The Empire State Building Observatory (admission to the 86th floor and the right to return after dark the same night for a second visit)
- And 3 more attractions (either the Top of the Rock Observation Deck, the ferry to Ellis Island and the Statue of Liberty, the 9/11 Memorial & Museum, a Circle Line sightseeing cruise, the USS Intrepid, or the Guggenheim Museum).

Individual tickets to all these sites combined would cost 42% more.

CITYPASS 3: This covers only three attractions and offers slightly less savings, but you have a wider choice, as all of the sites above are possibilities, plus the Museum of Modern Art and the Edge. Cost for this one is $109/adult and $86/child. With this one you could save about 41% over individual tickets for all of the attractions covered by the pass.

C-ALL: This one gives you access to all 10 attractions listed above, but since three are observation decks, I think this is the least useful of the passes, because of the repetitiveness of these experiences. But for the oddballs who were planning to knock off these 10 experiences in 9 days, using the pass will net a 42% savings.

Significantly, CityPass is not a coupon book: It contains actual tickets, so you can bypass lengthy lines (though advance reservations will also do that, and for some attractions you're required to make advance reservations, even with the pass). CityPass is good for 9 days from the first time you use it. It's sold at all participating attractions and online at **citypass.com/city/ny**. You can download and self-print the pass or you may buy the pass at your first attraction (start at an attraction that's likely to have a shorter admission line, such as the Guggenheim). If you begin your sightseeing on a weekend or during holidays, when lines are longest, online purchase (with online timed reservations) is the smarter way to go.

Wall Street and the New York Stock Exchange ♥ ICON Unfortunately, the NYSE is no longer open to the public for tours. But if you're in the vicinity, stop by for a look at this imposing structure, and the diminutive sculpture outside (for more on both, go to p. 266 for our walking tour of the Wall Street area). One odd fact about the Stock Exchange: Though it's associated in the popular imagination with Wall Street, its facade actually fronts Broad Street, not Wall.

11 Wall St. nyse.com. Subway: J, Z to Broad St.; 2, 3, 4, 5 to Wall St.

The Woolworth Building ♥ ICON This soaring "Cathedral of Commerce" cost Frank W. Woolworth $14 million worth of nickels and dimes in

1913. It was the tallest edifice in the city from 1913 until 1930, when it was surpassed by the Chrysler Building. (At its opening, President Woodrow Wilson pressed a button from the White House that illuminated the building's 80,000 electric light bulbs.) Called the "Mozart of skyscrapers" by architectural critic Paul Goldberger, the neo-Gothic architecture is festooned with spires, gargoyles, flying buttresses, vaulted ceilings, 16th-century-style stone-as-lace traceries, castlelike turrets, and a churchlike interior. Alas, you can only see it from the outside today.

233 Broadway (btw. Park Place and Barclay sts.). Subway: 2, 3 to Park Place; 4, 5, 6 to Brooklyn Bridge/City Hall; A, C to Chambers St.

Lower East Side

International Center of Photography ♥♥ MUSEUM Founded in 1974 by Cornell Capa, brother of eminent war photographer Robert Capa, the ICP has a definite grounding in photojournalism. So when you visit, you'll often see probing photography that investigates the current zeitgeist, whether that be societal challenges (like a recent show about labor organizing), recent conflicts, or retrospectives of the work of important shutterbugs. The museum has moved several times over the years, and is now in a handsome, multi-floor space right across the street from the fab Essex Street Market (p. 95).

84 Ludlow St. (btw. Broome and Delancey sts.). icp.org. ✆ **212/857-0000.** Admission $18 adults, $14 seniors/people with disabilities/military, $12 students; free for ages 14 and under. Wed–Mon 10:30am–6:30pm (Thurs until 8pm). Subway: F, J, M, Z to Essex St.

Provocative photography draws visitors to the International Center of Photography.

Museum at Eldridge Street ♥♥ SYNAGOGUE An 1887 synagogue, the oldest house of worship in the city for Eastern European Jews, the Museum at Eldridge Street has the kind of grandeur one normally associates with the cathedrals of Europe. There's a poignancy to the place as well, as the building was abandoned for 40 years before restoration began in the 1990s, and it's crumbling away picturesquely in places. You can do a self-guided tour, but a better idea is to visit at 11am, 1pm, 2pm, or 3pm for the "From Bottom to Top" tour, which covers the history of the synagogue and the issues involved in its restoration. Don't skip the superb videos, shown in a room next to the entrance, about all the work that went into the transformation of the synagogue.

12 Eldridge St. (btw. Canal and Division sts.). eldridgestreet.org. ✆ **212/219-0302.** Admission $15 adults, $10 seniors/students, $8 children 5–17; free for children 4 and under; pay-what-you-wish Mon and Fri. Sun–Fri 10am–5pm; closed all national and Jewish holidays. Multiple docent-led tours daily, plus self-guided tours. Subway: B, D to Grand St.; F to W. Broadway.

New Museum of Contemporary Art ♥ MUSEUM Perhaps the greatest sign of New York City's ever-increasing prosperity is the fact that now, even the gritty, grimy Bowery (birthplace of the term *bowery bums* for the unhoused people who used to swarm its cheap bars and bunk in its missions) has a museum. Opened to great fanfare in 2026, the museum is housed in a cutting edge, glamorous building by starchitects Rem Koolhaas, Cooper Robertson, and Shohei Shigematsu. As with much art of the moment, exhibits range from the sublime to the silly (I was stopped dead in my tracks at an exhibit by a cardboard box and a big plastic bag among all the sculptures—was it art or the container the art came in? I knew the answer intellectually, but my heart kept crying out: Recycle that bag and box and do something

AN art invasion ON THE LOWER EAST SIDE

In just the past few years, the Lower East Side has become a mecca for art galleries. Rising rents in Chelsea (p. 186) pushed a number of them into this neighborhood, but the transformation of the area from immigrant enclave to haven for the hip also played a role.

Because the neighborhood is not solely art-focused (like the gallery area of Chelsea), finding galleries can sometimes feel like a scavenger hunt. Not all of them are on street level—you'll often have to ascend steep staircases in (mostly) unmarked buildings, or head onto side streets that, at first glance, appear to be all bars and boutiques.

These galleries tend to represent up-and-comers rather than established art world names, so it can be difficult to pin down each one's aesthetic. I've picked the following galleries because they have a track record for shining a light on exciting new talents. *Take the B or D subway to Grand St.* to access all of these galleries except Tibor de Nagy (the *J or Z to Bowery* is best for that).

- **Hoffman Donohue Gallery,** 99 Bowery, 2nd floor (hoffmandonahue.com)
- **Shin Gallery,** 322 Grand St. (shin-gallery.com)
- **Sperone Westwater,** 257 Bowery (speronewestwater.com)
- **Marc Straus Gallery,** 299 Grand St. (marcstraus.com)
- **The Hole,** 312 Bowery (theholenyc.com)
- **Tibor de Nagy Gallery,** 11 Rivington St. (tibordenagy.com)

In addition to this list, go to the *New York Times* website for its monthly piece "What to See in NYC's Galleries Right Now," which calls out the more thought-provoking current shows, both on the Lower East Side and elsewhere in the city. You can also take a look at this online map for visit-worthy galleries in this neighborhood (despite the fact that the map title is "Henry Street): m23.co/henry-street-gallery-map.

The Museum at Eldridge Street preserves a grand synagogue, built in 1887 for a congregation of Eastern European Jews.

useful with them!). Wall text is hard to find, so buttonhole one of the gallery guides wearing big "ask me" buttons; sometimes their explanations will be more interesting than the art itself.

235 Bowery (at Prince St.). newmuseum.org. ✆ **212/219-1222.** Admission $25 adults, $19 seniors/people with disabilities/students; free for ages 18 and under; free admission Thurs 7pm until closing. Tues–Sun 11am–6pm (Thurs until 9pm). Subway: 6 to Spring St.; N, R to Prince St.

The Tenement Museum ♥♥♥ MUSEUM At first glance, this museum looks just like many brownstone buildings on this Lower East Side block . . . and that's exactly the point. The first-ever National Trust for Historic Preservation site that was *not* the home of someone rich or famous, the Tenement Museum's first building was preserved to tell the story of the immigrants who once lived within (97 Orchard St.). Those stories are rich and varied: This five-story tenement housed some 10,000 people from 25 countries between 1863 and 1935. A visit here makes an excellent follow-up to Ellis Island (p. 165). Most visits to the museum are by **hour-long guided tour** (2 tours are 75 min. long). Visitors have a choice of eight programs, each of which illuminates the lives of different sorts of tenants: from 19th-century garment workers who did piecework in their apartment, to a family that survived not one but two depressions, to the German family that ran a saloon in the

The Tenement Museum tells the story of New York City's immigrants through historically restored apartments, like this one where an Eastern European Jewish family of garment workers lived in 1911.

basement, to a Black family in the late 1800s who struggled to create a community in NYC. The "Meet Victoria" tour features an actor, in costume, playing a teenage Italian émigré (this is the one to pick if you're traveling with children). Set in 103 Orchard, the museum's second building, the "100 Years Apart" program is the least compelling of the bunch, contrasting the experiences of immigrant women who lived in these buildings in the 1880s and the 1980s. Most visitors will prefer learning about the area's earlier history in the original building, which is also a more evocative space. Tours aren't appropriate for children 7 and under, and some are only for those 12 and up; see the website for details. The museum also offers walking tours of the neighborhood (pair one with one of the programs above for a 40% discount) as well as culinary experiences, tours combined with "talk back" sessions, and rotating exhibits. Tours are limited in number and sell out quickly, so it's smart to buy tickets in advance, though that does incur a $2.50 online booking fee.

Reception area at 108 Orchard St. (btw. Delancey and Broome sts.). tenement.org. ✆ **212/431-0233.** Tours $30. Daily 10am–5pm. Subway: F to Delancey St.; J, M to Essex St.

TriBeCa, Chinatown & SoHo

Jackie Robinson Museum ♥ MUSEUM As much about the Civil Rights Movement as it is about baseball, this two-room museum takes a detailed, clear-eyed look at the life of a great American hero and his times. It does so with the use of well-produced videos, a smattering of artifacts, and a savvy timeline plastered to the walls that juxtaposes milestones in Robinson's life with important world events. However, for an attraction that will take most visitors about 45 minutes to see, the admission price feels steep.

75 Varick St. (at Canal St.). jackierobinsonmuseum.org. ✆ **866/288-5593.** $18 adults, $15 seniors/students/children ages 5–17; free for children 4 and under. Thurs–Sun 11am–6pm. Subway: 1 to Canal St.

Leslie-Lohman Museum ♥ ART MUSEUM The first LGBTQ+ art museum in the world—and now the largest—was born from the collections of Charles W. Leslie and Fritz Lohman, pioneers who started collecting and exhibiting this genre in 1969. Along the way, they acquired genuine masterworks by such big names as David Hockney, Keith Haring, and Jean Cocteau. Much of the art by less well-known artists is as accomplished, and it is all accompanied by wall text that gives real insight into the lives of the artists and the issues they were illuminating. ***Note:*** Some of the material is highly erotic, which may make some viewers uncomfortable.

26 Wooster St. (btw. Grand and Broome sts.). leslielohman.org. ✆ **212/431-2609.** Suggested donation $10. Wed noon–5pm; Thurs–Sun noon–6pm. Subway: A, C, E, N, Q, R, 1, 6 to Canal St.

Merchant's House Museum ♥♥ MUSEUM New York City has never been very good at preserving its past (perhaps we have too little room . . . or patience), but on East 4th Street this precious sliver of history has survived utterly intact. In fact, this is the *only* Victorian-era structure in New York City

The elegant formal parlor at the Merchant's House Museum, a window into a bygone era of New York City life.

preserved both inside and out. A handsome Greek Revival town house, it was once the home of the Tredwell family, who furnished it in the highest style of the day, all silk upholstered couches, bronze gas chandeliers, and deep burgundy curtains. These furnishings, the clothing of the 10-person family, their cookware, and anything else you might want to see are all on display, thanks to the efforts in 1936 of a preservationist (before there really was such a thing) named George Chapman. A lovely garden and frequent ghost sightings add to the home's appeal. In 2026, it was discovered that this home was a "safe house," on the Underground Railroad and used to shelter enslaved people who were on the run. Just how the hidden crawl space will be displayed to visitors was being discussed as we went to press.

29 E. 4th St. (btw. Lafayette and Bowery). merchantshouse.org. ✆ **212/777-1089.** Admission $15.50 adults, $10.50 seniors/students; free for children ages 11 and under. Wed–Sun noon–5pm; guided tours at noon ($5 extra). Subway: 6 to Astor Place; N, R to 8th St.; F, B to Broadway/Lafayette.

Museum of Chinese in America ♥♥ MUSEUM The story of the Chinese immigrant experience in the U.S. is very different from that of most other ethnic group that came here. These Chinese Americans, like the African Americans who brought here as slaves, experienced governmentally mandated racism that shaped their lives in cruel ways. At the museum, you'll learn about the limited work they were allowed to do and the "Chinese Exclusion Act," a federal law barring further Chinese immigration that separated countless families. The tales of what they endured give this small museum true power. Maya Lin, famed for the Vietnam Veteran's Memorial in Washington, D.C., was the museum's original designer.

215 Centre St. mocanyc.org. ✆ **212/619-4785.** Admission $10, $5 seniors/students/visitors with disabilities; free for children 11 and under. Wed–Sat 11am–6pm, Sun 11am–4pm. Subway: 6, N, R, Q, J, M to Canal St.

Old St. Patrick's Cathedral ♥♥ TOUR Funnily enough, though the tour of this church is called "Catacombs by Candlelight," the catacombs aren't the highlight of this sweep through the Old St. Patrick's Cathedral. What makes this experience so absorbing is how the talented, humorous guides retell the history of the city—and country—through the lens of Catholic immigration. Visitors are on the move while this happens. Over the course of the tour, you'll roam through a historic graveyard, into the church sanctuary, into side rooms of the structure, and yes, into the dimly lit burial place below what had been the city's first cathedral.

263 Mulberry St. (near Prince St.). takeawalk.com. No phone. Tour $38 adults, $32 seniors/veterans/children 11 and under. Thurs–Mon 10am–4pm. Subway: 3 to Spring St.; N to Prince St.

Greenwich Village/Meatpacking District

Stonewall National Monument ♥♥ HISTORY MUSEUM While the fight for LGBTQ+ rights didn't begin here, it was kicked into high gear when police raided the Stonewall Inn, a gay bar, in 1969 (more of the story on p. 297). Statues of gay and lesbian couples, plus some wall text, mark that event in a pocket park across from the bar. Nearby, a one-room visitor center presents videos, artifacts, and text about the ongoing struggle for civil rights. Alas, the Trump administration has decided to rewrite history, removing any mention of transgender people from the site, despite the fact that one of the major figures of the Stonewall riots, and subsequent LGBTQ+ battles, was a trans woman named Martha P. Johnson. She was so important that she has a park named for her in Brooklyn. We are worried that other changes could be coming to try and neuter the powerful story being told here.

At 53 Christopher Street and in the park across the way, near Seventh Ave. nps.gov/ston. Free entry. Visitor center Tues–Sun 10am–4pm. Subway: 1 to Christoper St./ Stonewall.

Whitney Museum of American Art ♥♥♥ ART MUSEUM The canon of American art is celebrated, and, in some ways, was *created* by the Whitney Museum. It was Whitney curators, after all, and Whitney founder Gertrude Vanderbilt Whitney, who championed such now-iconic artists as Edward Hopper, Georgia O'Keeffe, Alexander Calder, and Jasper Johns at the start of their careers, collecting many of their most important works. In most cities that would be enough, but the Whitney's crew has greater ambitions—ambitions that have been turned into smooth concrete, steel, and glass in Manhattan's hippest neighborhood, the Meatpacking District. A little over a decade ago, the new Renzo Piano–designed home for the Whitney opened right next to the High Line park (p. 257), and it is, in many ways, reshaping the idea of what this institution, and art museums in general, can and should be.

And what they should be is flexible. "We have no idea what artists will be doing [this year], let alone later than that," Dana Miller, former chief curator of the permanent collection, told me. "So we wanted spaces that could be reshaped in dozens of ways." What that means is a building that's not a looker

Abstract art from the Whitney Museum's permanent collection.

(I think) but that allows artists to be as creative as they want: Floors can be drilled into, all interior walls are moveable, and every inch of the place is wired, which should make installing electronic art a snap. For visitors, this means they will have a wildly different museum experience each time they come: Not only will the art change, but the environment will cocoon them in different ways. I use the word *cocoon* quite deliberately, because this is one of the few museums that takes into account the comfort of its patrons. Many rooms are flooded with natural light and the floors are sprung on "sleepers," so there's no foot fatigue, even after hours of standing and looking at art. (And there are few neighborhoods more fun to explore, before or after a visit, than the Meatpacking District.) Most importantly, the Whitney's home is 60% larger than its old Upper East Side digs, allowing the best-known pieces from its epochal permanent collection—Calder's *Circus* (along with a video of the artist moving all the little figures), bleak beauts by Hopper, blossoms by O'Keeffe, and more—to be always on display on the fifth and sixth floors (go there first if you have limited time). The museum now has more room for its famed **Biennial,** a show that displays the most important American art of the previous 2 years and often shapes perceptions of what contemporary art should be.

99 Gansevoort St. whitney.org. ✆ **212/570-3600.** Admission $30 adults, $24 seniors/students; free for visitors 25 and under; free Fri 5pm until closing, and second Sun each month. Wed–Mon 10:30am–6pm (Fri until 10pm). Subway: A, C, E to 14th St.; L to Eighth Ave.

Chelsea

Artechouse ♥ GALLERY/SHOW Immersive digital art pieces by contemporary artists are mounted here, with a new show every 3 months or so, held in the 6,000-sq.-ft. former boiler room of Chelsea Market (p. 118). Shows range from thought-provoking works to ones that are inscrutable and dizzying (the movement of the images makes some viewers queasy). Since you never know what the quality of the current show will be, budget a bit to hit the bar—it might improve the experience.

439 W. 15th St. (btw. Ninth and Tenth aves.). artechouse.com. No phone. Admission $26.50 adults, $21 seniors/students/active military, $18 ages 4–15; free for ages 3 and under. Sun–Thurs noon–7pm; Fri noon–8pm; Sat 10am–10pm. Subway: A, E, C, L to 14th St.

The Museum at FIT ♥♥ MUSEUM You don't have to be a fashionista to appreciate NYC's premier design school's museum. Yes, you'll see a lot of clothing but exhibits here tend to explore cultural history through the lens of fashion, looking at such topics as how denim went from factory wear to club gear; the history of uniforms; or how Black designers reshaped stereotypes. A visit should take less than an hour.

Seventh Ave. at 27th St. fitnyc.edu/museum. ✆ **212/247-4558.** Free admission. Wed–Fri noon–8pm; Sat–Sun 10am–5pm. Subway: 1, N, R to 28th St.; A, C, E, F, M to 23rd St.

Flatiron District

Flatiron Building ♥♥ ARCHITECTURE You'll probably know the Flatiron Building even before you see it, thanks to the famous photos by Alfred Stieglitz, who snapped it numerous times, calling the Fuller Building

Overlooking Madison Square, the iconic Flatiron Building (to the right of the clock) lends its name to this neighborhood around 23rd Street and Broadway.

CHELSEA CALLING: MEET NYC'S art district

More than 250 galleries are on the blocks spanning 19th to 29th streets between Tenth and Eleventh avenues in West Chelsea, effectively making the Big Apple the planet's premier marketplace for contemporary art. Gallery after gallery has taken over the former warehouses and industrial spaces of this dusty old 'hood, creating an eminently walkable arts district. You can have a perfectly lovely time simply getting lost in the area and wandering blindly from one space to the next, although you might hit a lot of clunky exhibitions (as with any collection of new art, some are better than others)—but so what? If you want to take this course of action, start on 24th Street, which has the largest assortment of "name" galleries. A better tactic might be to catch a tour of the area (see below) or to concentrate on the eight galleries listed here, which offer consistently thought-provoking shows. Your best subway option is either the C or E line to 23rd Street.

Note: Chelsea galleries are generally open Tuesday to Saturday 10am to 6pm (June–Aug closed on Sat). On Thursday evenings, and sometimes Wednesdays and Tuesdays, galleries have opening parties, complete with open bar, that are open to the public. To find out if one of these fetes is happening during your trip—they're a lot of fun—follow **@thirstygallerina** on Instagram.

Another note: Because of rising rents in Chelsea, a number of excellent galleries have moved in the last few years to the Lower East Side (p. 178), Tribeca, and Williamsburg, Brooklyn.

303 Gallery 555 W. 21st St. (303gallery.com; ✆ **212/255-1121**). The Whitney biennial has this gallery on speed dial, having picked up works by several of the young to mid-career cutting-edge photographers and painters who present here.

Barbara Gladstone Gallery 515 W. 24th St. and 530 W. 21st St. (gladstonegallery.com; ✆ **212/206-9300** or 212/206-7605). Come here to see artists who have emerged as honchos in the last 2 decades or so, such as Matthew Barney and Richard Prince. Gladstone features conceptual, often highly political art—most prominently photography and videos, but also sculpture and paintings. The gallery now has other showrooms at 130 E. 64th St. and in Brussels, Los Angeles, and Seoul.

David Zwirner 519, 525 & 533 W. 19th St. and 537 W. 20th St. (davidzwirner.com; ✆ **212/727-7020**). This is not the place for people with delicate sensibilities, but if you don't mind seeing art that's really on the edge, you'll often find something that will get your adrenaline pumping. A *New York Times* profile praised Zwirner's "idiosyncratic roster, with great oddballs like R. Crumb and

(its original name) "a picture of new America still in the making." Many consider it the first skyscraper in New York; it certainly was one of the first to use a steel frame, the classic skyscraper structure. Its unusual triangular shape was architect Daniel Burnham's solution to a space problem: The building rests on the bow-tie intersection where Broadway and Fifth Avenue cross each other. In order to produce a decent amount of rentable space, he built it to a towering 375 ft. on every sliver of land available to him. The front tip is just 6 ft. across at its narrowest point. When it was first erected in 1902, crowds used to gather

Raymond Pettibon alongside institutional darlings like Stan Douglas and Francis Alÿs." Also at 34 E. 69th St. and 52 Walker St.

Gagosian 541 & 555 W. 24th St. and 522 W. 21st St. (gagosian.com; ✆ **212/741-1111**). A massive, important family of galleries (with another three uptown, one in California, one in Hong Kong, several in Europe), Gagosian presents blockbuster shows of such major 20th- and 21st-century figures as Nam June Paik, Gerhard Richter, Takashi Murakami, and Nan Goldin.

Lisson Gallery 504 and 508 W. 24th St. (lissongallery.com; ✆ **212/404-0370**). Founded in London, Lisson shows cutting-edge international art, with a particularly strong roster of Asian and Indian subcontinent artists including Ai Weiwei, Tatsuo Miyajima, and Anish Kapoor. Other spaces in Asia and Europe.

Pace Gallery 510 & 540 W. 25th St. (pacegallery.com; ✆ **212/929-7000**). Another "Blue Chip" gallery, with two outposts in Chelsea, as well as ones in Europe, Asia, California, and Florida, Pace has been a powerhouse since the 1960s. Musician David Byrne's artwork was featured in 2026, as were pieces by filmmaker David Lynch, Gideon Appah, Wang Guangle, and Kiki Smith.

Paula Cooper 521, 529 & 534 W. 21st St. (paulacoopergallery.com; ✆ **212/255-1105**). Cooper opened her first gallery in the late 1960s and was instrumental in the careers of many major conceptual and minimalist artists. Today her galleries regularly show the works of such titans as Mark di Suvero, Claes Oldenburg, Sol LeWitt, Walid Raad, and Donald Judd.

Yossi Milo 245 Tenth Ave. (yossimilo gallery.com; ✆ **212/404-0370**). One of my personal favorites, Milo works almost exclusively with photographers and has a terrific eye for the next big thing. He also runs a very friendly gallery—he and his staff are always happy to talk with interested patrons. Because he represents photographers, some of them selling multiple editions of their work, you just may be able to afford to buy something here.

A gallery tour: New York's foremost expert in the Chelsea Gallery scene—he visits 50 to 70 shows a week just to keep current—is Raphael Risemburg of **NY Gallery Tours** ♥ (nygallerytours.com; ✆ **212/946-1548**). Risemburg, a former professor at Keane College in New Jersey, has a droll, friendly manner and leads his tours in Socratic fashion: He'll tell you what he thinks of the art and then asks your opinion on the unanswered questions it poses. His open tours, which cover four to five galleries, are offered almost every Saturday ($31); he also leads private tours for $195 to $300 depending on group size.

in Madison Square Park across the street to wait for it to fall down! Later men were drawn here by the urban myth that the building's shape caused strange wind patterns that were effective in lifting up women's skirts. The cops who dispersed these groups of gaping men on 23rd Street would call out "23 skidoo!" and so a slang term was born. (It means, roughly, "So long, sucker.") One of the most beloved buildings in the city, it has been compared to a mighty ship sailing up Fifth Avenue.

175 Fifth Ave. (at 23rd St.). Subway: N, R to 23rd St.

MIDTOWN

Hudson Yards

At 28 acres, Hudson Yards is the largest private real estate development in American history. Amazingly, it was built in the most crowded city in the United States without displacing a single resident. That's because the area it occupies, from 30th Street to 35th Street, and Tenth Avenue to the river, covers the rail yards that extend from Penn Station (p. 382). An extraordinary feat of engineering created a platform above some 30 active railway tracks, with the massive skyscrapers of Hudson Yards resting partially on that platform, partially on caissons drilled down into Manhattan's bedrock. The platform is wired with communication cables; rainwater collected on building rooftops is filtered for on-site irrigation and drinking needs; cooling units in the platform make sure the heat of the train yards doesn't affect the 28,000 trees, grasses, wildflowers, and other plants in the development's park areas.

But for all these state-of-the-art innovations, this is one of the most unpopular projects in recent New York memory. Many locals compare it unfavorably with Rockefeller Center (p. 197), the city's last large-scale development, a place of unparalleled architectural harmony and symmetry. Unlike that project, which had a team of architects and designers working in tandem, Hudson Yards is simply a cluster of unrelated skyscrapers, created by half a dozen different architectural firms. The often-sneaky use of public funds to underwrite this private luxury development has also been galling to many New Yorkers.

The centerpiece of the Hudson Yards development is a massive statue known as Vessel, laced with staircases and walkways for visitors to roam inside.

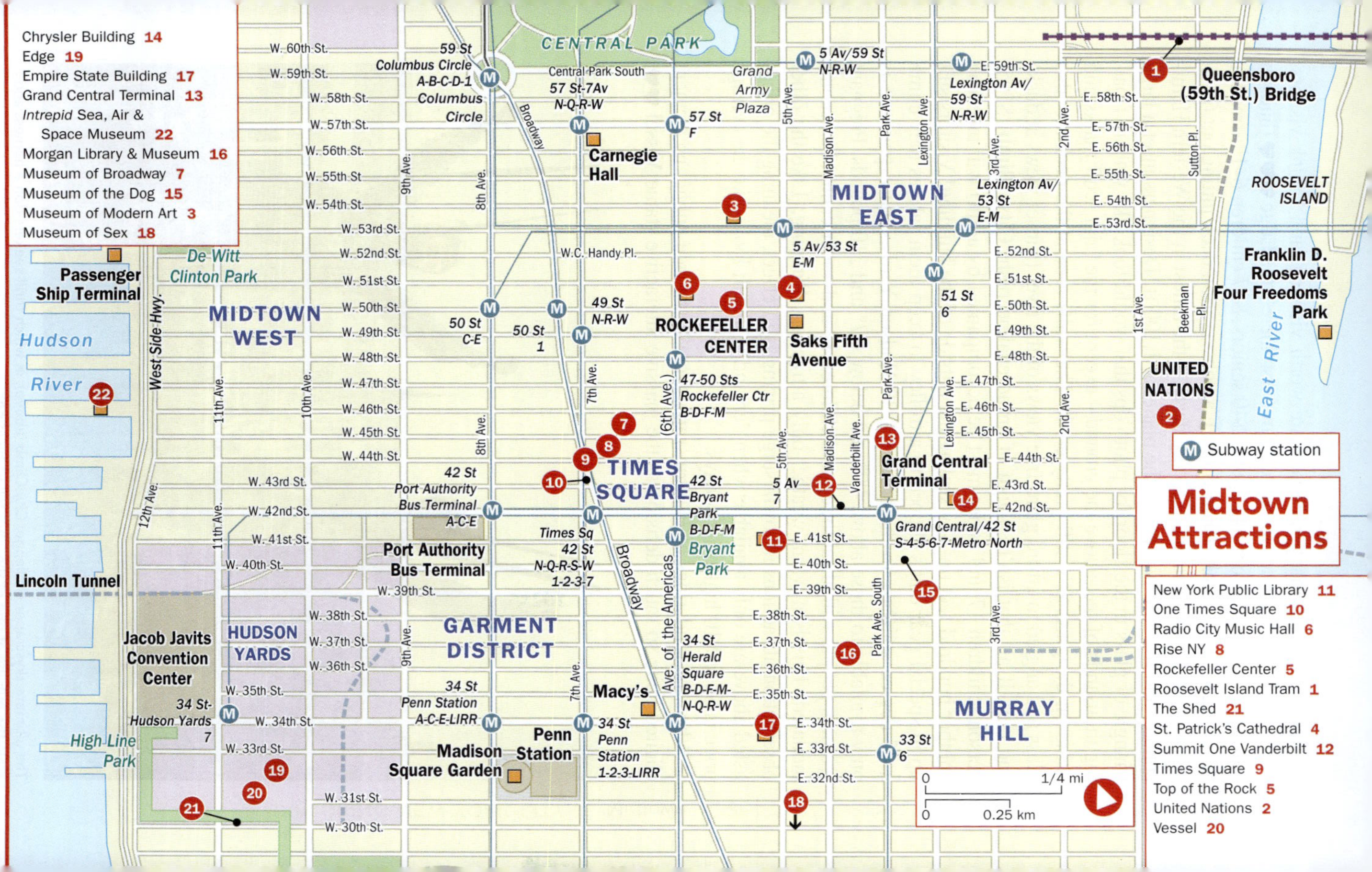
Midtown Attractions
Chrysler Building 14
Edge 19
Empire State Building 17
Grand Central Terminal 13
Intrepid Sea, Air & Space Museum 22
Morgan Library & Museum 16
Museum of Broadway 7
Museum of the Dog 15
Museum of Modern Art 3
Museum of Sex 18
New York Public Library 11
One Times Square 10
Radio City Music Hall 6
Rise NY 8
Rockefeller Center 5
Roosevelt Island Tram 1
The Shed 21
St. Patrick's Cathedral 4
Summit One Vanderbilt 12
Times Square 9
Top of the Rock 5
United Nations 2
Vessel 20
Subway station
0 1/4 mi
0 0.25 km
CENTRAL PARK
MIDTOWN EAST
MIDTOWN WEST
TIMES SQUARE
ROCKEFELLER CENTER
GARMENT DISTRICT
HUDSON YARDS
MURRAY HILL
ROOSEVELT ISLAND
UNITED NATIONS
Queensboro (59th St.) Bridge
Franklin D. Roosevelt Four Freedoms Park
Carnegie Hall
Saks Fifth Avenue
Grand Central Terminal
Bryant Park
Macy's
Penn Station
Madison Square Garden
Port Authority Bus Terminal
Jacob Javits Convention Center
Passenger Ship Terminal
De Witt Clinton Park
High Line Park
Lincoln Tunnel
Grand Army Plaza
Hudson River
East River
Broadway
West Side Hwy.
Ave. of the Americas
W.C. Handy Pl.
Central Park South
59 St Columbus Circle A-B-C-D-1
57 St-7Av N-Q-R-W
57 St F
5 Av/59 St N-R-W
Lexington Av/59 St N-R-W
Lexington Av/53 St E-M
5 Av/53 St E-M
51 St 6
50 St C-E
50 St 1
49 St N-R-W
47-50 Sts Rockefeller Ctr B-D-F-M
42 St Port Authority Bus Terminal A-C-E
Times Sq 42 St N-Q-R-S-W 1-2-3-7
42 St Bryant Park B-D-F-M
5 Av 7
Grand Central/42 St S-4-5-6-7-Metro North
34 St Herald Square B-D-F-M-N-Q-R-W
34 St Penn Station 1-2-3-LIRR
34 St Penn Station A-C-E-LIRR
34 St-Hudson Yards 7
33 St 6

That being said, many sites here are worth viewing, and I think visitors, especially, will find much to excite them. First, there's the **Edge** ♥♥♥ (hudsonyardsnewyork.com; from $44 adults, $40 seniors, $37 children 6–12; free for those 5 and under; daily 10am–10pm), an observation deck jutting out 65 ft. from its skyscraper, making it a "sky deck"—the tallest in the Western Hemisphere, and the fifth highest on the planet at 1,100 ft. Designers inset a large triangle of glass in the floor for photo ops that would look like you are floating thousands of feet above the ground—except for the faint scuff marks and shine on the glass (it's still pretty cool). The walls around the deck are also glass and angled to afford glare-free views of the river (sunset views at dusk) and city. If all that isn't enough of an adrenaline rush, **City Climb** ($195/person; children 17 and under must be accompanied by adult) will take you another hundred feet up—by scaling the outside of the building! Visitors suit up in special gear that's clipped to a trolley to keep them safe as they climb a 45-degree staircase to the crown of 30 Hudson Yards. The experience is only available to those above 4'9" and below 6'7" and 310 pounds. Pregnant women, people with disabilities, and children 12 and under cannot be accommodated. This is a warm-weather-only attraction. ***Warning:*** Like the other observation attractions in town, surge pricing is in effect, meaning the prices listed above are only available when demand is low. It looks like the average price is $8 to $10 higher most days.

When the renderings of Hudson Yards were first made public, no element elicited quite so much derision as the massive interactive statue **Vessel** ♥♥.

The ultimate skyscraper challenge: City Climb (above), in which thrill-seekers don a harness and scale the outside of one of the city's tallest buildings.

getting high: WHICH OBSERVATION DECK TO CHOOSE

With so many observation decks debuting in the last decade or so, choosing the right one has become complicated yet essential—they're pricey, and it's an experience you want just once per trip. Here's a quick look at the contenders, in order of preference.

1. **Empire State Building:** Our top choice. Not only does it have the highest observation deck in the city, but it does a bang-up job of teaching visitors *why* this building holds a revered place in the city's history. See p. 203.
2. **Summit One Vanderbilt:** For shutterbugs, this observation deck reigns supreme, thanks to its wacky all-mirrored interior (making it easy to take truly artful photographs), its clear-floored jutting balconies, and its floating orb room. See p. 210.
3. **Edge and Climb:** The pick for adrenaline junkies, this Hudson Yards deck not only has a pane of clear glass in its center, allowing visitors to look down into a dizzying vortex, but true adventurers can opt to scale the building's exterior, the world's highest skyscraper climb. See p. 188.
4. **One Times Square:** The newest of the decks, it is the best to visit at night, thanks to its position in the very heart of Times Square and all its blazing, dancing lights. See p. 195.
5. **Top of the Rock:** A classic, with the best views of Central Park, though it now feels overcrowded thanks to the addition of silly amusement park rides that take up valuable viewing space. See p. 199.
6. **One World Observatory:** Our last-place pick, thanks to its lack of an outdoor area (it's thrilling to feel the wind whipping around you that high) and its location at the tip of Manhattan, rather than in the heart of the action. See p. 169.

One big warning: The city's observation decks now all engage in dynamic pricing, which means prices soar at sunset, early in the morning when other attractions have yet to open, and during the more popular visitation periods. To save a bit, go after sunset (fewer crowds then, too, except at One Times Square), and avoid all the needless extras they push, like VIP entry. They're just money grabs.

Rockefeller Center's Top of the Rock observation deck.

Designed by Thomas Heatherwick, the open tower of copper-colored stainless steel is shaped like either a basket, a pineapple, or shawarma (depending on your Freudian disposition), with 154 sets of stairs interlinking in a complex fashion to 80 platforms. I was ready to dislike it, too, but it takes on a certain kooky majesty in person. Climbing this folly now costs $10 and involves going through airport-like security (sadly there have been several suicides here). But the views, and the experience, warrant the outlay. You can get advance reservations, but you don't really need them as there's never a long wait to get in.

Other draws include the **Shops at Hudson Yards** mall (p. 302) and the audacious arts complex **The Shed** ♥♥ (p. 344), set on massive wheels that can be "nested" into the tower behind it, creating an open-air pavilion for outdoor performances. Its exterior is covered with what looks like a giant silver puffy coat (like a ski parka). Inside is a maze of spaces—some with redwood-tree-height ceilings, others a bit more intimate—but all easily reconfigured for different uses, from art exhibits to performances, meaning The Shed will wear a different face each time you visit.

Hudson Yards. hudsonyardsnewyork.com. Subway: 7 to 34th St./Hudson Yards.

Times Square/Midtown West

Intrepid Sea, Air & Space Museum ♥♥♥ MUSEUM/HISTORIC SITE How's this for an all-star lineup? Not only does the Intrepid Sea, Air & Space Museum display the space shuttle *Enterprise,* it's got the world's only tourable nuclear submarine, the famed Concorde jet, nearly two dozen grounded

Jets are parked on the deck of the retired aircraft carrier *Intrepid,* which is also packed with subs and spacecraft and all manner of military hardware.

jets, a Revolutionary War–era submarine, and is itself a World War II–era aircraft carrier. Whew! Even those who profess no interest in aviation or military history will find themselves wowed by the breadth and depth of this collection. You'll likely have to devote a good 3 hours or more to get your fill here, so arrive early.

You'll want to begin your visit at the **USS *Growler*** submarine, built in 1958 and so narrow that only small groups can enter at a time (which keeps the lines here long). You'll be taken on a brief, thrillingly claustrophobic tour introduced by a terrific exhibition center, with videos and text about life onboard. Children 5 and under are not admitted. Next, make your way to the **Concorde,** the oversize luxury lawn dart that, after flying half-empty for a number of years, was finally taken out of commission in 2003. (The jet isn't in the classic bent-nosed pose; that was only used for take-offs and landings.) This ultra-deluxe flying bus carried a mere 100 passengers at a time, most of them paying $6,000 each way for the privilege of crossing the Atlantic faster than the speed of sound (it went from 0–165 mph in just 2½ seconds). Take a close look at places A and B, the seats reserved for Queen Elizabeth II and Prince Philip of England.

Visiting the pavilion of the **space shuttle *Enterprise*** is another highlight, thanks to its terrific exhibit exploring what day-to-day life on a space shuttle is like. Then turn your attention to the ***Fighting I,*** the main focus of your visit, a 40,000-ton aircraft carrier that had one of the greatest survival stories of World War II. Though it was hit by five kamikaze planes (two of them in a single day) during its tours of duty, it continued to serve (the Japanese called it "The Ghost Ship" because it couldn't be sunk). Go directly to the Information Center on the hangar deck to inquire if there's a tour starting anytime soon. ***Tip:*** If you've visited before, start your visit with the Intrepid's newest exhibit (added in late 2024): a rare World War II FG-1D fighter-bomber. It is surrounded by artifacts and interactive displays explaining its importance.

You can wander through the ship on your own, but you'll get more out of the experience with the hour-long guided tour, led by highly informed docents, most with military backgrounds.

Pier 86 (W. 46th St. at Twelfth Ave.). intrepidmuseum.org. ✆ **877/957-7447** or 212/245-0072. Admission $38 adults, $36 seniors/students, $28 ages 5–12; free for active or retired military and children 4 and under. Various combo tickets add extras like space shuttle or simulator rides. Free entry 1 Fri evening each month (check website for dates). Daily 10am–5pm (Apr 1–Sept 30 Sat & Sun until 6pm). Closed Thanksgiving and Christmas Subway: A, C, E to 42nd St./Port Authority. Bus: M42 Crosstown.

Museum of Broadway ♥♥ MUSEUM When a Broadway show needs new cast members, it puts an ad in *Playbill,* the long-running theater industry publication. The Museum of Broadway does the same when it's looking for gallery guards, and these eager, knowledgeable theater geeks (most are would-be actors) are the heart and soul of this museum. I found myself turning to them in many of the galleries and being treated to wonderful, often dramatic, tales about the exhibits and the shows they highlighted. Which was a

Among the many ready-made Instagram backgrounds at the Museum of Broadway: this groovy exhibit on the musical *Hair*.

blessing, because the wall text at MOB can be intimidating, with panel after panel of often encyclopedically dense theater history, starting in the 18th century and weaving through minstrel shows, vaudeville, classic musicals, kitchen-sink dramas, and juke box musicals to the Broadway of today. The curators have smartly devoted entire rooms to genre-shifting shows like *Oklahoma* (it has a wonderful video of Agnes de Mille describing how she created the dream ballet), *West Side Story* (with Tony's jacket from the original run), *Rent,* and others. Along the way are Instagram moments where visitors can pose in "environments" from their favorite shows, plus cute interactive pieces (like an oversized jigsaw puzzle devoted to composer Stephen Sondheim), lots of artifacts, and spellbinding videos of famed set designers, directors, composers, playwrights, and other theater pros discussing the evolution of their famous shows. The bottom floor is devoted to the intricacies of how Broadway shows come to life, with videos about the art of lighting, wig making, lyric writing, stage managing, and more. Most visitors will need about 2 hours to see it all, but real theater fanatics could linger for double that amount of time.

145 W. 45th St. (btw. Sixth and Seventh aves.). themuseumofbroadway.com. ✆ **212/239-6200.** Admission $39 adults, $34 seniors, $31 students and ages 14 and under; $5 service fee for online bookings. Mon–Wed 9:30am–4pm; Thurs–Sun 9:30am–6:30pm. Subway: B, D, F, M to 47th–50th sts./Rockefeller Center; 1, 2, 3, N, Q, R, W, S to Times Square.

Museum of Modern Art ♥♥♥ ART MUSEUM MoMA, as it's nicknamed, doesn't want for masterpieces. This is where you'll find seminal works by Picasso, van Gogh, Brancusi, Dalí, and Matisse, among others. But which ones you find here is often in flux: It's the museum's policy to rehang works throughout the museum every several months, so that the visitor experience is constantly shifting, based on the way different pieces interact with one another. It may also mean some favorites are taken out of rotation (in 2019, there was a hubbub when Andrew Wyeth's famed ***Christina's Word*** was put in storage for several months). The **Abby Aldrich Rockefeller Sculpture Garden,** one of the city's most delightful spots to linger, tends to change less often.

Though there are many masterworks in the museum, be sure you give yourself enough time for the following highlights, which are always on view:

- Vincent van Gogh's ***Starry Night,*** which has a vivid impact when viewed in person, the thickness of the brush strokes making it as much sculpture as painting. Created a year before his suicide, when van Gogh was in an insane asylum, the painting is filled with premonitions of what was to come, the foreground taken up with a soaring cypress tree, symbol of death.
- Pablo Picasso's ***Desmoiselles d'Avignon,*** a massive brothel scene in which Picasso experimented with a number of art styles—look closely and you'll see that one of the women's heads looks like an African mask, another profile is taken from Egyptian art, the woman in the middle assumes a classical Venus-like pose, and a leg of one of the figures devolves into cubist abstraction. Reportedly, Picasso painted the work when he was suffering from syphilis, which may be why the women appear so threatening.
- Salvador Dalí's ***Persistence of Memory,*** in which watches melt and a long-nosed figure (some say it was a self-portrait of Dalí; others think it represents an unborn baby) lies prostrate on the ground. You may be surprised at how small this seminal work is.

Soaring sculptures by Brancusi, vibrantly colorful masterpieces by Matisse, Jackson Pollock's splatter art, and painted metaphors by Magritte are among the other wonders of the museum's collection, the most important in the world for art of this era.

Note: MoMA has a museum-wide Wi-Fi network so that visitors can access audio tours and commentary on their wireless devices; this includes specialized versions for children, teens, and the visually impaired.

11 W. 53rd St. (btw. Fifth and Sixth aves.). moma.org. ✆ **212/708-9400.** Admission $30 adults, $22 seniors/people with disabilities, $17 students; free for ages 16 and under if accompanied by adult. Daily 10:30am–5:30pm (Fri until 8:30pm). Subway: E, M to Fifth Ave.; B, D, F to 47th–50th sts./Rockefeller Center.

One Times Square ♥♥ OBSERVATION DECK NYC's newest observation deck (it debuted in 2026) has a lot of bells and whistles to try to distinguish it from the city's other aeries. First and foremost: its location above the buzzing, bustling heart of Times Square, a spectacular vista, especially after dark. One Times Square's free app explains the background of the surrounding buildings, even surfacing decades old photos for a now-and-then view. Visitors can pair this 360-degree observation deck either with a trio of

The atrium just past the main entrance of the Museum of Modern Art is often home to massive, temporary exhibitions.

multimedia presentations about the history and culture of this iconic square; or with an up-close visit to the Waterbury Crystal-laden ball that drops every New Year's Eve at midnight from the top of this tower. Big spenders can even take home one of the crystals, replacing it with a crystal that is programmed to send out a morse code of their wish for the coming year, on New Years Eve. (No, I'm not kidding—there are 5,280 crystals, and they'll do this swap until they're sold out of crystals.) Those who choose the ball experience will also visit a large hall hung with balls from decades past, including a replica of the darlingly dorky original ball which was striped with lightbulbs. Final, and oddest attraction here: **Eye Candy NY,** which is a trick or treating activity for families—and possibly high adults—during which visitors traipse through four floors of cartoony, rainbow-colored versions of New York venues (the Central Park Zoo, Chinatown, even a NYC jail, to name a few) gathering candy of all kinds from each area in a jar big enough for 2 pounds of sweets, which they can then take home. It's either a brilliant way to entertain the wee ones—or the prelude to the biggest, sugar-rush-induced crash out ever.

1 Times Square (entrance on 42nd St.). onetimessquare.com. Daily 10am–10pm (most seasons). Starting at $30, but prices vary by season, hour, and add ons. Subway: 1, 2, 3, N, Q, R, S, 7 to Times Square.

Rise NY ♥ ATTRACTION An amusement park with the soul of a museum, Rise NY's marquee attraction is a ride that makes you feel like you're swooping over the city. It takes place in a 40-ft.-tall dome with 180-degree views of well-executed 3D videos, plus a soundtrack of every damn song ever written about the city. Think: Disneyland's California Adventure . . . but on the other coast. Since the ride only lasts about 5 minutes, Rise NY also includes a faux subway ride that barrels through time and space, from the debut of the subway up to, well, Pizza Rat. There are also a dozen galleries which look at the many, many items invented in New York—the Singer sewing machine, the Otis elevator, the Broadway musical, hip hop—and how they made the city central to the industries they spawned. Most guests seemed to be dashing through the exhibits to get to the rides when I was there, but those who linger will actually learn something—and that's an unusual occurrence this near to Times Square. ***Three tips:*** Don't pay extra for VIP access, as long lines are rare; buy tickets on site to avoid the online fee; and don't go if your child is shorter than 40" as they won't be allowed on the marquee ride here.

160 W. 45th St. (off Seventh Ave). riseny.co. No phone. Admission $45 adults, $42 ages 3–12; free for children 2 and under. Sun–Thurs 10am–6pm; Fri–Sat 10am–8pm. Subway: 1, 2, 3, N, Q, R, S to Times Square.

Rockefeller Center ♥♥ ARCHITECTURE Gotham's splendid "city within a city" was built in the 1930s at the height of the Depression. Thanks to the jobs it gave construction workers, it was the city's second-largest employer at the time, surpassed only by the federal Works Progress Administration (WPA). And it remains a marvel of elegance and aspiration, a several-blocks-wide collection of 19 buildings that, despite their mass, create a space

HOLIDAY traditions

Starting the day after Thanksgiving (and often even before that), New York City dresses up for Christmas, stringing lights, hanging tinsel, and inserting computer chips into all the moving figurines that have hijacked the windows of the city's large department stores. The best street to see the trimmings, by far, is **Fifth Avenue,** between 39th and 59th streets. Along with the spectacular windows at the big stores—**Saks Fifth Avenue, Bergdorf Goodman,** and **Tiffany's**—you'll also want to admire the massive fir tree at **Rockefeller Center,** off Fifth Ave., at 51st St. (lit in late November; rockefellercenter.com). The windows at **Macy's,** 34th St. at Broadway, are also deservedly famous, as is Macy's indoor winter wonderland display, at the heart of which is a Santa waiting to hear your tots' Christmas wishes (just like in *Miracle on 34th Street* except that now you'll need to go online to get a timed-entry slot in advance). **Madison Avenue,** between 55th and 60th streets, is also worth a stroll, and if you have the time, drop by **Bloomingdale's,** Lexington Ave. (btw. 59th and 60th sts.), for its display.

In addition to the ***Radio City Christmas Spectacular*** (p. 392) and the New York City Ballet's staging of ***The Nutcracker*** (p. 392), traditional holiday events include an exquisite medieval creche display at the **Metropolitan Museum,** a holiday train show at the **NY Botanical Garden,** and the National Chorale's singalong performances of **Handel's *Messiah*** (nationalchorale.com). The *Messiah* is also staged in many churches and other venues throughout the city. Check local listings.

Chanukah is also a big deal in this city, with the largest Jewish population outside of Israel. On Fifth Avenue at 59th Street, a **giant menorah**—at 32 ft. it's the largest in the world—is lit each year on the first night of Chanukah and for 7 nights thereafter. On the first and final evenings, steaming latkes (potato pancakes) are distributed at sunset, and live music accompanies the electric candle-lighting. December 24 will be the first night of Chanukah in 2027.

that is airy and light, a welcoming haven for both tourists and residents. No matter how many times I come here, I still get goosebumps on the walk from Fifth Avenue through the gardened central path—called "The Channel," as it runs between the French and British buildings. Follow this boulevard down to the **ice-skating rink** (the first commercial one in the world), and the golden statue of ***Prometheus,*** or "Leaping Louie," as wits have called him over the years, his prone position under the soaring vertical of the RCA building making him look like he just jumped. (Directly behind the statue, a plaque marks the space where the 70-ft.-plus Christmas tree is set on November 20 each year.) The rink is open for ice skating October to early April; the rest of the year, it hosts roller skating. Hours are Monday to Thursday 11am to 10pm, Friday until midnight, Saturday 9am to midnight, and Sunday 9am to 10pm. Hourlong skating sessions, including skate rental, are "dynamically priced" (ugh!) which means you could pay anywhere from $29 to $66 most dates and times if you're 6 or older (prices start at $15 for younger tots). It looks like there are some savings to be had by purchasing tickets well in advance, and for the morning hours (some of the pricing is ridic—the top end, according to the site, is $120!).

Take a left and walk toward 49th Street to the small side street with the glassed-in TV studio on the corner, where NBC's ***Today Show*** is taped. Sign-waving crowds gather in this street area every morning Monday to Friday as early as 4am, to attempt to get their faces on TV. (When the show has musical performances, people line up days before, and guests play on a stage in this narrow alley. It looks much bigger on TV, doesn't it?) There's no fee to stand in the cold for a taping. Stroll over to Fifth Avenue between 50th and 51st streets, where *Prometheus*'s brother, mighty ***Atlas,*** the finest piece of art in the complex (by artist Lee Lawrie), hoists a giant globe on his shoulders, muscles rippling. From the back, *Atlas* looks a bit like a Christ figure, especially superimposed on St. Patrick's Cathedral across the street (p. 210). Go into the International Building lobby directly behind the *Atlas* statue for a peek at one of the city's most magnificent public spaces, the walls bedecked with a rare, swirling Greek marble, the gold "curtains" at the side creating an ever-changing dance of shadows on the ceiling.

The iconic gilded statue of Prometheus presides over the plaza at the heart of the Rockefeller Center complex.

I'm on the fence about recommending the **Rockefeller Center Tour** ($27). Yes, the tales associated with this city-within-a-city are fascinating, but on the two occasions I've taken the tour, it was clear the guides were bored with their jobs, which made the experience less compelling than it should have been. History fans will still enjoy it, but others will likely head straight to the 70th-floor observation deck at Rockefeller Center, **Top of the Rock** ♥, 30 Rockefeller Plaza (topoftherocknyc.com; ✆ **212/698-2000;** basic tickets $42–$71 adults, $40–$64 seniors, $36–$60 ages 6–12, free for children 5 and under; see website for other combo packages; daily 9am–11pm). While not as high as the decks in the Empire State Building or One World Observatory, it has its own striking views (including a much better vista of Central Park). In late 2023, "The Beam Experience" opened on the 69th floor (additional $25), a downright stupid experience that lasts just a hair over 1 minute which lets visitors re-create the classic photo of workmen sitting on an open beam, taken during the creation of Rockefeller Center. Unlike those daredevils, participants get a seatbelt, a back rest, and rubber construction tools to pose with and are hoisted 25 ft. above the observation deck. There are better uses for $25, and that goes for Skylift, too, a circular cup that hoists 15 people about 35 ft. above the observation deck, while rotating. Alas, these rides have taken up valuable real estate on the observation deck, making the experience far more crowded than it used to be. This is a case of "improvements" that substantially degraded the visitor experience.

The **Tour at NBC Studios** ♥, 30 Rockefeller Center (hours vary by date and season; $48 adults, $42 seniors and children), is led by shockingly earnest NBC Pages (they really *are* like Kenneth in *30 Rock*), and combines studio visits with a number of slick but informative videos about the history of the network. In the course of the tour, you'll visit two studios, though they can't guarantee in advance which ones they'll be (options range from the Saturday Night Live Soundstages, to the news offices, to Jimmy Fallon's theater). It feels like a long commercial for NBC, but it's pretty fun (I won't give away here what happens at the end of the tour, but suffice it to say that you'll go home with a souvenir video).

For those traveling with children over the age of 4, the **FDNY Fire Zone** ♥, 61 W. 48th St. (fdnysmart.org/firezone), is a free, highly interactive look at fire safety. It will bore kids over 11, but may make a nice distraction for younger tots.

Finally, there's **Radio City Music Hall,** 1260 Ave. of the Americas at 50th St. (radiocity.com; ✆ **212/247-4777;** $50–$400 show tickets, tour daily $44 adults, $39 seniors, students, and children 12 and under), which remains a kitschy, thrilling delight: The Christmas Spectacular is a marvel of excess, with dozens of people and hooved animals on stage; orchestras magically rising from the pit; and best of all, the Rockettes chorus line, that superhuman all-leg dancing machine. Even if you don't get tickets to a show, you can take an hourlong tour, well worth it to view the exquisite Art Deco features of this sensational pleasure hall. ***Note:*** during the time of year the Christmas Show runs, the tour includes a photo op with a Rockette. Tour tickets are available on the website or at the Radio City box office without the $7 service fee; they take place several times a day (times vary).

Frequent daily tours explore Radio City Music Hall, with its soaring Art Deco lobby.

Note: In the past couple of years Rockefeller Center has become a genuine foodie destination. For our summary of the best places to eat here, see p. 123.

Btw. 48th and 50th sts., from Fifth to Sixth aves. radiocity.com. ✆ **212/247-4777** (tour info). Subway: B, D, F, M to 47th–50th sts./Rockefeller Center.

With pedestrianized spaces and amped-up signs, Times Square dazzles after dark.

Times Square ♥ ICON Adam Gopnik wrote about Times Square in *The New Yorker,* "No other part of New York has had such a melodramatic sensitivity to the changes in the city's history, with an image for every decade." Think for a moment and those visions of Times Square should start flooding your mind: snazzy clubs and peroxide blonde chorus girls in the 1920s and '30s, sailors kissing girls at the end of World War II, the wisecracking small-time hoods of *Guys and Dolls* in the '50s, and, of course, the bleak urban decay of the '60s and '70s when, as Gopnik put it, "everything fell apart and Hell wafted up through the manhole covers."

Times Square is back on the upswing now, the porn shops banished and crime held (mostly) at bay. To get the full effect of today's Square, it's imperative you visit at night. It's then that the rainbow glitter of the flashing lights from the dozens of billboards, giant TV screens, electronic news crawls, and headlights of cars whizzing by wash over the Square, sweeping all the litter and crowds into the background. The effect is like watching fireworks. (This tradition of massive "spectaculars" is codified into law—in the 1980s, ordinances were passed requiring that new buildings abutting the Square have 16,000 sq. ft. of light shows on their facades, with "moving elements" that are sufficiently bright.) One of the best views is from the massive stairs atop the TKTS booth at 46th Street. In recent years, the city pedestrianized large parts of the square, creating 110,000 sq. ft. of walkable space. Also added: an outdoor performance space for frequent events during lunch hour (noon–2pm), happy hour (5–7pm), and temporary art installments.

Beyond this theater of the streets is the legitimate theater: Times Square still has more playhouses per acre than any other area in North America (p. 362). For dawn theater, peer into the sidewalk-level television studios of *Good Morning America* (44th and Broadway); the show also offers advance tickets to be part of the studio audience (go to ABCNews.go.com/gma for full info).

In 2026, the square added an observation deck (p. 195). And hey, don't beat yourself up if you feel claustrophobic when you stand at the corner of 47th and Seventh Avenue: Studies have shown that it's the most congested spot in the Western Hemisphere. ***Warning:*** If you take a photo with any of the costumed characters or "painted ladies" roaming Times Square, you'll be expected to tip them.

Subway: 1, 2, 3, 7, N, Q, R, S to Times Square; A, C, E to 42nd St./Port Authority.

Midtown East

Chrysler Building ♥♥♥ ARCHITECTURE In the Chrysler Building we see the Roaring-'20s version of what Alan Greenspan called "irrational exuberance"—a last burst of corporate headquarter building before stocks succumbed to the thudding crash of 1929. Throughout the previous decade, real estate speculators had been flinging up building after building, adding almost 100 skyscrapers and utterly transforming the skyline of the city. Automaker Walter P. Chrysler commissioned architect William Van Alen to top them all, instructing him that he wanted a building "higher than the Eiffel Tower," the tallest in the world at that time. What Chrysler would soon learn was that the gentlemen behind the Bank of America had the same ambition, and they had hired Van Alen's former partner (and sworn enemy) H. Craig Severance to build *them* the tallest building on the planet down on Wall Street. Soon the race was on, as each architect returned continually to the drafting board, adding 10 more stories of penthouses here, a lantern or a 50-ft. flagpole there. In the fall of 1929, Severance was sure he had won, so he completed the Bank of America building at 927 ft. Van Alen then unveiled the *coup de grâce* that he'd been hiding in an elevator shaft—a silver spike to crown his building, making it, at 1,046 ft., an unbeatable 117 ft. higher than his rival's. Not only taller, the Chrysler was the more striking of the two buildings, its scalloped spire set like a jaunty jester's cap atop a sleek tower. Take a look at the sharp stainless-steel eagles that jut out just below the roof; the "gargoyles" below those on the 61st floor are modeled after the hood ornament of the 1929 Chrysler Plymouth. The Chrysler remains one of the most impressive Art Deco buildings ever constructed—but it

The Chrysler Building holds court over Lexington Ave. and 42nd St.

The Scourge of Dynamic Pricing

Artificial intelligence has become a major player in attraction pricing in New York City. Not only is it terrible for the environment (with data centers using as much energy as entire cities) and puts tens of thousands of people out of work, it has made it a lot easier for attractions to incrementally raise prices. Today, every single observation deck in the city, plus a number of other non-museum attractions like the skating rink at Rockefeller Center and the Intrepid Museum, are crunching historic attendance numbers to shift prices to match—not just by the season or by the day, but by the *hour.* It's a rough situation for visitors, as it makes it far harder to figure out what your sightseeing expenditures will likely be. I've tried to game the system for you, pointing out the cheaper times, but I worry that's a moving target.

wasn't the tallest for long. Less than a year after it was completed, the Empire State Building assumed that mantle and held it until the World Trade Center came along. ***Note:*** The Chrysler Building is only viewable from the outside. 405 Lexington Ave. (at 42nd St.). chryslerbuilding.com. Subway: S, 4, 5, 6, 7 to 42nd St./Grand Central.

Empire State Building ♥♥♥ ARCHITECTURE There's no better introduction to New York than a visit to the Empire State Building. It's an apex of the New York skyline, both literally (at 102 stories and 1,454 ft.) and figuratively, and the view from its observation deck is at once instructive and exhilarating. From your bird's-eye perch, you orient yourself geographically and see, with a clarity not possible on the ground, the miracle of Manhattan, that runt of an island that couldn't get much wider or longer, and so did what no other city before it had done and expanded to the skies, becoming a dense, pulsating city of boxy towers set on a painfully narrow strip of land.

Look first to the **south,** where the Financial District's powerful skyscrapers loom over the field of lower, mostly residential housing that stands between it and midtown. Beyond the Financial District, in the harbor, are the Statue of Liberty to the right and the Brooklyn Bridge to the left (the most graceful of the three bridges you'll see in this direction). **Right below** you will see the triangular Flatiron building (p. 185), one of the most thrillingly odd in Manhattan (it was Frank Lloyd Wright's favorite building). Just to the side of it are the glittering gold roof of the Metropolitan Life Tower and the World Life Insurance Towers, once centers of New York's high society and now just part of the landscape. Drift to the **north side** of the building and you will be among a riot of skyscrapers, thrown up in a manner that seems wildly chaotic from this vantage point. This strip of midtown contains more office space per acre than any other area in the world. Peer through the curtain of buildings to catch a glimpse of Central Park, looking like a modest lawn from this great height. To your right, take a good look at the shiny, scalloped spire of the Chrysler building (p. 202; many have said it was designed to look like the grillwork of 1930s–era Chrysler cars).

The observation deck at the Empire State Building is a classic site for aerial views of Manhattan and beyond.

The Empire State Building has done an excellent job in recent years of spreading out guests with advance timed reservations, so the crowding issues that plagued the building a decade ago have pretty much disappeared. Still, there are some ways to get the most out of your visit here:

- **Don't rush through the exhibits you walk through before getting to the views.** There are 9 darn informative exhibits that cover everything from the remarkably fast construction of the building, to clips from the 600 appearances the building has made in major TV shows and films over the decades (and video games, comic books, and commercials). One of the most weirdly compelling exhibits gives you glimpses of the offices of famous companies in the building, another explains the smart ways the ESB has become one of the world's greenest tourist attractions. The QR codes in the wall text are worth scanning for additional info and videos. And note that you won't be coming back the same way you entered, so if you rush through, there's no opportunity to return after you've seen the views.
- All guests are offered the opportunity to **take the stairs** (from the 79th to the 86th floor) rather than the elevator. Doing so can shave a good 10 to 20 minutes off your wait time.
- I'm on the fence about whether the top deck is worth the uptick in price. Go there and you do have bragging rights: you've seen the city from the tallest observation deck in Gotham. But because the top deck is totally enclosed in glass, it's not as exciting as the one several floors below, and the view isn't $35 better (to my mind).

The Empire State Building—in Brief

- Opened in 1931 after just 14 months of construction (total cost: $25 million).
- Tallest building in the world from 1931 to 1970, when the World Trade Center took the title. It's still the 32nd tallest building on the planet.
- The oddly shaped spire at the top was meant to be a landing port for blimps, but high winds kept dirigibles from ever being able to anchor here.
- In 1945, a plane accidentally crashed into the building, killing 17 people.
- Every Valentine's Day, 14 couples are married for free on the observation deck.

There is no snack bar on the observation deck but there is a souvenir shop as you exit (coolest gift: Empire State Building zipper pulls).

350 Fifth Ave. at 34th St. esbnyc.com. © **212/736-3100.** 86th Floor Observatory admission from $44 adults, $42 seniors, $38 ages 6–12; free for children 5 and under. Top deck: add $35 to each ticket price. Hours vary by date and time of day, with opening hours and sunset times generally highest. Daily 10am–11pm much of the year, with closing an hour or two earlier in winter, and opening earlier in the warmer months. Subway: B, D, F, N, Q, R, M to 34th St.; 6 to 33rd St.

Grand Central Terminal ♥♥ ARCHITECTURE In ancient Roman times, the entrances to great cities were framed with monumental arches, meant to awe all who passed through. When Grand Central Terminal was

Storied Grand Central Terminal, built in 1913, is more than just a thriving transit hub, as you'll discover on a walking tour.

being built at the turn of the 20th century, it was recognized that our railroad terminals were our grand gateways, the first view a traveler would have of the metropolis. So, the architects of both Grand Central and the late, great Pennsylvania Station (the original, torn down in the 1960s) created as much pomp and stateliness as possible, filling these spaces with the symbols and architecture of imperial Rome. On Grand Central's south facade, 10 colossal Doric fluted pillars tower over Park Avenue; above them a massive statue of Mercury, the god of travel, spreads his arms in welcome as Hercules and Minerva, gods of strength and wisdom, lounge at his feet. (The face of the clock below the sculpture is the largest piece of Tiffany glass in the world.) The station's interior is no less impressive, its concourse soaring nine stories to a vaulted ceiling on which the signs of the zodiac are created from 59 fiber-optic lights and 2,500 painted stars. The side walls feature massive windows that throw shafts of light onto the acre-long Tennessee marble floor. Not that the station needed them: One of its innovations was the use of electric lights, so you'll see bare bulbs sprinkled throughout the station and on the massive chandeliers that overhang the concourse. Two hundred buildings were demolished to make way for the station, which opened on February 2, 1913, bearing a price tag of $80 million.

As you walk through, take in all of the trendy shops and food markets housed in the arteries of the main concourse; another dining concourse below, with the famed **Oyster Bar** at its heart (p. 132); and a huge Apple Store on one balcony. If you're traveling with children, take them to the "whispering gallery" right outside the Oyster Bar. Stand on one side of the arch there and have your child stand on the other, and then whisper to each other back and forth; a trick of acoustics allows sound to travel from one side of the vault to the other.

A PARK & a ride

On October 24, 2012, a small miracle occurred: **Franklin D. Roosevelt Four Freedoms Park** on Roosevelt Island finally opened. An austerely beautiful tribute to the four-term president, it was designed by star architect Louis Kahn shortly before his death in 1974. It took an intervening 38 years for the project to finally come to fruition (mostly due to the efforts of Kahn's son, who created a documentary about his father's vision that helped raise the millions necessary to build the monument). The park offers wonderful views of the Manhattan skyline, as well as a serene break from the bustle of NYC.

But perhaps one of its greatest lures is the amusement park–like ride one takes to the island aboard the **Roosevelt Island Tram** (rioc.ny.gov/community/transportation/tram; ✆ **212/832-4555**). This is the aerial vehicle you have probably seen in countless movies, most notably *Spider-Man*. It originates at 59th Street and Second Avenue, costs $3 each way, and takes about 5 minutes to traverse the East River to Roosevelt Island, where there are a series of apartment complexes (part of the fun is peering into the apartments as you swoop by). The tram operates daily from 6am until 2am (Fri & Sat until 3:30am).

Three reasons to visit the Morgan Library: rare books on display, exquisite interior architecture, and excellent rotating shows in the contemporary wing.

Informative, 90-minute **walking tours** of the station are offered daily at 11am and 3pm. Adult tickets are $39, and they must be pre-booked at takewalks.com.

42nd St., at Park Ave. grandcentralterminal.com. ✆ **212/532-4900.** Subway: S, 4, 5, 6, 7 to 42nd St./Grand Central.

The Morgan Library & Museum ♥♥ LIBRARY/MUSEUM Famed Canadian scientist George Mercer Dawson once wrote that a great library contained "the diary of the human race." With that definition, very few libraries come as close to greatness as the Morgan, which contains examples of the written word from the beginning of recorded time—from pictorial Mesopotamian cylinder seals (4th millennium B.C., a precursor to writing); to papyrus rolls from ancient Egypt, Greece, and Rome; to brilliantly colorful medieval illuminated manuscripts. Its crowning jewels are three editions of the Gutenberg Bible, the first book to be created using movable type. (This is the only collection in the world to boast three editions; scholars come from around the globe to study them, as each is unique.) Also in the collection: manuscripts by Mark Twain, Jane Austen, Charles Dickens, the Brontë sisters, Galileo, Bob Dylan, Alexander Calder, and James Joyce. One of the 25 known surviving copies of the Declaration of Independence is another highlight, along with a First Folio of Shakespeare. (The fragility of these treasures means they can't be constantly on display, but you'll usually see one of the Gutenbergs when you visit, along with other exquisite books.) When you visit, be sure to set aside at least an hour and a half to take in the ever-rotating special exhibitions. In 2026, these included tarot cards from the Renaissance through today and objects from Austria's Mozarteum tracing the life story of Wolfgang Amadeus Mozart. Set for 2027 is a look at Medieval European block books, the first printed picture books.

The Morgan in the library's name, 19th-century billionaire J. Pierpont Morgan (1837–1913), collected more than just books; after his death, many of his greatest artistic acquisitions were donated to the Wadsworth Atheneum (in Hartford, Connecticut) and the Metropolitan Museum. The original library, a marble villa in High Renaissance style, was designed by Charles Follen McKim (of the famous firm of McKim, Mead & White). Contemporary sections of the library, designed by lauded architect Renzo Piano, added massive steel-and-glass pavilions in 2006, doubling the size of the facilities. Unfortunately, they're showing signs of wear and tear; Piano didn't create an easy way to clean the glass, and so its outside skin is often covered with grit, and even trash. A gift store, cafe, and restaurant are on-site.

225 Madison Ave. (btw. 36th and 37th sts.). themorgan.org. ✆ **212/685-0008.** Admission $25 adults, $17 seniors and visitors with disabilities, $13 students; free for ages 12 and under; free admission Fri 5pm to closing. Tues–Sun 10:30am–5pm (Fri until 8pm). Subway: 6 to 33rd St.

Museum of Sex ♥ MUSEUM Though it tries hard to avoid a carnival atmosphere, with voluminous and often soporific wall text, this museum still has a major "wink, wink, giggle, giggle" quotient. If you're interested in the subject from an anthropological perspective, you may be disappointed. For the rest of us, including all of the folks who seemed to be out on dates (or perhaps they met there?), the museum is good, dirty fun. ***Warning:*** Due to the graphic nature of its exhibits, this museum is not for everyone. ***Tip:*** Save $4 by buying tickets at the door rather than in advance online.

233 Fifth Ave. (at 27th St.). museumofsex.com. ✆ **212/689-6337.** Admission $36; ages 18 and over only. Mon–Thurs 1–10pm; Fri 1pm–midnight; Sat noon–midnight; Sun noon–10pm. Subway: N, R, 6 to 28th St.

Museum of the Dog ♥ MUSEUM Founded by the American Kennel Club, this attraction welcomes four-legged museumgoers as well as their two-legged companions. All get to experience the fun interactive exhibits on service dogs and the differences breed-to-breed, and a (mostly) mediocre collection of canine portraiture from the Victorian era through today.

101 Park Ave. (entrance on 40th St.). museumofthedog.org. ✆ **212/696-8360.** Admission $15 adults, $10 seniors/students/active military, $5 children age 3 to 12; free for children 2 and under—and dogs. Wed–Sun 11am–6pm. Subway: 4, 5, 6, S to 42nd St./ Grand Central.

New York Public Library ♥♥ LIBRARY/LANDMARK Many art historians consider this the finest Beaux Arts building in the United States. It certainly is one of the grandest, completed in 1911 at a cost of more than $9 million and built by the famous firm of Carrère and Hastings. The exterior takes its inspiration from the twin palaces on the north side of the Place de la Concorde in Paris and is done in the same French Renaissance style, a perfect

The New York Public Library's splendid Main Reading Room befits the Beaux Arts grandeur of this landmark building.

harmony of columns, pediments, and statuary—all guarded by the famous stone lions, said to roar whenever a virgin passes by. Want to use the library? Well, you will be "reading between the lions" (sorry, I couldn't resist). The library itself holds thousands of volumes, many of them housed underground below what is now Bryant Park. A "non-browsing" facility, it uses an ancient dumbwaiter system to retrieve books for readers—tomes are stacked into a small elevator and sent up when requests are made. The permanent **Polonsky Exhibition of The New York Public Library's Treasures** showcases astonishing manuscripts, recordings, letters, and images (both moving and still) from the library's massive collection. These include cuneiform tablets from the 3rd century B.C., a pen knife morbidly fashioned from the paw of a deceased pet that belonged to Charles Dickens, sheets of music hand-written by Mozart and Beethoven, and much more. In addition, there are changing exhibits on topics as varied as the history of children's literature, New York literary figures, innovations in photography, and more. Near the major exhibit hall is a small theater for showings (on the half-hour and hour) of a really terrific 23-minute film about the library's history. Don't skip the Lionel Pincus and Princess Firyal room, which houses one of the world's most extensive collections of maps (it's magnificent after a $5-million renovation). Entrance is always free, as are exhibits and the film, and the palatial interior, with its expanses of marble and carved oak ceilings, is worth a look-see. Download the Bloomberg Connections app (free) to access its audio tour of the building's highlights; excellent hourlong docent tours are Monday to Saturday at 11am and 2pm. Too much of a time commitment? Take a 20-minute tour of just the main reading room at 11:20 am, 1:30, and 3pm.

Fifth Ave. (at 42nd St.). nypl.org. ✆ **917/275-6975** (exhibits and events) or 212/930-0800 (general number). Free admission. Mon–Sat 10am–6pm (Tues & Wed until 8pm); Sun 1–5pm. Tours Mon–Sat 11am and 2pm; Sun 2pm. Subway: 1, 2, 3 to 42nd St./Broadway; B, D, F, M to 42nd St./6th Ave.; S, 4, 5, 6 to Grand Central/42nd St.; 7 to Fifth Ave.

St. Patrick's Cathedral ♥ CATHEDRAL The largest Roman Catholic cathedral in the United States, St. Pat's is also the seat of the Archdiocese of New York. Designed by James Renwick, begun in 1859, and consecrated in 1879, St. Patrick's wasn't completed until 1906. The vast cathedral seats a congregation of 2,200; if you don't attend Mass, pop in between services to get a look at the impressive interior. The St. Michael and St. Louis altar came from Tiffany & Co. In 2025, a new mural was added at the front, celebrating the importance of immigrants to the Catholic Church, and the United States as a whole. A self-guided audio tour, available on the website for $20, provides an erudite introduction to the cathedral's history and architecture, narrated by retired Cardinal Timothy Dolan. We also highly recommend visiting the original St. Patrick's Cathedral down in SoHo for a tour of its catacombs (p. 183).

Fifth Ave. (btw. 50th and 51st sts.). saintpatrickscathedral.org. ✆ **212/753-2261.** Free admission. Daily 6:30am–8:45pm. Check website for Mass schedule. Subway: B, D, F, M to 47th–50th sts./Rockefeller Center.

Summit One Vanderbilt ♥♥♥ OBSERVATION DECK Can an observation deck be a work of art? That's the provocative question the developer SL Green Realty posed when it hired artist Kenzo Digital to create an immersive experience at the top of its newest skyscraper. Set right on 42nd Street, Summit One has the sort of heart-of-the-action, glorious views that the Empire State Building has (with even better views of the Chrysler Building, since it's just a few buildings over). But thanks to Kenzo Digital's imagination (before this he was best known for collaborations with Beyoncé), those views are amplified and fractured by mirrors that cover most of this 1,750,212-sq.-ft. space. (***Warning:*** The floors are

Mirrored orbs, glass-floored boxes, and digital effects amplify the stunning city views from Summit One Vanderbilt.

A tour of the United Nations headquarters (advance ticket required) reminds visitors of all this international body has done for world peace and progress.

mirrored too, so unless you're an exhibitionist, don't wear a skirt here.) It's a dazzling effect, and one that will delight shutterbugs. In addition to the mirrored spaces are other surprises, like three fully transparent "sky boxes" jutting out from the side of the building, allowing brave visitors to stare down 1,063 ft. to the sidewalk below; a room with floating mirrored orbs; and another space with a digital screen that shows visitor's faces transposed onto clouds over the view. I'll leave it up to you whether all this is "art" but it's certainly artful—and pretty darn wonderful. The only real disappointments here? "Ascent": a glass elevator, with the world's largest see-through elevator floor, that climbs up the outside of the building. The latter sounds more exciting than it actually is, as part of the roof sits below the elevator at all times, and the views three stories up aren't appreciably better anyway. Don't waste the $20 it costs to ride. ***Tip:*** This attraction does sell out, so though booking online adds a $3 processing fee, we suggest doing so well ahead or you could be turned away at the door.

45 E. 42nd St. (at Vanderbilt, entrance in Grand Central on main concourse). summitov.com. No phone. Admission from $44 adults, $38 children ages 6–12; free for ages 5 and under; price varies by date and time. Daily 9am–midnight.

United Nations ♥♥ ARCHITECTURE/HISTORIC SITE It's this 7-block stretch of international territory that makes New York City the capital of the world. No, really. It's become fashionable of late in some political circles to denigrate the UN. Though some reform is obviously necessary, a tour here will remind you of just how much the United Nations has done since its inception. Perhaps more importantly, a visit here will remind you of how much potential the UN still has for effecting meaningful progress in numerous fields, from the elimination of disease and poverty to the resolution of ethnic conflicts.

Those who take the hour-long tour will visit not only the **General Assembly** (where Khrushchev once famously pounded his shoe in anger) and the **Security Council,** but also the less well-known **Economic and Social Council Room** that oversees the work of UNICEF, the World Health Organization (WHO), and 28 other UN programs of development. (Little-known fact: It's thanks to recommendations by the WHO that most countries have expiration dates stamped on milk.) It's in this room that officials are working to create standardized tests for avian flu, vaccinate the world's children against polio, and promote the cause of world literacy. The Nobel Peace Prize won by the UN Peacekeeping forces in 2001 is displayed just outside the council room, along with an enlightening exhibit on the important work these troops are still doing throughout the world. Along with the interior rooms, visitors view the lobby of the General Assembly building with its free exhibits (photojournalism mostly), a meditation room, and the memorial stained-glass window Marc Chagall created in 1964 for former Secretary General Dag Hammarskjöld (to the right of the entrance). An international gift shop, with trinkets from across the globe, and the UN post office are in the basement.

Important note: Due to increased security, the UN no longer allows on-the-spot tour ticket purchases. Only those who've bought a ticket online in advance, and registered with UN security, will be admitted into the building Monday to Friday (Sat & Sun visitors can see the visitor center 10am–4:30pm without a ticket, but there are no tours). Many days sell out entirely, so buy tickets as far in advance as possible. Visitors are required to show government-issued ID, so be sure to bring a driver's license, passport, or other form of official identification with you. In addition to the standard tours are regularly offered tours that focus on the building's gardens, architecture, art works, and more. Guided tours may be canceled when heads of state are speaking and tend not to take place in September and October when the General Assembly is in session.

First Ave. at 47th St., visitor check-in office at 801 First Ave. un.org/en/visit/tour. ✆ **212/963-8687.** Guided tours $29 adults, $21 seniors/students, $18 ages 5–12; children 4 and under not permitted. Tours Mon–Fri 9am–4:45pm (except Sept & Oct). Subway: S, 4, 5, 6, 7 to 42nd St./Grand Central.

UPTOWN

Upper East Side

Cooper Hewitt National Design Museum ♥♥♥ MUSEUM Architect Mies van der Rohe famously said "God is in the details." That could be the motto for the Cooper-Hewitt, which has made a name for itself by taking subjects from the world of design—cutlery or superstrong textiles, say—and dissecting them down to their foundational elements, in a way that enraptures

Intricate design details come to life at the Cooper Hewitt museum, a branch of the Smithsonian.

the visitor. That textile exhibit, as an example, showcased a wide range of truly unusual fabrics, like the material used in space suits, artistically strung netting that stops soil erosion, and a shoulder implant that looks like a crocheted snowflake (it moves inside the body with the flexibility of a sweater). More recent exhibits have unpacked how people are shaped by domestic spaces; how design enhances and visualizes musical experiences; and the role design could play in achieving world peace. All of the exhibits take place in the baronial manor house of steel magnate Andrew Carnegie, so part of the fun of visiting is seeing the bones of this exquisite home (take some time to study the interactive panels that show historic photos of different rooms within the home). The Cooper-Hewitt is a branch of the Smithsonian, and the only design museum in the nation to cover both contemporary and traditional design, which gives its exhibits a breadth and depth that are quite unusual for this subject matter.

2 E. 91st St. (at Fifth Ave.). cooperhewitt.org. ✆ **212/849-8400.** Admission $22 adults, $16 seniors, $10 students and people with disabilities; free for ages 18 and under. Pay-what-you-wish from 5pm until closing. Daily 10am–6pm. Closed Thanksgiving and Christmas. Subway: 6 to 86th St.; 4, 5 to 96th St.

Frick Collection ♥♥♥ MUSEUM Arguably the best small museum in the nation, the Frick provides a deeply satisfying experience on a number of levels. There's the highbrow fun of seeing some of the world's greatest masterpieces; the lowbrow kick of getting a firsthand peek at the home of one of the super-rich and famous; and the somewhat macabre thrill, akin to a séance in a way, of communing with someone long dead through his choices in art.

- American Folk Art Museum **2**
- American Museum of Natural History **6**
- Cathedral of St. John the Divine **15**
- Children's Museum of Manhattan **7**
- The Cloisters **18**
- Cooper Hewitt National Design Museum **11**
- El Museo del Barrio **14**
- Frick Collection **3**
- Hispanic Society Museum & Library **17**
- The Jewish Museum **12**
- Metropolitan Museum of Art **8**
- Museum of Arts and Design **1**
- Museum of the City of New York **13**
- Neue Galerie New York **9**
- The New York Historical **5**
- Solomon R. Guggenheim Museum **10**
- Sotheby's **4**
- Studio Museum **16**

Uptown Attractions
0 1/4 mi
0 0.25 km
Subway station
Upper Manhattan
Uptown
Midtown
Downtown
East River
UPPER EAST SIDE
Carl Schurz Park
ROOSEVELT ISLAND
Harlem Meer
Jacqueline Kennedy Onassis Reservoir
The Great Lawn
CENTRAL PARK
Central Park Zoo
Wollman Rink
Central Park South
Transverse
Mt. Sinai Hospital
MUSEUM MILE
Fifth Ave.
Madison Ave.
Park Ave.
Lexington Ave.
Third Ave.
Second Ave.
First Ave.
York Ave.
East End Ave.
FDR Dr.
103 St 6
96 St 6
96 St Q
86 St 4-5-6
86 St Q
77 St 6
72 St Q
68 St/ Hunter College 6
Lexington Av/ 63 St F-Q
Lexington Av/ 59 St N-R
5 Av/ 59 St N-R
59 St 4-5-6
Roosevelt Island Tram
Queensboro (59th St.) Bridge
E. 105th St.
E. 104th St.
E. 103rd St.
E. 102nd St.
E. 101st St.
E. 100th St.
E. 99th St.
E. 98th St.
E. 97th St.
E. 96th St.
E. 95th St.
E. 94th St.
E. 93rd St.
E. 92nd St.
E. 91st St.
E. 90th St.
E. 89th St.
E. 88th St.
E. 87th St.
E. 86th St.
E. 85th St.
E. 84th St.
E. 83rd St.
E. 82nd St.
E. 81st St.
E. 80th St.
E. 79th St.
E. 78th St.
E. 77th St.
E. 76th St.
E. 75th St.
E. 74th St.
E. 73rd St.
E. 72nd St.
E. 71st St.
E. 70th St.
E. 69th St.
E. 68th St.
E. 67th St.
E. 66th St.
E. 65th St.
E. 64th St.
E. 63rd St.
E. 62nd St.
E. 61st St.
E. 60th St.
E. 59th St.
3
4
8
9
10
11
12
13
14

Housed in industrialist Henry Clay Frick's ornate neoclassical mansion, the Frick Collection is a testament to his taste as a collector.

In the end, the Frick Collection is as much about Henry Clay Frick (1849–1919) and the world he created as it is about the art itself.

And that's a good thing, as Frick was a fascinating if controversial figure, an entrepreneur in the steel and coke industries with only 3 years of formal schooling, who became a self-made millionaire by the time he was 30. On his death, he bequeathed his enormous art collection and the grandly colonnaded neoclassical mansion that housed it (built by Carrere and Hastings, architects of the N.Y. Public Library) to the formation of a public museum for the purpose of "encouraging and developing the study of the fine arts" in the United States. A long-overdue renovation, begun in late 2020 and completed in spring of 2025, opens up the second floor to visitors for the first time ever. This exciting development should inspire return visits from those who've only seen the first floor (some of the art works upstairs are revelatory).

In each of its galleries are wonders to behold: paintings and sculptures from nearly every great artist in the Western canon. Unlike the Barnes Collection in Philadelphia, Frick gave his trustees the right to change the arrangement of the works and acquire new ones; a full third of what you'll see was purchased after Frick passed away. But most of the great pieces are from Frick's era and are a testament to his astute taste as a collector. This is a man who not only collected Rembrandts (a trifecta of them!), but chose none but the most intriguing works, such as the portrait of fur merchant Nicholas Ruts, Rembrandt's first commissioned portrait and the one that launched his career. Masterpieces by Vermeer (three of the meager 36 that still exist today), Renoir, Degas, Velazquez, El Greco (his *St. Jerome,* of which the Metropolitan

Museum's version is a copy), and more are also on view. The most famous painting in the collection is Holbein's portrait of Sir Thomas More. In an ironic move, it hangs across from Holbein's portrait of Thomas Cromwell—More's longtime political rival, who was also executed by Henry VIII—so that the two can stare each other down through eternity.

Before you visit, download the Bloomberg Connects app to listen to curators discuss the art. You may also want to see if there are any special concerts, lectures or tours taking place during your visit.

1 E. 70th St. (off Fifth Ave). frick.org. ✆ **212/288-0700.** Admission $30 adults, $22 seniors/visitors with disabilities, $17 students; free for youth ages 10–18; pay-what-you-wish Wed 1:30pm to closing. Children ages 9 and under not admitted. Wed–Mon 10:30am–5:30pm. Closed all major holidays. Subway: 6 to 77th St.

The Jewish Museum ♥♥ MUSEUM The "modest" goal of this intriguing museum is to explore 4,000 years of Jewish culture through Judaica, art, and artifacts. Surprisingly, it succeeds much of the time. It used to present the story in chronological fashion, but in 2025 curators reimagined the core exhibit as an exploration of different themes of Jewish life through the ages. I worried that the new structure wouldn't be as illuminating, but I discovered I was wrong on a recent visit. When you're shedding light on a people divided across a diaspora for thousands of years, learning the wildly diverse stories of individuals and communities is a satisfying approach—and one that may better reflect the complexity of the subject.

The Jewish Museum holds a collection of objects and art exploring the history of Jewish culture around the world.

Start your visit on the fourth floor, where a dazzling display of menorahs speaks to the different lifestyles, and challenges, of Jews through time and across the globe. Two of the most moving objects here are a wooden menorah successfully hidden by its maker at the Theriesenstadt concentration camp during World War II and a Korean War-era menorah crafted by an American soldier from a spent artillery shell and bullets. On that same floor is a look at Jewish portraiture and artifacts from religious practice and daily life from 1500 B.C. to today. The third floor has more artworks and artifacts, as well as a room recounting the history of Jews in the United States. What finally emerges is a portrait of a people who have not

The Metropolitan Museum is an immense palace of fine art. Advance planning can help you find the artworks you most want to see without experiencing museum overload.

only managed to survive against the steepest odds but have become magnificently diverse in the process.

Galleries on the first and second floors are a bit more hit or miss, presenting changing exhibits, such as past shows on musician Leonard Cohen, artists Marc Chagall and Anish Kapoor, and fashion designer Isaac Mizrahi. Bottom line: the museum should be of great interest to Jews and non-Jews alike.

1109 Fifth Ave. (at 92nd St.). thejewishmuseum.org. ✆ **212/423-3200.** Admission $15 adults, $10 seniors/students; free for kids 18 and under; free admission Sat. Thurs 11am–8pm; Fri 11am–4pm; Sat–Mon 11am–6pm. Subway: 4, 5, 6 to 86th St.; 6 to 96th St.

Metropolitan Museum of Art ♥♥♥ ART MUSEUM The giant among New York museums both figuratively and literally: At 1.6 million sq. ft., it's not just the biggest museum in the city, it's the largest one in this hemisphere. And I'd argue the Met competes in stature with the Louvre in Paris, the Prado in Madrid, the Uffizi in Florence, and the British Museum in London. Whatever your interests in art—and even if you usually have no interest in art—you will find something here to astonish you, to enlighten and enrich your life. I solemnly promise. No, really, I do.

The Met was founded fairly late, as great museums go, conceived in 1870 by a group of wealthy businessmen and artists. A decade later, Calvert Vaux, one of the architects of Central Park, was brought in to create the first red-brick building on this site (you can see that facade still—it's the side wall of the European Sculpture Court). A little over a decade later, an expansion was necessary, so famed architect Richard Morris Hunt was tapped to create the majestic, neoclassical Indiana-limestone edifice you see today, awing the visitors who climb its mountain of steps and walk past its redwood-height pillars. Never a static institution, the museum and its collection have continued to grow, with the Met currently owning more than 3 million works of art spanning 5,000 years. Its temporary exhibits are often blockbusters.

The Met truly has something for everyone among its vast and varied halls. Seen here, the Arms and Armor gallery.

Obviously, there's no way to see it all in one, two, or even five visits. You must choose carefully among the 18 curatorial departments and decide what interests you most. On view are masterworks from nearly all the world's cultures—from Egyptian mummies to ancient Greek statuary to Islamic carvings to Renaissance paintings to Native American masks to 20th-century decorative arts. One way to focus your time is to take one of the hour-long scholarly **Highlight tours**—free with admission and offered about five times a day—led by volunteer docents. These enthusiastic art lovers are treasures in and of themselves, highly trained and well-spoken. They'll run you all over the museum, pointing out and expounding upon the various gems of the collection, offering a quick taste of the museum's highlights so that you can come back yourself and feast upon what really interests you. Also excellent: the **Collection Tours** which concentrate on one genre of art at a time, like Chinese or Medieval European art.

If I had to pick the top five highlights, I'd select:

- **The European paintings collection** on the second floor (which fully reopened after a 5-year-long rehang, and now spotlights some 700 works) with such jewels as Velazquez's truer-than-life portrait of Juan de Pareja (the enslaved man whom the painter respected enough—you can see it in the painting—to set free); El Greco's brooding landscape of Toledo; 20 Rembrandts including *Aristotle Contemplating the Bust of Homer* (three great Greeks in one painting—notice the pendant of Alexander the Great hanging from his shirt); five light-kissed Vermeers; a roomful of van Goghs; and works by Manet, Monet, de Goya, Breughel, Van Eyck, and every other master you read about in your college art-history course.
- **The period rooms,** which re-create dozens of important chambers, including Louis XIV's state bedroom in Versailles; an Arts and Crafts living room from Frank Lloyd Wright; and the stunning Cubiculum from Boscoreale, a perfectly preserved, brilliantly colorful room from a villa near Pompeii that was buried when Mount Vesuvius erupted in A.D. 79. Whenever I visit these rooms I'm reminded of the terrific children's novel *From the Mixed-Up Files of Mrs. Basil E. Frankweiler,* in which the protagonists slept each night in a historic bed. Share it with your tweens and they'll be dying to come here.
- **The American Collection,** the most comprehensive in the world, featuring masterworks by Sargent, Homer, Tiffany, Leutze (his sentimental but rippingly fun *Washington Crossing the Delaware*), and many more.
- **The Egyptian Collection** includes some pieces discovered by the Met's own teams of archaeologists, such as the miniature figures found in a tomb in Thebes that show in intricate detail what daily life for a wealthy Egyptian was like. There's also elaborate statuary; mummy cases; jewelry; wall paintings; and the Temple of Dendur, an actual temple to the goddess Isis (ca. 15 B.C.) that was saved from the rising waters of the Nile after the construction of the Aswan Dam.
- The hidden **Hall of Art from Japan,** with its famed Iris Screens (reproduced on many Metropolitan Museum products), as well as architectural-looking suits of armor, delicate woodcuts, and dazzling kimonos. To my mind, this is one of the most ravishingly beautiful sections of the museum.
- The fully reworked **Michael C. Rockefeller Wing,** which reopened in 2025 with some 1,800 artworks now on display, illuminating important artistic traditions from Africa, the ancient Americas, and Oceania. A highlight: the exquisite ivory pendant mask of *Iyoba Idia*, the Queen Mother of the Court of Benin in the 16th century. Look closely at her hair: you'll see

Portuguese traders carved there, the source of much of the kingdom's wealth, and mud fish, a symbol of resilience as they can live both in water and on land.

The Best Times to Visit the Met

On Friday and Saturday evenings, the Met remains open 'til 9pm not only for art viewing but also for cocktails in the Great Hall Balcony Bar. Classical music from a string ensemble accompanies the tippling. A slate of after-hours programs (gallery talks, walking tours, family programs) is also offered. The restaurant at Petrie Court Café and Wine Bar stays open until 10:30pm (last reservation at 8:30pm), and dinner is usually accompanied by piano music. Best of all, the crowds dwindle after dark—in the galleries, if not near the bars.

Along with all the art, the Met has half a dozen cafes and restaurants, fab gift shops and bookstores, and tremendously engaging art and culture programs for children of all ages (see website for info). Its offshoot museum, **the Cloisters** (p. 228) allows for free entry the same day you visit the Met—but that seems to me like too much museum time in one day, frankly.

Fifth Ave. (at 82nd St.). metmuseum.org. ✆ **212/535-7710.** Admission $30 adults, $22 seniors, $17 students; NY State resident w/ID pay-what-you-wish; free for ages 11 and under. Sun–Tues and Thurs 10am–5pm; Fri–Sat 10am–9pm. Subway: 4, 5, 6 to 86th St.

Museum of the City of New York ♥♥ MUSEUM Thanks to a recent overhaul, this century-old museum (founded in 1923) is finally making good on the promise of its name. Today, it offers visitors a textured, dramatic, suavely interactive look at the improbable tale of a tiny, obscure Dutch colony that blossomed—and burned, and conned, and fought its way into a world capital. Start your visit in the basement, where an absorbing 30-minute film (narrated by Stanley Tucci) outlines the story. Next stop should be ground floor, where one gallery traces Gotham's history from Native American days through the 1900s, displaying artifacts of all sorts, accompanied by electronic panels offering biographies of New Yorkers both well-known and obscure—everyone from Alexander Hamilton to a murdered prostitute—that illuminate different strands of the story. The panels, with their interactive maps, reproduced paintings and drawings, newspaper clippings, graphs, and more, are hugely absorbing (on my last visit I looked up and an hour had passed). Its twin gallery traces the yarn from 1901 through today with the same panache. Also on this floor: the Future City Lab, an exhibit that allows visitors to try to solve the city's problems with sustainability, population density, and other unique-to-New York City woes on individual tablets that are later screened for all to see (kids will love this room). Upstairs are changing exhibits, a famed dollhouse, galleries with Gilded Age frippery, and an excellent permanent exhibition on activism in NYC.

1220 Fifth Ave. (at 103rd St.). mcny.org. ✆ **212/534-1672.** Admission $23 adults, $18 seniors, $14 students; free for ages 19 and under; free admission Wed. Mon–Fri 10am–5pm; Sat–Sun 10am–6pm. Closed Thanksgiving, Christmas, New Year's Day. Subway: 6 to 103rd St.

Neue Galerie New York ♥ ART MUSEUM Most notable for its jewel-toned paintings by Gustav Klimt (including the famed *Woman in Gold*), its "Didn't I sit on that in the '70s?" Bauhaus furniture, and its collection of drawings by such Teutonic masters as Dix, Schiele, and Breuer, the Neue Galerie offers a swift but effective overview of German and Austrian arts and design. Because some of these drawings are a bit racy, children 11 and under are not admitted, and ages 16 and younger must be accompanied by an adult. Also on-site: a transporting Viennese cafe (p. 140), a theater for lectures and films, and a pricey gift shop. ***Note:*** There's often a line outside for entrance to the cafe. If you're just going to the museum, you can head right in.

1048 Fifth Ave. (at 86th St.). neuegalerie.org. ✆ **212/628-6200.** Admission $28 adults, $18 seniors, $15 students (ages 12–16)/educators/visitors with disabilities; admission free 1st Fri of month 4–7pm. No children 12 and under. Wed–Mon 10am–6pm. Subway: 4, 5, 6 to 86th St.

Frank Lloyd Wright's bold spiral design makes the Guggenheim Museum a distinctive backdrop for modern art.

Solomon R. Guggenheim Museum ♥♥ ART MUSEUM/ARCHITECTURE New York is the city of the rectangle, of the sharp right angle. Our streets form a grid, our buildings are boxy and regular. Until you get to the Guggenheim, that is. Frank Lloyd Wright's delirious spiral of a museum sits among the towers of Fifth Avenue like a steroidal peacock among guinea hens. Architectural critic Herbert Muschamp described the look best when he wrote, "What else but a building brought back from a dream would be windowless, have walls and floors that tilt and twist, begin on the top floor, and spiral in towards the center like an enigma?" Visiting this 1959 masterpiece and trudging up the ramps of curving halls transforms the standard museum experience into a profound journey (and sometimes a battle against vertigo), no matter what art is displayed. Early critics dismissed the museum (*Newsweek*'s insipid review was headlined "Museum or Cupcake?"), but I think today even the most jaded visitor will feel the power of the place, the symbolic weight of infinite circle upon circle. (And to answer the question nobody ever voices aloud: No, there haven't been any suicide jumps from over the low-slung rails, nor has anyone ever accidentally fallen to their death.)

Beyond the architecture, the museum is popular, thanks to its curators' skill at mounting retrospectives on top contemporary artists (like Rashid Johnson, Cecilia Vicuña, and Beatriz Milhazes). Permanent gallery space is also given to the stars of the Guggenheim's collection, towering figures such as Chagall, Brancusi, Mondrian, Miró, Kandinsky, and other modernists.

1071 Fifth Ave. (at 89th St.). guggenheim.org. ✆ **212/423-3500.** Admission $30 adults, $19 seniors/students/visitors with disabilities; free for kids 11 and under; pay-what-you-wish Tues and Sun 4pm until closing. Daily 10:30am–5:30pm (Sat until 8pm). Subway: 4, 5, 6 to 86th St.

Sotheby's ♥♥ GALLERY Works by the world's most famous artists, publishers, wineries, and artisans regularly land on the loading dock of Sotheby's, and have since 1744 when the famous auction house was founded in London. That's no secret. What's less well known is that 2 weeks before an auction, all the goods go on display at one of Sotheby's 13 auction houses worldwide, and anyone is welcome to come in and gawk. There's no one checking to see if you have an extra million—or 20—squirreled away in your mattress for a buying spree. In fact, Sotheby's lets all comers in for free. And now that the auction house has placed its flagship in the famed Breuer Building (originally built as the home of the Whitney Museum), it's a snap to combine a visit here with museums just a block away on Museum Mile. Pop over to the Sotheby's website first for a preview of what you will see, as that can vary greatly from auction to auction. ***Tip:*** A big part of the fun of visiting here is seeing what the art works will likely cost; estimated prices for what the work will go for at auction are displayed alongside the pieces.

945 Madison Ave. (at 75th St.). sothebys.com. Free admission. Hours vary, check website. Subway: 6 to 77th St.

Upper West Side

American Folk Art Museum ♥

ART MUSEUM Self-taught artists and their stories (told in wonderful detail by the wall text) are the focus of this small museum, which illuminates the art in invigorating ways. You'll see works from the 18th century to the present, and the breadth and variety of the art can be quite stunning. The terrific book-and-gift shop is filled with one-of-a-kind pieces.

2 Lincoln Square (Columbus Ave., at 66th St.). folkartmuseum.org. ✆ **212/595-9533.** Free admission. Wed–Sun 11:30am–6pm. Subway: 1 to 66th St.

Exhibitions at the American Folk Art Museum give rich context to intriguing works by self-taught artists, contemporary as well as historic.

American Museum of Natural History ♥♥♥ MUSEUM/PLANETARIUM Since 1869, this institution has served as both the country's preeminent private scientific research facility and its top museum for paleontology, zoology, anthropology, and, in recent years, astronomy. It's this constant flow of energy and insight between the research side and the curatorial side that has kept the museum fiercely vital, fresh, and unique. Just a few decades ago, for example, scientists concluded that dinosaurs had not dragged their tails as had long been thought but waved them in the air as they walked. The curators responded, painstakingly dismantling the museum's famed dino skeletons and reassembling them with tails erect and off the ground. Then, in a brilliant stroke, they placed one skeleton atop a section of a Texas riverbed where they had found fossilized dino footprints (sans tail-dragging marks), giving museumgoers a peephole into how scientific theories emerge.

This double spotlight on the science itself and on how science is "made" is one of the pleasures of a visit here, with many exhibits focused on current "educated guesses" and the scientists who are making them. An extraordinarily interactive museum, it challenges visitors to figure out which theories make the most sense via computer stations, wall text, videos, soundscapes, and, of course, the artifacts themselves. That effort became even more cutting-edge in 2023, when the $431-million **Richard Gilder Center for Science, Education and Innovation** opened, transforming the museum-going experience. It

The American Museum of Natural History's new Gilder Center for Science, Education and Innovation showcases a number of interactive exhibits in a dazzling contemporary building.

Planning Tips for the Museum of Natural History

Timing your visit: Because the museum is so popular with school groups, it can get crowded, particularly midmorning. Also, since it's so popular with families, attendance is often in inverse proportion to the weather: When it's lovely outside, the crowds will be sparse within. When it's blustery or rainy . . . watch out. Weekdays tend to be less crowded than Saturday and Sunday. Note that timed tickets are available starting 2 months before the date of visit.

An overview tour: First-time visitors should consider taking one of the guided introductory tours that begin at 30 minutes past every hour from 10:30am to 3:30pm. Led by highly knowledgeable volunteer guides (they take classes for 6 months), tours vary by guide and will hit different highlights of the museum over the course of 75 minutes. The museum also has a free app with an overview tour of the entire museum, helpful interactive maps, videos, quizzes, and additional info about the exhibits and the *Night at the Museum* films.

Especially for kids: Families with children will want to visit the **Discovery Room,** an educational center where kids can pretend to dig up dinosaur bones, do a scavenger hunt, peer through microscopes, and more. Timed free tickets are given for admission here, so be sure to grab one early in the day before they run out. Some hours are dedicated for certain ages, so check online or at the front desk before heading over.

houses 12% of the museum's collections in a new 230,000-sq.-ft. structure including an insectarium, a permanent butterfly vivarium, open storage exhibits showing the span of the museum's collections, and a 360-degree-view **Invisible Worlds Theater,** a mesmerizing high-tech show about the networks that underlie all life (it's hard to describe, but a real wowzer of an experience). If you enter the museum through this new center, notice how the dazzling, contemporary architecture of its lobby mimics curving Southwestern American canyons, a sinuous look created by spraying structural concrete directly onto rebar.

If it's your first visit to the museum, we suggest you do the awe-inspiring insectarium in the Gilder Center first and then head to the dinosaur rooms on the **fourth floor.** The museum has the largest such collection in the world, and the hot questions surrounding dinosaurs—How did they die out? Did they care for their young? Did they live in organized herds? Are birds their descendants?—are imaginatively explored. **Floors 2 and 3** are diorama-driven, with half the floors devoted to the anthropological study of various peoples of the world, the other half to African and North American mammals. If you're short on time, take the mammal route, which features the poetic work of taxidermist/zoologist/sculptor Carl Akeley, who pioneered a new technique of sculpting papier-mâché, then covering it with actual animal skins, antlers, and hoofs, often using the animal's bones for structure as well. The results are remarkably lifelike. (Akeley died in Africa while collecting animals to display.) The exhibit fulfills his mission to conserve these animals and their environment for future generations—many of the wilderness areas depicted have changed beyond recognition in the past 50 years.

Other highlights include the **Hall of Ocean Life,** with its famed 10-ton blue whale replica hanging from the ceiling; the **Hall of Planet Earth** with its humongous (and disturbing) interactive media wall about climate change; and the **Spitzer Hall of Human Origins,** an extraordinarily persuasive argument for the theory of evolution. The dazzling **Hall of Minerals,** another must-see, with its Fabergé-carved gems and the largest star sapphire in the world, reopened recently with a new design to celebrate the museum's 150th anniversary. You'll also want to save time for the **Rose Center for Earth and Space ♥♥♥**, a monumental 120-ft.-high glass box enveloping a colossal sphere, which is the virtual reality theater, the Hayden Planetarium. The planetarium's stellar (sorry, I couldn't resist) space show is narrated by astrophysicist Neil deGrasse Tyson, the planetarium's director and former host of PBS's *Cosmo.*

Central Park W. (btw. 77th and 81st sts.). amnh.org. ✆ **212/769-5100.** Admission $30 adults, $24 seniors/students, $18 ages 3–12; pay-what-you-wish for NY/NJ/CT residents w/ID; free for children 2 and under. Additional charges for IMAX movies and some special exhibitions. Daily 10am–5:30pm. Closed Thanksgiving and Christmas. Subway: B, C to 81st St.; 1 to 79th St.

Cathedral of St. John the Divine ♥♥ CATHEDRAL/ARCHITECTURE

Little-known fact: The largest cathedral in the world is *not* St. Peter's in Rome (which is technically not a cathedral but a basilica), it's St. John the Divine in upper Manhattan. Odder fact: Despite the popish name, it isn't Catholic, it's Episcopalian. Oddest fact: Though construction began on the cathedral in 1892, the building is yet to be completed, and many estimate that it will take another 100 years for that to happen. All of which makes this a fascinating building to visit. You'll see a bit of how the ancient cathedrals of Europe were erected—the 121,000-sq.-ft. structure, a blend of Romanesque and Gothic elements (thanks to the varying tastes of the architects who worked on it over the past century), is being built without steel, in the classic Gothic manner. (To that end, in 1979 a master stonecutter was brought from England to train Harlem youths in the art of traditional stonecutting.) There's still much work to be done (including a lot of fundraising!) but what is in place—and there's a lot—is quite beautiful,

The Peace Fountain is a funky 1980s addition to the campus of St. John the Divine, an immense Episcopal cathedral that's still a dynamic work in progress.

At the Museum of Arts and Design intriguing themed exhibitions can vary from a retrospective on Barbie dolls to an examination of turned wood sculpture.

especially the Rose Window in the apse, the largest in North America. You can explore the cathedral on your own or on the **Highlights Tour** ($18) Mondays, Wednesdays, Fridays, and Saturdays at 1pm (sometimes also at 11am). Also inquire about the **Vertical Tour** ($25, Fridays and some Saturdays, at 2pm), which takes you on a hike up an 11-flight circular staircase to the top, for spectacular views.

Services here tend to be among the most musical and progressive in the city. I particularly recommend the New Year's Eve service, featuring original work from some of the best composers in town; the Halloween concert; and the Blessing of the Animals (on the feast day of St. Francis of Assisi, usually early Oct), a ceremony in which New Yorkers bring their pets—ranging from puppies to pythons to thoroughbred horses—to be blessed.

1047 Amsterdam Ave. (at 112th St.). stjohndivine.org. ✆ **212/316-7490.** Admission $15 adults, $12 seniors, $10 students; free for ages 12 and under. Highlights Tour $18 adults, $15 seniors, $12 students. Mon–Sat 9:30am–5pm; Sun noon–5pm. For worship schedule, see website. Subway: B, C, 1 to Cathedral Pkwy.

Museum of Arts and Design ♥♥ MUSEUM It's not easy to get a New Yorker's attention, but this museum does that consistently—it's one of the few museums in town where you'll see more locals than visitors, drawn in by creative, sometimes wacky, exhibitions on design. One, for example, was a blockbuster about Taylor Swift, exhibiting her costumes, stage sets, and more; another explored the design ethos and influence of the Barbie doll. On the top floor, artists in residence work at their craft—furniture, textiles, you name it—making the exhibits below feel that much more vital. It also has one of the best gift stores in the city (p. 326) and a lovely top-floor restaurant.

2 Columbus Circle. madmuseum.org. ✆ **212/299-7777.** Admission $20 adults, $16 seniors, $14 students; free for ages 18 and under; half price on Thurs. Tues–Wed and Fri–Sun 10am–6pm; Thurs noon–8pm. Subway: 1, A, B, C, D to 59th St./Columbus Circle.

The New York Historical ♥ MUSEUM When you're NYC's oldest museum (founded in 1804), your attic gets mighty full. In past years that fourth floor "attic" felt like a treasure hunt, its open storage units overflowing with telling artifacts from the museum's holdings—a Tiffany lamp here, a pair of historic pistols there, the plaster model head created by sculptor Daniel Chester French for Washington's Lincoln Memorial in another corner. Alas, the curators decided to tidy up, and replaced the open storage with three not-so-successful permanent galleries including a large room with themed glass cases of artifacts that illustrate—but don't do enough to illuminate—different facets of New York City life through the ages, and a center for women's history, which has created several yawner exhibits since its opening. On lower floors permanent displays include paintings from the Hudson Valley School, and Audubon drawings, making the museum feel more dedicated to art than to history. Luckily, the powers-that-be had the wisdom to keep the superb 18-minute film that welcomes visitors to the museum. It is reason alone to come here, as are some, but not all, of the temporary exhibits—recent offerings have covered 2.5 centuries of pet owning in NYC, the archives of author Robert Caro *(The Power Broker),* and a look at the life of Justice Ruth Bader Ginsburg.

170 Central Park W. (at 77th St.). nyhistory.org. ✆ **212/873-3400.** Admission $24 adults, $19 seniors/military/educators, $13 students, $6 children 7–13; free for ages 6 and under; pay-what-you-wish Fri 6–8pm. Tues–Sun 11am–5pm (Fri until 8pm). Subway: B, C to 81st St.; 1 to 79th St.

Harlem & Upper Manhattan

The Cloisters ♥♥♥ ART MUSEUM/ARCHITECTURE An offshoot of the **Metropolitan Museum** (p. 219), the Cloisters is the only museum in the United States devoted wholly to medieval art. And it shows its masterworks in a setting that seems to have been airlifted, utterly intact, from some remote corner of the Pyrenees or from a castle-rich town in Bavaria. Opened in 1934, the museum was, in fact, built in the United States, but 30% of its architectural elements—columns, pedestals, naves, doorframes, exquisite stained-glass windows—were salvaged from medieval European structures. It's a stunning mirage—even the land across the river was bought by patron John D. Rockefeller to thwart development and safeguard the Cloisters' view. At its heart are four cloisters, garden areas centered with a fountain and surrounded by covered walkways of the type seen in every monastery and abbey in Europe. Off these tranquil gardens lie galleries devoted to different periods of art and

The Cloisters, constructed from fragments of European monasteries, has many peaceful spots for contemplating medieval art.

architecture—a peak-ceilinged Gothic chapel here; a squat, Romanesque hall there—each housing treasures of that era.

Though you can see the entire museum in an hour or so, pay special attention to the **Unicorn Tapestries,** one of only two full sets with a unicorn theme in the world (the other is in Paris). These richly detailed tapestries can be enjoyed on a number of levels: Many scholars see the unicorn as a symbol of Christ, and the hunt to slay it as evocative of the Passion. Others write that the work is a metaphor for courtly love, with the hunt itself courtship, and the last tapestry of the unicorn trapped inside a wedding ring–like fence symbolizing marriage (despite its captivity, the unicorn does look happy). Whatever you decide, they are strikingly beautiful, an evocative slice of the past when nobles only hunted in packs of six, and unicorns were thought to be real (hence the long narwhal tooth in this room, which medieval man thought came from unicorns). The other must-see items are kept in the climate-controlled Campin Room (bring a sweater), where you'll view Robert de Campin's breakthrough **Merode altarpiece** (ca. 1425) which placed the Annunciation—the moment when an angel informs the Virgin Mary that she will bear the child of God—in a secular setting rather than a church. It's also quite dramatic for its use of Jewish objects, including a prayer shawl and a vase with Hebrew-looking lettering, to establish Mary's background. Nearby is the so-called **Cloisters Cross,** one of only three known ivory crosses preserved from the 12th century—and the most complex, at that, with over 90 figures and inscriptions painstakingly carved into the walrus tusk ivory. I highly recommend timing your tour to coincide with one of the curator-led gallery talks or garden walks (usually held at 1pm).

North end of Fort Tryon Park. metmuseum.org/cloisters. ✆ **212/923-3700.** Admission $30 adults, $22 seniors, $17 students; free for ages 11 and under; NY State residents w/ID pay-what-you-wish. Admission includes same-day entrance to Metropolitan Museum (p. 219). Thurs–Tues 10am–4:30pm. Subway: A to 190th St., then 10-min. walk north along Margaret Corbin Dr. Bus: M4 Madison Ave. (Fort Tryon Park/the Cloisters).

El Museo del Barrio ♥ MUSEUM This showplace for the art of Latin America and the Caribbean owns hundreds of pre-Columbian pieces, contemporary and modern paintings and sculptures, and, most significantly, 500

Santos de Palo, mostly from Puerto Rico. These very beautiful hand-carved, wooden saints are well worth a visit to see. The museum also throws fun parties for Latin and Caribbean holidays and hosts changing exhibits.

1230 Fifth Ave. (at 104th St.). elmuseo.org. ✆ **212/831-7272.** Admission $9 adults, $5 seniors/students; free for ages 12 and under. Thurs–Sun 11am–5pm. Subway: 6 to 103rd St.

Hispanic Society Museum & Library ♥♥ MUSEUM Set in a majestic Belle Epoque complex, the Hispanic Society has been collecting the art of Spain, Portugal, Latin America, and the Philippines since 1904. A lengthy and costly ($20 million) renovation kept it out of the public eye for a number of years until spring 2023, when it reopened with a flourish—and a show of the Goyas, Picassos, El Grecos, and other treasures that it owns. Later exhibitions focused on paintings that illustrated contemporary fashions during the Renaissance, archeological finds from ancient Iberia, and the works of 19th-century Peruvian painter Pancho Fierro. Always on view is Joaquín Sorolla's room-wrapping mural showing richly detailed scenes of Spanish life in the early 20th century.

613 W. 155th St. (entrance on Broadway). hispanicsociety.org. No phone. Free admission but visitors are asked to reserve a visit time online in advance. Thurs–Sun noon–5pm. Subway: 1 to 157th St., C to 155th St.

Masterpieces by Goya and El Greco are part of the rich collections of the Hispanic Society Museum & Library.

ENJOYING THE gospel OF HARLEM

Harlem has over 400 churches. Some are large and ornate, while others are small, one-room churches housed on the ground floors of brownstones. And many of those churches, large or small, feature fiery sermons and magnificent gospel services every Sunday. Gospel tours (p. 264) of these churches have become big business, mainly drawing foreign visitors who line up on Sunday mornings and pay handsomely. There's something uncomfortably voyeuristic about the scene, but the pastors and the churches that attract the crowds—and their donations—aren't complaining. If you want to skip the guided tour and go to services on your own, here are several that are worth visiting:

- **Abyssinian Baptist Church,** 132 Odell Clark Pl. (abyssinian.org; ✆ **212/862-7474;** subway: A, B, C to 135th St.)
- **Canaan Baptist Church,** 132 W. 116th St. (canaanbaptistcoc.com; ✆ **212/866-0301;** subway: 2, 3 to 116th St.)
- **First Corinthian Baptist Church,** 1912 Adam Clayton Powell Jr. Blvd. at 116th St. (fcbcsermons.com; ✆ **212/864-5976;** subway: A, B, C to 116th St.)
- **Greater Refuge Temple,** 2081 Adam Clayton Powell Jr. Blvd. (greaterrefugetemple.org; ✆ **212/280-5268;** subway: 2, 3 to 125th St.)

Most services begin promptly at 11am; seating for non-members is on a first-come, first-served basis. Make sure you arrive in plenty of time; there will most likely be a line. At some churches, tour groups get preference over walk-ups; call in advance to find out that particular church's policy. Service lengths vary but expect at least 2 hours and up to 3. Most tours leave after the gospel choir and before the sermon—you'd think that would be disrespectful, yet because this is a profitable venture for the churches, the faithful take it all in stride.

The Studio Museum ♥♥ ART MUSEUM The Studio Museum in Harlem finally has a space as big as its ambitions. After an 8-year-long closure, the museum reopened in late 2025 in a $300 million, custom-built building so handsome and airy it's now a joy to view the art here (the roof deck has fab views of Harlem). What will you see? Founded in 1968 to support and display Black artists at a time when U.S. museums and galleries rarely, if ever, showed the work of people of color, the Studio Museum has always been the place to view cutting edge art and thoughtful retrospectives. Exhibitions change—the permanent collection is *not* on permanent display—but they regularly show works by such big names as Jean-Michel Basquiat, Romare Bearden, and Faith Ringgold.

144 W. 125 St. (btw. Malcolm X Blvd and Adam Clayton Powell Jr. Blvd.). studiomuseum.org. ✆ **212/864-4500.** Admission $16 adults, $9 for seniors/students/people with disabilities; free for ages 16 and under. Wed–Sun 11am–6pm. Subway: A, B, C, D to 125th St.

THE OUTER BOROUGHS

The Bronx

Note: See p. 153 about exploring Arthur Avenue, a much more authentic Italian American enclave than Manhattan's Little Italy.

Bronx Zoo ♥♥♥ ZOO If you count number of animals as well as acreage, the Bronx Zoo is the largest zoo in the United States, an innovative, unbeatably entertaining place to spend the day. But with over 4,000 animals and 24 exhibits, it requires strategy to see what you want without meltdowns from the younger set. When I visited with kids, I made a direct path first to the **Congo Gorilla Forest,** a remarkable exhibit of silverback gorillas that begins with a short film. Once the film is over, curtains dramatically part to reveal floor-to-ceiling windows, with cavorting gorillas galore (unlike other animals at the zoo, the gorillas are awake if you visit in the daytime; along with the adults, there always seem to be a half-a-dozen baby gorillas in sight as well). From here we hop over to the nearby "bug carousel" or the butterfly exhibit (a tent with thousands of beautiful butterflies fluttering about your head), or to lunch at Flamingo Park. Then we blow off steam at the children's zoo—with all the usual farm animals, plus a spider-web jungle gym and a prairie dog park where children crawl into tunnels and pop their heads up right next to the critters. Dozens of other animals, a fun monorail ride, feeding shows, and more keep you entertained. ***Tip:*** To beat the crowds, try to visit on

The Congo Gorilla Forest is a crowd-favorite exhibit at the Bronx Zoo.

a weekday or a nice winter's day. In summer, come early, before the heat sends the animals back into their enclosures. Expect to spend an entire day here—you'll need it.

Getting there: The BxM11 express bus, which makes stops on Madison Avenue, will take you directly to the zoo. By subway, take the no. 2 train to Pelham Parkway and then walk west to the Bronxdale entrance. For info on both, go to **bronxzoo.com/visitor-info/getting-here**.

Fordham Rd. and Bronx River Pkwy. bronxzoo.com. ✆ **718/367-1010.** Admission $29 adults, $27 seniors, $21 children ages 3–12; free for children 2 and under; free admission Wed but you must apply in advance online. Extra charges for special exhibits. Apr–Oct daily 10am–5pm (Sat–Sun and holidays until 5:30pm); Nov–Mar daily 10am–4:30pm. Transportation: See "Getting There," above.

New York Botanical Garden ♥♥ GARDEN An equal to the Brooklyn Botanic Garden (see below) in both scope and interest, the New York Botanical Garden boasts the world's largest Victorian greenhouse; a "home gardening" section with classes and demonstrations for all the green thumbs out there; a children's garden and play center; and a 50-acre native forest. If there's any difference between the two gardens—they're both wonderful and both world-class—the wealth of hands-on programming just may give this place the edge. That being said, NYBG is now far pricier to visit than the Brooklyn Botanic Garden (the two used to be equivalently priced), so if you're only going to go to one garden in the city, do that one.

A glorious Victorian greenhouse means there's always something blooming year-round at the New York Botanical Garden.

Getting there: Take Metro-North (mta.info/mnr; ✆ **212/532-4900**) from Grand Central Terminal to the New York Botanical Garden station, a 20-minute ride. By subway, take the D or 4 train to Bedford Park, then take bus Bx26 or walk southeast on Bedford Park Boulevard for 8 long blocks.

200th St. and Kazimiroff Blvd. nybg.org. ✆ **718/817-8700.** Admission $35–$39 adults, $31–$35 seniors/students, $25–$27 ages 2–12; free for children 1 and under. NYC residents grounds-only pass $15 adults, $7 seniors/students, $4 ages 2–12. Tues–Sun 10am–6pm (Jan–Feb until 5pm). Transportation: See "Getting There," above.

Brooklyn

Brooklyn Botanic Garden ♥♥ GARDEN Right down the street from the Brooklyn Museum (see below), the Brooklyn Botanic Garden is not only one of those necessary green safety valves, it's also quite an innovative garden in many ways. It was the first in the world to have a "children's garden," allowing local kids to develop green thumbs (it's still here, along with a fun play area for youngsters). There's also a "fragrance garden" for sight-impaired visitors, where everyone is encouraged to sniff and touch the plants; and an authentic Japanese garden, complete with a large pond, pagodas, and plants from that Asian region. The best time of year to visit is spring, when the gardens' many cherry trees are in bloom, though there are seasonal displays, both outdoors and in the on-site greenhouses, year-round.

900 Washington Ave. (at Eastern Pkwy.); entrances also at 455 Flatbush Ave. & 990 Washington Ave. bbg.org. ✆ **718/623-7200.** Admission $22 adults, $16 seniors/students; free for ages 11 and under. Dec–Feb Tues–Fri pay-what-you-wish. Mar–Aug Tues–Thurs 8am–7:40pm, Fri–Sun 8am–6pm (May–Aug Tues–Thurs until 8pm); Sept–Feb Tues–Sun 10am–4:30pm. Subway: Q to Prospect Park; 2, 3 to Eastern Pkwy./Brooklyn Museum.

Brooklyn Museum ♥♥♥ ART MUSEUM Though not as big as the Metropolitan Museum (what is?), this "mini-Met"—covering almost all eras of history in its holdings—is a superb museum on its own terms. Its **Egyptian Collection,** while not as extensive as the Met's, arguably has more masterpieces. (When an ancient Egyptian piece comes up at auction, dealers often ask, "Is it Brooklyn quality?"—the Brooklyn Museum's collection being the benchmark for this sort of artifact.) Among the collection's many wonders are a tiny 5,000-year-old, pre-dynastic terra cotta sculpture of a woman, which curators have nicknamed "Birdwoman" for her beaklike face, one of very few intact sculptures from this long-ago era. The Cartonnage of Nespanetjerenpere is another highlight, a mummy case that looks like it was swiped from the set of *Revenge of the Mummy,* its colors electrically bright and unfaded.

Second most popular among the museum's offerings are the **Decorative Arts Galleries** (fourth floor), which re-create important rooms from different eras of American history, including John D. Rockefeller's "Moorish Smoking Room," an over-the-top Victorian version of the Middle East, every bit of space lavishly carved, gilded, inlaid, or embroidered. Also worth a look: the museum's **American Collection** (works by such masters as Albert Bierstadt, Thomas Eakins, Winslow Homer, and Georgia

The impressive Brooklyn Museum—home to permanent collections such as the extensive Egyptian Collection and the Sackler Center for Feminist Art—holds its own against Manhattan's heavy hitters.

O'Keeffe); the **Elizabeth A. Sackler Center for Feminist Art** (permanent and rotating exhibitions of art made by women, including Judy Chicago's *The Dinner Party*); and whatever special exhibitions are taking place (they're often stellar). Be sure to download the free Bloomberg connections app, which offers several well-produced audio tours of special exhibits and areas of the permanent collection. One final thing the Brooklyn does better than the Met: party. The first Saturday of most months, the museum hires DJs and performers of all sorts and throws a free fiesta from 5 to 11pm.

200 Eastern Pkwy. (at Washington Ave.). brooklynmuseum.org. ✆ **718/638-5000.** Admission $20 adults, $14 seniors/students; free for ages 11 and under; free admission first Sat of month. Special exhibits additional $5. Wed–Sun 11am–6pm. Subway: 2, 3 to Eastern Pkwy./Brooklyn Museum.

Brooklyn Navy Yard ♥♥ HISTORIC SITE At its peak usage during World War II, when it employed some 70,000 men and women, the Brooklyn Navy Yard was the biggest industrial complex in U.S. history—no other site has yet to top that employment figure. But its importance to America began far before then, during the American Revolution, when the British docked their infamous prison ships here; conditions aboard them were so atrocious that more than 11,500 Americans perished here, more than the combined number of U.S. casualties in all the battles of the American Revolution. (Most of their bodies were simply dumped overboard into the water, making these waters the largest Revolutionary graveyard in the States.) Today this 300-acre property is owned by the city of New York, which maintains its historic working dry docks. It also rents out space to dozens of manufacturers and artisans, including the company that builds the sets for *Saturday Night Live;* the soundstage where *The Marvelous Mrs. Maisel* was filmed; and businesses that manufacture clothing, medicines, custom furnishings, and more. You'll learn all of this and then some at the excellent (and free!) on-site museum, which displays historic artifacts and offers several well-crafted videos and oral histories (those dealing with the women who worked here during World War II are especially moving). Outsiders are not allowed to walk around the Navy Yards, however, except as part of a tour, so I recommend pairing a visit to the museum with one of the excellent 2-hour tours run by **Turnstile** (p. 265). Most tours are devoted to the Yard's history, though a few times a month, midweek Turnstile tours visit the manufacturers and soundstages of today's Navy Yard. Since the site is so large, most tours involve a bus, though you will get off the bus often, for a closer look.

East River waterfront (btw. Williamsburg and Manhattan bridges; most entrances off Flushing Ave.). Museum at Building 77, 141 Flushing Ave. brooklynnavyyard.org. ✆ **718/907-5900.** Free admission. See website for dates and times. Ferry to Brooklyn Navy Yard. Subway: B, D, N, Q, R, W to DeKalb Ave. (see website for shuttle info from subway).

City Reliquary ♥ MUSEUM A tiny museum that seems to take its aesthetic from flea markets, City Reliquary illustrates strands of NYC's tale through oddball collections of seltzer bottles, Statue of Liberty figurines, and paintings of Jackie Robinson, among other artifacts. Touring here is a fun 30 minutes, but if you're not nearby you can skip it without regret.

370 Metropolitan Ave. (at Havemeyer St.), Williamsburg. cityreliquary.org. ✆ **718/782-4842.** Admission $10 adults, $5 seniors/students; free for children 12 and under. Sat–Sun noon–6pm. Subway: G to Metropolitan Ave.

Coney Island ♥ ICON/BEACH/AMUSEMENT PARK Honky-tonk paradise, Coney Island has been rescued from extinction a few times (first from developers and most recently from severe Hurricane Sandy damage). Parts of it are given over to brand-new amusement parks and rides, but it's still possible to try some of the classic attractions from times past, including the **Wonder Wheel** (a Ferris wheel with gliding compartments) and the **Cyclone**

Generations of Coney Island visitors have ridden the Wonder Wheel, a giant Ferris wheel with rocking compartments.

(a huge wooden roller coaster, one of the scariest you'll ever ride, because you'll do so knowing that nearly a dozen people have been killed on it over the years). If you visit in summer, don't skip the **Coney Island Circus Side Show** (formerly known as "The Freak Show"; $15 adults, $12 kids ages 12 and under), which features a "human pincushion," a snake charmer, a man who hammers nails up his nose, and other odd performers. It's one of the last shows of its kind in the U.S., and though it sounds unsavory, it's G-rated. Then there's the beach itself, a motley swatch of sand where gaggles of Brooklynites gather in summer to pitch umbrellas, practice kung fu, blast music, picnic, and swim. It's a fascinating social scene, with many different ethnic groups—Russian and Ukranian emigrees from the neighborhood and folks from all over the Caribbean and Latin America, foremost, but just about everyone else, too—represented. ***Note:*** Luna Park recently expanded to add a darn good ropes-and-zipline course, perfect for active tweens and teens.

coneyisland.com. Subway: D, F, N, Q to Coney Island–Stillwell Ave.

Green-Wood Cemetery ♥♥♥ HISTORIC SITE As you wander through New York City, you'll notice a number of streets named for the important Gothamites you'll also encounter at Green-Wood. The "first families" of the city were all interred here, as were such notables as DeWitt Clinton (a presidential candidate who was the mastermind behind the Erie Canal), Leonard Bernstein (composer of Broadway's *West Side Story*), and artists Louis Comfort Tiffany and Jean Michel Basquiat. Heck, even pets were buried here . . . until the funeral of a devoted horse convinced the cemetery's staff to stop the practice in 1870 (the cemetery itself was founded in 1837). It's not hard to understand why New Yorkers would pick Green-Wood for their eternal rest: Set on the highest point of Brooklyn, it's a stunning place, considered an arboretum as well as a cemetery for the 7,000 or so trees that grow here. The monuments are equally beautiful, hand-carved in dozens of different styles, from Tiffany-glass-adorned mausoleums to bronze and marble statuary. A final lure: The staff here, determined to prove that cemeteries can be fun, host a number of events: sporadic trolley and walking tours ($20), lectures, nighttime concerts, "death cafes" (free-form guided discussion groups about what happens after we pass), and even history happy hours at sunset, where people

The Green-Wood Cemetery is the resting place of many famous New Yorkers. Its historic chapel is just one of many architectural beauties within its grounds.

learn the stories behind the tombs with cocktails in hand. The cemetery has also released a free app with interactive maps and self-guided audio walking tours, which tell about both the graves and the area's history (an important Revolutionary War battle took place here).

Main entrance Fifth Ave. at 25th St., Sunset Park. green-wood.com. ✆ **718/210-3080.** Free admission. Daily 8am–6pm.

Industry City ♥♥ ENTERTAINMENT COMPLEX Distinctively Brooklyn entertainment, shopping, and dining experiences are the draw here. There's an escape room, an indoor/outdoor pétanque club, a climbing gym, a board game club, art installations, an ice rink (in season), concerts with local bands, and a lecture/seminar series. Shopping enters the equation with the excellent **Powerhouse** bookstore, and massive discount outlets for **West Elm, RH** (formerly Restoration Hardware), **Design Within Reach,** and **ABC Carpet & Home** (p. 322), along with smaller quintessentially Brooklyn clothing and gift boutiques. Rounding out the offerings are three food halls (one run by the iconic Middle Eastern grocer **Sahadi's** [p. 321], another devoted to Japanese fare, the third holding Brooklyn's much-snarked-about "all avocado" restaurant), as well as a beer brewery, the city's first sake brewery, a distillery for whiskey, and another for ginger liqueurs (the latter is also a liquor store and bar serving only brands created in New York State). It's all a lot of fun. The 16-building complex was first developed by Irving T. Bush in the 1890s as a multi-use manufacturing and warehouse site. By the 1970s, much of it had become derelict, but then, as happened in the SoHo and DUMBO areas, it was rehabbed by artists. Alas, just as in those two neighborhoods, private developers priced out the artists, and most have had to move to cheaper spaces.

Btw. 33rd St. and 41st St., from Gowanus Expressway to waterfront. industrycity.com. Subway: D, N, R, W to 36th St.

New York Aquarium ♥♥ AQUARIUM The marquee attraction here is the whiz-bang **Ocean Wonders** center, dedicated to sharks and the Grand-Canyon-deep underwater "Hudson Canyon," just 40 miles off the city's coastline. Its massive walk-through tanks get visitors up close, but not too personal, with great whites, leopard sharks, giant rays, endangered Atlantic sturgeons, and other sea life; it also holds dozens of educational-but-not-preachy interactive exhibits on sustainable seafood, ocean trash, and the importance of sharks to the ecosystem. On its roof, adults can relax at an open-air cafe while their kids explore touch tanks just steps from the tables. In addition to Ocean Wonders, there's a sea lion show; outdoor pools for black-footed penguins, seals, and sea otters; the **Playquarium,** a kelp-forest-themed play space for visitors age 8 and under; and **Conservation Hall,** which displays massive Amazonian river fish and other sea life.

502 Surf Ave. (at W. 8th St.), Coney Island. nyaquarium.com. ✆ **718/265-FISH** [3474]. Admission $30–$33 adults, $28–$30 seniors, $26–$28 children ages 3– 12 (higher amounts for "peak" times); free for children 2 and under. Daily June–Oct 10am–6pm; Nov–Mar 10am–3:30pm; Apr–May 10am–4pm; last entry 1 hr. before closing. Subway: F, Q to W. 8th St.

Shopping and entertainment have replaced manufacturing at the rehabbed Industry City complex.

New York Transit Museum ♥ MUSEUM Best for kids and train nuts, this underground museum (yes, it's in a former subway station) covers the storied history of the NYC subway system. The museum houses a number of handsome vintage subway cars, turnstiles, and mosaics that used to adorn the stations. If you're in Grand Central Terminal, pop into their off-shoot gallery and store (off the Main Concourse).

Boerum Place and Schermerhorn St., downtown Brooklyn. nytransitmuseum.org. ✆ **718/694-1600.** Admission $10 adults, $5 seniors/visitors with disabilities/children ages 2–17; free for kids 1 and under. Wed–Sun 10am–4pm. Subway: A, C to Hoyt St.; F to Jay St.; M, R to Court St.; 2, 3, 4, 5 to Borough Hall.

At the New York Transit Museum, in downtown Brooklyn, model trains and underground artifacts explain the history of the city's iconic subway system.

Queens

Isamu Noguchi Garden Museum ♥♥ ART MUSEUM Utterly unique, it's one of the only museums in the nation to be founded by an artist in his lifetime, dedicated to his work and curated by him. Because Noguchi (1904–88) was a genius in a number of fields—sculpture, architecture, ceramics, furniture design—he was more than up to the task and created a space that is at once balanced and (often) rapturously beautiful. On-site are also a small store and a Zen sculpture garden (one of the most serene spots in the city). Gallery talks, held at 2pm each day, are helpful for those not familiar with Noguchi's work, as they illuminate the complex engineering issues and intentions behind his large, sometimes slablike, non-representational works.

9-01 33rd Rd. (at Vernon Blvd.), Long Island City. noguchi.org. ✆ **718/204-7088.** Admission $16 adults, $6 seniors/students; free for children 11 and under; free admission first Fri of month. Wed–Sun 10am–5pm. Subway: N to Broadway. Walk west on Broadway to Vernon Blvd.; turn left on Vernon and go 2 blocks.

Louis Armstrong House/Armstrong Center ♥♥ HISTORIC HOME/MUSEUM The visitor experience here is as gracious, warm, and intriguing as the man himself, thanks to the marvelous guides (all ex-musicians and jazz historians) who lead visitors through this historic home every hour on the hour. The only house that this traveling musician ever owned, it was perfectly preserved after his wife Lucille died in 1983 (Armstrong himself passed away in 1971) and opened to the public in 2003. There's an eerie sense that someone still lives here—you may find yourself expecting Satchmo to emerge from the kitchen, turn on the stereo, and tell a joke. In the course of your tour, you'll

In the living room of the Louis Armstrong house, you can imagine Satchmo himself regaling guests with memories of his musical life.

learn Louis's rags-to-riches history (son of a prostitute, learned to play trumpet in a juvenile detention center, made his name in mobster-owned clubs). It's a fairly modest two-story home, but he and Lucille lavished it with every luxury, from custom-made 24-karat bathroom fixtures to Baccarat chandeliers and a state-of-the-art audio system. The highlight: tape recordings of everyday life that Armstrong captured—your guide will play them as you wander through, allowing you to hear the family and visiting musicians talking, laughing, and jamming together. In 2023, the **Armstrong Center** opened across the street, offering a treasure trove of videos about Satchmo and the times in which he lived, touching on the racism of Hollywood, Armstrong's participation in the Civil Rights movement, and much more. Be sure to give yourself another half hour, either before or after the house tour, to see all the exhibits.

34-56 107th St., Corona. louisarmstronghouse.org. ✆ **718/478-8274.** Admission $20 adults, $14 seniors/students/children; free for ages 3 and under. Tours on the hour, Thurs–Sat 11am–4pm. Subway: 7 to 103rd St./Corona Plaza. Walk north on 103rd St., turn right on 37th Ave., turn left on 107th St.; the house is a ½-block north of 37th Ave.

The International Express

The **no. 7 train**—which originates in Manhattan at Times Square, makes three stops in that borough, and then snakes, mostly above ground, through the heart of Queens—is also popularly known as the International Express. Built by immigrants in the early 1900s, the no. 7 IRT (Interborough Rapid Transit) brought those same immigrants to homes on the outer fringes of New York City.

That tradition has continued as immigrants from around the world have settled close by the no. 7's elevated tracks. Get off in Sunnyside and see Romanian grocery stores and restaurants; a few stops farther in Jackson Heights, you'll see South Asian women in saris and Sikhs in turbans; explore Roosevelt Avenue, home to "Little Caracas" for the recent Venezuelan arrivals; go all the way to Flushing and you'll think you are in Chinatown. (You are—Queen's Chinatown is bigger than Manhattan's.) In 1999, the Queens Council on the Arts nominated the International Express for designation as a National Millennium Trail, and that resulted in its selection as representative of the American immigrant experience by the White House Millennium Council, the United States Department of Transportation, and the Rails-to-Trails Conservancy.

Museum of the Moving Image ♥♥♥ MUSEUM For sheer unadulterated fun, no museum in town can beat this one. The first museum anywhere to look at TV, film, and video games together (a heretical concept when the museum opened in 1988), it's not simply an archive of past shows. Instead, it explores the craft and technology behind these arts with startlingly imaginative interactive exhibits, commissioned art works, video sequences, and, of course, artifacts. Just how much fun is all this? Well, CitySearch ranked it the best place in the city for a family outing, while *Time Out* magazine called it the number-one place to go when you're "baked"—if that doesn't hit all the bases, I don't know what does.

Creative exhibits at the Museum of the Moving Image bring museumgoers deep into the worlds of TV, film, and video games.

Start your visit with the museum's core exhibit, **Behind the Screen,** which explores the many technical issues behind moving images, from explanations of how the eye is tricked into seeing movement in rapidly repeating images, to the intricacies of sound and film editing. You'll have a chance to dub your own voice into such classics as *My Fair Lady,* create original computer animation, transmute the musical score of a famous film scene, and more. Several times a day, working editors, animators, and educators demonstrate how these techniques are used on actual productions. Other sections cover design concerns, exploring how makeup, costumes, sets, and publicity stills help create the image the director (or studio) is looking for. If you've been harboring a secret yen to play *Galaga* just one more time, you'll have your chance in the playable video games exhibit. Next, you'll likely want to take in whatever blockbuster special exhibit is on; recent ones have covered TV shows *(Mad Men, The Walking Dead),* the phenomenon of Internet cat videos, and the dangerous artistry of deep fake videos. On the first floor, the museum's full-size movie theater screens feature films from around the world, often followed by discussions with the artists involved, including such big names as Glenn Close, Tim Burton, David Cronenberg, or Jennifer Connelly. And at some time during your visit, take the elevator: It screens custom-made GIFs by some of the top GIF-makers working today (yes, that is a now a career path!). This part of Queens was where many early American films were made—the 98,000-sq.-ft. museum was built on the grounds of Kaufman Astoria Studios. The overall experience illuminates how far the art form has come in so brief a span of time, and just how powerful the human imagination is.

35th Ave. at 37th St., Astoria. movingimage.us. ✆ **718/777-6800.** Admission $20 adults, $12 seniors/students, $10 ages 5–18, $5 visitors with disabilities; free for ages 4 and under; free admission Thurs. Thurs 2–6pm; Fri 2–8pm; Sat–Sun 11am–6pm. Subway: R, M to Steinway St.; N to 36th Ave.

P.S. 1 Contemporary Art Center ♥♥ ART MUSEUM At this proving ground for young artists, the work you'll see will be challenging, of the moment, and sometimes downright wacky. "P.S. 1 is mythological," says former assistant director Brett Littman. "Wherever I go, people know that there's this crazy building in Long Island City where you see crazy art. They come here to put a notch on their culture belt." That "crazy building" was once a public school (hence the name), and its somewhat decrepit charm is part of the experience. Because it's not a fancy white box of a space (like its sister institution the Museum of Modern Art), P.S. 1 allows artists to create full-blown, sometimes invasive, installations in the space. (One summer several years ago, an artist blasted holes in the brick wall of a gallery.) It uses all kinds of unusual spaces to house art, such as the basement boiler room. The bulk of the work you'll see here will be in changing exhibits, as the museum does not collect art; visitors are usually greeted with as many as 14 different shows in all parts of the building. As I've said, some can be quite, well, bizarre. In its retrospective of New York City art several years back, one framed sculpture turned out to be the actual hand of the artist who was sitting on the other side of the wall, personifying her art. Now if that's not worth $10, I don't know what is. ***A note for summer visitors:*** On summer Fridays (4–10pm), P.S. 1 throws rowdy, fun Warm Up "beach parties" (sand is dumped in the outdoor areas), complete with live music, food, and various games.

22-25 Jackson Ave. (at 46th Ave.), Long Island City. ps1.org. ✆ **718/784-2084.** Free admission. Thurs–Mon noon–6pm (Sat until 8pm). Subway: E, M to 23rd St./Ely Ave. (walk 2 blocks south on Jackson Ave.); 7 to 45th Rd./Court House Square (walk 1 block south on Jackson Ave.).

Changing art installations at P.S. 1 feature challenging work by emerging artists.

Queens Museum ♥ MUSEUM Long before there was Google Earth, there was the Panorama of the City of New York. A diorama of 9,335 sq. ft., it was created for the 1964–65 World's Fair with the help of photographers who swooped in helicopters over the city, taking over 7,000 photos to capture every building in the five boroughs. The Panorama is still a wonder today, and the heart of the Queens Museum. It was fully updated in 1992, and subsequently, building owners can pay to have their newer edifices added, which makes for some odd anomalies. I highly recommend taking the museum's free guided tour (offered several times a day) as the docent does a masterful job of making the geography come alive, with discussions of the city's history and what on the map is wrong and right. Other exhibits cover the museum building's storied history: It was erected for the 1939 World's Fair and served as the site of the United Nations during its first 5 years. There's also a lovely exhibit of Tiffany lamps (a nod to the fact that the Tiffany factory was in Corona, Queens) and changing art exhibits.

Flushing Meadows Corona Park, Queens. queensmuseum.org. ✆ **718/592-9700.** Free admission. Wed–Fri noon–5pm; Sat & Sun 11am–5pm. Subway: 7 to Mets–Willets Point.

ESPECIALLY FOR KIDS

Museums

In addition to the museums specifically for kids detailed below, consider the **American Museum of Natural History** ♥♥♥ (p. 224), whose dinosaur displays are guaranteed to wow both you and your children; the **Museum of the Moving Image** ♥♥♥ (p. 242), where you and the kids can learn how movies are actually made (and play vintage video games); and the **New York Transit Museum** (p. 240), where young 'uns can explore vintage subway cars and other hands-on exhibits. Note that even museums that would be considered more "adult," like the **Whitney** (p. 183), the **Museum of Modern Art** (p. 194), and the **Metropolitan Museum of Art** (p. 219), now offer free activity books and/or audio tours for younger visitors, to help engage them with the art.

"Game" places for slightly older kids can be good for blowing off steam, like **Escape the Room** (several locations and varying rates; escapetheroom nyc.com), in which groups are locked into a room and have 1 hour to solve riddles and find clues that will help them get out. It's tons of fun.

The Brooklyn Children's Museum ♥♥ MUSEUM The very first museum of its type in the nation, the Brooklyn Children's Museum isn't easy to get to from Manhattan, but it rewards those who make the trek (there's a shuttle from the nearest subway stop many days of the week; check the museum's website). Inspired by the idea that children love to play at working, the museum gives them a number of places in which to toil: a garden where they can plant things and learn about botany, a pretend restaurant and grocery

At the Brooklyn Children's Museum, kids can "shop" at a play grocery store.

store where they can "feed" their parents, a "building brainstorm" area that teaches the basics of architecture and engineering with blocks and other building toys, and more. For those who end up spending hours here (it happens!), there's an on-site cafe.

145 Brooklyn Ave. (at St. Marks Ave.). brooklynkids.org. ✆ **718/735-4400.** Admission $15; free admission Thurs 2pm until closing. Wed–Sun 10am–5pm. Subway: 3 to Kingston Ave.; A to Nostrand Ave.; C to Kingston/Throop Ave.

Children's Museum of Manhattan ♥ MUSEUM At this slick hands-on attraction, changing exhibits highlight the kiddie zeitgeist of the moment: Red Grooms, Maurice Sendak, and William Wegman's dog art were just a few recent exhibit themes. Those with toddlers should go directly to the Child Development Center on the fourth floor, where kids can finger-paint to their hearts' delight, play with little stoves, and send rubber balls rocketing down a twisted tube from a loft to the floor (there were days when I never got past this room). Older children will want to take part in the classes and special exhibits; since these fill up fast, stop by the sign-up desk right when you enter.

212 W. 83rd St. (btw. Broadway and Amsterdam Ave.). cmom.org. ✆ **212/721-1234.** Online admission $17 adults, $14 seniors (add $1 if you buy at the door); free for children 1 and under; free admission first Fri of month 5–8pm. Tues–Sun 10am–5pm. Subway: 1 to 86th St.

Museum of Illusions ♥ ATTRACTION You want to be in a group of three or more for this attraction: Many of the photo ops are for two posers, requiring another person to snap the shot. And that's mostly what this "museum" is about: taking funny photos to post on social media. Tweens will love it . . . and parents will try unsuccessfully to engage them in conversation about the science behind optical illusions. On weekends, there's often a line out the door, but this place really isn't worth waiting for (you can see the entire attraction in about 20 minutes, a disappointment at these prices and after an hour-long line).

77 Eighth Ave. (at 14th St.). museumofillusions.com. ✆ **212/645-3230.** Admission $35 adults, $31 students/seniors, $28 ages 6–13; free for kids 5 and under. Mon–Thurs 10am–11pm; Fri–Sat 10am–midnight. Subway: L, A, E, C to 14th St./Eighth Ave.

New York Hall of Science ♥♥ MUSEUM Set in one of the few remaining buildings from the 1964 World's Fair, this museum is a big hit with science-attuned youngsters, as most of its exhibits are hands-on and interactive. For those who just want to blow off steam, there's a minigolf park in good weather and an excellent science-themed playground. The only negative for most visitors—and it's a serious one—is how remote it is from Manhattan (it can take a good hour on the subway each way). Still, if you've been to NYC with your kids a few times and want something new, this is definitely a good option.

47-01 111th St., Corona, Queens. nysci.org. ✆ **718/699-0005.** Admission $22 adults, $19 seniors and children 2–17 (additional costs for special exhibits, films, and mini-golf); free for kids 1 and under. Wed–Sun 10am–5pm. Subway: 7 to 111th St.

Hands-on activities absorb young visitors at the New York Hall of Science.

PARKS & GARDENS

Central Park ♥♥♥

Manhattan's 843-acre green oasis is the yin to the city's neon, concrete, and office tower yang. It serves as the city's backyard, its concert hall, its daytime pick-up bar, and, in the summer, when dozens don bathing suits to soak up the rays, its green beach. The marvel of the park, besides its size (a full 6% of the total area of Manhattan), is its ability to provide just the right sort of

One of Central Park's loveliest features, Bethesda Fountain, presides over Bethesda Terrace, near West 72nd Street.

experience for the myriad of very different personalities who think of it as their own. I think it's that chameleon-like quality that makes it such an interesting place for visitors to tour. Seeing it from an outsider's perspective, it's much easier to recognize that the park is a great mirage and paradox.

Because, let's face it, very little here is natural. Every tree, every shrub, every lake, and most of the rolling hills were designed, planted, or blasted into existence by landscape architects Frederick Law Olmsted and Calvert Vaux back in the 1850s, and their efforts still shape our experiences today. These two geniuses took a 2½-mile tract of swampland, farms, and suburban towns and created an Arcadia that had no resemblance whatever to what had come before. Underneath the park, 95 miles of drainage pipes were installed, many to fill and periodically empty the four lakes that were created; at ground level the site was transformed using six million bricks, 65,000 cubic tons of gravel, 26,000 trees, and 250,000 shrubs. Even the dirt was imported; the natural topsoil was so poor that 500,000 cubic feet of topsoil was shipped in from New Jersey. As Olmsted once wrote, "Every foot of the park, every tree and bush, every arch, roadway and walk, has been fixed where it is with a purpose."

And what was that purpose? No less than the health of the city. Those who rallied for its creation felt that it was crucial to create a place where New Yorkers could blow off steam and get away from the stresses of urban life. Moreover, Olmsted wanted to create a park that would be a bridge between classes.

"There need to be places and time for re-unions," Olmsted wrote, "[where] the rich and the poor, the cultivated and the self-made, shall be attracted together and encouraged to assimilate." Though that didn't happen when the park was first finished—it was too far from the homes of poor New Yorkers for them to visit it—that ideal was realized when the city itself began to wrap around the park, making it finally a true *central* park.

Many sights I list below may feel familiar to American visitors: Central Park was and remains the most influential piece of landscape architecture in the United States, and many parks around the country were directly copied from this one. In your strolls around the park, you'll encounter three different types of landscapes: **pastoral vistas** such as the Sheep Meadow, which are meant to evoke a cultivated countryside; **primitive portions** where dense forestation shuts out any view of the city; and **promenade zones,** which were once used by the city's aristocracy as an extension of their parlors, a place to strut and be seen. I've created a brief list of highlights that includes all three, but feel free to ignore the list altogether and just wander the curving paths of the park, exploring its hidden nooks, surprise vistas, ball fields, and playgrounds. There's no right way to see or do this park.

ORIENTATION & GETTING THERE The park runs from 59th Street (also known as Central Park South) at the south end to 110th Street at the north end, and from Fifth Avenue on the east side to Central Park West (the continuation of Eighth Ave.) on the west side. A 6-mile rolling road, Central Park Drive, circles within the park, with separate designated lanes for bikers, joggers, and in-line skaters. A number of transverse (crosstown) roads cross the park at major points—at 65th, 79th, 86th, and 97th streets—but they're built down a level, largely out of view, to minimize intrusion. Several subway stops serve the park; which one you take depends on where you want to go. To reach the southernmost entrance on the west side by subway, take an A, B, C, D, or 1 to 59th Street/Columbus Circle. To reach the southeast corner entrance, take the N or R to Fifth Avenue. There's now an app, **Central Park Entire** ($2.99) that will guide you around Central Park and comes complete with GPS should you get lost and need to find a nearby exit. It was created by the Park Service.

CENTRAL PARK HIGHLIGHTS

Belvedere Castle and the Delacorte Theater ♥♥♥ FOLLY/THEATER Olmsted and Vaux's "folly" (or fantasy building), this turreted castle sits atop the second-highest elevation in the park. Inside is a nature observatory with good rainy-day activities for children. In front of the castle is the **Delacorte Theater ♥♥**, where the famed **Shakespeare in the Park** (p. 344) is performed, a star-studded and free evening of theater staged in the summer only. From Belvedere, you'll also look down on the **Great Lawn,** which has gone through a number of incarnations, first as a reservoir and later

Belvedere Castle & the Delacorte Theater **3**
Bethesda Terrace **6**
The Carousel **10**
Central Park Zoo/ Tisch Children's Zoo **12**
Cleopatra's Needle **2**
Conservatory Garden **1**
Conservatory Water **5**
The Dairy **11**
Loeb Boathouse **4**
The Mall **9**
Sheep Meadow **8**
Strawberry Fields **7**
Wollman Rink **13**

M Subway station
Playground

0 1/10 mile
0 100 meters

in the 1930s as "Hooverville," the shantytown where hundreds of homeless families lived out the Depression. Today it's laid out in ballfields and often used as a concert space: Simon and Garfunkel reunited here in the 1980s in a widely televised concert.

Enter the park at either 72nd or 79th St. For info on Shakespeare in the Park: publictheater.org. ✆ **212/539-8500.** Free admission.

Central Park's Victorian-era Carousel.

The Carousel ♥♥ CAROUSEL A Victorian spinner, this is most children's favorite park stop (it certainly was my daughters'). Though it's not the original carousel (the first burned down in the 1950s), it's a beaut, built in Coney Island in 1908, and featuring some of the tallest merry-go-round horses in the U.S. It's also a much more humane carousel than the original, which was rotated by a blind mule and horse toiling in the basement.

At approximately 65th St., in the center of the park. centralpark.com. $4 per ride. Daily 10am–dusk.

Central Park Zoo/Tisch Children's Zoo ♥♥ ZOO Because of its small size, the zoo is at its best with its displays of smaller animals. The indoor multilevel **Tropic Zone** is a real highlight, its steamy rainforest home

Playgrounds, Carriages & Bird-Watching

A word on playgrounds: With a few exceptions, most of Central Park's 22 playgrounds are located on the rim of the park near the entrances. They tend to pop up every 5 blocks or so, with some of the more elaborate playgrounds located on the south end of the park (conceived as the children's side of the park because it was nearer to where lower-income families lived at the time of the park's opening).

Horse-drawn carriage rides: At the entrance to the park at 59th Street and Central Park South, you'll see a line of horse-drawn carriages waiting to take passengers on a ride through the park or along certain of the city's streets. A ride is $100 to $150 for 20–30 minutes (plus tip), but I suggest skipping it. Not only are the horses sad looking (there have been publicly aired allegations many are mistreated), the "tour" you'll get is likely to be filled with misinformation.

Wildlife in the park: Birders from all over the city flock to the park for the variety of species it hosts, the most coveted sightings being of the endangered red-tailed hawks that make their nest on Woody Allen's Fifth Avenue building (at Fifth Ave. and 74th St.).

to everything from black-and-white colobus monkeys to Emerald tree boa constrictors to a leaf-cutter ant farm; look for the poison-dart-frog exhibit, which is very cool. So is the large penguin enclosure in the **Polar Circle,** which is better than the one at San Diego's SeaWorld. Despite their pool and piles of ice, however, the polar bears still look sad. The zoo is good for short attention spans; you can cover the entire thing in under an hour. It's also very kid-friendly, with lots of well-written and illustrated placards that older kids can understand. For the littlest ones, the nearby **Tisch Children's Zoo** ♥ has goats, llamas, potbellied pigs, and more in a petting zoo and playground that's a real blast for the 5-and-under set. ***Note:*** Admission to the immersive 4-D theater is $6 extra, but it's a worthwhile show.

830 Fifth Ave. (at 64th St., just inside Central Park). centralparkzoo.com. ✆ **212/439-6500.** Online admission $16 adults, $13 seniors, $10 children 3–12; free for ages 2 and under. In-person purchase $6 more but includes 4-D theater. Nov–Mar daily 10am–4:30pm; Apr–Oct daily 10am–5pm (Sat–Sun and holidays until 5:30pm). Last entrance 30 min. before closing. Subway: N, R to Fifth Ave.; 6 to 68th St.

Cleopatra's Needle ♥♥ MONUMENT This handsome obelisk was a gift to the United States from Egypt in 1881, in recognition of the help this country gave in the construction of the Suez Canal. Transporting the 200-ton pillar took 38 days from Alexandria to New York by ship, and then another 144 just to get it from the Hudson River to Central Park. It originally stood at the Temple of the Sun in Heliopolis, and is believed to have been erected in 1600 B.C. The Romans moved it in the 12th century to the front of a temple built by Cleopatra, hence the name. A plaque at the base translates the hieroglyphics.

Near the back of the Metropolitan Museum at roughly 83rd St.

Conservatory Garden ♥♥♥ GARDEN The park's only formal gardens are simply stunning, which may be why this is a favorite spot for wedding photographers. Walk around and you'll notice that each of the garden's three sections has a different ambience; one is meant to mimic the gardens of France, another those of Italy, and the third pays tribute to Britain's blossoms.

Enter at Fifth Ave. and 105th St.

Conservatory Water ♥♥♥ POND Here's the model boat pond where Stuart Little had his fabled race. You can rent a model boat to float around (via remote control), take a look at the Hans Christian Andersen statue (where storytelling takes place on summer Saturdays), or visit the Alice in Wonderland statue, an artistic jungle gym for the city's youth.

Enter at 79th St. on Fifth Ave.; the pond is directly uptown of the entrance, down a hill.

The Dairy ♥ ARCHITECTURE/TOURS Completed in 1871, this frou-frou-laden Gothic structure was an actual dairy set up to give city children access to fresh milk. Today it serves as the park's visitor center, so it's a good place to stop to pick up maps. Most of the Central Park Conservancy's free tours start from this point; see below for info on their scheduling.

At roughly 65th St., closer to Fifth Ave. Go to centralparknyc.org/tours for tour info.

The Mall, Bethesda Terrace & the Loeb Boathouse ♥♥♥ PARK LAND In their original plans for the park, Olmsted and Vaux called the area known today as the Mall "the Promenade," and intended for it to be an "open air hall of reception." Today when you visit you'll be greeted by a grand elm-lined walkway bedecked with statues. At its uptown end is an underused band shell, and west of that is one of the park's premier party places: an unofficial rollerblading rink where regulars dance-skate for hours each weekend to blasting disco music. It's quite a scene. At the uptown end of the mall (just across the road), **Bethesda Terrace** is, without a doubt, the architectural heart of the park. You're likely to see a bride or two here, as many use this extraordinarily lovely area as a backdrop for wedding photographs. If you approach it from the Mall, you'll come to two massive posts on either side of the stairs, carved with symbols representing day and night (the side with the witch on a broom is "night"). Take a look as well at the carvings on the stairs down to the fountain area; they represent the four seasons, and no two are alike. Bethesda Fountain commemorates the opening of the Croton Aqueduct, which finally solved New York's water problems in 1842 (the fountain was finished in 1864). Sculpted by Emma Stebbins, the first woman to receive this type of commission from the city, the statue represents the angel Bethesda. She blesses the water with one hand, carrying a lily—the symbol of purity—in the other. Added to the park in 1874, **Central Park Boathouse** is where you rent the boats that you see bobbing on the lake, and dine (at either the cafe, which has salads and sandwiches, or the sit-down restaurant. Carrie and Mr. Big, of *Sex and the City,* fell into the water together at the end of a disastrous date on the dock that pushes out from the cafe.

At approximately 74th St. off Park Dr. centralparkboathouse.com. ✆ **212/517-2233.** Boat rentals $25 per hour Apr–Nov Mon–Thurs and $30 per hour Fri–Sun.

Sheep Meadow ♥♥ MEADOW The premier see-and-be-seen spot for New York's teenagers, who turn this expanse of grass into a sunbathing party come spring and summer. They're following a long tradition: This is where New York's hippie "be-in," a day of non-political grooviness created by Abbie Hoffman, took place in 1967. The meadow got its name in 1864 when park commissioners set sheep to graze here in an attempt to stop the First Division of the NY National Guard from using the meadow as a parade ground (it didn't work). In 1934, the sheep were exiled to Prospect Park in Brooklyn.

Between 64th and 68th sts., toward the West Side.

Strawberry Fields ♥ MEMORIAL A memorial to John Lennon, who was shot to death in 1980 in front of the Dakota apartment house (1 W. 72nd

To experience Central Park as so many locals do, join a group run with NY Running Tours (p. 264).

St.) just across the street from here. Many come here to play music and leave flowers at the "Imagine" mosaic on the ground.

Enter at 72nd St. and Central Park West and follow the crowds.

Wollman Rink ♥♥ SKATING RINK A wonderfully scenic place to skate, you may remember it from the movies *Home Alone 2, Serendipity,* and *Love Story.* In the summer and spring months, the rink hosts varied events, from concerts to "sip and paint" classes.

Enter at Central Park S, across from the Plaza Hotel. wollmanrinknyc.com. Admission $16–$38 adults (depending on time), $11 seniors and children 4–12; $12 skate rental. Skating: late Oct–Apr Mon–Tues 10am–2:30pm, Wed–Sun 10am–9pm (Fri & Sat until 10pm).

More Parks in New York City

Battery Park ♥♥ PARK At the southernmost tip of Manhattan, Battery Park has been growing kudzu-like for the past several decades. It's now a string of eclectic park spaces hugging the waterfront from just above the original Battery Park (where the Statue of Liberty ferry terminal is located) all the way up to Chambers Street (21 acres in all). At the downtown-most park are a number of stirring war monuments and the **Seaglass Carousel** (Thurs–Sun 11am–6pm; Fri–Sat until 7pm, weather permitting; $6/ride), which dips and swoops riders around on massive plexiglass fish. Walking uptown from the original battery, you'll encounter expansive lawns, a riverside promenade that runs the length of the park, terrific playgrounds, and a yacht marina. My favorite parts are the South Cove (on the Esplanade between First and Third places), an artfully varied collection of quays, bridges, and meandering walkways with great river views; and the **Irish Hunger Memorial,** a grassy outcropping direct from Ireland, complete with a real Irish stone fence.

From State St. to New York Harbor. thebattery.org. ✆ **212/344-3491.** Subway: R to Whitehall St.; 1 to South Ferry; 4, 5 to Bowling Green.

Brooklyn Bridge Park ♥♥♥ PARK Many visitors who walk over the Brooklyn Bridge from Manhattan find the urge to linger in this handsome 85-acre waterfront park. Once an industrial area, it's home to a spectacular 1922 carousel (surrounded by a pavilion by contemporary star architect Jean Nouvel); the bouncy and architecturally significant **Squibb Park Bridge;** and several dozen play spaces including basketball, volleyball, handball, bocce, and shuffleboard courts as well as terrific playgrounds for the little ones. Free guided tours are periodically offered, and events of all sorts make this an exciting place in the warm weather months (see website for more info). Do I need to mention that the views of Manhattan are killer from here?

East River waterfront from Manhattan Bridge to Brooklyn Bridge. brooklynbridgepark.org. Subway: A, C to High St.; F to York St.; R to Court St.; 2, 3, 4, 5 to Borough Hall.

Bryant Park ♥♥ PARK Just behind the New York Public Library, this park is a welcome respite from the endless high-rises and crushing crowds of midtown, a 4-acre lawn surrounded by benches, statuary, and London planetree–shaded promenades (like the Tuileries Gardens in Paris). It's notable for its extensive programs of public concerts, movies, even free juggling classes every good weather day at noon. Worthwhile free park tours are offered every other Wednesday at 11am. From roughly May through October, the Sixth Avenue

Among the many daily activities scheduled in midtown's Bryant Park: winter ice skating.

Brooklyn's Domino Park has creatively adapted relics of an old sugar refinery.

end of the park is set up as a stage, where Broadway performers often give concerts, free movies are shown on summer Monday nights, and other events take hold. In winter a small "pond" is set up for free ice skating (skate rentals have a fee; advanced reservations are available online). They also have bumper cars on ice for the shocking price of $23 per ride. On the 40th Street side is the elegant little merry-go-round **Le Carrousel** ($5–$6/ride, depending on the season; June–Aug daily 10am–8pm; Sept–Dec 11am–8pm, Jan and Mar–May 11am–7pm; Feb 11am–6pm). A good spot for a picnic, Bryant Park has a bunch of chain restos across the street; pricey, so-so restaurants are on the north side of the park (go for drinks, not dinner).

Behind the New York Public Library, at Sixth Ave. (btw. 40th and 42nd sts.). bryantpark.org. Subway: B, D, F, Q to 42nd St.; 7 to Fifth Ave.

Domino Park ♥♥♥ PARK/HISTORIC SITE Who knew "adaptive reuse" could be this sexy? One of two privately owned parks on this list, Domino Park is open to the public and sits on a quarter acre of riverside property once owned by the Domino Sugar Refinery. In adapting the land, designer Lisa Switkin (of the firm behind the High Line; p. 257) protected that landmarked structure, making the hulking factory a spooky centerpiece of the park, and re-using other industrial artifacts found here to wonderful effect. That includes a gantry, basically a massive platform that holds two cranes, painted the same shade of turquoise that once lined the refinery's walls; it's now an elevated walkway affording spectacular Manhattan views. In front of it is a playground that looks like a mini-refinery, a volleyball court flanked by old syrup tanks, and a grove of metal corkscrews the height of Christmas trees (they were once used to stir syrup). Right in front of the old factory **Domino Square** hosts ice skating in the winter ($20 admission; $12 skate rental) and all sorts of events the rest of the year. Notably, one of the city's only open-air riverfront restaurants is here, as is top pizzeria **Roberta's** (p. 121), just outside the park, along with a brewery and an ice-cream parlor. If this had been publicly funded, we doubt there'd be this many for-profit eateries here, and it makes the park especially attractive for sunset drinks or dinner.

In Williamsburg, Brooklyn, on the river, btw. S. 5th and Grand sts. dominopark.com. Daily 6am–11pm. Subway: G to Metropolitan Ave.; L to Bedford Ave.

Governors Island ♥♥ PARK/HISTORIC SITE Situated a half-mile south of Manhattan, the 172-acre Governors Island was for many years a Coast Guard installation. Before that, it was an army post for nearly 200 years

Car-free cycling with killer New York Harbor views makes Governor's Island a fun getaway spot.

and played a part in the Revolutionary War. In April 2010, New York City took over. Because it had been a military base for so long, few New Yorkers, much less tourists, had visited Governors Island. But that has changed. Much of Governors Island is now a public park, and 22 acres are a national monument, centered around two 1812-era fortresses. One part of the parkland here is crowned by four artificial hills, giving visitors even more stellar views of Manhattan. The island is open to visitors year-round, with transportation via either the NYC ferry's yellow line from Brooklyn (go to ferry.nyc for a map of docks) or the Trust for Governor's Island ferries, which depart from the Battery Maritime Building adjacent to the Staten Island Ferry in lower Manhattan. On the island, you can walk or bicycle in a car-free environment and attend activities from jazz concerts to pop-up museum exhibits. There's a fun slide park for kids and glamping options in warm-weather months for those who'd like an overnight stay.

govisland.com. ✆ **212/440-2200.** Free admission. Ferries depart from Battery Maritime Bldg. (next to Staten Island Ferry terminal); in Brooklyn ferries depart from Pier 6, at foot of Atlantic Ave.; check website for schedules, as the timing for the last ferry back varies. Late May–Oct Fri–Sun. Subway: 1 to South Ferry; 4, 5 to Bowling Green.

High Line ♥♥♥ PARK For years, a secret, untamed garden hovered above the cityscape of Chelsea and Hell's Kitchen. Formed from the wild grass, flower, and weed seeds that randomly blew onto the tracks of a 1½-mile abandoned elevated railway, it became a hidden-in-plain-sight oasis for those New Yorkers brave (and limber) enough to scale the trestles. When the city started planning to tear down the historic rail structure (constructed 1929–34), a movement was born to save it and create a "grand public promenade," with easy access from the street. Opened in 2009, it's beautifully landscaped (in many places with the "weeds" that once grew there naturally, replanted in areas where they wouldn't destroy the rest of the plants), with benches and gourmet food vendors galore, and a unique vantage for viewing surrounding buildings and the streets below—it's become THE place to head for a stroll on a balmy summer evening.

From Gansevoort St. to W. 34th St. (btw. 10th and 12th aves.). thehighline.org. ✆ **212/500-6035.** Dec–Mar 7am–8pm; Apr–Nov 7am–10pm. Subway: A, C, E, L to 14th St.; 7 to Hudson Yards.

Hudson River Park ♥♥ PARK This 500-acre park runs for 4 miles, transforming once industrial waterfront into a variety of parks and playspaces. They include Sheep Meadow–like expanses of grass, marvelous landscaping, terrific views of the Hudson River, innovative playgrounds (including a science-based one that opened in 2023), public art installations, and more. This is an ideal place to bring the kids for a sunny afternoon, especially to one of the park's pride and joys: a custom-designed 36-passenger **carousel** with all

Playgrounds, minigolf, and a carousel make Hudson River Park a favorite destination for New Yorkers with young kids.

the hand-carved animals indigenous to the greater New York City area (it's at Pier 62, near 23rd St.). The free skate park and minigolf course are also fun.

Enter between N. Moore and 56th sts. on the far west side. hudsonriverpark.org. ✆ **212/627-2020.** Carousel $3.50/ride (children under 42 in. tall must be accompanied by adult); daily 11am–6pm, weather permitting. Minigolf $10, $5 for ages 12 and under; daily 10am–6pm (until 5 Mon and Tues). Skate park 8am–dusk.

Little Island ♥♥♥ PARK Gotham's newest park seems to float like a watery mirage in the Hudson River. The engineering and architecture by Thomas Featherwick (of Vessel; p. 188 and p. 190) is stupendous, with a set of 132 concrete "tulips," all of differing heights, emerging from the water and connecting to form the base of the isle. On top of that Seuss-like structure, hills were built, and amphitheaters, and eateries, all connected by a network of sinuously winding paths, stairs, and boulder scrambles. Landscaping superstar Signe Nielson was in charge of the greenery, and she spared no expense—it's been reported she spent $5 million to cover the island with some 35 species of trees, 65 species of shrubs, and 270 varieties of perennials, grasses, vines, and bulbs. Many were chosen for their appeal to bees and birds, as it's hoped this will be a sanctuary for those critters. Like Domino Park (p. 255), the structure is open to the public but is a private enterprise: It's a gift to the city from media mogul Barry Diller, who spent $260 million for its construction and has pledged to supply money for its upkeep into the foreseeable future. The park is the hilly green yin to the city's flat and gray yang—it's a bewitching new addition to Gotham.

Hudson River between 13th and 14th sts. littleisland.org. Subway: A, C, E, L to 14th St.

Prospect Park ♥♥♥ PARK Designed by Frederick Law Olmsted and Calvert Vaux after their success with Central Park, this 562-acre expanse of woodland, meadows, and ponds is considered by many to be their masterpiece and the *pièce de résistance* of Brooklyn. The best approach is from **Grand Army Plaza,** presided over by the monumental **Soldiers' and Sailors' Memorial Arch** (1892) honoring Union veterans. For the best view of the lush landscape, follow the path to Meadowport Arch and proceed through to the Long Meadow, following the path that loops around it (it's about an hour's walk). Other park highlights include the 1857 Italianate mansion **Litchfield Villa** on Prospect Park West; the **Friends' Cemetery** Quaker burial ground (where film actor Montgomery Clift was laid to rest); the wonderful 1906 Beaux Arts **boathouse;** an **ice skating rink** in winter; and a 1912 **carousel,**

A neoclassical gem built in 1906, the boathouse on the lake in Prospect Park contains an Audubon Society nature center.

The Little Red Lighthouse

Also known as Jeffrey's Hook Lighthouse, this historic beaut under the George Washington Bridge in Fort Washington Park on the Hudson River was the inspiration for the 1942 children's book classic, *The Little Red Lighthouse and The Great Gray Bridge*, by Hildegarde Swift and Lynd Ward. Built in New Jersey in 1880 and reconstructed and moved to its current spot in 1921, it was operational until 1947. The lighthouse was to be removed in 1951, but because of its popularity there was a public outcry and it was saved. It's now a New York City landmark and on the National Register of Historic Places. It's a fun place for the kids to explore and a scenic picnic spot in nice weather. It's sporadically open to the public, with guided tours (for more info go to historichousetrust.org) from spring through fall. We suggest biking there on the sheltered path up the Hudson (it's easy enough for families).

with white wooden horses salvaged from a famous Coney Island merry-go-round (Apr–Oct Thurs–Sun; rides $4; it's one of the only wheelchair accessible carousels in the U.S.). On the east side is the **Prospect Park Zoo** (prospectparkzoo.com; ✆ **718/399-7339**), a modern children's zoo where kids can walk among wallabies, explore a prairie-dog town, and more (admission $11 adults, $9 seniors, $8 children 3–12; free for kids 2 and under).

At Grand Army Plaza, bounded by Prospect Park W, Parkside Ave. and Flatbush Ave., Brooklyn. prospectpark.org. ✆ **718/965-8951** (general info). Subway: 2, 3 to Grand Army Plaza (walk down Plaza St. W 3 blocks to Prospect Park W) or Eastern Pkwy./Brooklyn Museum.

Riverside Park ♥♥ PARK Another masterwork by landscapers Olmsted and Vaux (the visionaries behind Central Park and Prospect Park). As its name suggests, Riverside Park has always had one advantage over Central Park: glorious river views. Many of its garden-laced promenades make the most of these vistas, as does the lovely boat basin and rotunda area at 79th Street (a hopping bar enlivens evenings at the boat basin). As in Central Park, there is a smattering of playgrounds; there's also a skate park with assorted ramps and half-pipes; and a handful of monuments, including **Grant's Tomb,** at 122nd St. (daily 9am–5pm), the largest mausoleum in the United States at 8,100 sq. ft. (And the answer to who's buried in Grant's tomb is: No one. Ulysses S. Grant and his wife are not buried; their sarcophagi lie above ground.)

From 72nd to 158th St. along the Hudson River. nycgovparks.org/parks/riversidepark.

Tompkins Square Park ♥♥ PARK This would be my pick for the city's funkiest green space. It's seen its share of political protests, but today it's better known for the very free expression it gives home to. The yearly Dance Parade (danceparade.org; p. 390) ends here with a smorgasbord of dancing of all sorts; live music is also a fixture on weekends. Best is the daily sidewalk catwalk of pierced, tattooed, fashion-forward locals. Incorporated as a park in

1878, Tompkins Square has a number of meditative green spaces, playgrounds, a swimming pool, and a smattering of undistinguished monuments. It used to have a band shell where an early version of the Grateful Dead made their East Coast debut, but that has since been torn down.

Located btw. aves. A and B, btw. 7th and 10th sts. Subway: L to First Ave.

Union Square Park ♥ PARK/MARKET The spirit of the 1960s is still very much alive here, though Union Square Park's tradition of political activism goes back to the first Labor Day Parade in 1882, which ended in the park. Since that time, it has become soapbox central, a place where orators come on a daily basis to blast whatever current administration is in power, weighing in on all the big topics of the day. George Washington, in the second public equestrian statue ever created in the United States, watches over these proceedings, as does a statue of Gandhi, a gift of the Indian people, with a fresh wreath of flowers always draped about his neck. Along with the political folk, Union Square hosts the finest **greenmarket** in the city (on the western side of the park) every Monday, Wednesday, Friday, and Saturday. Most days you'll find 30+ vendors hawking regionally grown produce, organic wines, flowers, artisan cheeses, even honey from a rooftop in Brooklyn. It's a lot of fun to visit. Two playgrounds and a dog run are also on-site.

14th to 17th sts. (btw. Park Ave. S and Broadway). nycgovparks.org/parks/unionsquarepark. Subway: 4, 5, 6, L, N, Q, R to 14th St./Union Square.

Washington Square Park ♥♥ PARK This park is nothing if not tuneful and has long been a place for amateur musicians to gather in groups, lugging along instruments for impromptu concerts each weekend (and many weeknights when the weather is nice). The round fountain in the center of the park serves as a stage for a dozen or so regular comedians, acrobats, and dancers who are good enough to draw crowds of 100 people or more. Entertaining as well are the intense chess matches played from noon to sundown on the park's southwest corner (the regulars are real sharks). Children will enjoy the two playgrounds on the park's north side. For history buffs, there's much to mull over here—see the full story in our walking tour of Greenwich Village (p. 289).

South end of Fifth Ave. (where it intersects Waverly Place, btw. MacDougal and Wooster sts.). Subway: A, C, E, F, M to W. 4th St. (use 3rd St. exit).

Pass-the-hat concerts are a long-standing tradition in leafy Washington Square Park.

ORGANIZED TOURS

Harbor Cruises

Note that some of the lines below may have limited schedules in winter, especially for evening cruises. Call ahead or check online for current offerings.

Bateaux New York ♥ The most elegant and romantic of New York's evening dinner cruises, aboard a boat designed for 300 guests with two suites, one dance floor, two outdoor strolling decks, and windows galore. Dinner is a formal, three-course sit-down affair (though the food is just so-so). A live quartet entertains with jazz standards and pop vocal tunes.

Departs from Chelsea Piers, W. 23rd St. and Twelfth Ave. cityexperiences.com. ✆ **866/817-3463.** 3-hr. dinner cruises around $150/person. Subway: C, E to 23rd St.

Circle Line Sightseeing Cruises ♥♥ A New York institution, led by witty, informed guides (many are also actors), the Circle Line takes travelers round the harbor on 3-hour, 2-hour, and 90-minute cruises, 60-minute cruises that simply cover the water at the downtown tip of Manhattan, and 50-minute "Express" ones that only zip out and back to the Statue of Liberty. That last option seems like a bad value to us, considering that a public ferry trip to-and-from Staten Island would be free, and would also get within snapshot range of Lady Liberty. The longest makes a complete circle of Manhattan, but I'd recommend the 90-minute "Landmarks Half Island" cruise instead. You'll miss Yankee Stadium and the view of the Palisades (the wooded cliffs of New Jersey) on that one, but all of the other highlights—the Statue of Liberty, the lower Manhattan skyline, the Empire State Building, the Chrysler Building, the Brooklyn Bridge—are included. Unfortunately, the company recently changed its ticketing policy and now offers two tiers of seating, which makes

THE ATTACK OF THE double-decker buses

If you were to climb aboard any public bus (cost $3), turn to the person next to you, and ask, "What building is that?" you'd probably get a response as informative, accurate, and interesting as what you'll find on the much pricier hop-on, hop-off bus tours of New York City. I rode a slew of them doing research for this book, and I was appalled by the poor quality of the guides and audio guides. I think New York is best appreciated on foot, or on public buses and subways. Not only do you learn more about the city that way, you meet locals, rather than peering at the streets from afar, almost as if you were watching it all on TV. And you'll actually see more than you will if you waste time waiting . . . and waiting . . . and waiting for the next of these hop-ons to arrive, rather than just footing it to the next sight. If you insist, the top bus tour is **Big Bus** (bigbustours.com; ✆ **800/669-0051**). Tours depart from various locations. Hop-on, hop-off bus tours start at $60 adults for a 24-hr. downtown Manhattan loop (though the buses only run between 9am and 5pm)—more if you get a 48-hour pass going all around Manhattan.

Seeing the city from the water is a treat, especially when you do so in the company of the expert guides of the Circle Line.

it harder to snag good views without coughing up extra dough. ***Note:*** Because the top-deck, premier seats require climbing stairs, they are not an option for travelers with mobility impairments. Whichever tier of pricing you pick, try and sit on the right side of the boat, facing inward as you enter (that's the side that faces Manhattan; ask the staff if you're unclear). It can get very chilly on the water, so be sure to dress in layers, or take a seat inside.

Departs from Pier 83, at W. 42nd St. and Twelfth Ave. circleline.com. ✆ **212/563-3200.** Check website or call for schedule. 90 min. cruises $34–$45, depending on date; add $26 for upgraded seating and early boarding. Combo tickets with other attractions, especially CityPass (p. 176), are a smart way to save. Subway to Pier 83: A, C, E to 42nd St.

Specialty Tours

CULTURAL ORGANIZATIONS

The **Municipal Art Society** ♥ (mas.org; ✆ **212/935-3960**) offers excellent historical and architectural walking tours. Each is led by a highly qualified guide; topics range from "Subway Art" to "Gilded Age Mansions off Fifth Avenue." Tours cost $35 and do sell out (book early).

We're also huge fans of the free and personal tours offered by **Big Apple Greeter** (p. 38).

INDEPENDENT OPERATORS

Big Apple Jazz Tours ♥♥♥ (bigapplejazz.com; ✆ **917/863-7854**), hosted by New York jazz experts Gordon Polatnick and Amanda Hones, are the real deal for music buffs. If you're into bebop, book the Harlem tour: It hits Minton's Playhouse, the jazz club that was the supposed birthplace of bop, along with other active Harlem clubs. If you're into the 1960s bohemian Village scene, the Greenwich Village jaunt is what you want as it covers the joints popular during the golden era of Village jazz clubs (and today). The tour fee starts at $99 for 4 hours, and includes entrance fees and transportation, but not drinks.

Big Onion Tours ♥ (bigonion.com; ✆ **888/806-WALK** [9255]) are led by local graduate students, most of them studying history. The emphasis therefore is on the history of the area you may be visiting—Greenwich Village, Times Square, Central Park—and the lectures tend to be complex, illuminating portraits of those places. My only quibble with these tours is that the talk is often only tangentially related to the building or park you may be viewing at the time, so the walking tour can feel more like a classroom lecture than an afternoon's exploration. Adults $30, seniors and students $20 for 2-hour tours.

Harlem Heritage Tours ♥♥ (harlemheritage.com; ✆ **212/280-7888**) offers multimedia history tours ($40) and gospel and jazz tours of Harlem that can be combined with a soul-food meal. Prices start at $45 for a "Harlem Gospel Walking Tour" and go up from there based on length and activities/ meals.

Inside Out Tours ♥♥ (insideouttours.com; ✆ **800/258-7359**) focuses on the city's "hidden history," which may mean tours that explore the city's role during the slave trade and as a stop on the Underground Railroad; a gospel tour of Harlem; or human-centered looks at several Brooklyn neighborhoods, and the Financial District, among others. Inside Out Tours is proudly Black-owned by a former adjunct professor of New York City history. Tours start at $49 adults, $42 for children.

Laid off from his corporate job, Keith Taillon spent 2020 walking every street in Manhattan and doing deep historical research on the buildings he passed. He then shared his knowledge and photos with a growing number of fans on Instagram (@KeithYorkCity). Eventually, Taillon founded a walking company, **Keith York City** ♥♥♥ (keithyorkcity.com), and though his tours are pricy at $150, his passion for the city, and ability to unpack *why* it developed as it did, make his tours top of the line for history lovers. Plus, they're 3 hours long, rather than the usual two. (In 2026, Taillon added a handful of 90-min. tours for $75, but most are still full length and full price.)

"Sweat and sightsee simultaneously" is the tagline at **NY Running Tours** (cityrunningtours.com; ✆ **877/415-0058**), an operation that offers both group and private runs in various pedestrian-friendly areas. Their most popular offerings are daily runs across the Brooklyn Bridge and in Central Park ($49). Stops are made in front of top sights to allow participants to rehydrate while listening to the guide's commentary. They say they can accommodate runners of all speed and endurance levels.

On Location Tours visit NYC filming sites, such as the firehouse used in Ghostbusters.

On Location Tours ♥ (onlocationtours.com; ✆ **212/209-3370**) has the "as seen on screen" version of NYC, basing its tours on sites made famous by *Gossip Girl, Sex and the City, Marvelous Mrs. Maisel, Real Housewives,* and classic movies. Schedules and departure points vary depending on what tour you take, and tickets range from $40 to $65 per tour (walking tours are cheaper than bus tours). Reservations are required; many tours sell out in advance.

Turnstile Tours ♥♥♥ (turnstiletours.com; ✆ **347/903-8687**) is run by a husband-and-wife pair who team with important historic sites around the city not only to lead tours, but also to help them build out their on-site museums and oral history projects. This means that a lot of what you'll learn on their history-rich outings comes from direct research, not from reading someone else's books, making the tours unusually compelling. Turnstile is the sole tour operator for the Brooklyn Navy Yard and Brooklyn Army Terminal; it also offers food-cart tours and Prospect Park tours. Regular tours are $25, dining tours $60.

Untapped New York ♥♥ (untappednewyorktours.com; ✆ **347/903-8687**), founded by professor and journalist Michelle Young, is a hybrid company (it also publishes books, a podcast, and a blog about the city) that has partnered with a number of classic NYC sites, like Grand Central Terminal and the Metropolitan Opera, to offer tours on their behalf. It also has smartly curated food tours, walks that explore the Gilded Age on Manhattan's Upper East Side, and an especially cool underground subway tour. This and the Gilded Age tour are great options for cold winter days and hot summer ones, as you are indoors for the first, and the second ducks into embassies and museums along the route to look at their architecture—and get warm or cool. Tours start at $39.

For shopping tours, see p. 317. For art gallery tours, see p. 187.

6 WALKING TOURS

In the pages ahead, you supply the feet and the eyes, and I supply the commentary. I've picked three neighborhood walks that will envelop you in the sweep of the city's history, architecture . . . and gossip. The first of them visits Lower Manhattan, the oldest area of New York City, full of historical resonance. The second, a Harlem tour, touches on Revolutionary War history, along with 20th-century issues. The third roams around Greenwich Village, for centuries a haven for outcasts and artists. I'm willing to bet that one of these itineraries will be the highlight of your visit (it's a fine exercise for natives, too).

WALKING TOUR 1: HISTORIC LOWER MANHATTAN

GETTING THERE:	**Take subway 4 or 5 to Battery Park; walk from there into Battery Park and toward the river.**
START:	**Battery Park: Stand at a spot where you can see the river.**
FINISH:	**The 9/11 Memorial**
TIME:	**2 hr.**
BEST TIMES:	**Weekdays during the daytime.**

Not only is this the most historic part of the city—New York reached no farther than Wall Street for its first 100 years—it also affords the best overview of architectural styles in the city. Buildings range from jazzy Art Deco structures, to pseudo-Greek temples, to the soaring glass rectangles of the "International Style" heyday, one rubbing up against the other like guests at a fantastic costume party where Martha Washington cha-chas uninhibitedly with Jamie Dimon. All the sites inhabit a compact, eminently walkable area.

More importantly, Lower Manhattan is the area of the city that has seen the most tragedy, having endured terrible fires, a cruel occupation by the British during the Revolutionary War that left the city in rubble, and not one but four terrorist attacks over the years (I describe them below). The scars of these events, the weight of the tears shed, and the lives lost give this area a resonance and presence unlike those found in most other areas of the United States.

Start your tour of lower Manhattan from Battery Park, a stretch of green beneath skyscrapers at the waterfront.

1 Battery Park

Look out at the river. It's the reason this great city was built. When Henry Hudson and his crew of 16 sailed up it in 1609, mistakenly thinking they'd find Asia at its mouth, little did they know they were setting into motion a chain of events that would still be shaping lives over 400 years later. Hudson's reports about the trading possibilities of the area (particularly for valuable animal pelts), plus his amazement at the great natural harbor here, spurred the Dutch to create settlements in the area. They guessed, rightly it turned out, that the harbor of New York would be the linchpin that would connect Europe (via the Atlantic Ocean) with the interior of this vast and wealthy continent (via the Hudson River). Later, after the building of the Erie Canal, which connected the Hudson with the Great Lakes, NYC became the most powerful city in the nation.

Walk toward the circular stone building known as:

2 Castle Clinton

Go inside if the building is open. Though it doesn't look like much now, this circular structure (it was taller in some earlier incarnations) has, over the years, been at the center of New York life. In 1807, the West Battery, as it was then called, was built as a fort on a landfill island in the water off

Manhattan to ward off British invasions (it never saw action, however—the Brits attacked Washington, D.C., instead, during the War of 1812). In 1823, the federal government ceded the site—renamed Castle Clinton in 1817, in honor of Mayor De Witt Clinton—to the city, and it became an extremely popular entertainment center called Castle Gardens (the "Swedish Nightingale," Jenny Lind, was a headliner here in 1850). In 1855, the space was transformed once more, into the city's first immigrant processing center. Over eight million new arrivals, a full two-thirds of those who came to the United States at this time, spent their first hours in the United States here registering their names with the government, exchanging money, and getting information on jobs, medical care, and lodgings. By 1890, the vast number of immigrants—and the growing problem of outsiders scamming them—necessitated a move to a larger and more easily patrolled offshore space, Ellis Island. You can see Ellis Island from here, to the right of the Statue of Liberty. Its main hall reaches into the sky with four little spires.

But back to Castle Clinton: The famed architectural team of McKim, Mead, and White then stepped in and transformed the site into the nation's first aquarium, visited by about 90 million people until it was moved in 1941 to Coney Island. After the site stood empty for many years, the National Parks Service took it over and restored the Castle Clinton of the original fort.

Walk around Castle Clinton, past the ferry terminal, and head inland (northeast) toward the tall buildings. Soon you'll come upon:

3 Large Flagpole

At its base is a bas relief sculpture depicting the historic scene of Dutch official Peter Minuit "buying" Manhattan from Native American residents in 1626 in order to consolidate the Dutch colony in one easily defended spot.

Just how the "sale" of the island went down is still a matter of controversy. Most likely the "sellers" were the Canarsie People who, according to a letter by Dutch merchant Peter Schagen, let the island go for 60 guilders (the equivalent of $24). But did the Canarsie know they were selling the island, or did they think that they were simply accepting shiny trinkets as part of a welcome ceremony? And were the Canarsie even in a position to sell it, as it had long been a communal hunting ground used by a number of tribes? We'll never know the truth of the matter or even if it happened on this spot, but this is the one place in Manhattan where the most infamous real estate deal in history is memorialized.

As for Peter Minuit, he was recalled from his post in Manhattan in 1631 (much to his dismay) but returned on behalf of the Swedish government in 1638 to set up a rival "New Sweden" colony on the Delaware River (today's Wilmington, Delaware).

Walking Tour 1:
Historic Lower Manhattan
1 Battery Park
2 Castle Clinton
3 Large Flagpole
4 National Museum of the American Indian
5 Bowling Green Park
6 Fraunces Tavern
7 Goldman Sachs Building
8 Stone Street
9 Mill Lane
10 Hanover Square
11 Wall Street
12 Pier 16
13 Federal Reserve Bank
14 40 Wall Street
15 Federal Hall
16 The NY Stock Exchange
17 1 Wall Street
18 Trinity Church
19 Canyon of Heroes
20 Zuccotti Park
21 9/11 Memorial and Museum
0 1/10 mi
0 0.10 km
Subway station
start
finish
North Tower Pool
South Tower Pool
CITY HALL PARK
BATTERY PARK
HUDSON RIVER
EAST RIVER
Zuccotti Park
St. Paul's Churchyard
St. Paul's Chapel
N.Y. Vietnam Veterans Mem.
World Trade Ctr E
Cortlandt St R-W
Fulton St 4-5
Fulton St J-Z
Fulton St 2-3
Rector St 1
Rector St R-W
Wall St 4-5
Broad St J-Z
Wall St 2-3
Bowling Green 4-5
Brooklyn Bridge
Robert F. Wagner Sr. Pl.
Park Row
Broadway
Vesey St.
Beekman St.
Spruce St.
Ann St.
Fulton St.
Gold St.
Frankfort St.
Nassau St.
Maiden Ln.
Cedar St.
John St.
Platt St.
Pearl St.
Water St.
Peck Slip
Front St.
South St.
Fletcher St.
William St.
Pine St.
Exchange Pl.
Liberty St.
Trinity Pl.
Rector St.
Greenwich St.
Washington St.
West St.
South End Ave.
Albany St.
I-478
New St.
Beaver St.
Broad St.
Battery Pl.
State St.
Bridge St.
Old Slip
FDR Dr.

Now home to the National Museum of the American Indian, the ornate Alexander Hamilton U.S. Customs House once presided over the Port of New York.

Walk farther inland to the plaza in front of the:

4 National Museum of the American Indian

You are now standing at the foot of Broadway, the famous thoroughfare that leads all the way to the top of Manhattan, 13 miles away. The original Dutch fort stood in this exact place. But what you see in front of you is a building of just as much significance. Designed by Cass Gilbert, this was one of the most important structures in the city when it was built—the Alexander Hamilton U.S. Customs House. Before 1913, when the federal government instituted the personal income tax, the federal government's revenue came almost entirely from customs on goods imported into the States. And a full 75% of this revenue came from the Port of New York, where it was processed in this appropriately grand Beaux Arts colossus, completed in 1907 and comprising over 450,000 sq. ft. of interior space.

It's a wedding cake of an edifice, with dozens of bright white sculptures adorning the gray granite facade. Daniel Chester French was the sculptor—he also did the moving sculpture of Lincoln at the Lincoln Memorial in Washington, D.C.—and his choice of symbols could be used as a treatise on the prejudices of Victorian-era America. The four women seated at the front represent the four "great" continents of the world. From left to right as you look at them, they are Asia; the Americas (South America, barely present, is tellingly represented by the Aztec-like structure that North America has her foot on); Europe; and Africa. America and Europe look full of vigor and purpose, but Asia has her eyes closed (perhaps in meditation?), and Africa—in a metaphor for her lack of vision and power?—is in a deep slumber. America is sheltering a new immigrant who crouches to her left, and the immigrant is pushing forward a wheel with wings on it, those of the Roman god Mercury, the divine overseer of commerce (a comment, some think, on the essential role immigrants were playing in the expanding economy).

At the top of the building are 12 more figures, meant to represent the great trading nations of history: Greece, Rome, Phoenicia, Genoa, Venice, Spain, Holland, Portugal, Denmark, England, France, and Belgium. Why Belgium, you ask? The official story is that during World War I, "vandals" carved BELGIUM across the shield of the figure that had originally been "Germany." No explanation has ever been given on how vandals could surreptitiously make such a big change to one of the most visible and heavily guarded buildings in the city.

If you have the time, and are here during opening hours, go inside the building for a peek at the WPA murals in the rotunda (depicting the great conquistadors—ironic, as the building now houses the **National Museum of the American Indian** ♥; p. 168); the staircase on the right as you enter (meant to evoke the look of the inside of a nautilus shell); and, in what is now the museum's gift shop, the elaborate, imposing rows of teller windows where merchants would pay their Customs taxes. Entry to the museum is free.

Turn around and walk into:

5 Bowling Green Park

This was the city's first official park (est. 1733). Had you been a soldier during the British Colonial era, you would have been stationed at the fort that once stood here, Fort George, and likely you'd have passed your leisure time lawn bowling where the park now stands (hence the name Bowling Green Park).

On July 9, 1776, the Declaration of Independence was read aloud (near City Hall) and a small battalion of agitated colonists marched here to behead the statue of King George that stood in the center of the park. It had been erected just 5 years previously by many of these same men, in gratitude for the king's part in repealing the odious Stamp Act (the one that provoked the "no taxation without representation" movement). Though it can't be proven, legend has it that the lead statue was then melted down and used for cannon balls and bullets in the war against the

British. The fence that rings the park is the original, one of the few colonial structures of any sort left in Manhattan (when it was first erected, its spokes had royal crowns at their tips; these, too, were destroyed by the colonists).

Before you go to the center of the park, look up at the great skyscrapers that now shadow it. On your left, the building with the Egyptian motif (5 Broadway) was the headquarters of the White Star shipping line. It is here that distraught relatives came to learn the fate of their loved ones after the sinking of the *Titanic.* (There's a famous photo of a stricken Jacob Astor exiting the building after learning that his son had perished.) Across the street, to your right at 26 Broadway, is the former headquarters of Standard Oil, the company that made John D. Rockefeller his millions. Depending on where you're standing, you may be able to see the representation of an elaborate oil lamp at the top.

The *Charging Bull* sculpture in Bowling Green Park is a popular Financial District photo op spot.

Walk to the uptown end of the park to view ***Charging Bull.*** In 1989, a recession inspired artist Arturo Di Modica to create the sculpture as a symbol of bull markets to come. The city hadn't asked for this work of boosterism, though: Di Modica trucked it over to Wall Street in the dead of night and dumped it below a giant Christmas tree in front of the N.Y. Stock Exchange. The 7,000-lb. statue proved so popular the city decided to let the "gift" stay, though not in its original spot.

Walk out of the park, going toward the National Museum of the American Indian and then walking on the side of the museum on Whitehall St. until you reach Bridge St. Turn onto it and walk to Broad St. Take a right, and in front of you will be:

6 Fraunces Tavern

The bad news first: This is not what Fraunces Tavern actually looked like, but a hopeful reconstruction completed in 1904 and based on the architectural styles of the period (about 40% of the building is original). Nonetheless, it was here that the Sons of Liberty met on dozens of occasions to discuss plans for evicting the British. Once the Revolutionary

War was over, Fraunces Tavern was the place where George Washington delivered his famous "Farewell to the Troops" and where Alexander Hamilton set up his first Office of the Treasury.

On a more sobering note, in 1975 Fraunces Tavern was bombed by the Armed Forces Puerto Rican National Liberation Front. Four people were killed and dozens injured. The choice of this site for the bombing had dual reasons: Not only is it a symbol of American ideals, it is one of the few important historic buildings in New York that has a Caribbean connection, as Samuel Fraunces was an immigrant from the West Indies.

Look behind you, diagonally across the street, to see the:

7 Goldman Sachs Building

Directly across the street from the tavern is the headquarters of Goldman Sachs, the massive glass-and-brownstone skyscraper that cuts Stone Street in two. When it was being constructed, crews found the foundations of old **Governor Lovelace's Tavern,** another colonial-era watering hole, and briefly seat of the colonial government. In a compromise with local archaeologists, part of the site was left open with a glass viewing pane atop it. If you walk around the perimeter of the skyscraper in the same direction that you've been going, you should be able to see these excavations through glass panels in the sidewalk (they're at the end of the rows of benches, one under the colonnade, one in the open air). Take a moment to read the plaques and gaze down.

George Washington delivered his famous "Farewell to the Troops" at the colonial-era Fraunces Tavern.

By the way, this street is known as Pearl because it was once the beachy edge of the island, and it was where residents went to look for oysters. They were one of the most common foods served in New Amsterdam; some biologists have estimated that New York's waters once contained as much as half the entire world's supply of oysters.

Continue to walk northeast, curving around the Goldman Sachs building until you spot:

8 Stone Street

Here you'll have a remarkably accurate snapshot of what the city looked like in about 1837. This narrow winding street (it's the next street from Pearl St.) was the first to be paved in New Amsterdam and the only street that is thought to still be where the Dutch colonists originally placed it. All of the buildings were constructed in the period immediately following the great fire of 1835, which devastated the city, wiping out 20 square city blocks. Many blamed the volunteer firefighters of the time who, working in rival squads for cash payment, spent more time fighting one another than fighting the flames (Martin Scorsese's 2002 film *Gangs of New York* dramatically re-creates a similar firefighter battle).

The buildings we see today are classic Greek Revival structures of straight up-and-down brick with granite bases. They were built as

The historic 1885 *Wavertree* sits docked at the South Street Seaport, where visitors can learn about the sailing trade that made New York City wealthy.

counting houses and warehouses for local merchants. **57 Stone St.,** you'll notice, has a very Dutch steplike gable, added in 1908 by architect C. P. H. Gilbert as a nostalgic nod to New Amsterdam.

Continue to the middle of the street and then step to the left onto:

9 Mill Lane

Mill Lane has the distinction of being the shortest street on Manhattan (and yes, there was once a mill here). Folk tradition had it that it was here that Peter Stuyvesant, the Dutch Director-General of New Amsterdam, signed a treaty of surrender when the British invaded. Thanks to recently uncovered documents, we know that historic act actually happened at Stuyvesant's farm, in what is today the East Village. Stuyvesant surrendered unwillingly, having torn to pieces the first letter sent by the British warship commander. City leaders then pieced the letter painstakingly back together. Upon seeing the favorable terms it presented the colonists (they would be allowed to keep their land and businesses), 93 leading citizens—including Stuyvesant's 17-year-old son, a traitorous young upstart—demanded Stuyvesant surrender the colony to the British. Stuyvesant did so but mourned the loss of the colony for the rest of his life.

At the end of Pearl St. lies:

10 Hanover Square

One of the only places in New York City to retain its "royalist" title after the American Revolution, it was named for the House of Hanover, from which the era's British monarchy was descended. Once the center of the social and political life of the city, this was where the colony's first newspaper was published. The cotton exchange dominated one corner. When he was still considered a respectable citizen, notorious pirate Captain Kidd lived here in bourgeois splendor with his wife (they were known for their grand dinner parties). India House, on the west side of the square, is a perfectly preserved example of a brownstone banking house from the 1850s.

Continue walking to the uptown point of the triangle that is Hanover Square and hook a left onto Hanover St. You're now entering the "canyons of Wall Street," so named because the skyscrapers are so close together that the sidewalk gets little light. Walk until you come to:

11 Wall Street

You are now standing at what was the boundary of the city during Dutch Colonial times. If you had been alive then, you'd be staring at a 9-ft.-high wooden wall erected to keep out British invaders, who, it was thought (wrongly), would be more likely to invade by land than by sea. If you walk to **74 Wall St.** you'll be standing in the heart of what was once the United States' largest slave market, a bastion of inhumanity that held more auctions than any other in the U.S. The sale of humans began here in 1711, and was not fully outlawed in New York until 1827, making it one of the last two northern states to do so. (A small plaque about the market at is at Water and Wall streets, but most scholars think it was actually here, not there.)

Continue walking east until you get to South Street. Turn left, and cross the highway at the nearest green light, walking to

12 Pier 16

Docked at the pier will be the 1908 **Lightship Ambrose** and the **Wavertree**, an 1885 cargo sailing vessel. Both are part of the **South Street Seaport Museum** (p. 170) and the Wavertree is visitable via free, self-guided tour in the warmer weather months, and by scheduled 30-minute tours in winter (the Ambrose is usually an add-on to those tours and not open as regularly). If you have time, climb aboard for a look-see, but seeing these ships from afar is still evocative, giving you a glimpse of what this part of the harbor would have looked like when it was one of the busiest mercantile ports on the planet.

Go downtown to Maiden Lane and follow it inland until you get to 33 Liberty Street, the entrance to the:

13 Federal Reserve Bank of New York

No currency is printed in this fortress-like structure—that function was moved from this site to New Jersey in 1992—but this building holds more lucre than any other place on the planet. Down several stories, behind a door that's a good 5 feet thick, the Fed keeps over $500 billion worth of gold bars, a full 25% of all the gold reserves in the world, far more than is kept in Fort Knox. Ninety-five percent of the gold stored here belongs to foreign nations, who use this facility, embedded in the bedrock of Manhattan and guarded by a small army of marksmen (they have their own on-site firing range for practice), because it's considered the safest place in the world for this type of storage. Tours used to be offered to the public, but now only school groups are allowed inside.

Retrace your steps back to Williams Street and continue going in the direction you were heading before until you reach Wall Street. Turn right and walk to:

14 40 Wall St.

Here is New York's greatest monument to thwarted ambitions. Architect H. Craig Severance had a dream: He wanted to build the tallest building in the world, taller than the Woolworth Building (which held the record from 1917–30). Problem was, his former partner and archrival William Van Alen had the same aspirations, and in the summer of 1929, at the height of the bubble that preceded Black Tuesday (the great stock market crash), they began a "race to the top," Severance at 40 Wall St. and Van Alen at the Chrysler Building (p. 202). In a record 11 months, Severance completed this building for the Bank of Manhattan at 40 Wall St., certain that the Chrysler Building was completed and his structure would be the tallest. But once Severance finished construction, Van Alen administered the *coup de grâce* that he'd been hiding in the elevator shaft of his building: the Chrysler Building's iconic Art Deco spire, which added an unbeatable 125 ft. onto the building. I can only imagine that Severance felt some small measure of satisfaction when the Chrysler's title was snatched from it 1 short year later by the Empire State Building. Take a moment to gaze up at 40 Wall St.; it's still an impressive achievement and a beautiful building, with all of the ziggurat-like step-backs (cascading layers) of the prototypical late '20s skyscraper. Those setbacks were added to allow more light to reach the street below—a change you'll feel after having walked through the "canyons."

Keep walking in the same direction until you get to the corner of Wall St. and Broad St. Our next stop is:

15 Federal Hall

The most historically significant piece of land in the city, Federal Hall is a quintessential Greek Revival edifice, a modified version of the Parthenon (can't get much more Greek than that!), completed in 1842. Note the statue of George Washington; it was here, perhaps on the very spot where the statue now stands, that George Washington took the oath of office to become president (though not in this actual building, but in an earlier one located on this spot). That momentous occasion would be enough to secure its place in history, but matters just begin there. In this former British City Hall (transformed into "Federal Hall" when the Brits quit the city), the famous 1735 Zenger Trial, which helped secure freedom of the press, was held; in 1765, the pre-Revolutionary Stamp Act Congress met to rail against "taxation without representation"; and after the war, the new nation's first Congress met here to draw up the Bill of Rights. Head inside to see the magnificent rotunda, one of the loveliest public spaces in the city. Admission is free.

A statue of George Washington marks the spot where he was sworn in as the United States's first president.

Note the austere, somewhat anonymous-looking building across the street from the hall; it was the headquarters of banker J. P. Morgan (the window of his former office is above the flagpole). If you look closely at the side of the building that faces Federal Hall, you'll notice that it is pocked with small indentations. These are the scars of the Financial District's first terrorist attack, which occurred in 1920. One bright and sunny morning (isn't it odd that these events always seem to occur on beautiful days?), a horse and carriage loaded with explosives parked here. Moments later a huge explosion shook the street, killing 31 people and wounding scores more. The blast was so powerful that all that was ever found of the horse was a horseshoe. The police used this piece of evidence to trace the blacksmith who made it; he had vague recollections of shoeing the horse of an Italian man, and on this scanty piece of evidence the police (and press) decided that the blast must have been the work of Italian anarchists. No one was ever charged with the crime.

Next, walk toward:

16 The New York Stock Exchange

You are now gazing at the most famous (some would say infamous) financial institution in the world. The building's towering columns, crowded ornamental pediment, and huge flag trumpet louder than any opening bell that this is a place of incomparable might and prestige (it's a much more imposing building than the government's plainer Federal Hall across the street). The building was completed in 1903, but what you see today is *not* all original to that time: in the 1930's, pollution caused the marble statuary in the pediment to start crumbling, and the structural integrity of the facade was put in jeopardy. So those sculptures were replaced with copper replicas coated in white paint in 1936. In front of the Stock Exchange is a scraggly buttonwood tree, meant to invoke the buttonwood that New York's first traders stood under in 1792 when they met to begin brokering the Revolutionary War debt—the first stock market in

The statue *Fearless Girl* stands her ground in front of the New York Stock Exchange.

America. Also in front is the bronze statue of a fierce young girl, fists on hips—***Fearless Girl,*** she's called. In March of 2017 she was set in a face-off with the *Charging Bull* statue in Bowling Green (stop 5 on this tour) as a statement on the need for more women working in finance. The bull's sculptor loudly objected to her presence, but she was such a popular photo op, the city moved her here in 2018.

Continue crosstown on Wall St. toward Broadway until you arrive at:

17 1 Wall St.

Take a moment to gaze at this absolutely stunning Art Deco building, once one of the priciest addresses in the city. The beautifully fluted, curtainlike limestone of the facade; the spider-web pattern of the cathedral window above the entry; and the sumptuous, soaring lobby remind us of a time when such excess and exquisite workmanship were the norm for places of business (which were, in the heady times before the Stock Exchange crash, conceived as temples of commerce).

Many famous New Yorkers are buried in Trinity Church's graveyard.

Cross the street to:

18 Trinity Church

For a full description of the history and architecture of Trinity Church, go to p. 174. Do wander the graveyard here; it has the remains of Alexander Hamilton and other notables.

Exit the graveyard and look uptown on Broadway, as you are now in the:

19 Canyon of Heroes

Look down as you amble along at the brass plates with names and dates listing the ticker-tape parades that have been held along this swatch of Broadway. Had you been here on one of those occasions in the 1930s or '40s, the crowds around you would have been shoulder-to-shoulder, and above your head, hundreds would have been standing at the windows, showering the street with the long paper ribbons of stock market quotations that spewed from their machines, marking the dance of the stock market. Read the plates. The catalogue of names is an interesting retread of American history and political alliances; along with athletes, astronauts, and presidents, you'll find parades for the American hostages released from Iran (1982), pianist Van Cliburn (1958), and the controversial President Sukarno of Indonesia (1956).

Walk uptown on Broadway and turn left on Liberty St.:

20 Zuccotti Park

There's not much to see anymore, but this private 1-block-long park is where the "Occupy Wall Street" movement started in September of 2011, bringing the concept of the power of the 1% into modern political discourse. Activists occupied the park for almost 2 months before being forced out on November 15 by the police.

Continue walking on Liberty St. to Church St. You'll pass the Oculus (p. 24). Follow the signs to:

21 The 9/11 Memorial and Museum

Be sure to reserve advance tickets online so that you can skip some of the lines at this sobering museum. If you don't have time for the museum, be sure to walk around the 8-acre 9/11 Memorial Plaza, which is centered on the 1-acre footprints of both towers. For more information, see p. 160.

WALKING TOUR 2: HARLEM

GETTING THERE:	**Take the 2 or 3 subway to 125th St.**
START:	**Walk downtown to 120th St. and Malcolm X Blvd. (also known as Lenox Ave.).**
FINISH:	**The Apollo Theater, 253 W. 125th St.**
TIME:	**1 hr.**
BEST TIMES:	**Daylight hours**

More than in any other place in the city, you need a strong imagination and social sense to really enjoy touring Harlem. The tragic fact is that much of what made this area unique, lively, and . . . well, Harlem, during the fabled Jazz Era (aka the Harlem Renaissance), crumbled beneath the wrecking ball decades ago. What you now see—wide avenues, rows of brownstones, elegant apartment buildings—are somewhat an accident of history, the physical face of an area that housed a people but wasn't necessarily "of" that people (I'll explain below). Despite all this, Harlem remains the African-American capital of the United States (sometimes called the "capital for Africans throughout the world"), a one-of-a-kind area with much to recommend it. Architect Zevilla Jackson Preston best sums up its appeal in the book *HarlemWorld,* in which she writes, "Ultimately it is the energy on the street, the beat on the street—all of the beautiful Black people on the streets—that make the experience unique."

Harlem was settled by a number of different groups over the years—Dutch farmers first, followed by their British counterparts, then poor Irish and Italian immigrants. But development only took off in the years just prior to 1904, when the city's first subway line opened, a 9½-mile snaking tunnel connecting Lower Manhattan with points as far north as 145th Street. In anticipation of

Handsome Greek Revival town houses line Harlem's side streets.

this event, an unprecedented housing boom hit the neighborhood, with developers slapping up Victorian row house after row house for the crowds of upwardly mobile immigrants—middle-class Jews and Germans, primarily—they were certain would soon flood this newly commutable neighborhood. What they didn't anticipate were recessions and panics in 1893, 1907, and 1910, which deflated the housing market and badly affected the development of large numbers of homes on the Upper West Side.

Left with hundreds of unrentable homes, property owners soon began doing what nobody else had done in the history of the United States: renting or selling brand-new, often beautifully appointed buildings to the race of people that had, until that point, always made do with the tumble-down ghetto housing no other group would accept. In 1905, pioneering real estate agent Philip Payton persuaded a white landlord to rent him 31 W. 133rd St. so he could re-lease it to African Americans. The landlord accepted the offer because Payton promised to pay far more than the going rate, a substantial $5 more per tenant per month (a lot of money in those days). Several other white landlords panicked and bought the building in order to evict the Black tenants, but by then it was too late. Payton had the funding to buy several other buildings, and Black migration into the area began in earnest. What you see in Harlem today are homes and businesses that were not created by or for African Americans. These lovely buildings, however, did allow for an unprecedented standard of living and security, primarily in the 1920s, '30s, and '40s, for African Americans.

Another thing you won't see in Harlem today are the Jazz Era nightclubs and theaters for which the area was famed. Tragically, those historic sites were torn down. But we will visit places where the great figures of Harlem, men and women such as Langston Hughes, Malcolm X, Mother Hale, and Adam Clayton Powell, Jr., lived, worked, and made history.

A note about this tour: Harlem is by far the largest neighborhood in Manhattan, stretching from approximately 116th Street all the way up to the river. There's no way to see it all in one walk, but this tour gives you a taste of the area's history from different eras. I'd urge you to go back and see such historic gems as Striver's Row (138th and 139th sts. btw. Adam Clayton Powell and Frederick Douglass blvds.), Sugar Hill (127th to 155th sts. from Edgecomb Ave. to Amsterdam Ave.), and Alexander Hamilton's home (414 W. 141st St.).

1 Mt. Olivet Baptist Church

Stand across the street (120th St. and Malcolm X Blvd., aka Lenox Ave.) so that you can get a better look at this prominent Harlem Church (over the years, presidential candidate Howard Dean and the late Venezuelan President Hugo Chavez have addressed the congregation). If you look closely, you'll notice something that one doesn't usually see on the facade of a church: several Stars of David. This church epitomizes the neighborhood's transformation over the years; it was built (in 1907) to be the neighborhood's first synagogue. The architect, the first Jewish architect licensed in New York State, based its design on that of the Second Temple in Jerusalem, which had just been excavated, making worldwide headlines. Remember the name Louis Blumstein, a prominent member of this congregation, as he'll reappear later in this walking tour.

Walk uptown on Malcolm X Blvd., turn left on 122nd St., and walk to 152 W. 122nd St., which is:

2 Hale House

We jump forward now a century to 1969 when an act of kindness changed the lives of thousands of children. A young woman named Lorraine Hale was driving on 146th Street when she saw a mother nodding off on the street from the effects of heroin, her 2-month-old baby almost slipping from her arms. Ms. Hale got out of the car and told the mother she needed to get treatment and that she could leave the baby with her own mother—Clara McBride Hale—while she got sober. The next day the mother did just that, and soon hundreds of babies were being left with "Mother Hale," who pioneered methods of treating babies born with addictions (and also took in a lot of HIV-positive babies).

This all happened during the 1960s, '70s, and '80s, a period of steep decline for Harlem. Racist redlining policies made it impossible for Harlem residents to get housing loans and mortgages. A number of predatory landlords bought neighborhood buildings and rented them out but stopped maintaining and even abandoned the buildings once they'd leached as much profit as they could get out of them (in 1960, a census showed only 50% of the housing in Harlem to be deemed sound, as opposed to 85% elsewhere in the city). Harlem became synonymous with urban decay, and Hale House, though a controversial institution later, was one of its few rays of hope. You can read more about the house and its mission on the plaque at the door.

Walk back to Malcolm X Blvd., cross the street, and walk east on 122nd St. until you get to:

3 Church of the Holy Trinity (230 Malcolm X Blvd)

Completed in 1885, this Romanesque Revival Church was designed by a very prominent New Yorker: William Appleton Potter, who later served as the architect for the federal Department of the Treasury. He commissioned Louis C. Tiffany to decorate the interior, and no expense was spared: the final bill came in at $210,500 or $5 million in today's currency. It took the congregation until 1910 to pay off the debt, when an anonymous check for $35,498 hit the collection plate on Thanksgiving Day. Alas, two devastating fires destroyed the interior, the roof, and parts of the exterior in 1925 and 1939, so it doesn't have its original majesty. Among the famous congregants was Civil War hero Major General Abram Duryee, who later became a villain when, as Police Commissioner of the city, he sent mounted policemen in to break up a labor protests in 1874, one of the city's most violent episodes.

Look across the street to no. 242, the corner of an 1888 row of buildings with mansard roofs, that wouldn't look out of place in France. In

1890, a dentist named William S. Hollingsworth moved here and did pioneering work in the new field of orthodontia. He felt that piano wire was best for yanking recalcitrant teeth into place (ouch!), according to industry magazine *The Dental Cosmos*. He died a wealthy man in 1929, leaving $270,000 in his will (roughly $5 million in today's dollars).

Continue walking east on 122nd St. until you get to:

4 4-16 W. 122nd St.

This is not a famous building, but a very beautiful one and another good example of the kind of talent that was enlisted to build Harlem's brownstones when the neighborhood was first being developed. This one is by architect William Tuthill, who went on to design Carnegie Hall later in his career. As in many Gotham brownstones, the main entrance is on the second, not the ground, floor. Why? The streets were stinky places at the time of this construction, littered with horse poop and trash. So the kitchen and servants' quarters were placed on the ground floor, and the owners lived above to escape the stench.

In Marcus Garvey Park (formerly Mount Morris Park), this cast-iron tower was built in 1857 as a fire lookout.

Look toward the park at the east end of the street. It used to be called:

5 Mount Morris Park

Named for General Roger Morris, this park was created in honor of the very first American victory in the Revolutionary War. It was in the vicinity of where you're standing now, on September 16, 1776, that George Washington engaged in what he called a "brisk little skirmish" with the Redcoats. Just 1 month earlier, the largest British expeditionary fleet in history had sailed into New York Harbor, bringing with it 21,000 troops, a full 40% of all the men serving in the Royal Navy at that time. In quick order, these trained soldiers slaughtered approximately 2,800 American militiamen at the Battle of Brooklyn, forcing Washington to escape Brooklyn under cover of night and hightail it to the northern reaches of Manhattan. At the small battle on this site, called the Battle of Washington Heights, enemy buglers taunted the colonists by playing the call that traditionally ended a foxhunt. Enraged, Washington called for reinforcements and drove the Redcoats back to what is now the Upper West Side. It was the first time his soldiers had won an engagement and did much to boost morale. Many years later, in 1969, the park hosted the outdoor Harlem Cultural Festival—sometimes called "the Black Woodstock"—celebrated in the 2021 Oscar-winning documentary *Summer of Soul.* In 1973 the park was renamed Marcus Garvey Park, in honor of the founder of the Universal Negro Improvement Association.

If you have the time and the stamina, follow the path to top of the park (it's on a steep hill) where you'll see the last remaining fire tower in the city. Starting in the 1850s, watchmen were positioned here night at day to alert the neighborhood, via different combination of bell patterns, where fires had broken out. Once every neighborhood in the city had these towers.

Exit the park at Fifth Ave and 124th St. and continue walking uptown to 127th St. Turn east and walk to 20 E. 127th St.:

6 The Former Home of Poet Langston Hughes

Hughes bought this brownstone in 1947, likely with the royalties he received for writing the libretto to the Broadway musical *Street Scene.* His was an open house, with other writers, musicians, and friends from the neighborhood dropping by at all hours. He was particularly known for his kindness to the children of the neighborhood; he called the garden in front of his house "The Children's Garden" and let the little ones plant whatever they wanted to there. It was in this house that he wrote his famous book-length poem, *Montage for a Dream Deferred.*

Walk back to Fifth Ave. and continue uptown to the corner of 128th St. Here, you'll see:

7 Collyer Park

Are you a fan of the TV show *Hoarders?* This pretty pocket park marks the site where the most famous hoarders of the pre-television age once lived, a pair of reclusive brothers who occupied their home here from the 1880s until their deaths in 1947. Though rumors swirled about their compulsive behavior, nobody knew the extent of their hoarding until both were found dead in their home, surrounded by 140 tons of stuff—books, musical instruments, towering stacks of newspapers, baby carriages, guns, furniture, and all manner of junk, all set with booby traps to ward off outsiders. It took over a year to clear out the house, which was eventually razed—it was rotting on its foundations.

Walk back to Malcolm X Blvd. and walk downtown to 126th St.

Take a Break

If it's meal time, head to celebrity chef Marcus Samuelson's **Red Rooster Harlem** for a bite to eat. For our full review, see p. 141.

Continue down Malcolm X Blvd. to 125th Street. Turn right (west) and proceed on to:

8 The Corner of Adam Clayton Powell Jr. Boulevard and 125th Street

Abuzz with history, this intersection is one of the most important in Harlem. Look over first at the windswept northeast corner, where **the statue of Adam Clayton Powell, Jr.,** Harlem's first African-American congressman, stands. This is also the spot where Malcolm X spent many hours lecturing to Harlem residents on behalf of the Nation of Islam. His message—"We are Blacks first and everything else second"—was so powerful, and he was such an effective orator, that before he left the NOI that organization had nearly half a million members (it dwindled rapidly after he resigned). His controversial message, which rejected non-violence and condemned integration as cultural suicide, went directly against the goals of the NAACP, the largest civil rights organization of the time.

A statue on 125th Street, Harlem's main thoroughfare, commemorates NYC's first African-American congressman, Adam Clayton Powell, Jr.

Now, look across the street at the tall white building with geometric patterns climbing up its facade, the former **Hotel Theresa.** If your olfactory glands have any imagination, you may detect a hint of Cuban cigar smoke in the air. In 1960, a young Fidel Castro was scheduled to speak at the United Nations, but no hotel in town would take him and his contingent. After he threatened to set up camp on the lawn of the United Nations, the government ordered city hotels to accommodate him, but Castro got into an argument with the midtown hotel he'd picked, the Shelburne Hotel. After a conversation with Malcolm X, he moved up here to the Hotel Theresa—a dramatic gesture Castro hoped would show his solidarity with Black Americans (and perhaps encourage a few to join the Communist Party). Repeated clashes between pro- and anti-Castro forces outside the hotel kept busy the 258 police officers assigned to guard him. On his second day at the Theresa, Nikita Khrushchev came to visit; his police contingent plus Castro's created the greatest show of force Harlem had ever witnessed (to this day, it hasn't been matched).

Four years later, when Malcolm X broke with the Nation of Islam to found his own Organization of Afro-American Unity (open to people of all religions), he held his press conference at the Theresa and soon afterward moved his offices here. When he was assassinated in 1965, just 1 year later, this is where crowds gathered to mourn, until they were dispersed by the police.

Walk farther west until you get to 230 W. 125th St., the former:

9 Blumstein's Department Store

When it opened its doors in 1900, this was the neighborhood's largest and most exclusive store, built at a cost of $1 million (notice the beautifully worked copper ornamentation on the facade, a mix of Art Deco and Spanish Renaissance in its patterning). And yes, it was owned by Louis Blumstein, whom we discussed at the beginning of this tour. At the time of its construction, it was an important resource for the Jewish community, as downtown department stores had signs in their windows announcing that Jews and dogs were not allowed to enter.

As the neighborhood changed, the vast majority of its clientele became African American, but Blumstein's refused to hire any Black store clerks (a particularly maddening policy in the Great Depression, when jobs were scarce). In 1934, the Urban League began a campaign, spearheaded by Reverends John H. Johnson and Adam Clayton Powell, Jr., to boycott and picket the store until it changed its hiring practices. The action lasted 2 months, with picketers carrying signs with the simple but effective request DON'T BUY WHERE YOU CAN'T WORK. Blumstein's finally relented, hiring 34 African-American women as clerks. Dr. Martin Luther King, Jr. often spoke of this strike in his speeches as an example of the power of nonviolent protest.

In 1958, Dr. King himself was at the center of history at Blumstein's. He was seated at a table signing copies of his book *Strides Towards Freedom* when a Black woman named Izola Ware Curry got to the front of the line. After asking, "Are you Martin Luther King?" she began shouting "You Communist, you Communist!" and stabbed him in the chest with a letter opener. Dr. King was rushed to Harlem Hospital with the blade still in (had it been removed, he would have bled to death) and underwent surgery. The next morning, the *New York Times* reported that had King sneezed, he would have died, as the blade was touching his aorta. From his hospital bed, King issued a letter of forgiveness to Wade, who was committed to an insane asylum for the act (she had had a long history of mental instability).

Cross the street, and you'll see the marquee of:

10 The Apollo Theater

For years, 125th Street was known as the "Great Black Way," in comparison to Broadway's "Great White Way." This was the theater district of Harlem. Only a few of these great show palaces still exist, but right in front of us is the most famous and influential: the Apollo Theater (253 W. 125th St.). A whites-only burlesque house until 1934, it changed its policy and its lineup, becoming a music hall in January of that year and introducing the legendary "Amateur Night" a few months later. Among the many big names who jump-started their careers at Amateur Night: Sarah Vaughn, James Brown, Lauryn Hill, and most famously Ella Fitzgerald, who was planning to dance but fortuitously changed her mind backstage right before she went onstage. Amateur night continues here every Wednesday at 7:30pm, and it's as raucous as ever, with wild cheers for the performers the audience enjoys and painfully cruel shouts and boos for those who get the axe. The gift shop inside the Apollo is open during the day time, so step inside and see it and the lobby.

An impressive roster of Black musicians has performed at Harlem's Apollo Theater.

WALKING TOUR 3: GREENWICH VILLAGE

GETTING THERE: **Take the N or R subway to 8th St. or the 6 to Astor Place.**

START: **Walk west on 8th St. to Fifth Ave., and then walk downtown to the Washington Square Arch (you should be able to see it from 8th St.).**

FINISH: **Stonewall Inn, 53 Christopher St.**

TIME: **1½ hr.**

BEST TIMES: **Day or night**

Greenwich Village started as its own village, a place where, as in Boccaccio's *Decameron,* the well-to-do fled on a near-yearly basis to escape the plagues of colonial Nieuw Amsterdam and then New York City (recurrent bouts of yellow fever, mostly). Building began in earnest in the 1820s and 1830s, with wealthy families building row house after row house in what was then a suburb. Soon, of course, the city caught up, the hoi polloi were living just down the block, and the bluebloods did the 19th-century version of urban flight and moved a mile uptown to newer suburbs. Their swank houses were subdivided into cheap apartments and boarding houses or torn down entirely to create factories. The neighborhood became home to immigrants and later, artists.

The Village always retained its status as a place apart, however, thanks to the confusing configuration of its streets, a jumble of twisting byways and narrow streets. "The streets have run crazy and broken themselves . . . into strange angles and curves," O. Henry wrote. "One street crosses itself a time or two." In the 1960s and '70s, the charm of this urban topography, the quiet of the tiny streets cut off from upper Manhattan's bustle, brought the well-to-do back, and the neighborhood became once more a hideaway for wealthy New Yorkers.

In this walking tour, I hope to give you a taste of all the varied groups of people and social movements that shaped this neighborhood over the years.

1 Washington Square Park

Hangings, protests, burials, parades . . . if there's another spot in New York that's seen as much drama as Washington Square Park has, I've yet to hear of it. Located north of the first Dutch settlement in Manhattan, the area was originally a marshland, fed by the stream that still runs under nearby Minetta Lane (see stop 10, below). Its first settlers were several enslaved people who, in 1641, were given partial freedom in return for farming this then-dangerous and remote acreage. Primarily older men and women (they'd outlived their usefulness to their masters), their freedom was a mixed blessing: They had to hand over a large part of their harvests to the colony, and, perhaps more disturbingly, they became human watchdogs, set here to alert the Dutch should local Native Americans or British forces try to attack.

In 1797, the drained swamp was designated a potter's field; it was put to good use a year later when yellow fever swept through what was by then New York City. Over 5% of the population of the city died that muggy, mosquito-infested summer, the poorest of whom were buried here, nearly 20,000 of them. In 1826 it became a military parade ground; tales were told of soldiers doing their drills, boots slipping through the crust of the dirt and crunching down on shroud-covered skeletons. If all this weren't haunting enough, the square was often used for public hangings; a massive, and hundreds of years old, elm tree stands on the park's northwest corner and was long thought to be where these executions took place, though recent evidence suggests otherwise.

The magnificent white marble arch at the foot of Fifth Avenue was designed by Stanford White, the second such arch he created (the first, made of wood and plaster, was erected in 1889 to mark the centennial of George Washington's inauguration and to raise funds for this permanent arch, completed in 1892). The sculpture on the right side of the arch, depicting Washington as *President, Accompanied by Wisdom and Justice,* was added in 1918 by Alexander Stirling Calder, father of the great modern artist and mobile-maker Alexander Calder. On the other side, we see *Washington as Commander-in-Chief, Accompanied by Fame and Valor* by Herman Atkins MacNeill, also tacked on in 1918.

Spread around its iconic arch, Washington Square Park is the unofficial center of Greenwich Village and its *de facto* living room.

Walking Tour 3: Greenwich Village
1 Washington Square Park
2 22 Washington Square North
3 Washington Square North
4 29 Washington Place
5 Judson Church
6 New York University Law School
7 Provincetown Playhouse
8 130 MacDougal Street
8a Caffe Reggio
9 Minetta Tavern
10 Minetta Street
11 Bleecker Street
12 One If By Land, Two If By Sea
13 Stonewall National Monument & Stonewall Inn
Subway station
"Take a Break" stop
0 100 y
0 100 m
GREENWICH VILLAGE
WASHINGTON SQUARE PARK
start
finish
Washington Square Arch
Washington Square Fountain
Hangman's Elm
Washington Square West Chess Tables
Garibaldi Plaza
Washington Square North
Washington Square West
Washington Square South
Washington Square East
5th Ave.
Washington Mews
Washington Pl.
LaGuardia Pl.
Thompson St.
W. 3rd St.
Sullivan St.
MacDougal St.
W. 4th St.
Minetta St.
6th Avenue (Avenue of the Americas)
W. Washington Pl.
Waverly Pl.
MacDougal Alley
W. 8th St.
W. 9th St.
West 4 St-Wahington Sq A-C-E-B-D-F-M
Cornelia St.
Jones St.
Bleecker St.
Barrow St.
7th Avenue South
Sheridan Square
Grove St.
Christopher St.
Christopher St 1

Over the years, the arch has become a choice target for protesters. In 1918, Dada daddy Marcel Duchamp climbed up the 110 interior steps with his fellow members of the Liberal Club (including a woman who called herself "Woe," so she could declaim, "Woe is Me!"), carrying Chinese lanterns, food, wine, and cap guns, to declare Greenwich Village an "independent republic." They were soon brought down by an unamused constable. Less lighthearted was a 1968 takeover by the Students Against Racism and War, who barricaded themselves inside to hang a banner protesting the Vietnam War. The door to the inner stairway has been bolted ever since.

Cross the street, turn left (west), and walk until you see:

2 22 Washington Square N

Dash-dot-dot-dash: You've now reached the birthplace of the telegraph. Inventor Samuel Morse lived in this New York University building (he was a painting instructor) when, in 1836, he formulated the rudiments of the telegraphic alphabet, better known as Morse Code. A year later, on September 2, 1837, he was able to gather 1,700 ft. of copper wire, which he coiled around his room, sending the world's first wire dispatch from one end to the other.

Retrace your steps and cross Fifth Ave., looking at the magnificent row houses of:

3 Washington Square North

You're now looking at the longest unbroken string of Greek Revival town houses anywhere in the United States. Aren't they lovely? New York University owns most of these (in fact, they own much of the neighborhood), but in the 1830s, when these were built, they were strictly for individual owners of the highest social class. Henry James' grandmother lived here, and he used the area as inspiration for the famed novel *Washington Square* (later turned into the play and film *The Heiress*).

The use of Greek Revival architecture was no accident. In the mid-1820s, support for the Greeks—a Christian nation fighting for independence from the "heathen" (their term) Ottoman Empire—was all the rage among the upper echelons of Manhattan society. It's one reason (along with the notion that America was a modern version of ancient Greek democracy) why classical columns started popping up on buildings all over town, with Greek symbols incorporated into fences (as you'll see in front of you), pedestals added to facades, and so on.

By the early 20th century, this strip had become run down, and many of the Village's best-known "Bohemians" moved in, including painters Edward Hopper and Thomas Eakins, and writer John Dos Passos. All three lived at no. 3 Washington Square North, though not at the same time.

Turn right (downtown) onto Washington Square E, then take a left onto Washington Place and walk to the corner of Greene St.:

4 29 Washington Place (at the corner of Greene St.)

On March 25, 1911, a horrific tragedy on this site reshaped the laws of New York State and the history of the American labor movement. On that Saturday, some 600 young women, mostly Jewish and Italian immigrants between the ages of 13 and 23, were hard at work in a garment factory on the eighth, ninth, and tenth floors of this building. At 5pm, just as the workers were getting ready to leave, a fire sprung up in the southeast corner of the eighth floor—no one has ever been able to determine the cause—and within minutes all three floors were an inferno. An inescapable one, it turned out, because many of the doors had been locked from the outside (to prevent theft, the owners said later). Minutes after that, one of the fire escapes collapsed, and the elevator operator fled in terror. A brave pedestrian named Joseph Zito ran into the building, got the elevator working, and made five trips up through the flames, saving 25 to 30 workers on each trip. Fleeing the flames, several young women jumped to their deaths in front of horrified passersby. Those trapped inside suffocated from the smoke, while still others were crushed in a heap at the locked doors. In all, 146 people were killed at the Triangle Shirt Waist Factory, most within the first 10 minutes of the hour-long blaze.

After many protests, the state legislature responded to the tragedy by re-writing the labor code, making it the most stringent in the nation. The labor movement, struggling up to this point, gathered steam and the International Ladies Garment Workers Union (ILGWU) became a force in the industry.

Walk back to Washington Square and follow the perimeters of the park south to 4th St. Turn right and walk to Thompson St.:

5 Judson Church (239 Thompson St.)

This boxy Romanesque church from 1929 was another masterwork by architect Stanford White, who took his inspiration from the churches of Florence—hence the thin, ochre bricks. The church was a center for immigrant life at the turn of the 20th century and became known in the 1950s and '60s for the progressive politics of minister Howard Moody, who sheltered protestors from the police and helped to overturn a short-lived ban on folk singing in the park. Today's performers (and there are *always* groups making music in the park) owe a debt of gratitude to Moody.

Facing onto the south side of Washington Square Park, Judson Church has a rich legacy of social activism.

Keep walking west, passing:

6 New York University Law School

When journalist John Reed (the subject of the Warren Beatty bio-pic *Reds*) was a tenant of a famous boardinghouse that once stood here, he wrote a poem about his artsy neighbors, whom he called "Inglorious Miltons by the Score/ And Rodins, one to every floor." Be sure to take a look at the street names on this side of Washington Square Park. All were chosen to honor Washington's Revolutionary War generals.

Walk west to MacDougal St., turn left, and stop beside the legendary:

7 Provincetown Playhouse (133 MacDougal St.)

The more theatrical strain of Greenwich Village bohemianism found its home at the little theater that once stood here (only the name remains), at one time one of the most influential playhouses in the city. That's thanks largely to Eugene O'Neill, who managed it, and whose important early works were first performed here, including *Emperor Jones, The Hairy Ape,* and *The Great God Brown.* Overturning barriers, the theater cast African Americans to play African Americans and even featured a kiss between a Black man and a white woman (a radical move in 1926, and one that resulted in threats from the Ku Klux Klan). Other famous names who contributed to the theater include Edna St. Vincent Millay (her anti-war classic *Aria de Capo* debuted in 1919), John Reed, and e. e. cummings. Among the famous actors who trod these boards, Bette Davis made her stage debut here.

Stroll south, crossing W. 3rd St. until you see:

8 130 MacDougal St.

This perfect little brick federal town house is where Louisa May Alcott probably wrote *Little Women* (can't you just picture Professor Baer calling on the young writer here?). Alcott never had her own Professor; her health damaged by her work as a nurse in Washington, D.C., during the Civil War, she never married, instead spending her limited energies on writing and lobbying for women's suffrage.

Take a Break

For a pastry and some java, head to **Caffe Reggio** ♥♥♥, 119 MacDougal St. (caffereggio.com; ✆ **212/475-9557**). Founded in 1927, it claims to have introduced cappuccino to America, and has the huge copper machines to prove it. The Caffe has been featured in such films as *Godfather II* and *Inside Llewyn Davis*. For something a bit more substantial, go one door down for the city's

Stop for a coffee break at Caffe Reggio—a Village gathering place for nearly 100 years.

best pita sandwiches at **Mamoun's Falafel** ♥♥, 119 MacDougal St. (mamouns.com; no phone).

Continue downtown until you reach Minetta Lane and take a look at:

9 Minetta Tavern (113 MacDougal St.)

Among the literary landmarks on MacDougal Street, Minetta Tavern has kept many features of its first incarnation as a speakeasy.

Formerly a speakeasy called the Black Rabbit, this was a major literary hangout back in the day, serving poetry-inspiring booze and heaping plates of spaghetti to such notables as Ezra Pound, e. e. cummings, and Ernest Hemingway in the '20s; and Allen Ginsberg, Jack Kerouac, and Alan Corso in the '50s. Little-known fact: The very unbohemian *Readers Digest* was founded on this very spot, published from the basement of the restaurant for half a dozen years before moving into proper offices. Today the restaurant is owned by Keith McNally of Balthazar (p. 100) and retains most of its original 1937 fixtures.

Turn onto Minetta Lane and walk halfway down (if you reach Sixth Ave., you've gone too far) to an unmarked, twisting street that's actually:

10 Minetta Street

Listen carefully: A stream still runs below this street, and on the rare quiet day, it's possible to hear it gurgling faintly below your feet. The Algonquin called it Manette, which means "Spirit Water." The Dutch term for it was "Mintje Kill" (little stream). Minetta is a corruption of one of those two terms—or perhaps both. Though the street is now one of the most charming in the city, when the stream was at street level this area was a muddy ghetto called "Little Africa," inhabited entirely by free Blacks in the 1820s and beyond. In 1863, when the riots surrounding the Civil War's first draft lottery morphed into race riots, this was one of the few safe places in the city for Black Americans. For 5 days, hundreds of white hooligans raged through the streets beating and lynching Blacks, even burning down an orphanage for Black children. It was the most violent riot of the century; 105 people were killed and many more maimed for life. But the narrow layout of Minetta Street allowed armed residents to successfully guard their homes and families from harm.

Soon after the Civil War, Minetta Street became known for its "black and tan" clubs, the few spots in the city where Black and white New Yorkers would socialize. In the Prohibition era, nearly half the buildings on the street housed hidden speakeasies. In the 1950s, a coffee house called The Commons was on the street and was a center for the Beatnik movement of the time, hosting jazz and poetry readings. It was replaced by music and comedy club The Fat Black Pussycat (look at the wall above the Mexican restaurant to see its name fading on the brick). Mama Cass Elliot made her debut here as did Bill Cosby, Richie Havens, and Tiny Tim.

Head back to Minetta St. and walk west to Sixth Ave., crossing it and walking west on:

11 Bleecker Street

This stretch of Bleecker Street contains some of the finest noshes in the city, as it's home to historic **Faiccos Italian Specialties** (at no. 260) owned by the same family since its founding in 1900 and selling the best sopressata in the United States (no joke). When the store opened it was just one of many Italian stores in what was then the part of the city's much larger Little Italy, which flourished from the 1890s well into the early 1970s. Inhale deeply—this is the most aromatic stretch of this walking tour.

Walk to Seventh Ave., but instead of crossing, loop to the right to Barrow St. Continue in the same direction until you get to:

12 One If by Land, Two If by Sea (17 Barrow St.)

Attention *Hamilton* fans! In the 1790s the widowed Aaron Burr moved into this 1767 carriage house with his daughter Theodosia. After the tragic duel, Burr lost not only his political career but much of his property, including this building. The structure then became an engine house for the local firehouse, and in the 1890s a saloon and brothel. The restaurant that's here today is still a stop on ghost tours, as many claim it's haunted by Aaron, Theodosia, and some of the ladies of the night who worked here. The specters are blamed whenever a customer's earring goes missing.

Continue walking to W. 4th St., turn left, and walk to the:

13 Stonewall National Monument and Stonewall Inn

Oddly enough, it was an organized-crime sting operation that precipitated the raid that gave birth to the contemporary gay rights movement. By the 1960s, the Genovese crime family owned most gay bars in the Village, where they served watered-down liquor to a community that didn't have many other places to meet; they also blackmailed wealthier customers with the threat of outing. The family regularly paid off the police, but on June 28, 1969, the Stonewall wasn't tipped off in advance. When eight police officers showed up at 1:20am and started loading employees and customers into a police van, patrons began pelting them with pennies, cans, bottles, and bricks. As the melee escalated, thousands of people rioted for another 5 days before order could be restored. While these protests weren't the start of the gay rights movement, many feel that they were the galvanizing force. Today, pride celebrations in New York, and worldwide, take place on the anniversary weekend of the riots.

The Stonewall Inn, a rallying point for gay rights during the 1969 Stonewall Riots.

In 2016, President Barack Obama designated as a national monument the Stonewall Inn, Christopher Park, and the surrounding streets. It became a National Park in 2024 (p. 183). If you want to end your tour with a celebratory toast, head into the Stonewall Inn for a beer or cocktail. It's still a gay bar, and a very friendly place (all are welcome).

SHOPPING

Why do the highest numbers of visitors to New York descend on the city in fall and early winter? They come here to shop. In the run-up to Christmas, Chanukah, Kwanzaa, and other big-spender holidays, avid shoppers storm the city because they know that if you can't find it in the Big Apple . . . well, it simply doesn't exist. In this chapter, I attempt to bring some order to the massive number of shopping options in the Big Apple, concentrating on the locally owned shops, NYC-based designers, and shopping experiences that can be had only in NYC.

SHOPPING BY AREA

Often in Gotham, finding what you want has less to do with picking the right store than with choosing the right area in which to shop. Similar types of stores tend to cluster together, making it quite easy for shoppers to flit from one to the next, comparing merchandise and prices. Here, beginning at the bottom of Manhattan and working my way north and then to Brooklyn and Staten Island, is my list of the city's best shopping streets and their areas of specialty.

Downtown

FINANCIAL DISTRICT

Several chichi malls operate in the vicinity of the 9/11 Memorial. The largest one, set under the dazzling ribbed ceiling of the **Oculus**—a spectacular transit hub designed by architect Santiago Calatrava—offers such brands as the Apple Store, John Varvatos, Cole Haan, and Pop Mart. Across the street at **Brookfield Place,** 230 Vesey St., the shopping frenzy continues with Adam Lippes, Louis Vuitton, and Tory Burch, among other boutiques. *(Subway: 2, 3, 4, 5 to Fulton St.; N, R, W to Cortland St.)*

TRIBECA

Today, Tribeca is second only to Chelsea when it comes to the number of art galleries per block. If you want to see the latest in fine arts, and perhaps buy a piece yourself, this is an excellent area to visit. *(Subway: 1, 2, 3 to Chambers St.)*

CHINATOWN

Canal Street between Mott and Lafayette: It's best for super-cheap knockoff accessories: purses in the style of Gucci and Dior, watches of all types, sunglasses, and luggage. If you're planning to buy a T-shirt to commemorate your New York vacation, buy it here for half of what you'd spend in Times Square. ***Tip:*** Very few stores in this area use price tags, because bargaining is expected. Be prepared to walk away if the price seems too high—often the mere gesture of turning toward the door will halve the cost.

For browsing: Fish and herbal markets along **Canal, Mott, Mulberry,** and **Elizabeth streets** are fun for their bustle and exotica—as well as for a handful of Italian joints from the pre-Chinese days when this area was known as Little Italy. The **Two Bridges Mall,** 75 East Broadway, set under the Manhattan Bridge, has a bustling food market on the ground floor, complete with tanks of giant crabs and other living seafood, and above, an array of hip vintage and designer clothing stores, including **Eckhaus Latta** (eckhauslatta.com), founded by hot NY-based designer Mike Eckhaus. *(Subway: 1, 2, 3, 4, 5, 6, N, Q, R to Canal St.).*

Shopping in Chinatown takes you through several narrow streets crammed with stores.

LOWER EAST SIDE

Orchard, Allen, Delancey, and Ludlow streets: A number of art galleries that were priced out of Chelsea (p. 178) have moved to the Lower East Side in the last few years. They join a vibrant array of indie fashion stores (p. 314) and natural wine stores, making the LES tops for offbeat shopping. *(Subway: B, D to Grand St.; F to Delancey St.; J, M, Z to Essex St.)*

Bowery between Kenmare Street and East Houston: Restaurant supply wholesalers line this stretch, and their prices are often a fraction of what you'll find in shops geared toward consumers (most *are* open to the general public).

SOHO & NOLITA

Broadway between West Houston and Canal: If you're between the ages of 15 and 29, and want affordable flashy fashions or sports gear, this is where to shop. Both Brandy Melville and Converse have flagship stores here, with similarly sprawling spaces devoted to Nike, Steve Madden, Uniqlo, Lacoste, North Face, and other big brands. Many shoppers end up in the selfie paradise known as the **Museum of Ice Cream,** 558 Broadway at Prince St. (museumoficecream.com). You won't learn anything here, but hey, there are sweet treats, slides, and photo ops.

Nearby, **smaller side streets** (Spring, Elizabeth, Mott, Mulberry) offer an entirely different scene, with couture mavens and unique perfumeries next to high-fashion consignment stores and such stellar names as the Museum of Modern Art Design Store (p. 326). Several galleries are also along West Broadway and sprinkled throughout SoHo. **Lafayette Street** has recently become a mecca for antiques and fashion. *(Subway: R, Q to Prince St.; 6 to Spring St.)*

THE EAST VILLAGE

9th Street between Second Avenue and Avenue A: New, younger designers populate this street, so you'll find a terrific assortment of "only in New York" fashions, along with several well-curated vintage stores, a sake purveyor, and several stores with children's goods (clothing and books). If you have time, wander down to **St. Marks Place** (the continuation of 8th St.) and **7th Street** for similar stores, though not in the same density. St. Marks between Second and Third avenues is fun for teens, filled with vintage clothing shops and sunglasses stands. *(Subway: 6 to Astor Place; L to First Ave.)*

GREENWICH VILLAGE

Bleecker Street between Seventh and Eighth avenues: If cutting-edge style is your thing and you have the pocketbook to support that appetite, the boutiques along this block-long stretch have all the latest fashions, with friendlier service than you'll find uptown. You'll also find a number of pop-ups from chic clothing brands that are usually online only. And oddly, Bleecker Street between Sixth and Seventh avenues is foodie paradise, selling all the fine cheeses, chocolates, cupcakes, and other goodies that will prevent you from fitting into the fashions an avenue further west! *(Subway: A, E, C to 14th St.)*

The farmers market in Union Square (p. 261) is an essential stop for local cooks and chefs.

UNION SQUARE/THE FLATIRON DISTRICT

Union Square has many American mall standards, with **Barnes & Noble, DSW (Designer Shoe Warehouse), Reebok, Sephora,** and **Burlington,** along with other stores. It is also the site of the city's best open-air food market (p. 261).

For more mall-type stores, **Fifth Avenue between 14th and 23rd streets** mixes home furnishings with brand-name clothiers (Eileen Fisher, Aritzia) and kiddie magnets (Harry Potter New York, CAMP). At 23rd is the original Eataly, as much tourist site as food store. *(Subway: 4, 5, 6, N, Q, R, L to Union Square; N, R, 6 to 23rd St.)*

CHELSEA/MEATPACKING DISTRICT

West of Greenwich Avenue between 12th and 14th streets, the **Meatpacking District** (once a slaughterhouse area) was made famous by *Sex in the City,* and most stores here would appeal to that show's characters (Christian Louboutin, Hermès, Diane von Furstenberg), alongside a few more middle-of-the-road retailers (Lululemon, the Apple Store). Above 14th Street, west Chelsea between Tenth and Eleventh avenues has become the **Chelsea Art District** (p. 186), with more than 200 galleries. *(Subway: A, C, L to Eighth Ave.; 7 to Hudson Yards).*

Chelsea Market (p. 118) also has excellent shopping options, including Artists and Fleas, a maker's market where you can find unique jewelry, graphic Ts, and gifts; a Moroccan goods store; **Posman Books** (p. 311); an offshoot of the Asian goods superstore **Pearl River Mart** (p. 306); and many fab food options. On Saturdays and Sundays, **Chelsea Flea** sets up shop on 25th Street between Fifth and Sixth avenues, a treasure trove for vintage clothing, architectural salvage, antiques, and posters.

Midtown

HUDSON YARDS

The **Shops at Hudson Yards** (hudsonyardsnewyork.com), a marble-clad four-level behemoth, has the ambiance of a high-end Asian shopping center. Its 100-plus shops include major luxury brands, mall standards like H&M, Aritzia, and Mango, and an impressive range of eateries. *(Subway: 7 to 34th St./Hudson Yards)*

HERALD SQUARE & THE GARMENT DISTRICT

Herald Square—where 34th Street, Sixth Avenue, and Broadway converge—is dominated by **Macy's,** the self-proclaimed "biggest department store in the world," but it also has a number of other name-brand retailers. *(Subway: 1, 2, 3, B, D, F, M, N, Q, R to 34th St.)*

FIFTH AVENUE FROM 38TH ST. TO 57TH ST.

This is a window-shopper's paradise, with such grand old beauties as Saks Fifth Avenue, Tiffany's, and Bergdorf Goodman, along with flagship stores

A Pilgrimage to Woodbury Commons

Set on a campus meant to look like a small New England town—there's even a fake clock tower at the center—**Woodbury Commons,** 498 Apple Court Rd. (Central Valley, NY; premiumoutlets.com), may be the outlet mall to end all outlet malls. It carries every single American and European brand of note, including names one *never* sees at outlets, like Alexander McQueen, Moncler, Gucci, Fendi, and Givenchy. All in all, it's more than 150 stores. Since Woodbury Commons is an hour outside the city, you need to be a dedicated shopper to go, but you will see drastic discounts. If you don't have a car—and why would you on a trip to NYC?—the easiest way to get there is via the mall-sponsored bus (woodburybus.com). It picks up at 51st street and Broadway and costs $45 round-trip.

for Dyson (their "demo" store), Bulgari, and others. *(Subway: E, M to Fifth Ave./53rd St.)*

Uptown

MADISON AVENUE FROM 57TH ST. TO 86TH ST.

This stretch is home to the world's most expensive retail real estate, selling pricey baubles and garments for the 1%. Along with Vera Wang's original shop, you'll find flagships of Ralph Lauren, Chanel, Hermès, Dolce & Gabbana, and Prada. Visit madisonavenuebid.org for a shop list. *(Subway: 6 to 59th, 66th, or 77th sts.)*

Chelsea Market (p. 118) has a bustling food hall, plus multiple shops of New York artisans, in a complex that stretches a whole city block.

LEXINGTON AVENUE FROM 70TH ST. TO 80TH ST.

This 10-block stretch sells ladylike apparel and the types of home decor items preferred by Upper East Side doyennes. Happily, prices tend to be about 25% less than you'd pay two avenues over, on Madison. *(Subway: 6 to 66th or 77th sts.)*

125TH STREET FROM FREDERICK DOUGLASS BLVD. TO ADAM CLAYTON POWELL JR. BLVD.

Harlem's famed shopping strip is going strong with big box stores like Target and factory outlets for Banana Republic and the Gap. Nearby, on 116th St. near Malcolm X Boulevard is the **Malcolm Shabazz African Market,** a covered market where vendors sell dashikis, beads, shea-butter products, and handmade African folk art of all kinds. *(Subway: A, D to 124th St.)*

Brooklyn

DOWNTOWN

City Point, 445 Albee Sq. W (citypointbrooklyn.com), has turned downtown Brooklyn into a prime shopping and eating destination, particularly for its underground food hall, the **DeKalb Market** (p. 143). Popular shops include McNally Jackson bookstore, a brick-and-mortar location for the online furniture giant Joybird, and an outlet for the high-fashion/low-cost European chain Primark. *(Subway: B, D, N, Q, R to DeKalb Ave.; 2, 3 to Hoyt St.; 4, 5 to Nevins St.; A, C to Hoyt-Schermerhorn)*

GREENPOINT

50 Norman, at that address on Norman Street is an exquisite mini-mall of high-quality Japanese goods, from artisanal dashi broths (with tasting stations!) to fine knives, cookware, flatware, and clothing. Nearby, around the part of **Greenpoint Ave.** that intersects with **Franklin and West streets,** are a number of adorable boutiques, some devoted to teas, others to fine Asian stationery, still others selling locally cobbled shoes and accessories. This is also a top neighborhood for vintage stores. The website theshopkeepers.com has excellent maps and shop lists. (*Subway: G to Nassau Ave.)*

PARK SLOPE

"I shopped small—the OTHER Fifth Avenue" is the hashtag used to promote **Fifth Avenue** in Brooklyn, a bustling stretch of mom-and-pop restaurants, vintage clothing stores, and truly unique boutiques—it's completely different from Manhattan's flagship-laden strip. Favorites include **Annie's Blue Ribbon General Store** (no. 232, a fab gift shop), **Beacon's Closet** (no. 92, recycled designer clothing), and **Sterling Records** (no. 121, vinyl, CD's, music books, and posters). *(Subway: 2, 3 to Bergen St.; B, Q, 2, 3, 4, 5, D, M, N to Atlantic Ave./Barclay Center).*

I'm also a HUGE fan of **Atlantic Avenue** for shopping, particularly the stretch between Bond and Hoyt streets. It has a wide variety of home goods stores with the types of pieces that will lend a chic Brooklyn aesthetic to any room, plus several offshoots of European and Canadian clothing boutiques that are nowhere else in the United States, including Meg (p. 316).

WILLIAMSBURG

Get off at the Bedford Avenue stop of the L train and just wander. Bedford Avenue, like the surrounding streets, is a treasure trove of hip boutiques,

If you're headed to Williamsburg for shopping, you'll find plenty of boutiques and markets selling hip, handmade, and local goods.

bookstores, galleries, vintage clothing stores, and the food fest **Smorgasburg** (p. 144). *(Subway: L to Bedford Ave.)*

Staten Island

Billing itself, correctly, as New York City's only outlet mall, **Empire Outlets New York City** (Richmond Terrace; empireoutlets.nyc) is right by the Staten Island Ferry terminal. While it doesn't have the top designer shops that lure New Yorkers out to Woodbury Commons (p. 302), it will have discounts on goods from such brands as Banana Republic, H&M, Nike, and Levi's. *(Take the Staten Island Ferry.)*

DEPARTMENT STORES

Beyond the stores listed below, you may want to wander into **Bergdorf Goodman,** 754 Fifth Ave. (bergdorfgoodman.com), to ogle some cutting-edge fashions, though I find it FAR too expensive to shop in.

Bloomingdale's ♥♥♥ Classier than Macy's (below) and a bit more logical in terms of layout, this shopping behemoth can keep shopaholics occupied for hours. Founded in 1872 as a hoop skirt store, the vast emporium is still in the forefront of fashion, with four complete floors just for garments (basement for men's; second, third, and fourth floors for women's). It also sells housewares, furniture, kids' clothing, luggage, kitchenware, accessories, cosmetics, and jewelry, but its strength is the clothes. 1000 Third Ave. (Lexington Ave. at 59th St.). bloomingdales.com. ✆ **212/705-2000.** Subway: 4, 5, 6 to 59th St. Also at 504 Broadway (at Broome St.). ✆ **212/729-5900.** Subway: N, R to Prince St.

Century 21 ♥ Felled by the pandemic, in 2023 Century 21 rose from the dead, to many shoppers' surprise. Its lure is still discounted high-end brand clothing, shoes, and handbags but the selection is noticeably more limited than it was pre-2020. There are still good values to be found here, so stop by if you're in the Financial District. 22 Cortland St. (btw. Church St. and Broadway). c21stores.com. Subway: 2, 3, 4, 5, J, Z, to Fulton St., R, W to Cortland St.

Dover Street Market ♥ An all-couture department store, Dover specializes in clothing ($7,000 dresses, $500 T-shirts, $2,200 denim jackets) from such NY-based and international labels as Comme des Garçons, Renli Su, and Alexander Wang. Goods are displayed as if at an art installation, and customers wander around uttering such only-in-Manhattan inanities as "When I bought my first pair of $400 shoes, people thought I was nuts. Now you can't GET a pair of shoes for less than $400!"—it's fascinating to visit from an anthropological perspective even if you can't afford a thing here. 160 Lexington Ave. (at 30th St.). doverstreetmarket.com. ✆ **646/837-7750.** Subway: 6 to 28th St.

Macy's ♥ With approximately one million items for sale and a huge two-building space that stretches the very long block between Broadway and Seventh Avenue, this, the World's Largest Store, is also one of New York's top tourist attractions. It has some of the best prices of the major department stores, though its fashions are definitely middle-of-the-road. The basement is devoted to cookware, of which there's a dazzling variety; the house brand of pots and pans (Tools of the Trade) is a great buy, well-made and usually quite affordable. And the return policy here is one of the most generous in the city, so mistakes are not irrevocable. However, you may want to pop a Valium before you attempt to visit Macy's. Its vast scale and the huge crowds it attracts are its Achilles heel. There's never a salesperson when you need one; on sale days the masses can be crushing; and even native New Yorkers get lost here. At Herald Square, W. 34th St. and Broadway. macys.com. ✆ **212/695-4400** or 212/494-7300. Subway: B, D, F, N, Q, R, 1, 2, 3 to 34th St.

Nordstrom ♥♥ Nordstrom has only been in NYC since 2019, but this is its largest store ever—a whopping 320,000 sq. ft. of luxury goods. It's known for its helpful staff, especially its personal shopping service, and beyond fashion has a well-stocked home goods section, including products from a number of New York makers. 225 W. 57th St. (near Broadway). nordstrom.com. ✆ **877/310-8537.** Subway: A, B, C, D, 1 to Columbus Circle.

Pearl River Mart ♥♥♥ If you're like me, Pearl River will unleash yens you never knew you had. You'll walk into this two-story department store dedicated to goods imported from Asia and suddenly realize how much you desperately need lacquered chopsticks, or a silk brocaded mandarin shirt, or that industrial-size bag of rice crackers. It happens every time. And prices are reasonable in the extreme. 452 Broadway (near Grand St.). pearlriver.com. ✆ **212/431-4770.** Subway: 6, N, Q, R, or W to Canal St.

SoHo's Pearl River Mart sells an irresistible mix of Asian imported housewares.

Saks Fifth Avenue ♥♥ Despite the fact that it's now a chain, there's still definite glamour to the original Saks. It's a classic, and unlike Macy's, its size is manageable. As for its prices . . . they may not be within reach for many people, but browsing here is a delight. The cosmetics department (now on the second floor) and the shoe department both include brands you won't find elsewhere in the United States. 611 Fifth Ave. (btw. 49th and 50th sts.). saksfifthavenue.com. ✆ **212/753-4000.** Subway: B, D, F, Q to 47th–50th sts./Rockefeller Center; E, F to Fifth Ave.

RECOMMENDED STORES

Antiques & Collectibles

New York has such a bounty of antiques stores that you often do better visiting them in packs, to get a well-rounded look-see at what's available. Head, for example, to **10th street west of Broadway** and you'll find half a dozen stores that carry only the best of French and American Art Deco pieces, Scandinavian heirlooms, and historic tapestries. Antiques hunters will also want to scout **East 59th, 60th,** and **61st streets** around Second Avenue, not far from the **Manhattan Art and Antiques Center ♥**, at 1050 Second Ave. between 55th and 56th streets (the-maac.com; ✆ **212/355-4400**), which is one of the largest antiques malls in the nation.

BK Antiques ♥♥ That would be Barbara Kirshbaum, the owner/founder who heads to France, England, Belgium, Sweden, Italy, Spain, and China several times a year to comb markets and bring back the treasures (lighting, art, and furniture) found here. It now also sells Art Deco- and midcentury modern-inspired furniture, created by local artisans, under the brand name **BK Limited.** 306 E. 61st St., 2nd floor. bkantiques.com. ✆ **212/888-8930.** Closed Sat & Sun. Subway: F, N, Q, R to 63rd St./Lexington Ave.

Dienst + Dotter Antikviteter ♥♥ Opened by Jill Dienst, a former curator from the Metropolitan Museum, this shop celebrates all that is old and Scandinavian, which means many of the pieces look more contemporary than those that were created yesterday. You'll find everything from rococo inlaid tables to low-to-the-ground Danish Modern armchairs. 411 Lafayette St. (btw. Astor Place and E. 4th St.). dienstanddotter.com. ✆ **212/861-1200.** Subway: 6 to Astor Place.

Dienst + Dotter Antikviteter specializes in elegant Scandinavian antiques.

Todd Merrill ♥♥ Merrill is both a store owner and the co-author of a seminal design history book, *Modern Americana.* Well before *Mad Men* hit the airwaves, he was stoking the craze for midcentury modern furnishings. Merrill now also makes custom contemporary furniture that's pretty darn snazzy. 80 Lafayette St. (btw. White and Franklin sts., visits by advance appointment). toddmerrillstudio.com. ✆ **212/673-0531.** Subway: 4, 6, J, Z to Canal St.

Beauty & Perfume

Aedes de Venustas ♥♥♥ Evoking a romantic boudoir out of the Victorian era, this whimsical spot offers very fine and hard-to-get perfumes, 95% of which are imported from France. 16A Orchard St. (btw. Canal and Hester sts.). aedes.com. ✆ **212/206-8674.** Subway: F to E. Broadway.

C.O. Bigelow ♥♥♥ The oldest apothecary shop in the nation (founded in 1838), Bigelow has become known for its huge range of beauty supplies, carrying European and Japanese products that aren't available anywhere else in the United States. Some of the products are quite unusual (like "frownies," an 1800s stick-'em-on cure for frown lines that claims to train the wrinkles to go in another direction as you sleep). Even if you don't need to buy anything, stop by to browse under the Victorian gas chandeliers (converted to electric, but still lovely). 414 Sixth Ave. (btw. 8th and 9th sts.). bigelowchemists.com. ✆ **212/533-2700.** Subway: A, C, E, F, M to W. 4th St.

DS & Durga ♥♥ "Perfume is armchair travel" is the poetically apt tagline adopted by the Brooklyn-based married couple who founded this perfumery.

C.O. Bigelow maintains its Victorian-era atmosphere, complete with antiques from its history as the nation's oldest apothecary.

Hand-crafted perfumes and scents open the senses at DS & Durga.

Self-taught perfumers, they opened their first store in 2008, to immediate success; today their scents are one of the hallmarks of Thompson Hotels, and are sold at small boutiques around the United States. Here you'll find their largest collection of eaux de parfums, candles, lotions, and other goods—you'll waft out smelling better than you ever have before. 255 Mulberry St. (at Prince). dsanddurga.com. ✆ **212/226-2981.** Subway: 6 to Spring St.; R to Prince St. Also at 1070 Madison Ave. and in Brooklyn at 126 N. 6th St.

Kiehl's ♥ Founded in 1867 as an apothecary shop—its specialty back then was such magic potions as "Money Drawing Oil"—in the 1960s it switched to more modern snake oil, facial creams and cleansers, and has been wildly popular ever since. Head to the original of this now-massive chain for the historic decor (the original chandeliers are still in use) and the generous gift of numerous small samples. 109 Third Ave. (btw. 13th and 14th sts.). kiehls.com. ✆ **212/677-3171.** Subway: L, N, R, 4, 5, 6 to 14th St./Union Square.

Books & Music

Beyond the bookstores below, consider a visit to the fusion wine bar/book purveyor **Book Club** (p. 357).

Barnes & Noble ♥♥♥ This famous chain—largest in the nation—was founded in NYC, and while the original store is now closed, the rest are a wonderland for bibliophiles with numerous branches throughout the city (see website). 555 Fifth Ave. at 45th St. barnesandnoble.com. ✆ **212/253-0810.** Subway: 4, 5, 6, L to Grand Central/42nd St.

Book Culture ♥♥ Professors and students from nearby Columbia University keep this store buzzing and mean that the selection of tomes is quite diverse, from best-selling thrillers to cookbooks to scholarly works. 536 W. 112th St. (near Broadway) and 2915 Broadway (at 114th St.). bookculture.com. Subway: 1 to 110th St.

Books Are Magic ♥♥♥ Founded by best-selling novelist Emma Staub—you'll often meet her behind the counter at the front—Books Are Magic has an influence well beyond Brooklyn, thanks to its superb near-nightly authors events. Regular browsing here is pretty great, too, with smart and sometimes quirky fiction selections (lots of local authors) and a robust children's section. 225 Smith St., Cobble Hill, Brooklyn. booksaremagic.net. ✆ **718/246-2665.** Subway: F, G to Bergen St.

Best-selling novelist Emma Straub and her husband Mike founded Books Are Magic, now with two Brooklyn locations.

Books of Wonder ♥♥♥ Do you remember the charming children's bookstore in the 1998 Meg Ryan rom-com *You've Got Mail?* It was inspired by Books of Wonder (Meg even worked here briefly to train for the role), and the real thing, jam-packed with great kiddie reads, is just as magical as the cinematic store. 18 W. 18th St. (btw. Fifth and Sixth aves.). booksofwonder.com. ✆ **212/989-3270.** Subway: L, N, R, 4, 5, 6 to 14th St./Union Square.

Drama Bookshop ♥♥♥ Lin-Manuel Miranda—the patron saint of Broadway! Not only did he make musicals a hot cultural phenom again with his hit *Hamilton,* but when this beloved theater community bookstore was about to fold he gathered a group of investors and bought the place. In its new incarnation—designed by *Hamilton* set designer David Krorins—it's as much theatrical hangout as store, with a cafe and a small stage for readings and shows. 266 W. 39th St. (near Eighth Ave). dramabookshop.com. ✆ **212/944-0595.** Subway: N, Q, R, 1, 2, 3, 7 to 42nd St. (Times Square).

OPEN FOR business?

Hours can vary significantly from store to store—even different branches of CVS can keep different schedules in this city!

Generally, stores open at 10 or 11am, with a dwindling number staying shuttered on Sundays; 7pm is a common closing hour. Both closing and opening hours tend to get later as you move downtown, with some East Village stores keeping their gates down until 1pm and staying open until 8pm or later. In the Financial District, some stores close for the weekend (this is the only part of the city, however, where that happens).

All the big department stores are open 7 days a week, with many staying open until 9pm on Thursdays. Nervous you'll show up and the doors will be locked? Call ahead or go on the internet to double-check hours.

Kitchen Arts & Letters ♥♥ A stellar cookbook store. Along with titles from the standard celeb chefs are out-of-print, rare, and even foreign language books, all just brimming with recipes and advice. 1435 Lexington Ave. (btw. 93rd and 94th sts.). kitchenartsandletters.com. ✆ **212/876-5550.** Subway: 6 to 96th St.

McNally Jackson Books ♥♥♥ Many bookstores post recommendations from their staff, but few are as right on as the ones here. A great place to take a break from the crowds of Rockefeller Center or find that book for the plane ride home. 1 Rockefeller Plaza. mcnallyjackson.com. ✆ **212/274-1160.** Subway: N, R to 50th St. Also at 4 other locations (see website).

Posman Books ♥♥♥ A friendly oasis in the middle of Chelsea Market, Posman does a brisk trade in classic fiction, and has a staff well-read enough to give excellent advice about that as well as contemporary books. In Chelsea Market, entrance on Ninth or Tenth aves. (btw. 15th and 16th sts.). posmanbooks.com. Subway: A, C, E, L to 14th St./Eighth Ave.

Rizzoli ♥♥ Lovers of majestic olde New York groaned when news came that Rizzoli would be losing its spectacular long-time home on 57th Street. Amazingly, Rizzoli found a new spot as palatial (high ceilings, fluted columns) and as appropriate to its wares: handsome coffee-table books on fashion, interior design, architecture, and art (you'll also find fiction and non-fiction tomes here). A truly grand shopping experience! 1133 Broadway (btw. 25th and 26th sts.). rizzolibookstore.com. ✆ **212/759-2424.** Subway: N, R to 23rd St.

Rough Trade ♥ London's punk rock mecca Rough Trade is now, oddly enough, a Rockefeller Center tenant. Outside the shop is all marble, inside a lot of colorfully staged grunge. But like the U.K. original, this is a top spot for records (yes, vinyl ones!) and books about rock 'n' roll. 30 Rockefeller Plaza (on Sixth Ave). roughtrade.com. ✆ **718/388-4111.** Subway: B, D, F to Rockefeller Center.

The Strand ♥♥♥ Grungy, maddeningly disorganized, stuffy, and crowded, the Strand is nonetheless one of New York's premier bookstores, a

Browsing is encouraged at the vast, book-crammed store The Strand.

place that rivals the legendary Library of Alexandria in its scope and variety. Its motto is "Eight Miles of Books," and it certainly feels like it has that many when you visit; best of all, many of these are "front list" books that are ordered directly from the publisher at a substantial discount (sometimes as much as 50%). Those looking for rare books should look no further: The Strand has the largest collection in the city. 828 Broadway (at 12th St.). strandbooks.com. ✆ **212/473-1452.** Subway: L, N, Q, R, 4, 5, 6 to 14th St./Union Square. Also at 450 Columbus Ave. (btw. 81st and 82nd sts.) and 2020 Broadway (btw. 69th and 70th sts.) and in a kiosk on Fifth Ave. and 60th St.

Clothing

Everlane ♥♥♥ On weekends, two lines snake down Prince Street in SoHo: one for the fabulous Prince Street Pizza (p. 100) and the other to enter this equally fabulous clothing store. On sale are finely crafted basics—blazers, jeans, T-shirts, simple dresses, khakis, flats, scarves—made at ethical factories (that is, places that offer fair wages, reasonable working hours, and a healthy work environment). Miraculously, these natty duds are very reasonably priced, some at Uniqlo levels (like the $19 T-shirts). Everlane sells mostly online; this was its first brick-and-mortar space, now joined by another in Brooklyn (104 N. 6th St.) and several others elsewhere in the United States. 28 Prince St. (btw. Mott and Elizabeth sts.). everlane.com. Subway: N, Q, R, W to Prince St.; 6 to Spring St. Also in Williamsburg, Brooklyn.

Uniqlo ♥♥♥ The flagship Fifth Avenue store is also the largest Uniqlo on the planet. Garments (and undergarments) here are among the least expensive in the city. Not only that, they come in quality fabrics, in a wide range of styles from streamlined basics (T-shirts, good wool cardigans, dapper khakis and shorts) to clothes that ape items you'll see in the fashion magazines (smartly cut blazers, billowy skirts, patterned sweaters, and more). Clothing for men, women, and children. 666 Fifth Ave. (at 53rd St.). uniqlo.com. ✆ **877/486-4756.** Subway: F to 57th St.; N, Q, R to Fifth Ave. See website for several other NYC locations.

Fashion basics in a range of colors at Uniqlo's Fifth Avenue flagship.

FOR KIDS

Ever After ♥♥ The place to come with hard-to-please 7-to-16-year-olds, Ever After offers some home-branded clothing (made in California) as well as carefully selected colorful-but-cool outfits from a wide variety of brands. 1162 Madison Ave (btw. 85th and 86th St.). everaftershop.com. ✆ **212/249-6781.** Subway: 4, 5, 6 to 86th St. Also at 349 Greenwich St. (at Harrison St.).

Greenstones ♥♥ Greenstones has a wide variety of trendy but tasteful clothing for newborns through tweens. For boys, that means everything from real suits to happy Ts. On the girls' side, the clothing ranges from rompers to dresses to casual wear, all of it on-trend without looking like it should be worn to a dance club (a problem with lots of girls' clothes these days). 454 Columbus Ave. (at 82nd St.). ✆ **212/580-4322.** Subway: B, C to 81st St.

Little Moony ♥♥ Clothing that's *almost* as adorable as your children is part of the appeal here, but a big reason to shop at Little Moony is the sustainability of their goods. All are designed by the owner and sewn by her mother in Los Angeles, from patterns that minimize waste, using fabrics from family-owned American companies. Along with clothing for newborns through 6-year-olds, the shop sells toys and books. 230 Mulberry St. (btw. Prince and Spring sts.). littlemoony.com. ✆ **646/852-8330.** Subway: 6 to Spring; R to Prince St.

FOR MEN

The Armoury ♥♥♥ An offshoot of the Hong Kong original, the city's most powerful power suits (plus shoes, leisure wear, and accessories) come from here. Those include ready-to-wear items expertly fitted on site, as well as bespoke clothing. Prices are high, but so is the quality. 13 E. 69th St. (near Madison Ave.). thearmory.com. Subway: 6 to 68th St. Also at 168 Duane St.

Blue in Green ♥♥ For the hip (or would-be hip) hunk in your life, this store carries a slew of small-production American designers (many NYC-based), as well as some of the most of-the-moment brands from Japan. You'll find everything from classic Ts to fashion-forward no-collar button-downs, well-tailored jeans, and more. 8 Greene St. (near Canal St.). blueingreensoho.com. ✆ **212/690-0555.** Subway: A, C, E, N, R, Q, W to Canal St.

Descendant of Thieves by Dres Ladro ♥♥ When you shop here, you're almost guaranteed you'll never see another dude strolling by in the same jacket. That's because Brooklyn-by-way-of-Sicily designer Ladro only manufactures limited 200-piece batches of each clothing item (as he told *Black Chalk* magazine, he's the "craft beer of fashion"). Surprisingly, that doesn't make the pieces outrageously expensive. You'll pay less than you would in neighboring boutiques for clothing built on rich fabrics, with subtle quirks (like pants that swagger, thanks to a slightly dropped crotch, or a button-down shirt in a surprisingly butch floral pattern). Even if you're not shopping, stop by: The shop was once gangster John Gotti's social club, and they've preserved the floors and some of the original fixtures. 247 Mulberry St. (near Prince St.). descendantofthieves.com. ✆ **646/858-4010.** Subway: 6 to Spring St. Also at 203 Bleecker St.

DESIGNED & MADE in nyc

Thanks to the Internet, it's now possible to shop for a t-shirt while preparing dinner in your Ohio kitchen. You can't try on the clothes, though, and you're more likely to find the big brand names online than the up-and-coming fashion designers who are creating the most exciting new styles. For the latter, come to NYC's Lower East Side, where a number of locally based indie designers have their own tiny shops selling their made-in-New York, often limited-production, items. You'll find a lot of them by simply wandering down Orchard Street between Canal and Delancey streets (subway: F, J, or M to Delancey St.) Or duck into these neighborhood faves:

Bode ♥♥♥, 58 Hester St. for menswear, 78 Worth St. for womenswear (bode.com). Limited-edition clothing, crafted either from historic fabrics or fabrics based on older patterns. The looks are dashing, with slouchy silhouettes and lots of special touches like quilting or applique. Designer Bode Aujla was named the Smithsonian Cooper-Hewitt Emerging designer of the year in 2022.

Kallmeyer ♥♥, 83 Orchard St. (kallmeyer.nyc). Daniella Kallmeyer is the queen of the contemporary woman's power suit, but also has a range of drapey dresses and wardrobe staples unique enough to elevate any look.

Santos by Monica ♥♥, 22 Ludlow St. (santosbymonica.com). This Latina-owned brand is all about sustainable bio-materials, but that doesn't mean the goods here aren't super chic. They include handbags made from cactus "leather" and clothing in soft and cool eucalyptus fabrics.

For other made-in-NYC shops outside this neighborhood, look at **Fine and Dandy** (p. 315), **Ulla Johnson** (p. 316), **DS & Durga** (p. 308), **Descendant of Thieves by Dres Ladro** (p. 314), **Jill Platner** (p. 324), and **The Locavore Variety Store** (p. 319).

Fine and Dandy purveys men's accessories with a distinct sense of style.

Fine and Dandy ♥♥♥ This specialist in men's accessories makes 80% of the natty bowties, neckties, silky socks, pocket squares, fedoras, suspenders, and other items of male glamor sold here. Need to buy the man in your life a really special gift? This is where to come. 445 W. 49th St. (off Tenth Ave.). fineanddandyshop.com. ✆ **212/247-4847.** Subway: C, E to 50th St.

State & Liberty ♥ The men who shop here have a very happy problem: They work out so regularly that their shoulders are too broad, and waists too nipped, for regular men's shirts. S & L's clothing is designed to fit their Adonis proportions, and it's all made from good-quality fabrics. Come to shop . . . or just to stare. 176 Fifth Ave. (at 22nd St.). stateandliberty.com. No phone. Subway: N, R to 23rd St. Also at 57 Spring St.

FOR WOMEN

Gudrun Sjödén ♥♥♥ No shade of the rainbow is off limits, as this eponymous Swedish designer uses both subtle pastels and neon hues in striking patterns for hippie-chic women's clothing and housewares. The brand is

Swedish designer Gudrun Sjödén brings her eco-conscious hippie-chic fashions to the United States in this SoHo store.

known for eco-conscious practices, fair pricing, and cuts that flatter all sizes, including plus sizes. This is one of only two U.S. outlets for this multinational chain (the other is in Minneapolis). 50 A Green St. (near Broome St.). gudrunsjoden.com. ✆ **212/219-2510.** Subway: 6 to Spring St.; N, Q, R to Canal St.

La Garçonne ♥♥ The first physical store of the esteemed online women's clothing marketplace, it sells its usual mix of chicly androgynous-looking basics, but here you can try them on. 465 Greenwich St. (at Watts St.). lagarconne.com. ✆ **646/553-3303.** Subway: 1 to Canal St.

Malia Mills ♥♥ Cruelty-free bathing-suit shopping for women—I'm not talking about the fabrics used, but the kind cuts of these suits and attitudes of the staff. Finding a new swim garment won't be torture here, no matter your age or size. 27 Wooster St. (at Grand St.). maliamills.com. ✆ **212/517-7485.** Subway: A, C, E to Canal St. Also at 1070 Madison Ave. (at 81st St.).

Meg ♥♥ You may not have heard of designer Meghan Kinney, but she's been a fixture in New York for over 30 years and has grown over the years to a Gotham-centric minichain (she has one other store in Toronto). Her designs have a unique fluidity and use kicky, unusual fabrics. I also like her reasonable pricing, the way she nips in the waist just so, and the fact that though the look is young, it doesn't look foolish on her middle-aged clients. 262 Mott St. (btw. Broadway and Prince St.). megest1994.com. ✆ **646/891-6553.** Subway: 6 to Bleecker St.; B, D, F, M to Broadway/Lafayette. Also at 376 Atlantic Ave., Park Slope, Brooklyn.

Sincerely Tommy ♥♥♥ Black-owned, and on the cutting edge of fashion, this Brooklyn boutique showcases emerging designers, many POC. The store also sells handsome housewares, accessories, and jewelry, and has a small cafe—a blessing in the middle of a long shopping day. 343 Tompkins Ave. (at Monroe St.), Brooklyn. sincerelytommy.com. No phone. Subway: A, C to Nostrand Ave.

Ulla Johnson ♥♥ Handmade fabrics from around the globe go into these casually elegant boho threads, created by a born-and-bred NYC designer. They're pricey, but the microfloral dresses, especially, are wonderfully whimsical. 15 Bleecker St. (at Elizabeth St.). ullajohnson.com. ✆ **212/965-0144.** Subway: 6 to Bleecker St.

VINTAGE & CONSIGNMENT CLOTHING

Front General Store ♥♥♥ The fashions here are highly curated by owner Hiro Yonekaway to feature vintage clothing from elite designers (Yohji Yamamoto, Issey Miyake, Prada, Comme des Garçons). In addition to the previously loved finds are some new clothing from of-the-moment designers, along with homeware and beauty goods. 143 Front St., near Pearl St., DUMBO, Brooklyn. frontgeneralstore.com. Subway: F to York St.

Housing Works Thrift Shop ♥♥ Do-gooder shopping: Not only will you find terrific fashion buys, but part of what you spend will go to help an

SHOP 'TIL YOU drop TOURS

It's an open secret in New York that you get the best bargains when you cut out the middleman and buy directly from the many designers who call Gotham home. But tracking down sample sales and getting into designer showrooms can be tricky, if not impossible, for outsiders.

Tours operated by **Style Room** (styleroom.com) contain the keys to the kingdom of fashion. They take would-be buyers into the inner sanctums of design (obscure offices in the Garment District filled with "sample" clothing, that is, goods that were created for runway shows or to show department stores). The savings can be ginormous! On one tour I took, I got a fabulous, real suede skirt for $20, a chic tweed dress for $40, two cashmere turtlenecks for $30 apiece, and about five lovely T-shirts for $15 total. I have no doubt that my savings more than paid for the cost of the tour.

There is, however, one major "gotcha" to these tours, and that's sizing. In general, the tours are not so hot for plus-size customers. You'll find the most options if you're a size 0 to a size 6.

unhoused person living with HIV or AIDS. Along with clothes by designers such as Calvin Klein, Perry Ellis, and Diane von Furstenberg, these stores carry wedding gowns and furniture. There are 12 outlets around the city; I always have the best luck at this one. Interestingly, in 2023 Housing Works became New York City's first legally licensed marijuana purveyor (you won't find weed at the thrift store—they have special locations for cannabis). 306 Columbus Ave. (btw. 74th and 75th sts.). housingworks.org. ✆ **212/579-7566.** Subway: 1, 2, 3, B, C to 72nd St.

Ina's ♥♥♥ This is where the *Sex and the City* costume department resold its clothes once the series ended. Though those clothes are now long gone (they sold out in 2 hours flat), no other place in the city helps you achieve Carrie's haute-but-wacky look so affordably. The men's part of the store has equivalently daring clothing for guys. There are now many outlets (see website for locations), but the one I list here has the best selection. 21 Prince St. (at Elizabeth St.). inanyc.com. ✆ **212/228-8511.** Subway: 6 to Spring St. Also at 207 W. 18th St., and 279 Mott St.

Michael's ♥♥♥ You'll find one-of-a-kind couture clothes (Gucci, Prada, Escada) at deep discounts here, including wedding gowns, all brought in by the doyennes of the Upper East Side. It also has the largest selection of hats and purses of any of the consignment houses. 1125 Madison Ave. (at 84th St.). michaelsconsignment.com. ✆ **212/737-7273.** Subway: 4, 5, 6 to 86th St.

Electronics

B&H Photo & Video ♥♥♥ I know people who visit New York City *just* to shop at B&H. Not only is it the largest camera store in the United States, it also boasts the best prices in the country (and that's a rarity for NYC). But you'd be mistaken if you think the store is just for shutterbugs—it's also tops for most everything electronic, from computers to mixing boards to chargers. Best of all: The staff is extremely knowledgeable, and, since so many customers now shop at the online store, these tech gurus have time to walk would-be buyers through all the options. (***Note:*** B&H is closed Sat.) 420 Ninth Ave. (at 34th St.). bhphotovideo.com. ✆ **800/606-6969** or 212/444-6615. Subway: A, C, E to 34th St.

Some shutterbugs make a special trip to NYC just to shop at B&H Photo & Video.

Gifts

Delphinium Home ♥♥ When a Broadway show opens, this is where friends of the creative team come to buy their celebratory gifts—it has the type of classy kitsch that community cherishes (it's owned by former musical theater performers). So, you might take home a "devotional candle" with the faces of the ladies from *Sex and the City*, or a board book called *B Is for Botox*. The shop also has some lovely NYC souvenirs, like handsome 6-in.-tall steel replicas of famous buildings. 353 W. 47th St. (btw. Eighth and Ninth aves.). delphiniumhome.com. ✆ **212/333-7732.** Subway: C, E to 50th St.

Gifts for pet-lovers are always popular at E.A.T.

E.A.T. Gift Shop ♥♥ Though this is an offshoot of a popular deli, only some of the goods here are food adjacent (candies, corkscrews, and the like). Others speak to the Upper East Side neighborhood's obsessions—lots of little golf gifties (like desktop sets), wind-up plastic pigeons, stuff for dog- and cat-lovers, and an unusual number of mushroom-themed objects (grow kits, butter containers, lights and more). Along with cards and party goods are toys galore for kids, adults, and those who don't want to be defined. 1062 Madison Ave. (btw. 80th and 81st St.). eatgiftsnyc.com. ✆ **212/861-2522.** Subway: 6 to 77th St.

Evolution Nature Store ♥♥ Who knew that there'd be a market for freeze-dried mice, stuffed piranhas, and pendants made from butterfly wings? Apparently the mad scientists behind Evolution did, and in 1993 they opened this mesmerizing store-cum-museum, where you can spend an engrossing hour staring at perfectly preserved skeletons (all types of animals), fossils, stuffed creatures, and bugs encased in plastic. A great place for kids. 687 Broadway (btw. 3rd and 4th sts.). theevolutionstore.com. ✆ **212/952-3195.** Subway: 6 to Bleecker St.

Forbidden Planet ♥♥ Know anyone who lives in a fantasy world? This is where you should buy their gifts. Forbidden Planet specializes in all the "geek" obsessions: sci-fi, horror, Japanese anime, comic books, and fantasy games. That includes gaming implements, figurines from such cult classics as *Game of Thrones* and *Star Wars,* and more ephemera. 832 Broadway (btw. 12th and 13th sts.). fpnyc.com. ✆ **212/473-1576.** Subway: L, N, R, 4, 5, 6 to 14th St./Union Sq.

Unique stylish items, strikingly displayed, fill the walls and shelves at John Derian.

John Derian ♥♥♥ Fabulous decoupage items, colorful candleholders handmade in Paris, Carrera marble fruit, and terra-cotta pottery are but a few of the delicious treats here. 6, 8 and 10 E. 2nd St. (btw. Second Ave. and the Bowery). johnderian.com. ✆ **212/677-3917.** Subway: 6 to Bleecker St.; F, M to Second Ave. Also at 18 Christopher St.

The Locavore Variety Store ♥♥ Everything here is made within 100 miles of New York City, with the majority of the goods coming from the city itself. Some of it seems like stuff that could only come from the Big Apple (cannoli-flavored candy bars, fresh pickles you fish from a barrel); other goods are surprising: packs of pencils, gardening supplies, fine terracotta pots. 434 Sixth Ave (at 10th St.). thelocavore.com/variety-store. ✆ **646/370-8349.** Subway: A, B, C, D, E, F to West 4th St.

More and More ♥♥♥ An apt name for such a cabinet of wonders, this tiny shop is jam-packed with delightful knick-knacks, toys, and housewares. It's the best store in the city for Christmas ornaments but also has some wonderful things to put under the tree: candleholders dripping with crystals, antique jewel-toned cut-glass sherry glasses, painted porcelain eggs, frog-shaped Scotch-tape holders, you name it. 378 Amsterdam Ave. (at 78th St.). moreandmoreantiques.com. ✆ **212/580-8404.** Subway: B, C to 81st St.

Gourmet Food & Sweets

Economy Candy Store ♥♥ Founded in 1937 and little changed since, this is the place to go for all those penny candies you can't find anywhere else, plus classic treats like bubble-gum cigars (remember those?) and wax lips. The halvah and house-dipped chocolates are swell. A trip down a very sweet memory lane. 108 Rivington St. (btw. Delancey and Norfolk sts.). economycandy.com. ✆ **212/254-1531.** Subway: F to Delancey St. Now also at Chelsea Market (p. 118).

Kalustyan's ♥♥♥ This 80-year-old international market just keeps growing and growing, now encompassing three buildings. But the aisles still feel cramped because they're so crammed with goodies from all corners of the globe: Korean chili paste, candied violets, Tunisian harissa, Sicilian pistachios, 100 different types of salt, za'atar spice mix from 17 countries, and every type of spice known to man. Best of all, the store doesn't let any herb or spice sit on the shelves for more than 3 months. For home cooks, Kalustyan's is mecca. 123 Lexington Ave. (btw. 28th and 29th sts.). kalustyans.com. ✆ **212/685-3451.** Subway: 6 to 28th St.

Murray's Cheese ♥ Cheese is the new wine, attracting obsessive devotees who, like oenophiles, can spend hours tasting, musing, comparing. Murray's was once at the epicenter of this movement, a cavernous emporium with a fanatical following. Alas, since it was bought by a grocery store conglomerate, the staff is no longer as expert or as interesting to talk with as they once were. Still, the store carries over 250 varieties of cheese from all over the world, meaning it'll always be a fun place to browse and taste. 254 Bleecker St. (btw. Sixth and Seventh aves.). murrayscheese.com. ✆ **212/243-3289.** Subway: A, B, C, D, E, F, M to W. 4th St.

Paquita ♥♥ A tiny temple of tea, Paquita pleases every sense. Shelves are lined by big bronze cannisters of loose tea, with a small domed cup in front of each, filled with leaves for

Canisters of loose tea line the shelves at Paquita.

At the iconic Upper West Side grocery/deli, Zabar's, the teeming food counters are only part of the story—don't miss the fabulous cookware department upstairs.

sniffing. Elegant hand-written descriptions detail the teas' properties, with a series of dots alerting the customer just how much caffeine each packs. On sale are also dainty tea sets and other gifts that please the eye. For the tongue there are bites and brewed tea and coffee available, with seating in the front. The entire place looks like it was lifted from a period film that might star Timothee Chalamet. 242 W. 10th St. (near Sixth Ave). No website. ✆ **646/504-6864.** Subway: 1 to Christopher St.

Sahadi's ♥♥♥ The first Sahadi's was started by Lebanese immigrant Abrahim Sahadi in lower Manhattan in 1896. Barrels of feta cheese, olives, or pink Lebanese pickles, plus huge sacks of dried fruits and nuts, were the mainstays back then, and still are today (the nuts are roasted in a Sahadi's facility). But Abrahim's descendants—this is still a family business—have added so much more over the years, some Middle Eastern foods (like the superlative tahini and hummus) and some representing the finest offerings of other cultures. ***Bottom line:*** If you want to bring home unusual edibles (fine tinned pate from France, say, or Italian chestnut puree), you'll likely find it at this three-building institution. A foodie experience. 187 Atlantic Ave. (btw. Court and Clinton sts.), Brooklyn. sahadis.com. ✆ **718/788-8500.** Subway: 2, 3, 4, 5, R, N to Court St./Borough Hall. Also in Industry City, and at Pier 57 in Manhattan.

Zabar's ♥ Featured in *Will & Grace, Seinfeld,* and countless other NY-based TV shows, this is New York's most famous grocery/deli, an iconic NYC

NYC IS chocolate city

With this many chocolate makers in town, the Big Apple could be renamed the Big Bonbon. Many sweet shops now turn out homemade chocolates that are so good, the stores, like four-star restaurants, are bona fide destinations.

What I like best about **Jacques Torres Chocolates ♥♥♥**—besides the fact that Jacques Torres is a dashingly handsome Frenchman who likes to cook (making him every woman's dream guy)—is its owner's willingness to blend common ingredients with splendid chocolates. He does this, for example, with two breakfast cereals—plain bran flakes and Cheerios—and the results are exquisite. You'll also want to pick up a can of his rich hot chocolate, which puts Hershey's to shame. Torres has locations in Grand Central Terminal and at 66 Water St. in DUMBO, Brooklyn (mrchocolate.com).

Just east of the Metropolitan Museum of Art, the Madison Avenue incarnation of the Paris import **La Maison du Chocolat ♥**, 1018 Madison Ave., at 78th St. (lamaisonduchocolat.us; ✆ **212/744-7117**), takes its handiwork very seriously, avoiding any bitterness in its chocolate by using nothing stronger than 65% cocoa. The chain has 5 other outlets including in Rockefeller Center and at the Shops at Columbus Circle.

One of the oldest chocolate shops in the city, the 1923-established **Li-Lac Chocolates ♥♥**, 75 Greenwich Ave. (li-lacchocolates.com; ✆ **212/924-2280**), is home to new batches of handmade fudge daily. What better souvenir to bring home than an edible Statue of Liberty or Empire State Building? Stores also in Grand Central Terminal (p. 205), Hudson Yards (p. 188), Chelsea Market (p. 118), Industry City (p. 238), and at 162 Bleeker St.

Myzel's Chocolates ♥♥♥, 140 W. 55th St., between Sixth and Seventh aves. (myzels.com), is run by Kamila Myzel, who is also its head chocolatier, using candy molds she brought from Poland when she emigrated in the 1980's. She has a wide variety of treats, from chocolate-covered matzoh and bits of ginger, to holiday themed bonbons for Easter and Thanksgiving. She's also famous for stocking 150+ types of licorice from all around the world.

And for a selection of artisanal chocolate bars from around the planet (as well as salts, bitters, and flowers), stop by **The Meadow ♥♥**, 240 Mulberry St., between Prince and Spring (themeadow.com; ✆ **212/645-4633**).

emporium. It has some unique edibles, but frankly, I come here for the competitively priced housewares and cookware on the second floor, of which there are a jaw-dropping range and variety. 2245 Broadway (at 80th St.). zabars.com. ✆ **212/787-2000.** Subway: 1 to 79th St.

Housewares

Also see the Japanese home goods at **50 Norman** (p. 303) and **Zabar's** (p. 321).

ABC Carpet & Home ♥♥ Once a two-building, multistory temple of home decor, ABC is now a much smaller two-story affair. The goods—rugs, throw pillows, lamps, candles, towels, textiles, and more—are still swoon-worthy, but this is no longer a one-stop shop for home goods. It also has an outlet store in Industry City, Brooklyn (220 36th St.; p. 238). 888 Broadway (at 19th St.). abchome.com. ✆ **212/473-3000.** Subway: L, N, R, 4, 5, 6 to 14th St./Union Square.

Big Night ♥♥ Unleash your inner host or hostess at this adorbs boutique dedicated to dinner- and cocktail-party necessities. Goods range from vintage glasses to plates by local ceramicists to condiments that will bring your home-cooked treats up a notch. 236 W. 10th St. (off Sixth Ave.). bignightbk.com. ✆ **646/370-6839.** Subway: 1 to Christopher St. Also in Brooklyn at 154 Franklin St.

Fish's Eddy ♥♥♥ Want to bring home a set of dishes with the New York skyline on them? You'll find those here, along with a slew of equally peppy, original plateware. Those who like vintage styles for modern tableware—like soda fountain and pint glasses—will find them here. 889 Broadway (at 19th St.). fishseddy.com. ✆ **877/347-4733.** Subway: L, N, R, Q, 4, 5, 6 to 14th St./Union Square.

Korin ♥♥♥ Hand-forged Japanese knives are the buy here, though Korin also has a large selection of handsome and affordable Japanese flatware and cooking implements. Go in and ask for a demonstration: the thinner, sharper blades on these beauties are life changing for home cooks. 57 Warren St. (near West Broadway). korin.com. ✆ **800/626-2172.** Subway: 1, 2, 3 to Chambers St.

Vintage-themed tableware piled high at Fish's Eddy.

Whisk ♥♥ The best kitchenware store in the city, it has every gadget, pot, and pan you'd ever need—and plenty you didn't know you needed until you walked in. 197 Atlantic Ave. (btw. Clinton and Court sts.), Brooklyn. whisknyc.com. ✆ **718/852-2665.** Subway: 4, 5 to Borough Hall.

Whisk sells all manner of kitchen gadgets and cookware.

Jewelry & Accessories

Catbird Jewelry ♥♥♥ Guilt-free baubles entirely crafted from recycled silver and gold, and diamonds that are either recycled, created in a lab, or mined in conflict-free areas. All the rings, bracelets, necklaces, and earrings are made in their Brooklyn workshop. Styles tend to be delicate and very feminine. 15 W. 49th St. (off Fifth Ave). catbirdnyc.com. ✆ **917/900-4769.** Subway: B, D, F, M to 47-50 St./Rockefeller Center. Also at 253 Centre St. and in Williamsburg, Brooklyn.

Jill Platner ♥♥ Ultra-modern designs mixed with unusual materials (many pieces are strung on a Gore-Tex–like thread called Tenara) make Jill Platner the go-to place for people who like to make a statement with their accessories. All the pieces are made in NYC, and, happily, many sell for well under $100. 165 Crosby St. (btw. Houston and Prince sts.). jillplatner.com. ✆ **212/324-1298.** Subway: N, R to Prince St.

The famous Tiffany & Co. flagship isn't just about jewelry—the tableware on display is pretty darn fantastic as well.

Tiffany & Co. ♥♥♥ Tiffany's flagship Fifth Avenue location is the original, and whether or not you decide to pose in front of it nibbling a Danish, you'll enjoy visiting the multilevel store, which received a glow-up in recent years and is now as much of a visitor attraction as it is a store. Start your visit on the 8th floor, where floor-to-ceiling windows offer excellent views of the surrounding blocks and nearby Central Park (there's also a chichi cafe here). Then head downstairs to 7, where the priciest baubles

The Diamond District

West 47th Street between Fifth and Sixth avenues is the city's famous Diamond District. It's said that more than 90% of the diamonds sold in the United States come through this neighborhood first, so there are some great deals to be had if you're in the market for a nice rock. The street is lined with showrooms, and you'll be wheeling and dealing with the largely Hasidic dealers, who are friendly but can be tough negotiators. For a complete intro to the district, including buying tips, go to **diamonddistrict.org**. Stores open Monday through Friday only.

are displayed. As you descend floor by floor, you'll see over-the-top displays of plateware, an exhibit about the film *Breakfast at Tiffany's*, an engagement ring section, and more. The staff are unusually friendly, and if you buy anything, as tradition dictates it will come in the store's iconic robin's-egg-blue box. 727 Fifth Ave. (at 57th St.). tiffany.com. ✆ **212/755-8000.** Subway: N, R to Fifth Ave. Also at 37 Wall St. (btw. William and Broad sts.).

Leather Goods & Shoes

Camper ♥♥♥ And lo', a miracle occurred at this Spanish chain of footwear stores (now colonizing other major U.S. cities as well): The maiden put on the soft-leather high heels and walked a mile . . . without remembering she wasn't wearing sneakers. That's the reason you'll want to visit this not-cheap but not-overly expensive store, which carries darn-chic shoes that cushion the foot no matter how high the heel. 221 Bowery (btw. Rivington and Stanton sts.). camper.com. ✆ **212/339-0078.** Subway: F to Second Ave, J, Z to Bowery. Also at 110 Prince St. in Soho.

Glam rock-star footwear fills the racks at John Fluevog.

John Fluevog ♥♥♥ Beloved by rock stars (you've seen these shoes in a number of music videos), this Canadian designer's kicks take their inspiration from a number of sources, from Louis XIV buckled heels to hook-and-eye Victorian-era styles to chunky work boots. They make any outfit more fun but are also wonderfully comfortable and durable. 67 Prince St. (near Mulberry). fluevog.com. ✆ **212/431-4484.** Subway: 6 to Spring St.; R to Prince St. Also in Brooklyn at 37 Main St., Dumbo.

Mooshoes ♥ Mooshoes, as you might guess from the name, sells "cruelty free" products—handbags, boots, pumps, men's dress shoes—all of which are crafted from plant-based fabric, but look like the finest suede and other forms of leather. Prices are good, too. 78 Orchard St. (btw. Grand and Broome sts.). mooshoes.com. ✆ **212/254-6512.** Subway: F to Delancey; B, D to Grand St.

Peter Hermann Leathergoods ♥♥ The owners of this swank SoHo shop search the world over for artisans who create unique and stylish bags, wallets, and scarves. Many pieces come from small producers in Europe and can't be found anywhere else in the United States. Recently these included vibrantly colorful purses with geometric embroidery, scarves with vivacious Indonesian patterns, and big, slouchy leather bags that just scream "shabby chic." 107 Thompson St. (btw. Prince and Spring sts.). peterhermannleathergoods.net. ✆ **212/966-9050.** Subway: C, E to Spring St.; N, R to Prince St.

Tip Top Shoes ♥ Here's where you come when your feet start complaining about all the walking you've been doing in New York City. Tip Top specializes in shoes that are comfortable without looking nerdy. And prices aren't bad at all. For men, women, and children. 155 W. 72nd St. (btw. Broadway and Columbus). tiptopshoes.com. ✆ **212/787-4960.** Subway: 1, 2, 3 to 72nd St.

Museum Stores

All of NYC's top museums boast superb stores on the premises. Below are my favorites. Don't be shy about buying goods at any museum in town; what's on sale will be unique and you'll be helping support these marvelous institutions.

Metropolitan Museum of Art Store ♥♥♥ Like something you've seen at the museum? It's likely you'll be able to bring it home . . . in the form of a mug, or a piece of jewelry, or a print for your wall. The Met is expert at turning the stars of its vast collection into lovely items for daily life. Also notable is the extraordinary selection of art books and posters. 1000 Fifth Ave. (at 82nd St.). store.metmuseum.org. ✆ **212/570-3894.** Subway: 4, 5, 6 to 86th St. Also at The Cloisters (p. 228).

MoMA Design Store ♥♥♥ Many of the iconic furniture items displayed at the Museum of Modern Art are sold here, in licensed reproductions, meaning you could take home an Eames recliner or Frank Lloyd Wright chair. The shop also has more affordable items, from nifty kids' toys to contemporary jewelry to swank cutlery. 44 W. 53rd St. (btw. Fifth and Sixth aves.). momastore.org. ✆ **212/767-1050.** Subway: E, F to Fifth Ave.; B, D, F, Q to 47th–50th sts./Rockefeller Center. Also in SoHo at 81 Spring St. (at Crosby St.).

Museum of Arts and Design Store ♥♥ As you'd expect from a museum devoted to cutting-edge design, the items here are pretty special, ranging from ultra-chic jewelry to home goods of all sorts to the most fetching umbrellas you've ever seen. The store is small, but it's packed to the gills with unique items, many of which are made just for this gift shop (in tandem with exhibits) and can't be found elsewhere. 2 Columbus Circle (at 59th St.). madmuseum.org. ✆ **212/299-7777.** Subway: 1, A, B, C, D to Columbus Circle.

Toys & Games

American Girl Place ♥ Sigh. Will you be able to avoid this place if you're traveling with a girl under the age of 8? Probably not, though many people find the place underwhelming and overcrowded (despite the fact that it's a massive store). To "do" the whole experience, you'll want to eat at the cafe, get a doll makeover at the salon, and head to the on-site theater. 75 Rockefeller Plaza. americangirl.com. ✆ **800/247-5223.** Subway: B, D, F, M to 47th–50th sts. / Rockefeller Center.

CAMP ♥♥♥ Toddler paradise! Kids ages 8 and under will adore this humungous 10,000-sq.-ft. new store-cum-play space, which is (mostly) hidden by a swinging bookcase/door. All around are play tables with blocks, trains, and other toys; in the back, salespeople lead arts and crafts sessions (for a fee), lead sing-alongs, and demonstrate products, like edible soap bubbles. On sale are non-electric toys and kids' clothing. A really smart, deliriously fun exercise in interactive commerce. 110 Fifth Ave. (btw. 17th and 18th sts.). camp.com. No phone. Subway: 4, 5, 6, N, Q, R, L to Union Square.

At the old school chess parlor Chess Forum, you can pop in for a game or browse the sets for sale.

Chess Forum ♥♥♥ Two generations or so ago there were chess parlors across New York City. This is one of the last holdouts, a hushed but friendly place where you can sit at a chessboard for a $5 game. It also sells handsome and unusual chess sets from around the globe. 219 Thompson St. (near Bleecker St.). chessforum.com. Subway: A, B, C, D, E, F, M to W. Fourth St. of R, W to 8th St.

F.A.O. Schwarz ♥♥ It's back! While this new iteration has roughly half the square footage of the iconic former space off Central Park, it has managed to retain much of the whimsical look of the original, with stations set up where young customers can interact with the merchandise. That might mean getting hair braided and bedazzled at a mini beauty salon; creating customized toy race cars; or playing with electricity in a science-themed area. Of course, there's a giant keyboard to jump on, a la *Big* (the movie). Interestingly, the shop has hired a lot of seniors as salespeople and toy demonstrators, and they bring a palpable joy to their jobs. 30 Rockefeller Plaza. faoschwarz.com. ✆ **646/809-9536.** Subway: B, D, F, M to 47th–50th sts./Rockefeller Center.

Shoppers of all ages get inspired by the creations of master Lego builders on display at the Rockefeller Center store. (Yes, that yellow cab is entirely made of tiny Lego bricks!)

Harry Potter NY ♥ One wand's length away from being a full-fledged indoor amusement park, the boy wizard's first flagship has virtual reality experiences, interactive wand duel stations, a Butterbeer bar, a scavenger hunt (exploring displays of actual props and costumes from the movies), and tons of merch. Collectors take note: Anything marked "New York" is exclusive to this location. 935 Broadway (at 22nd St.). harrypotterstore.com. No phone. Subway: N, R, 6 to 23rd St.

Kidding Around ♥♥♥ This store stays away from all those annoying beeping, buzzing, and flashing toys. Instead, the focus is on playthings that children manipulate themselves, hopefully learning something in the process. Prices are fair, and the shop has a number of unusual toys such as rubber horseshoes (hey, you can play in the living room), soap-making kits, musical instruments, and all kinds of dazzling costumes. 60 W. 15th St. (btw. Fifth and Sixth aves.). kiddingaroundtoys.com. ✆ **212/645-6337.** Subway: F to 14th St.

The Lego Store ♥♥♥ A creative toy, Lego has spawned equally creative stores, where patrons can not only buy Lego sets of all sorts (Star Wars, dollhouses, Spider-Man, and more) but play to their heart's content. Along with boxed sets are huge bins of different Legos, which shoppers can scoop into buckets to create their own custom sets. But I think most people wander in just to build stuff and look at the masterpieces (including a recreation of midtown Manhattan) that others have constructed. Within Rockefeller Center (near Fifth Ave. and 51st St.). lego.com. ✆ **212/245-5973.** Subway: B, D, F, M to Rockefeller Ctr. Also at 200 Fifth Ave. (at 23rd St.).

You'll probably buy more than expected at Toy Tokyo, which offers hundreds of collectible treasures for the young at heart.

Toy Tokyo ♥♥ Be careful! People walk into this store and end up buying far more than they expected, from tiny "jewels" in the shape of anime figures to adorn smartphones, to Hello Kitty and/or Star Wars and/or Godzilla—well, everything. The store is catnip for those who love collectibles from the '80s and '90s, and it also has an unusually wide selection of blind boxes (a package from a line of toys that hides its contents, so you don't know what you're getting until you open it). With hundreds of fist-size or smaller toys, it's primo for stocking stuffers. And yes, there are a ton of Japanese toys here (as the name suggests). 91 Second Ave. (btw. 5th and 6th sts.). toytokyo.com. ✆ **212/673-5424.** Subway: 6 to Astor Place.

ENTERTAINMENT & NIGHTLIFE

8

It isn't a boast but a plain fact: From opera to jazz, from nightclubs to bars, from concert recitals to theater and dance, New York offers the greatest variety and sheer quantity of evening entertainment in America.

It's a dizzying but important subject because most visitors enjoy New York's nightlife as much as they enjoy its daytime sightseeing. In New York, unlike most other American cities, the sidewalks aren't "rolled up" when darkness descends. In the Big Apple (one of the only cities in the country that operates its public transportation 24 hours a day), the bright lights stay on until 4am, and you owe it to yourself to take in all the after-dark excitement.

To make them easy to peruse, I've grouped the nighttime opportunities in this chapter by entertainment category.

THE NYC THEATER SCENE

You can traipse the entire Metropolitan Museum of Art, attend a Yankees game, and ascend to the top of the Empire State Building, but you can't really say you've *done* New York until you spend an evening at the theater. It's an essential element in a NYC vacation, like going to the beach in Hawai'i or slurping pasta in Italy. And though some predicted that the pandemic would kill off New York theater, somehow the corpse rose from its glittering grave, and in its first few seasons back produced Pulitzer Prize–winning plays, fine new musicals, and theatrical events of all sorts. It's these sorts of performances that just may shift your perspective an iota, give you a peephole into another culture, or perhaps illuminate, for 2 fleeting hours, the human condition.

Ticket Tactics

Let's start with a trade secret that no one in the theater industry wants you to know: Only suckers and out-of-towners pay full price for most Broadway and off-Broadway shows (see "Theater Basics," p. 332, for an explanation of the difference between the types of theater). I'd say that, on average, only five or six shows *per year* get away with charging full price for their seats eight shows per week. For the other 60 or so productions, discounts *are the norm,* not the exception. Don't believe anyone who tells you otherwise.

The Broadway Theater District lies between Sixth and Eighth avenues, from West 40th St. up to West 54th St., but there's theater to discover all over town.

BUYING TICKETS ONLINE

Booking tickets before you arrive in New York City is the most time-effective strategy. You're able to schedule your time in advance, get early dinner reservations, and not waste precious vacation hours standing on line at box offices. To do so at a discount, try **BroadwayBox.com** or the app **TodayTix.** In general, discounts will range from 35% to 50% off, though a handling fee will be tacked onto the cost of your ticket, varying by venue (it can be as much as $10). With the first company you buy your tickets through Ticketmaster, but with a discount code that saves you money; theater tickets are either mailed to you, sent via email, or held at the box office. With TodayTix (which offers tickets for up to 8 months in advance, despite the name), you buy direct through the app, and almost always use e-tickets on your phone.

For the big hits, you can use the sites above (though they won't be able to give you a discount) or deal directly with **Telecharge** (telecharge.com; ✆ **212/239-6200**) or **Ticketmaster** (ticketmaster.com; ✆ **212/307-4100**), both of which handle Broadway and off-Broadway shows and most concerts. For difficult-to-get theater (and sports and musical events) tickets, the website **SeatGeek.com** is probably the best bet, though you may pay top dollar. I don't recommend going through a broker not listed in this book, as their ticket prices can be outrageous.

THEATER basics

There are three types of theaters in NYC: Broadway, off-Broadway, and off-off-Broadway:

Broadway shows tend to be performed in the Times Square area (the one exception being the shows at Lincoln Center). They cost, without a discount, between $99 for a balcony seat (as little as $39 at some plays) to $229 for an orchestra seat, all the way up to $800 for a so-called "premium" seat at hit musicals.

Off-Broadway shows are performed in venues all over town, with a good many clustered in the Union Square area. Top prices for off-Broadway musicals rarely go above $159, with plays topping out (usually) at $90. Off-Broadway theaters are smaller than those on Broadway, pay less to cast and crew, and are thus able to present more controversial, less commercial plays and musicals. Many of the recent Pulitzer Prize drama winners (including *Hamilton* and *Fat Ham*) began as off-Broadway shows.

Off-off-Broadway shows are staged in very small theaters, often featuring experimental works or actors' showcases. Some of the best-known venues are La Mama (lamama.org) and Here Arts Center (here.org). Although you'll rarely see these shows advertised or even reviewed in the *New York Times*, they will be listed on *Time Out New York*'s website and at theatermania.com.

Schedule: Broadway and most off-Broadway shows perform eight times a week, most commonly Tuesday through Sunday, though some do play on Monday (instead of Tuesday or Sunday). Matinee (daytime) performances are usually presented at 2pm on Wednesday and Saturday, and 3pm on Sunday. Some shows also have Thursday matinees at 2pm, though that's not common. Evening performances take place 8pm Wednesday through Saturday, 7pm on Tuesday night—though increasingly, evening performances are taking place at 7pm on other nights of the week as well.

A sneaky strategy for getting tickets to insanely popular shows: Hunker down in a Times Square–area hotel lobby at about 6pm and access SeatGeek.com and/or Stubhub.com. If there's a ticket for the show you want to see there, monitor it until 40 minutes before show time. Usually, at that point, the seller will have gotten so desperate that they'll drop the cost of the ticket to face value. Buy it, and if it's not an e-ticket (most will be), ask the hotel if you can use their desk to print it out; all should let you do so. There's some risk, but if you're in Times Square already, you should be able to snag last-minute tickets to another show, either at the TKTS booth or over the web, if tickets to your dream show aren't obtainable.

GETTING YOUR TICKETS ONCE YOU'RE IN NYC

Tickets are sold directly at **theater box offices,** and by using them, you don't have to pay the service charge (though you rarely get a discount this way, unless you have a code from one of the websites above). However, by going to the box office, you may be able to score better seats. Often, on the day of performance, the "house seats" that are reserved for the use of the cast and crew (who pass them along to family members, friends, and investors) are sold to the general public. And these are primo seats, in the center and near the stage.

For the best discounts, and entrée to sold-out shows, joining the theater's **lottery** may be the way to go. Many shows sell the first two rows in the theater by online lottery (the views are considered too close for full-price ticketing). For some, like *Hamilton,* you'll need to download the show's app to join the lottery. There are also regular lotteries at **Lottery.BroadwayDirect.com**, **LuckySeat.com**, and the app **TodayTix.com** (download is free). Please note that sometimes lotteries are for performances 1 to 4 days in the future, so timing is crucial.

Last but certainly far from least is the discount-ticket **TKTS booth** for day-of-performance tickets. Its main branch is located on 46th Street, between Broadway and Seventh Avenue (Mon–Tues and Fri 3–8pm, Wed–Thurs and Sat 11am–8pm, Sun 11am–7pm). It also has a branch at the David Rubinstein Atrium on Broadway at 62nd Street (the official address is 61 W. 62nd St.; Tues–Sat 11am–6pm). TKTS often presents a greater breadth of shows than do the online discounters (you can see what's on offer at TDF.org), but you pay for that choice with your time—during busy periods, the wait on line can be up to an hour. Those who do brave the line are often rewarded with seats that are 50% off. There are ways to **"game" the TKTS line,** including:

- **Keep your ticket stubs if you go to more than one show in a week.** The staff at TKTS will let you jump to the front of the line if you can show a ticket stub purchased from TKTS within the past 7 days.

Deep discounts can be found at the TKTS booth, which sells day-of-performance tickets to both Broadway and off-Broadway shows.

- **Don't go early.** Tickets are released from the theaters to the booths throughout the day, so you don't necessarily increase your chances of getting the show you want by going early in the day, or waiting on line before the booth opens. Instead, go when it's most convenient for you.
- **Go to the theater on a Monday or Tuesday night,** the slowest nights of the week. You'll encounter almost no line and will have a much bigger selection than usual (at least on Tuesday; on Monday many shows are dark).
- Download **TKTS's free app,** so you can see what's being offered, and at what price, before you head over. That way you won't waste your time if the show you want to see isn't up for grabs or if it's too pricey.

Warning: Do not buy from the **scalpers** who roam up and down the line at TKTS. A few may be legitimate—say, a couple from the 'burbs whose companions couldn't make it for the evening—but they could be swindlers passing off fakes for big money. It's not a risk worth taking.

Here are a few additional methods of garnering discounts or getting into sold-out shows:

Rush tickets: A number of Broadway and off-Broadway theaters offer "rush tickets" for the first row of seats on the day of a show. The average price is $49 for these neck-benders (it's preferable to be a couple of rows back—the sightlines are better, and there's less danger of being spit on by performers). Sometimes these seats are only available to students, while in other cases any member of the public can get them (look at the show's website for details). These seats are given out on a first-come, first-served basis. ***Tip:*** If you're in the front row and the stage is high, ask for a cushion which will allow you to see better over the lip.

Standing room: Some sold-out shows offer "standing room" tickets on the day of the show only, to about 10 people per show (depending on the size of the theater). They are sold at 10am when the box office opens; for the really popular shows a line will form an hour earlier for these "standing spots" at the back of the house. These non-seats usually cost $45.

Student and youth discounts: Although Broadway theaters won't care how old you are, a number of off-Broadway houses do sell specially priced seats (sometimes for as little as $25) to students and those under 30. While some do this on the day of show only, others allow these theatergoers to purchase in advance with the correct identification. Among the theaters that usually discount in this way are the New York Theater Workshop, Lincoln Center Theater, and the Roundabout Theater Company.

CONSIDER SEEING AN OFF-BROADWAY SHOW

Because of the huge financial pressures on Broadway producers, they usually (but not always) stick with tried-and-true formulas, revivals, or shows with a clear marketing hook. For anything slightly edgy or intellectual, you often need to go to the smaller off-Broadway theaters (see "Theater Basics," p. 332). These theaters also tend to charge less for tickets. Although I can't

CHOOSING THE right show TO SEE

I'll admit it: I'm a walker. If I accidentally pick an awful show, I leave at intermission and grab dinner, rather than sitting through something dull. It doesn't happen that often, because over the years I've formulated the following rules to help me choose which shows to see.

Skip the long-running Broadway musicals: There should be an expiration date on Broadway musicals, just as there is on milk. After about 2 years, they turn sour. Here's why: The first cast usually leaves around the 1-year mark, and then a second cast is announced with much fanfare. When it comes to the third go-round, big-name actors aren't willing to take over the roles, so lesser-known pros get cast in the parts. These second-tier actors aren't any less talented, but because they have no clout, they never get to rehearse with the director and put their own mark on the role. Instead, they are "put in" by a stage manager and are expected to re-create what the previous actor did, which can lead to wooden performances. The chorus, which usually stays with the show for a few years, simply becomes bored and starts sleepwalking through their performances. That's why you'll often see a better show if you go to a newer one. To find out how long a show has been on, call the theater, ask the folks at the TKTS booth, look at telecharge.com (which lists when shows opened), or check *The New Yorker* magazine, which lists "long-running" shows separately in its theater section.

Beware the "un-nominated" Broadway shows: It doesn't matter which shows win a Tony Award—that's pretty much a crapshoot. But the nominating committee, which is made up of savvy theater professionals—actors, writers, producers, and the like—usually does a good job of rewarding the most interesting shows with nominations in late May. If a new play, musical, or revival can't manage to get a nod, take it as a sign that your theater dollars may be better spent elsewhere. Nominated shows trumpet that fact in their ads (but don't punish off-Broadway shows—only Broadway shows are eligible for Tonys). A good source for this information is Telecharge.com, which lists nominations and awards for each show.

Do some research before you buy: The web is a treasure trove of information, including past reviews of shows. Instead of going blindly to the TKTS line (p. 333), surf **nytimes.com** or **nymag.com** before you get to New York and pick a show that's garnered a fair number of good reviews. While the reviewers aren't always right, at least by reading up you'll have a better idea of what the shows are about.

Avoid "jukebox" musicals: *Mamma Mia* set off a frenzy of shows that simply take the catalogue of some famous pop composer and then string songs together with a silly, inorganic story. In most cases you'll hear better renditions of these songs at your local theme park—don't go!

guarantee you'll always see a great show, the following off-Broadway theater companies consistently produce exciting, award-winning works:

- **Atlantic Theater Company,** 336 West 20th St. (atlantictheater.org. ✆ **646/989-7996;** subway: C, E to 23rd St.). The Atlantic is a major incubator for new musicals. It also gets some of the biggest acting talents in the city to appear in its shows. **Biggest hits include:** *Kimberly Akimbo* (Tony Award), *Spring Awakening* (Tony), *The Band's Visit* (Tony).

KIDS TAKE THE STAGE: family-friendly THEATER

Broadway theaters do not allow children under the age of 5 to attend, nor do they give discounts to kids (with the exception of the **Kids' Night on Broadway** discount program—go to kidsnight onbroadway.com; discounts usually offered late Jan/early Feb only). But beyond Broadway there is affordable, often mesmerizing theater aimed squarely at the pre-puberty crowd. The following organizations in particular present consistently challenging and entertaining family shows.

The **New Victory Theater ♥♥♥**, 209 W. 42nd St., between Seventh and Eighth aves. (newvictory.org; ✆ **646/223-3010**), books shows from around the U.S. and abroad that are inventive and smart enough for the entire family to enjoy. One musical that made its debut here even moved to Broadway (now how about that for a kiddie show?). Past offerings have included quality puppet shows, acrobatic and circus troupes, "new vaudeville" acts, and theater pieces.

The **Swedish Cottage Marionette Theatre ♥♥** (cityparksfoundation.org/arts/swedish-cottage-marionette-theatre; ✆ **212/988-9093**) puts on surprisingly artistic marionette shows for kids at its 19th-century Central Park theater throughout the year. Reservations are a must.

Every summer, the marvelous touring theater company **Theaterworks USA ♥♥** (theaterworksusa.com) presents free musicals for kids at the Lucille Lortel Theatre, 121 Christopher St. (near Hudson St.). Written and performed by up-and-coming Broadway talents, they are among the most delightful shows in town for people of all ages.

Look for **Young People's Concerts ♥♥**, in which kids get to interact with orchestra members prior to curtain time, at the **New York Philharmonic** (nyphil.org/education; p. 339). Also check to see what's on for the entire family at **Carnegie Hall** (carnegiehall.org; p. 338), which offers family concerts at prices as low as $10, plus the **Carnegie Kids ♥♥** program, which introduces kids ages 3 to 6 to basic musical concepts through a 45-minute music-and-storytelling performance. And don't forget **Jazz for Young People ♥♥**, Wynton Marsalis's stellar family concert series at **Jazz at Lincoln Center** (jazz.org/education/public-programs/family-concerts; see box p. 348). At holiday time, the **Nutcracker** at the New York City Ballet (p. 341) and the **Radio City Music Hall Christmas Show** (p. 392) are also huge hits with the wee ones.

- **New York Theatre Workshop,** 79 E. 4th St., btw. Second Ave. and the Bowery (nytw.org; ✆ **212/460-5475;** subway: 6 to Astor Place). This is an intellectually heady and sometimes avant-garde company. **Biggest hits include:** *Once* (Tony Award), *Rent* (Pulitzer Prize), *Hadestown* (Tony), *Merrily We Roll Along* (the revival with Daniel Radcliffe; Tony), *What the Constitution Means to Me* (Tony).
- **Playwrights Horizons,** 416 W. 42nd St., btw. Seventh and Eighth aves. (playwrightshorizons.org; ✆ **212/564-1235;** subway: 1, 2, 3, N, R, S to Times Square; A, C, E to 42nd St.). Dedicated to nurturing the art of the writer (lyricists and librettists as well as playwrights), Playwrights has always had a great eye for talent, producing the works of Stephen Sondheim, Christopher Durang, A. R. Gurney, and Wendy Wasserstein. **Biggest**

The New Victory Theater, in the heart of the Theater District, has a full schedule of fun, high-quality productions designed specifically for young audiences.

hits include: *Driving Miss Daisy* (Pulitzer Prize), *Sunday in the Park with George* (Pulitzer Prize), *A Strange Loop* (Pulitzer Prize, Tony Award).

- **The Public Theater,** 425 Lafayette St., off Astor Place (publictheater.org; ✆ **212/564-1235;** subway: 6 to Astor Place). A strong emphasis on American playwrights, especially Asian-, Latin-, and African-American writers, has kept this theater relevant and popular since 1967. In all, Public Theater productions have been awarded 40 Tonys (for shows that moved to Broadway) and 138 off-Broadway or "Obie" awards. **Biggest hits include:** *Hamilton* (Pulitzer Prize, Tony Award), *A Chorus Line* (Pulitzer Prize), *Fun Home* (Tony Award).
- **St. Ann's Warehouse,** 45 Water St., Dumbo, Brooklyn (stannswarehouse.org; ✆ **718/254-8779;** subway: A, C to High St., F to York St. or 2, 3 to Clark St.). A bit different from the others on this list, St. Ann's acts as a second home for some of the most intriguing productions created by non-American

Productions at St. Ann's warehouse often embrace the avant-garde. Here, puppets star in *The Life & Times of Michael K.*

theater companies (like the National Theater of Scotland and London's Donmar Warehouse and Almeida Theater). It also puts on works by American avant garde artists. **Biggest hits include:** Daniel Fish's *Oklahoma* (Tony Award), Mark Rylance in *Measure for Measure.*

- **The Vineyard Theatre,** 108 E. 15th St., off Union Square (vineyardtheatre.org; ✆ **212/353-0303;** subway: 4, 5, 6, N, R to Union Square). Except for St. Ann's, the Vineyard is the biggest risk-taker of the major off-Broadway theaters, presenting out-and-out performance art alongside less far-out plays and musicals. When they're good, they're great; and when their shows miss the mark, they're still usually intellectually intriguing. **Biggest hits include:** *Avenue Q* (Tony Award), *Three Tall Women* (Pulitzer Prize), *How I Learned to Drive* (Pulitzer Prize).

CLASSICAL MUSIC, OPERA & DANCE

New York has grown into one of the world's major opera, music, and dance centers. The season generally runs September through May, but there's usually something going on at any time of year.

Classical Music

Carnegie Hall ♥♥ More than 135 years ago, Tchaikovsky himself presided over the opening performance of Carnegie Hall, just one of a legion of

The magnificent acoustics at Carnegie Hall, on W. 57th Street, enhance everything from symphony orchestras to chamber groups to world music ensembles.

LINCOLN CENTER: A one-stop shop FOR CULTURE

Lincoln Center—a giant complex of theaters on the west side of Manhattan, flanking Columbus Avenue between 62nd and 65th streets—hosts everything from major symphonic premieres to the Big Apple Circus. It's most famous for its presentation of classic works of music, dance, opera, film, and theater, and toward that end houses a number of permanent companies, as well as playing host to the world's leading performing arts organizations.

Resident companies include the **Chamber Music Society of Lincoln Center** (chambermusicsociety.org; ✆ **212/875-5788**), the **Film Society of Lincoln Center** (filmlinc.com; ✆ **212/875-5601**), and **Lincoln Center Theater** (lct.org; ✆ **212/362-7600**), the latter of which houses both a well-respected Broadway theater and an off-Broadway theater. For details on the center's other residents—the **Metropolitan Opera,** the **New York City Ballet,** the **Juilliard School,** the phenomenal **New York Philharmonic,** and the **American Ballet Theatre**—see "Classical Music, Opera & Dance" in this chapter. Most of the companies' seasons run from September or October to April, May, or June. Summer brings outdoor/indoor concerts and events on the plaza.

Tickets for performances at Avery Fisher, Lincoln Center Theater, and Alice Tully halls can be purchased through **CenterCharge** (✆ **212/721-6500**) or online at **lincolncenter.org**. Terrific **guided tours** of Lincoln Center that take you into the bowels of the theaters and sometimes even into rehearsals are also available via that link. Tours start at 1:35pm and 3:30pm on most weekdays and cost $22 ($18 seniors and students). The Metropolitan Opera also has tours during its season; see p. 265 for info on those tours.

great musicians who have graced this famous stage. Today, you may see such stars as Anne-Sophie Mutter, Itzhak Perlman, Cecilia Bartoli, Jon Batiste, the Berliner Philharmoniker, or more—all drawn by the unsurpassed acoustics and the honor of playing this magnificent hall (you can tour it Oct–June in the daytime; info online). Unfortunately, the hall is often rented out by school groups, so it's no longer a guarantee that there will be a great concert going on when you're in town. Ticket prices ricochet up and down, depending on the day of the week, the act, and, of course, the area in which you choose to sit. 154 W. 57th St. at Seventh Ave. carnegiehall.org. ✆ **212/247-7800.** Subway: N, Q, R to 57th St.

New York Philharmonic ♥♥♥ Wunderkind conductor Gustavo Dudamel, formerly of the Los Angeles Philharmonic, began his tenure as conductor during the 2025/2026 season—and classical music fans are ecstatic. The Philharmonic has become known in recent years for programming an eclectic mix of classic symphonies and film scores, and featuring lots of star power: Emanuel Ax and Renee Fleming were on the bill in recent performances. Most concerts are performed in the acoustically excellent David Geffen Hall at Lincoln Center. Philharmonic tickets range about $125 to $302, with $25 rush tickets available to students (with ID at pickup, purchased online up to 10 days in advance). A number of concerts feature pre-show talks and meet-the-artist events, which tend to be intimate and informative. There are also kids' concerts and free concerts in NYC parks over the summer. David Geffen Hall, 10 Lincoln Center Plaza, Broadway at 65th St. nyphil.org. ✆ **212/875-5656.** Subway: 1 to 66th St.

Opera

Metropolitan Opera ♥♥♥ Everything about attending an opera here is grand—from the entrance you'll make, past monumental Chagall murals, to the world-class singers you'll hear (such as Joyce DiDonato or Brian Jagde) to the pomp and glitz of the productions themselves. Though recent productions have received mixed reviews (one mentioned clunky scenery that, when moving, is louder than the singers), you can't miss if you see *La Bohème* or another of the Met's classic productions. And the lovely little secret about this house is that the cheap seats get the best sound. Sit in the pricey orchestra section and you may have trouble making out the words, but buy a "family circle" seat and the voices will float up to you in all their crystalline clarity. The Met makes $35 rush tickets available for all shows, at noon for evening performances (except for Saturday, when you must log on at 2pm) and 4 hours before matinees. The seats can only be obtained online, and an individual can only win two seats every 7 days. Often they sell out in minutes, so set an alarm so you're on time. See the Met website for more. ***Warning:*** Don't show up late unless you want to watch the first act on a video screen in the basement; the Met does not seat latecomers. ***Note:*** The Met's season runs from late September to mid-May. Metropolitan Opera House, Lincoln Center, Broadway and 64th St. metopera.org. ✆ **212/362-6000.** Subway: 1 to 66th St.

Dance

American Ballet Theatre ♥♥ ABT features more of an emphasis on story ballets than the New York City Ballet does—*Coppélia, Swan Lake, Sleeping Beauty*—and tends to produce more bravura stars than NYCB (where the emphasis is on ensemble work). Misty Copeland, the United States' first Black prima ballerina, came up through the ranks of ABT, though she no longer dances with them. ABT's season usually runs from mid-May to mid-July, for 2 weeks in the fall, and over the Christmas holidays. See website for dates. Metropolitan Opera House (in Lincoln Center). abt.org. ✆ **212/477-3030.** Subway: 1 to 66th St.

City Center ♥♥ Alvin Ailey, the American Ballet Theatre, and Paul Taylor perform here, along with other major dance companies. The splendid Moorish-revival space (formerly a temple) is perfect for these larger dance companies. In the basement are the stages of the excellent off-Broadway **Manhattan Theatre Club** (manhattantheatreclub.com). 131 W. 55th St. (btw. Sixth & Seventh aves.). nycitycenter.org. ✆ **212/247-0430** or 212/581-1212. Subway: F, N, Q, R to 57th St.; B, D, E to Seventh Ave.

A scene from *Swan Lake*, performed by dancers from American Ballet Theatre.

Joyce Theater ♥♥ Blockbuster modern dance shows tend to play the Joyce, and it's easy to see why: It's simply one of the best spaces in the city to see dance—there's not a bad seat in the house. In this renovated, Art Deco–era movie theater, the audience sits slightly above the dancers, meaning that you won't be seeing just the feet or just the bodies—you'll get the whole picture. In past years, this is where Pilobolus has played, as well as the Gauthier Dance, Trisha Brown, and Mark Morris Dance Group. 175 Eighth Ave. (at 19th St.). joyce.org. ✆ **212/242-0800** for tickets, or 212/691-9740 for theater. Subway: A, C, E to 14th St.; 1 to 18th St.

New York City Ballet ♥♥♥ NYCB was founded by Lincoln Kirstein and the 20th century's greatest ballet choreographer, George Balanchine. And it is for Balanchine's work that you still attend performances at the New York City Ballet; his choreography is the staple here and remains as diamond-sharp, elegant, and moving as when it was first performed as many as 50 years ago. Balanchine's version of *The Nutcracker* is a holiday classic and one of the most difficult tickets to get each Christmas season. NYCB's regular season runs from late September to mid-October, mid-January to early March, and mid-April to the beginning of June. David H. Koch Theater, 20 Lincoln Center Plaza, Broadway at 64th St. nycballet.com. ✆ **212/870-5570.** Subway: 1 to 66th St.

LANDMARK MULTIUSE VENUES

Apollo Theater ♥♥ It's a thrill just to walk into the legendary but intimate Apollo Theater, past the collage of all the greats who've played here (built in 1914, it looks much bigger on TV). Perhaps most famous for launching the careers of Ella Fitzgerald, Aretha Franklin, and Duke Ellington, today it's mostly used for comedy shows and Amateur Night (each Wednesday), a gladiatorial music battle where the winners may emerge stars and the losers are skewered with the unkindest of boos and shouted insults. In late 2023, the Apollo added two more stages, The Victoria Theater and the Apollo Music Café, so it can now present a wider range of events, from films to up-and-coming artists to visual arts shows. 253 W. 125th St. (btw. Adam Clayton Powell Jr. & Frederick Douglass blvds.). apollotheater.org. ✆ **212/531-5300** or 5301. Subway: B, D to 125th St.

Beacon Theatre ♥♥ They really knew how to build theaters back in the 1920s: Every seat at this Art Deco landmark has a good view, and the acoustics are remarkable. Which may be why this is such a favorite of the touring bands who make this their New York home. While you won't get the mega-names, you will see talented stars either on the way up or down, names such as Tedeschi Trucks Band, Jon Batiste, Rhiannon Giddens, and comedians Mike Birbiglia, and Sarah Silverman. Prices vary widely by show and seat. 2124 Broadway (at 74th St.). beacontheatre.com. ✆ **212/465-6500.** Subway: 1, 2, 3 to 72nd St.

Brooklyn Academy of Music ♥♥♥ Outside of Manhattan, BAM is the finest of the multiuse facilities. Along with the **Park Avenue Armory** (p. 343), it may well be the best place in the United States for challenging, inventive, and acclaimed international productions of music, dance,

NIGHTLIFE FOR skinflints

Down too many $22 cocktails, or pony up for several $200+ shows, and you could blow your vacation budget. Fear not—a few online sources can help you party in this party city for less:

- **TheSkint.com**: A low-tech, but high value website, listing of all the city's free and very cheap nightly events, from book readings to inexpensive comedy shows and concerts, to Native American pow wows, adult puppet shows, cheap yoga classes in breweries, performances by future stars at the renowned Julliard School, and more.
- **Thirsty Gallerina**: An Instagram account that shows which galleries have openings with free wine. The parties are usually between 6 and 8pm.
- **SecretNYC.co**: This website isn't as focused as the other two on cheap thrills, but you can often find them here nonetheless, as it lists unusual cultural events, like affordable candlelight concerts in some of the city's most magnificent churches, free horseback riding lessons in Queens, lesser-known (and inexpensive) outdoor ice-skating rinks, and on and on.

The Sing Harlem Choir performing at the BAM Opera House, a major arts complex in Brooklyn.

performance art, and theater. It's at BAM where you'll see highbrow theater straight from the West End (like Paul Mescal in *A Streetcar Named Desire*), Hannah Gadsby's new comedy show, or an opera by Richard Foreman. Along with the large **BAM Opera House** and the smaller **BAM Harvey Theater,** the organization has a dedicated movie theater (the **BAM Rose Cinema**) for art films, and a cafe space where up-and-coming talent perform. I've never been disappointed by anything I've seen here, though occasionally I've had difficulty getting a seat. ***Note:*** Discounts are sometimes offered to students and seniors, so inquire when purchasing a ticket. 30 Lafayette Ave. (off Flatbush Ave.), Brooklyn. bam.org. ✆ **718/636-4100.** Subway: 2, 3, 4, 5, M, N, Q, R to Pacific St./ Atlantic Ave.

Joe's Pub ♥ It's hard to classify just what Joe's Pub is, beyond a very handsome space in a landmark building that hosts performances and serves strong cocktails and pub food. Its show roster is all over the map—it has hosted spoken-word artists, rising singer/songwriters, jazz bands, pop stars, you name it. Nowadays the performers are more likely to be up-and-coming talent than big names, so it's a bit of a crapshoot what you'll get. 425 Lafayette St. (btw. Astor Place & 4th St.). joespub.org. ✆ **212/539-8778** or 212/967-7555 for advance tickets. Subway: 6 to Astor Place.

Park Avenue Armory ♥♥♥ This colossal former military space, with a 55,000-sq.-ft. drill hall at its core, has made a name for itself in recent years

park it! SHAKESPEARE, MUSIC & OTHER FRESH-AIR FUN

As the weather warms, NYC culture goes outside to play. Here are some top picks:

- **Shakespeare in the Park,** an offering of the Public Theater (p. 337), casts big stars (Lupita Nyongo, Peter Dinklage, Sandra Oh) in elaborate productions at the outdoor Delacorte Theater in Central Park (near 79th St. in the center of the park). Tickets are free, but hard to come by. Either sign up for the daily online lottery (at **publictheater.org**) or get on line in the park. Tickets are distributed at the theater free on a first-come, first-served basis (two per person) at 1pm on the day of the performance. Would-be theatergoers usually line up starting around 9 or 10am; for big hits, people have been known to camp overnight in the park!
- **New York Philharmonic:** Free concerts are held beneath the stars on Central Park's Great Lawn and in parks throughout the five boroughs. For schedules, go to **nyphil.org**.
- **SummerStage,** at several stages around the city, presents music, comedy, and dance. In recent years, they featured Lake Street Dive, Blues Traveler, and Spin Doctors. The season usually runs mid-June through August. For info, visit **cityparksfoundation.org/summerstage**.

for the prestige, scope (often huuuge), and quirkiness of the shows it has produced and/or brought in from all corners of the globe. They've included Anne Imhof's massive multi-disciplinary work *Doom* about creating new forms of hope through activism; an erotic look at Balkan folktales from Marina Abramović; Meredith Monk's latest immersive work; and dozens of musical recitals. Tickets aren't easy to come by, since so many of the performances are bona fide cultural events. 643 Park Ave. (at 66th St.). armoryonpark.org. ✆ **212/616-3930.** Subway: 6 to 68th St.

The Shed ♥♥ The Shed's mission is to explore "the future of art." That means it produces many more offerings than other similar venues (who simply bring shows in), but also results in a leaner schedule than its competitors. When The Shed has a show, it's often the hottest ticket in town, like the recent staging of Stephen Sondheim's last (and incomplete) musical; a recreation of a late 1980s "art amusement park" with works by Basquiat, Haring, Lichtenstein, and Hockney; and a play performed virtually, meaning the audience wore mixed reality glasses to watch Sir Ian McKellen, and others, act. The Shed is also host to major art fairs (p. 192). 545 W. 30th St. theshed.org. ✆ **646/455-3934.** Subway: 7 to 34th St./Hudson Yards.

Symphony Space ♥♥ For many years this has been where the National Public Radio show ***Selected Shorts*** taped. But that's just the beginning of the offerings at this always-busy theater. It also hosts yearly readings of James Joyce's *Ulysses,* dance performances, world music concerts, and a wonderful

The modernistic design of The Shed, at Hudson Yards, ensures maximum flexibility for its daring original programming.

series called **New Voices,** which features new musical works from Broadway composers (and would-be Broadway composers). The theater has two stages, a film theater, and a small cafe for cabaret performances and open-mic nights. 2537 Broadway (at 95th St.). symphonyspace.org. ✆ **212/864-1414.** Subway: 1, 2, 3 to 96th St.

Ticket-Buying Tips

Tickets for events at all larger theaters can be purchased through **Ticketmaster** (ticketmaster.com; ✆ **212/307-7171**). Advance tickets for an increasing number of shows at smaller venues—including Bowery Ballroom, Mercury Lounge, Jazz Standard, and others—can be purchased through **Ticketweb** (ticketweb.com; ✆ **866/468-7619**). Do note, however, that Ticketweb can sell out in advance of actual ticket availability. Just because Ticketweb doesn't have tickets left for an event doesn't mean it's completely sold out, so check with the venue directly or look at **SeatGeek.com.** Another excellent source: the social network ticketing website **Cash or Trade** (cashortrade.org), where tickets are always sold at face value. You can also visit **livenation.com** for tickets to many concerts.

Even a sold-out show doesn't mean you're out of luck. There are usually a number of people hanging around at show time, trying to get rid of extra tickets for friends who didn't show, and they're usually happy to pass them off for face value. You'll encounter pushy professional scalpers, too, who peddle forgeries for exorbitant prices and are best avoided (you'll probably know who the professionals are when you see them). Be aware that all forms of resale on-site are illegal.

ROCK, JAZZ, BLUES & MORE

If you're in town to see one of the mega-concerts, you probably already know to go to **Radio City Music Hall** (radiocity.com), **Barclays Center** (barclays center.com), **Madison Square Garden** (msg.com), **Forest Hills Stadium** (foresthillsstadium.com), or **Jones Beach** (jonesbeach.com). Add to that list these newer large venues: the **Coney Island Amphitheater** (seasidepark coneyisland.com), a 5,000-seat state-of-the-art outdoor (but covered) venue steps off the boardwalk; and **Terminal Five** (terminal5nyc.com) on the far west side of Manhattan. For slightly smaller, but still rewarding, concerts with artists like Grouplove, Lawrence, The Strokes, The Killers, Ripe, Melt, or Vulfpeck, your best strategy is to see what's on the roster at the following well-respected venues:

- **Bowery Ballroom,** 6 Delancey St. at the Bowery (boweryballroom.com; ✆ **212/533-2111;** subway: F to Delancey St., J, M, Z to Bowery)
- **Brooklyn Steel,** 319 Frost St. (Williamsburg, Brooklyn; bowerypresents.com/venues/brooklynsteel; no phone; subway: L to Graham Ave.)
- **Irving Plaza,** 17 Irving Place (1 block west of Third Ave., at 15th St.; irvingplaza.com; ✆ **212/777-1224** or 212/777-6800; subway: L, N, Q, R, 4, 5, 6 to 14th St./Union Square)
- **Music Hall of Williamsburg,** 66 N. Sixth St., between Kent and Wythe aves. (Williamsburg, Brooklyn; musichallofwilliamsburg.com; ✆ **212/260-4700;** subway: L to Bedford Ave)
- **Webster Hall,** 125 E. 11th St. between Third and Fourth aves. (websterhall.com; no phone; subway: 4, 5, 6, N, Q, R, W, L to Union Square)

Local Rock & Country Clubs

Brooklyn, and to a lesser extent Ridgefield in Queens, is where you go to hear the most exciting emerging talents in the world of Rock and Roll. Below are some of our favorite clubs for that. You might also consider downloading the app **Dice** onto your smartphone—it taps into your Spotify account, and then recommends concerts based on the bands and types of music you like, bringing users to both the big-name venues and the smaller clubs (like those below).

Baby's All Right ♥♥ The rare live-music venue with more-than-decent food and a space that doesn't seem too grungy to eat it in, Baby's All Right is the epitome of the Williamsburg scene: maybe a little too cool for school, but overall on-trend and friendly. Plus, the booker has real talent for discovering new talent. 146 Broadway (btw. Driggs Ave. & 6th St.). babysallright.com. ✆ **718/599-5800.** Subway: J, M, Z to Marcy Ave.

Brooklyn Bowl ♥♥ Yes, it's a bowling alley, and now a nationwide chain of venues, but you don't have to hit the pins to have a delightful night out here. A massive Williamsburg space with carny decor and a wide selection of beers, cocktails, and food, this is a great place just to come and hang out. Live DJs

The NYC-based indie-soul band Melt performing at Brooklyn Steel (p. 346).

spin catchy music on the nights that bands aren't playing. 61 Wythe Ave. (btw. N. 11th & N. 12th sts.), Williamsburg, Brooklyn. brooklynbowl.com. ✆ **718/963-3369.** Subway: L to Bedford Ave.; G to Nassau St.

Lucinda's Honkytonk ♥♥ As in Lucinda Williams, Grammy Award-winning singer/songwriter. She's one of the owners here, and regularly gets up and performs, though not always in ways you'd expect—at a recent live band karaoke night she played backing drums for the amateurs who got up to the mic to howl, apparently unaware they were being supported by a legend. There's music of some sort 6 nights a week here, ranging from line dancing to open mic nights for new songwriters, to rousing concerts from local country or bluegrass bands (yes, those exist in NYC). It all happens in a woodsy, fairy light-strung place that looks very much like a genuine Tennessee honkytonk. 169 Avenue A (at 11th St.). lucindasnyc.com. Subway: L to First Ave.

Union Pool ♥♥ Another Williamsburg stalwart, Union Pool's live music room looks like a saloon from the Wild West days, with circus posters on the walls, and a small stage with a square proscenium studded with Edison bulbs. The talent booked here is usually solid, ranging from guitar-strumming singer- songwriters to more experimental music types (on my last visit a harpist was playing with a countertenor, who sawed an electric violin as he crooned). In the front is a large bar with a DJ; to the side, an outdoor area with a taco truck and picnic tables. No pool tables: The name comes from this space's former life as a factory for pool equipment. 484 Union Ave. (at Meeker Ave). union-pool.com. Subway: L to Lorimer.

Jazz, Blues, Latin & World Music

Big-name jazz clubs can be really fun in New York, and likewise expensive. Music charges and bar-tab/drink minimums vary dramatically, depending on who's playing; beware especially of a dinner requirement at some, even for a late show. Reservations are almost always essential at top spots. We also recommend jazz tours for folks who want to hear music at several top venues. See p. 264.

JAZZ AT LINCOLN CENTER: not actually at LINCOLN CENTER

You've heard of food courts? This is the "jazz court," a massive three-theater facility that has been wedged into the uptown corner of the Columbus Circle Mall, which is, as its name suggests, a high-end shopping mall. Its centerpiece is the **Rose Hall,** a concert hall in the round (usually, though it can also be configured as a standard proscenium theater), with remarkable acoustics. Huge boxes of light change color throughout the night—from subtle creams to striking autumn-leaf colors—forming a glowing crown around the performance space. Some seats are actually behind the musicians, giving aficionados a chance to check out the fingering as the musicians perform. This is where Wynton Marsalis, the center's director, struts his stuff in concert with the Lincoln Center jazz orchestra. Programs are primarily focused on swing and New Orleans–style jazz. Though the hall can be intimidating, Marsalis does his best to keep an informal vibe, encouraging the audience to clap along and call out; usually by the end of the evening, they're doing just that.

The **Appel Room,** the center's second-largest space, has a configuration that can be switched to accommodate a dance floor, a seven-tier amphitheater, or cocktail table seating. Whatever the look, it's a splendidly beautiful room with a wall of glass behind the performing space, lending a Central Park backdrop to the music. **Dizzy's Club** is the most traditional of the theaters, a smaller cocktail and dinner jazz club (again with that transcendent view of Columbus Circle and the park), and the only one of the three facilities to operate year-round, serving as a showcase for some of the younger talents in jazz (called the "upstarts").

It's all in the Time Warner Center, at Broadway and 60th St. (jazz.org; ✆ **212/258-9800;** subway: 1, A, E, C to 59th St.).

Bar LunÀtico ♥♥♥ I get a "Frenchman Street in New Orleans" vibe from this railroad track-shaped bar, with its artfully distressed pressed tin ceiling, its collection of oddball knickknacks, and its small stage at the front. But beyond decor, its spirit is shaped by the respectful attention music gets here (nobody is chit chatting) and the quality of the sounds. The owners' have more than 20 years music biz experience and pick ferociously talented folks for the calendar, which swings from Afrobeats and Farro to Samba and Tango to Jazz. It's out of the way, but well worth the trek. 486 Halsey St. (off Lewis Ave.), Bedford-Stuyvesant, Brooklyn. barlunatico.com. ✆ **718/513-0339.** No cover, but audience members are asked to give $10 in cash per person to the performers. Subway: A, C to Utica Ave.

Bill's Place ♥ This tiny club is in the same historic Harlem brownstone where Billie Holiday was discovered (singing in a previous club there at the age of 17). It's a wee place, so reservations are required. Performances are on Friday and Saturday nights only, but by some great old-timers who know how to bend a note. No alcohol. 148 W. 133rd St. (btw. Lenox & Seventh aves.). billsplaceharlem.com. ✆ **212/281-0777.** Admission $36. Subway: 3 to 135th St.

Outings with Big Apple Jazz Tours (p. 264) are a great way for jazz lovers to explore the city's offerings, uptown and downtown.

Birdland ♥♥ Though this is not the original Birdland where Coltrane played, it still presents top acts. In fact, if your idea of jazz is a small battalion of men blowing horns, this is where to come, as the large space (4,000 sq. ft.) is able to accommodate big bands that other venues simply can't fit. My favorite night is Monday, when **Jim Caruso's Cast Party** takes place, and Broadway stars from nearby theaters stop by to sing standards and trade wisecracks. 315 W. 44th St. (btw. Eighth & Ninth aves.). birdlandjazz.com. ✆ **212/581-3080.** Subway: A, C, E to 42nd St.

Blue Note ♥ The Blue Note has the most corporate feel of all the clubs (perhaps because it's now a chain, with clubs in Europe and Asia). Tables are jammed together, the bar area is even more crowded, and the second floor is given over to a huge souvenir stand. But it still attracts some genuine jazz talent, so it can't be overlooked. 131 W. 3rd St. (at Sixth Ave.). bluenote.net. ✆ **212/475-8592.** Subway: A, B, C, D, E, F to 4th St.

The Jazz Gallery ♥♥♥ Where worker bees once toiled, trumpets now sound! This no-frills two-room venue, crafted from converted office space, draws the city's jazz luminaries not only to the stage, but into the audience (this is where musicians themselves come when they want to hear great music). Paying it forward, the venue commissions new works, and has programs pairing novices with pros for performances and seminars. A number of musicians nurtured by the Gallery have gone on to win MacArthur Genius grants and Grammy Awards; prices tend to be lower here than at the city's other jazz venues. 1160 Broadway (at 27th St.), 5th floor. jazzgallery.org. No phone. Subway: N, R to 28th St.

The Jazz Gallery is where jazz musicians themselves come to hear new talent.

Smoke ♥♥ Smoke is an intimate, classy spot to hear jazz. Such mainstays as Mike LeDonne and Eric Alexander—they helped launch the place—still make it their home for regular gigs. 2751 Broadway (btw. 105th & 106th sts.). smokejazz.com. ✆ **212/864-6662.** Subway: 1 to 103rd St.

The Village Vanguard ♥♥♥ Though it turned 90 in 2025, the Village Vanguard is still young at heart, featuring new talent and (often) cutting-edge jazz. It also looks the most like a jazz club *should* look. You enter a red door and descend a steep staircase to a battered, triangular room, cluttered with posters and pictures of all the greats who played and recorded albums here (Mingus, Davis, Monk, Marsalis). ***One warning:*** Sightlines can be problematic, so reserve ahead online to nab a front table. 178 Seventh Ave. S (just below 11th St.). villagevanguard.com. ✆ **212/255-4037.** Subway: 1, 2, 3 to 14th St.

CABARET

Sadly, most of New York's famed cabaret rooms have closed in recent years. For consistently good cabaret nowadays, you have two choices every night of the week (and do also look at the websites for **Joe's Pub** [p. 343] and **Birdland** [p. 349], two venues that often host cabaret singers).

Café Carlyle ♥♥ You come here for the big stars of the cabaret world: Alan Cumming, Sutton Foster, Dianna Agron (of *Glee* fame), and the like. The shows are terrific, the setting elegant, but being in this rarified atmosphere will be pricey: Admission ranges from $90 to $185, plus a drink minimum (the price varies widely by performer; bar seats are at the bottom of the scale). Carlyle Hotel, 35 E. 76th St. (at Madison Ave.). thecarlyle.com. ✆ **212/744-1600.** Closed July–Aug. Subway: 6 to 77th St.

Feinstein's/54 Below ♥♥ This is Broadway's cabaret. What that means is the vast majority of performers are playing hooky from their real jobs at the big Broadway houses nearby. They're often trying out new material, giving the shows a joyously loose feel, but because the talent is so stellar—in recent years Tony winner Norbert Leo Butz, TV's Tony Danza, Laura Benanti, and Lea DeLaria—it never feels like a rehearsal. And the club itself is charming, with a 1930s speakeasy decor, much better food than necessary, and great sightlines. A winner! 254 W. 54th St. (btw. Eighth Ave. & Broadway). 54below.com. ✆ **646/476-3551.** Subway: C, E to 50th St.

STAND-UP COMEDY

Here's a dirty little secret about most comedy clubs in New York City: In order for comics to make a living, they need to play at more than one comedy club an evening. So, you'll often see a very similar show from club to club, one that can feel stale, simply because the performer is doing the set for the third time that night after negotiating two long subway rides. That isn't *modus comicandi* at the clubs below (which is why these clubs were chosen; I think they give more, and fresher, laughs for the buck). ***Note:*** Most clubs charge a cover and a two-drink minimum. Reservations are recommended.

The Bell House ♥♥ Laugh then dance: This Brooklyn multi-room venue is home to both a dance and a comedy club. The latter has been known to host stars of SNL, as well as such recurring group shows as "Drunk Black History," "The Moth Story Slam," "Obitchuary," and more. Generally, this is the place for folks who appreciate smarty-pants humor. 149 7th St., Gowanus, Brooklyn. thebellhouseny.com. No phone. Subway: F, G to Carroll St.

Seth Meyers on stage at Caveat, where the comedy is also thought-provoking.

Caveat ♥♥ Not your typical comedy club, here brains are lubricated along with gullets. Every night different experts are brought in to present serious information—on science, history, political science, and more—in a playful fashion. So that might mean a battle between two teams trying to prove that birds are a better species than bees (or vice versa—the audience decides); a philosopher giving a clip- and laugh-laden talk on the ethical lessons to be gleaned from TV's *The Golden Girls;* or a hilarious interactive drinking game about the history of the Oregon Trail. An "only in NYC" experience. 21A Clinton St. (near Houston). caveat.nyc. ✆ **212/228-2100.** Subway: F to Delancey.

Comedy Cellar ♥ When Jerry Seinfeld, Ray Romano, and other equally famous New York–based comedians decide to "try out" material in front of an audience, they usually drop into this basement room in the Village. In fact, most of Jerry Seinfeld's documentary *Comedians* was filmed here. On nights when these "biggies" don't make an appearance (and their sets are never advertised in advance), newer headliners take the stage. In general, the comedy is "bluer" (read: vulgar) than at Gotham. 117 MacDougal St. (btw. Bleecker & W. 3rd sts.). comedycellar.com. ✆ **212/254-3480.** Subway: A, B, C, D, E, F, M to W. 4th St. (use 3rd St. exit). 2nd location around the corner at 130 W. 3rd St.

Gotham Comedy Club ♥ With more elbow room and a booker who picks the "cleaner" comics, Gotham tends to get an older, more sophisticated crowd than the other clubs. And sometimes the talent can be stellar; the TV show *Last Comic Standing* filmed its "duels" here. 208 W. 23rd St. (btw. Seventh & Eighth aves.). gothamcomedyclub.com. ✆ **212/367-9000.** Subway: F, N, R to 23rd St.

erudite EVENINGS

As home base for the American news media, New York is matched only by London in the number of lectures and readings taking place every evening. The folks in charge of creating buzz for a new book, product, or policy know that by getting it in front of opinion-makers here, they have a better chance of getting it out to the rest of the world. Readings can be some of the most inexpensive and entertaining events in town; many are free, while others charge only a small cover or require audience members to buy a book from the author.

Good daily listings of talks, readings, and more can be found at thoughtgallery.org. There's almost always a major author in town reading at one of the local Barnes & Noble stores (bn.com).

- **The 92nd St. Y ♥♥**, at Lexington Avenue (92y.org; ✆ **212/415-5740;** subway: 4, 5, 6 to 96th St.). The top venue in the city for lectures and "conversations" of all types, the 92nd Street Y (originally called the Young Men's Hebrew Association) has been a fixture of the Jewish community since 1845. And though many programs are devoted to Jewish topics, the vast range of talks in a Monday, Tuesday, and (sometimes) Thursday lecture series are more far-reaching, covering issues of health, politics, gastronomy, ecology, and the arts. Distinguished guests who've spoken here include scientist Neil deGrasse Tyson, author Malcolm Gladwell, columnist Maureen Dowd, and domestic diva Martha Stewart.
- **KGB ♥**, 85 E. 4th St., between Second and Third avenues (kgbbar.com; ✆ **212/505-3360;** subway: F to Second Ave., 6 to Astor Place). This tiny second-floor bar (sadly, not wheelchair-accessible) in an East Village brownstone was once a Ukrainian social club and is decorated with vintage Communist memorabilia. Tickets are less than $20; 7pm for most events. Theme nights are curated by individual writers for poetry, mystery tales, science fiction, and other genres.
- **Lectures on Tap** (lecturesontap.com). These 40-minute lectures—by best-selling authors, professors, and other brainy types—take place in bars around the city and tend to sell out weeks in advance. To see who will be talking when you're in town, go to the website . . . and do it early, or you may not snag a seat.

TV TAPING

Though it may seem odd to take time out of your vacation to do what you do at home—watch TV—it's the behind-the-scenes elements that make the experience here: the scurrying grips and cameramen, the "warm-up act" before the show, and seeing what the host does when the camera isn't on.

Attending tapings is a very popular activity, so it's important that you request tickets *far* in advance. In fact, 6 months ahead of time is not too early. If you can't plan that far ahead, or are rejected for an advance seat, all hope is not lost—standby seats are distributed for most shows. To snag one of these, you'll need to get up early and do a lot of waiting around, but many people on

Miley Cyrus performs on Rockefeller Center Plaza on the Today Show.

the standby list do get in. ***Warning:*** Standby tickets are given out by person, not by couple, so if you're traveling with someone else, both of you have to brave the line to attend the show. As for timing: Many of the late-night shows actually tape in the afternoons, so don't assume that you'll have to stay up past your bedtime to see a taping.

To see the ***Today Show,*** simply get up at dawn and head over to Rockefeller Center. You'll see where the crowds are that day.

Note: The better you dress, the more likely you are to get on camera (if that's important to you). And some shows will turn you away if you're wearing loud patterns or clothing that's too revealing, so read the rules carefully on all the sites below. Children under age 16, or 18 in some cases, are not admitted to tapings.

A company called **1iota** (1iota.com) provides access to most TV tapings in New York City; if you don't see the show you're interested in below, head to the website.

Some shows to try to see (with info on how to do so):

- **Last Week Tonight with John Oliver:** Go to lastweektickets.com (the ticket lottery takes place Tuesday at 3pm, with show tapings on Saturdays).
- **Late Night with Seth Meyers:** Sign up at 1iota.com/show/461/Late-Night-with-Seth-Meyers. A ticket calendar shows possible tapings for 6 weeks. Usually, applicants are notified 4 weeks in advance if they've gotten a ticket, but sometimes last-minute seats are available. Tapings are Monday to Thursday at 2 and 4:30pm; the audience is asked to arrive an hour and 15 minutes earlier.

- **Saturday Night Live:** This is the most difficult show of the bunch to get seats for (1 out of every 10,000 people who applies gets one!). Send an email in August *only* to snltickets@nbcuni.com. The show will then let you know if you've won its lottery and gotten a seat for the date you requested. If you haven't, you may be able to get in by going to NBC's online reservations portal (nbc.com/tickets/pages/tickets-and-nbc-studio-tour) at 10am ET on the Thursday before the show you want to see; request tickets for either the dress rehearsal (8pm Saturday) or the live show (max. 4 tickets per request). If you get a reservation number, you and all members of your party (all attendees must be 16 or older) must check in to pick up the tickets, between 6 and 7pm on the Friday before the show day at the in-person standby line, located at the 49th Street NBC Studios marquee of 30 Rockefeller Plaza.
- **The Drew Barrymore Show:** Go to 1iota.com/show/1217/the-drew-barrymore-show (tapings are generally Tues–Thurs at 11am).
- **The Daily Show:** Go to 1iota.com/show/1248/the-daily-show#t4. Shows are taped Monday to Thursday at 4:30pm.
- **Live with Kelly & Mark** (1iota.com/Show/385/The-View). For early birds! Shows tape at 7:45am and 10am, varying by date.
- **The Tonight Show with Jimmy Fallon:** Go to fallon.1iota.com/show/353/the-tonight-show-starring-jimmy-fallon. Tapings are Mondays through Thursdays at 3:45pm; standby cards are distributed in the NBC Universal Store at Rockefeller Center 10am to 2pm, but people often get there hours in advance, especially if Fallon has a popular guest scheduled.
- **The View:** Sign up at 1iota.com/Show/385/The-View. The show shoots live Monday to Thursday at 9:30am (Thurs a second taping at 12:15pm). The calendar will show you who the guest is.

BARS, COCKTAIL LOUNGES & DANCE CLUBS

Of the many thousands of bars in Gotham, I've chosen three dozen or so either because they'll (likely) be utterly different from those you'd find in your own hometown, or because they're the kinds of places where you can easily meet and mingle with locals. Obviously, this is just a small selection, so if you see a watering hole that intrigues you, head in and belly up to the bar!

Financial District & Chinatown

On warm summer nights, the outdoor party on **Stone Street** (p. 274) can be tons of fun. The pedestrian-only street becomes a sea of tables, serviced by the bars along the street (one's a German beer garden); it's a scene unlike anywhere else in the city. Go beyond Stone Street in this immediate area, and the streets are dead at night, though the hotel bars will be active (the bar at the **Beekman,** p. 48, is particularly buzzy, and beautiful to look at). The same can be said of Chinatown, with the exception of Apotheke (see below).

Apotheke ♥♥♥ This swank speakeasy takes its inspiration from classic apothecaries, so behind the imported Carrera marble bar are antique medicine bottles and test tubes—just for show. But herbs, medicinal and otherwise, are incorporated in many of the innovative cocktails here. I had the good fortune to down the "Siren's Call" on my last visit, which was created from gin, roasted seaweed, squid ink, ginger, lime, and agave—it tasted like something a mermaid would enjoy. I may go back to one of their weekly afternoon cocktail-making classes (see website) to learn how to make it! On many nights, live music and burlesque shows add to the fun. 9 Doyers St. (near Bowery). apothekemixology.com. ✆ **212/406-0400.** Subway: 6, J, Z, N, Q, R to Canal St.; B, D to Grand St.; F to E. Broadway. Also at 9 W. 26th St.

Dead Rabbit ♥♥♥ Just the type of bar you'd hope to find in the historic Financial District, Dead Rabbit is housed in an 1884 building and handsomely cluttered with relics of bygone eras: numerous black-and-white photos on the beams, Gay Nineties knickknacks, even trinkets from the set of the movie *Gangs of New York.* Despite the building's age, the bar itself only opened in 2013, but it's got old-fashioned hospitality down pat, and old-timey tipples to boot—scrumptious punches and 72 "historically accurate cocktails," as well as a craft beer selection. 30 Water St. (near Broad St.). deadrabbitnyc.com. ✆ **646/422-7906.** Subway: 1 to S. Ferry; N, R to Whitehall; 4, 5 to Bowling Green.

Overstory ♥♥ Though it's open year-round, it's best to come to this 64th-floor aerie in warm weather months, when there's service on the glass-fronted, wraparound patio. The appeal here—beyond rare whiskies and agave

Overstory is on the 64th floor, with views from its patio that are as good as you'll get at any of the city's observation decks. Plus, the cocktails are primo.

spirits and well-crafted cocktails—is drinking in the awe-inspiring views. When it's colder you'll imbibe inside a handsome, but windowless, Art Deco space—a pointless exercise when there are less expensive, and just as good, bars nearby (hello Dead Rabbit!). In fine weather though, this nightspot is at the apex of the city's nightlife scene (pun intended). 70 Pine St. (btw. Pearl & William sts.). overstory-nyc.com. No phone. Subway: 2, 3 to Wall St.

Lower East Side

You won't be short of choices when it comes to the LES (Lower East Side) bars, especially in the vicinity of Ludlow, Rivington, Orchard, and Allen streets.

The Back Room ♥♥ One of only two speakeasys that still operate where they did back in the Prohibition era, this one is an adventure to find. First, look for the address, but when you see it, double back to the unmarked stairway that goes into a dark alley. Go down the steps and walk through the spooky alley until you see another staircase leading up to some toy police cars. You're here! Inside they've done a nice job of evoking the original club, with chandeliers, fussy Victorian furnishings, pressed-tin ceilings, and cocktails served in teacups (though it's unclear whether that last touch is historically accurate). Most old-fashioned element? Ye olde metal cash register, complete with push buttons. 102 Norfolk St. (btw. Delancey & Rivington sts.). backroomnyc.com. ✆ **212/228-5098.** Subway: F, M, J, Z to Delancey St.

Bar Goto ♥♥ Named for owner Kenta Goto, this sophisticated drinkery puts a Japanese spin on its decor, cocktails, and snacks. That means liquors mixed with green tea powder, miso, a topping of marshmallow, or shochu and sake, served in a woodsy, square room that wouldn't be out of place in Kyoto. I have to admit, I considered putting this in the restaurant section, because the pub grub here may well be the tastiest in the city, particularly the cabbage pancakes *(okonomiyaki).* 245 Eldridge St. (near E. Houston). bargoto.com. ✆ **212/475-4411.** Subway: F to Second Ave. Also at 474 Bergen St. in Park Slope, Brooklyn.

A statue of an alligator devouring a chicken presides over the back bar at Double Chicken Please.

Double Chicken Please ♥♥ A perpetual favorite on *The World's 50 Best Bars* list (it was #1 in 2023, #7 in 2025, #41 in 2026), Double Chicken is one of the hottest cocktail lounges in Gotham. That means a line snakes down the block to try one of their headline chicken sandwiches (crunchy goodness!) and a mixed drink. Those in the know, however, make advance reservations for the wood-paneled back room, because that's where the conceptually dazzling cocktails are served (the front room has more standard drinks). Each is meant to mimic the taste of a type of food, ranging from "Burnt Pizza" (our fave—a pleasantly vegetal tipple tasting of parmesan and tomato), to one that pays homage to French Toast and comes with a house-made Oreo affixed to the rim of the glass. It's not the friendliest place; servers take your order even if you're sitting at the tasting-table-like bar, because the bartenders are apparently in too much of a cocktail-making trance to speak to folks 2 ft. away. 115 Allen St. (near Delancey St.). doublechickenplease.com. Subway: F, J, M, Z to Delancey/Essex; B, D to Grand St.

SoHo

Ear Inn ♥♥♥ The Ear Inn is set in one of the oldest buildings on the isle of Manhattan: a gable-roofed, two-story Federal town house built in 1817 by African-American Revolutionary War hero James Brown. It got its current name when the "B" on the neon sign outside went on the fritz. Today, this mini-museum of a bar (there's historical ephemera everywhere) is popular with a wide range of New Yorkers, from the city's motorcycle enthusiasts to its gallery owners. You're assured of an interesting conversation if you belly up to the bar. 326 Spring St. (near Greenwich St.). theearinn.com. ✆ **212/226-9020.** Subway: 1 to Canal St.; C, E to Spring St.

Milady's ♥♥ It's seems more than appropriate that three strong ladies—each bartenders and/or partners at some of the city's most celebrated watering holes—banded together to revive Milady's, a beloved locals' bars for nearly 70 years until it abruptly shuttered in 2014. Milady's 2.0, opened in 2024, no longer has a jukebox or a pool table, but it still has the unpretentious, fun air of the original, thanks to a disco ball lazily revolving over the bar, a beat-driven soundtrack, and a menu that includes fancy jello shots and the best artichoke dip in the city. Happy Hour (Mon–Thurs 4–6pm) cuts the cost of oysters down to $12 per half dozen, and highballs to $13. 160 Prince St. (corner of Thompson). miladysnyc.com. ✆ **646/484-6402.** Subway: C, E to Spring St.

The East Village

Book Club Bar ♥♥♥ In the front is a long bar, in the back dozens of bookshelves with titles for sale, but throughout this railroad space you'll find a joyous bookishness. It seems half the folks sitting at the bar are alone, scribbling into their journals between sips; in the back, bibliophiles browse the shelves for their next read, or listen to whomever is at the mic telling stories, reading poems, or discussing literary trends (there's a robust event series here). The "club" is a bookstore all day long, with the bar transitioning from coffee drinks to harder stuff once the sun sets. 197 E. 3rd St. (btw Aves A and B). bookclubbar.com. Subway: F, J, M, Z to Delancey St./Essex St.

BREEZES & booze: THE BEST OUTDOOR BARS

When the weather turns nice, New Yorkers like to take their tippling out-of-doors. Here are some lovely places to imbibe under the night sky:

Bohemian Hall Beer Garden ♥♥♥ Since 1910, this has been the go-to summer party place for Queens residents. Oompah music (and, on some nights, pop) is the soundtrack, 16 craft beers are on tap, and the food is authentically Czech. 29-19 24th Ave., Astoria. bohemianhall.com. ✆ **718/274-4925.** Subway: N, Q to Astoria Blvd.

Broken Shaker ♥♥♥ The rooftop bar of the Freehand Hotel (p. 64) offers a grand variety of outdoor and indoor spaces, including two tiki-decorated bars. All look out onto surrounding buildings (and into nearby apartments—voyeuristic fun). But what makes Broken Shaker stand out are the imaginative cocktails, a mash-up of tropical, Middle Eastern, and NY influences. My fave: "Hebrew Hammer," a scotch-and-rum concoction that swirls in tahini and holds a floating dreidel. 23 Lexington Ave. (at 23rd St.). brokenshaker.com. ✆ **212/475-1920.** Subway: 6 to 23rd St.

Grand Banks ♥♥ When the weather is pleasant, the *Sherman Zwicker*, an historic tall-masted schooner, turns oyster bar and cocktail haven. It's a bit pricey, but you're paying for splendid river breezes and views. Pier 25 at Hudson River Park and North Moore St. crewny.com. Subway: 1 to Franklin St.

Lucky Dog ♥♥ We'd say "lucky owners" because they're allowed to bring their canine companions to this laidback, backyard Brooklyn bar, and partake of one of the 20 beers on tap from Allagash and Ommegang. Didn't bring your pooch on vacation? You may be able to briefly borrow one while the dog "mom" or "dad" takes a turn on the shuffleboard court. 303 Bedford Ave., Williamsburg. Subway: L to Bedford Ave.

Maison Premiere ♥♥ The NOLA-themed drinkery has a nice backyard area, open in the more temperate months (p. 368).

The Frying Pan ♥♥ A permanently docked floating lighthouse turned bar, the Frying Pan is atmospherically grungy, and not a place for people who get seasick (you'll bob up and down as you drink). Luckily, there's also seating on the pier. And the views of the other boats on the river can't be beat, especially at sundown. Burgers and snacks are served, along with drinks. Pier 66, 26th St. off the West Side Highway. fryingpan.com. ✆ **212/989-6363.** May–Sept. Subway: A, E, C to 23rd St.

Stone Street ♥♥ One of the most historic streets in Manhattan (p. 274) turns into an outdoor beer hall when the weather is nice.

Also consider **Overstory** (p. 355) when the weather is nice and its outdoor patio is open.

Death & Company ♥♥♥ Cocktails here are as colorfully named as the bar itself—like the "Scallywag," which mixes five different types of rum (including a 75-year-old one) with two types of bitters, vanilla syrup, and demerara syrup; or the perfectly balanced "Mortal Enemy," blending locally made Dorothy Parker gin with crème de cacao, black currant cordial, absinthe, and lime juice. They're liquid art and can be enjoyed in a civilized fashion, as the bouncer at the door stops letting people in when all the seats are taken. The music is more likely to be tango or Dixieland jazz than pop. 433 E. 6th St. (btw. First Ave. & Ave. A). deathandcompany.com. ✆ **212/388-0882.** Subway: 6 to Astor Place.

Decibel ♥♥ A gritty, underground sake bar, Decibel is a center of social life for many Japanese expats living in NYC. Most of the clientele are Japanese, the soundtrack is Japanese rock, and the bar food is very much like what you'd find in Tokyo (dried squid, anyone?). But all are welcome, and if you feel out of place when you enter this Tokyo transplant, you'll relax once you tuck into any of the 30-odd sakes on offer here each evening. A real experience. 240 E. 9th St. (btw. Second & Third aves.). sakebardecibel.com. ✆ **212/979-2733.** Subway: 6 to Astor Place.

McSorley's Old Ale House ♥ If you're a man's man (which I'm obviously not), you'll like New York's oldest continuously operating pub (est. 1854), which famously kept out women until a 1970 lawsuit, a landmark case that ultimately outlawed discrimination in all public places in the city. With sawdust on the rough wooden floor, yellowing photos, newspaper clips chronicling all of the famous people who got smashed here (Abraham Lincoln was one), and a jumble of relics in every nook and cranny (the handcuffs hanging from the ceiling once belonged to Houdini), it's an evocative place to

McSorley's is often crammed with college students and visitors eager to quaff a pint in the city's oldest pub.

hang out . . . if you visit before 4pm in the afternoon. After that point it gets ugly—kind of like the frat parties I pretended to like in college—with out-of-towners jammed together tighter than on a rush-hour train, shouting over the din. 15 E. 7th St. (btw. Bowery & Second Ave.). mcsorleysoldalehouse.nyc. ✆ **212/473-9318.** Subway: 6 to Astor Place.

PDT ♥♥♥ The name stands for "Please Don't Tell" and is meant to speak to the exclusivity of this bar, which hides in the back of a hot dog stand (you enter through a hidden door in the old-fashioned phone booth—no, really!); and requires a reservation. The owners say it's because they don't want an overcrowded bar, so once the seats and stools are spoken for (the reservations line opens at 3pm), they turn would-be patrons away. It's a lot of rigmarole to get a drink, I admit, but the cocktails here are so unusual and tasty (many created on-site from liquor that's been specially doctored in-house) and the scene so urbane that once you're in, well, it's worth it. And the bar snacks—high-quality hot dogs and tater tots—hit the spot. 113 St. Marks Place (btw. Ave. A & First Ave.). pdtnyc.com. ✆ **212/614-0386.** Subway: L to First Ave.

Superbueno ♥♥♥ The name doesn't lie. Channeling the joyous nightlife of Mexico City, Super Bueno has a rollicking, (often) tuba-heavy dance music soundtrack; cocktails that successfully incorporate such Mexican culinary specialties as mole sauce, *huitlacoche* (a prized fungus), and high-end tequila (most notably in a green mango martini); and a bartending staff who dance with clients and periodically set the globe lights hanging above the bar swinging in time to the music. 13 First Ave (at 1st St.). superbuenonyc.com. ✆ **347/866-7739.** Subway: F to Second Ave.

Greenwich Village

Employees Only ♥♥♥ A crack staff of veteran bartenders run this joint, squeezing their own juices daily and infusing liquors with interesting additions, such as lavender (in the gin) and herbes de Provence (in the vermouth), which are then mixed into some of the most bizarre but delicious drinks in town. 510 Hudson St. (btw. Christopher & W. 10th sts.). employeesonlynyc.com. ✆ **212/242-3021.** Subway: 1 to Christopher St.

Mace ♥♥♥ Spices are the stars of the cocktails here, which sounds like a bad gimmick but leads to some wonderfully ingenious drinks. The delightful Frankincense, for example, comes with a head of smoke infused with that spice, and a vanilla-tinged bourbon. The Oregano is a play on a Bloody Mary, but with rum, tomato water, whey, and a moussaka spice mix. Yum! Siding the drinks are a number of tasty raw bar options, and veggie snacks. There's also a good happy hour, which cuts the cost of both food and drink significantly. 35 W. 8th St. (btw. Fifth & Sixth aves.). macenewyork.com. ✆ **347/866-7739.** Subway: A, E, C, D to W. 4th St.

Spices add an extra zing to the cocktails at Mace.

Chelsea, Flatiron District & Union Square

Flatiron Room ♥♥♥ That dazzling chandelier that softly lights the main seating area? It once hung in the Smithsonian. It's just one of the grand touches at this time capsule of a "dining and drinking parlor" (to use their term) where a jazz or blues band plays nightly on a velvet curtained–stage, while customers explore their way through a nearly 1,000-bottle whiskey library (in off hours they offer spirits tastings and classes). ***One warning:*** They have a dress code, so no sneakers or shorts—that would ruin the swellegant ambiance! 37 W. 26th St., off Broadway. theflatironroom.com. ✆ **212/725-3860.** Subway: R, W to 28th St.

Connoisseurs sample the whiskey library at the Flatiron Room.

Nubeluz ♥♥ This cocktail perch has a living saint behind it: José Andrés, the chef who founded World Central Kitchen, a non-profit that has served over a million meals in crisis zones (Los Angeles after the wildfires, Ukraine, and elsewhere). Knowing you're supporting such a good man may take the sting out of $32 cocktails, as will their balanced flavors, and the fact that you're sipping them in a suave lounge 500 ft. up, while gazing out over the glowing city all around. 25 W. 28th St. (at Broadway, top floor of the Ritz Carlton New York Nomad). nubeluzbyjose.com. Subway: R, W to 28th St.

Old Town Bar ♥ People have been tippling here since 1892 and that includes during Prohibition; if you check under the seats in the high-backed booths, you'll see the hiding spaces for bottles. With its 14-ft.-ceilings, memorabilia-laden walls, and Belle Epoque decor, few places are as quintessentially "olde New York." Sit near the dumbwaiter so you can watch the staff hand-crank the food and dishes up and down like they did a century ago. 45 E. 18th St. (off Broadway). oldtownbarnyc.com. ✆ **212/529-6732.** Subway: 4, 5, 6, L, N, Q, R to Union Square.

Patent Pending ♥♥♥ Hidden behind what is a coffee bar during the day, this was midtown's first truly successful speakeasy (it's now been joined by several others). It feels like a secret and looks like a movie-set ideal of a cool, exclusive Manhattan bar—brick walls, dim Edison-style bulbs hanging over the bar, model-handsome patrons. It's called Patent Pending because it's in the basement of the building where Nikola Tesla did his radio-wave experiments; following that theme, all of the tasty but slightly wacky cocktails have "electric" names—like the "Light Me Up," a play on an Old Fashioned using Szechuan peppercorn powder to give patrons' lips a tingle. 49 W. 27th St. (btw. Broadway & Sixth Ave.). patentpendingnyc.com. ✆ **212/689-4002.** Subway: 1, 2, N, R, W to 28th St.

Porchlight ♥♥ This is where conventioneers re-congregate, after enduring hours at the Javits Center. Happily, the dim, golden-hued lighting is recuperative after the glare of the convention hall, drinks are strong and balanced, and the vibe takes its cues from the American South (it feels like a night out in New Orleans or Charleston). Happy hour means $6 flasks of punch, $5 mugs of beer, and $11 cocktails. 271 Eleventh Ave. (btw. 27th & 28th sts.). porchlightbar.com. ✆ **212/681-2188.** Subway: 7 to 34th St./Hudson Yards.

Seed Library ♥♥ A London import from experimental mixologist Ryan Chetiyawardana (aka Mr. Lyan), cocktail nerds will appreciate the wizardry behind the bar's Coriander Gimlet (which gets its acidity not from lime but from coriander seeds), and its Beeswax Old Fashioned which gets its luscious mouthfeel from, yes, beeswax. This basement drinkery has a groovy, 1970's feel, thanks to low tables lit by mushroom shaped lamps. But we recommend sitting at the bar to chat with the gregarious bartenders. 51 E. 30th St. (off Park Ave S.). seedlibrarynyc.com. Subway: 6 to 33rd St.

Times Square & Midtown West

Aldo Sohm Wine Bar ♥♥ Don't gasp aloud, as I did, when you see the $90 glass of wine on the menu (welcome to Manhattan, kiddies!). Scan down and you'll see that there are also $16 glasses on offer, and the staff are too genteel here to look down their decanters at you if you go for the cheaper option. Whatever you drink, you'll feel like Midas, quaffing away in a room that's literally glittering—from the 20-ft.-high ceilings hang dozens of twinkling lights, and, around them, fine works of contemporary art. Grab a spot on a plush couch and pretend you're one of the "masters of the universe" who sip wine here regularly. 151 W. 51st St. (btw. Sixth & Seventh aves.; entrance on uptown side of plaza). aldosohmwinebar.com. ✆ **212/554-1133.** Subway: 1, 2, 3, N, R, Q, S to Times Square.

Dear Irving on Hudson & Dear Irving on Broadway ♥♥ What Overstory (p. 355) is to the Financial District, Dear Irving is to the Theater District: a view-rich aerie with accomplished mixology. At the Hudson location, you'll have very high views of midtown; the Broadway venue is a bit lower, but surrounded by lit up signs, which is fun. Neither have quite the personality of their downtown sibling at 155 Irving Place (curtained in glass beads, it looks like the type of joint Austin Powers would patronize) but the vistas make up for that deficit. ***Tip:*** You'll want to get advance reservations because they won't let you in if there's not a seat available—this is quite an adult drinkery, an appropriate spot for a romantic glass at the end of a celebratory night. 310 W. 40th St (in the Aliz Hotel, btw. Eighth & Ninth aves.) and 1717 Broadway (at 53rd St.). dearirving.com. No phone. Subway: 1, 2, 3, N, Q, R, W, S to 42nd St.

Don't Tell Mama ♥ As long as you don't mistake this place for a restaurant (the food is overpriced and underwhelming), you'll have a swell time at this long-established theater district piano bar. Everyone here sings—the pianist, the bartenders, the waiters, the bus boys—and since most are aspiring

Dear Irving on Hudson sets a tone for sophisticated imbibery.

Broadway performers, the talent level is high. Little time is given to customers who want to warble a tune, however (a disappointment for some guests, a relief to others). Off the main room are two cabaret rooms for nightly performances; they vary greatly in quality (unless you know the artists, we'd recommend sticking with the piano bar). 343 W. 46th St. (btw. Eighth & Ninth aves.). donttellmamanyc.com. ✆ **212/757-0788.** Subway: A, C, E, 1, 2, 3, N, Q, R to 42nd St.

Nothing Really Matters ♥♥ For those New Yorkers whose subway commute is driving them to drink, this underground bar serves hard liquor just beyond the turnstiles in the subway station at 50th Street and Broadway. It's a startlingly chic cocktail den, especially since you enter down a set of detritus-strewn stairs next to a Walgreens, following signs to the barbershop that once was here. As with the train, crowds tend to tumble into this place in waves, especially right before and after shows at the nearby Broadway theaters. Entrance downstairs on 50th St. just west of Broadway. nothingreallymatters.party. No phone. Subway: 1 to 50th St.

Pebble Bar ♥♥ In the 1920s when John D. Rockefeller was on his land-buying spree to build Rockefeller Center, he had one holdout: the saloonkeeper who owned this modest four-story town house. Eventually the massive complex went up all around this little building, which Rockefeller called "the pebble in his shoe." Today it's named Pebble Bar, and it's a very pleasant spot, with tasty cocktails and a crowd that mixes tourists and business folks. If you want a guaranteed seat, you'll need to make reservations for a table on the top floor. Otherwise, you can compete for a bar stool in the second-floor room and watch the crowds on Sixth Avenue coursing below the window. 67 W. 49th St. (off Sixth Ave.). pebblebarnyc.com. ✆ **646/669-7847.** Subway: R, W to 49th St.

The Rum House ♥♥ You don't expect to find a place that's both this hip and this unpretentious right in the heart of Times Square, but here it is. Set in the Edison Hotel, this classic old-time watering hole serves up a mean cocktail and decent bar food. On some nights, a live pianist adds to the ambience, softly playing hits from the days of Gershwin and Irving Berlin. 228 W. 47th St. (btw. Broadway & Eighth Ave.). therumhousenyc.com. ✆ **646/490-6924.** Subway: A, C, E to 42nd St.; N, Q, R to 49th St.

Midtown East

The Campbell Bar ♥♥♥ Hidden on the balcony level of Grand Central Terminal, the Campbell was once the private office of railroad magnate John Williams Campbell, a man who clearly had no self-esteem problems. The room is as grand as any created by Italy's Medici family, with a soaring coffered ceiling, leaded windows, an elaborate fireplace, and a Florentine elegance in the fixtures. The only aesthetic dissonance is the modern pop music the new owners have decided to pump in (when this bar was known as the Campbell Apartment, the soundtrack was jazz, which seemed more apropos). Make sure you go to the "bar"—there are now three Campbell drinkeries in

The Campbell Bar provides a palatial setting for imbibing in a private corner of Grand Central Terminal.

the terminal, but this is the most evocative. In Grand Central Terminal (enter at Vanderbilt Ave. and 42nd St.). gerberbars.com. ✆ **212/297-1781.** Subway: 4, 5, 6, 7, S to Grand Central.

The Flatiron Room—Murray Hill ♥♥ Like its sibling further downtown (p. 361), this venue resembles a glamorous supper club from the 1950s, with tufted leather booths, a crackling fireplace, and an Art Deco stage. A robust calendar of live jazz accompanies the drinking with no music fee, and the cellar bursts with rare whiskies and bourbons. You won't find any other drinkery this sophisticated in the shadow of the Empire State Building. 9 E. 37th St. (off Fifth Ave.). theflatironroom.com. ✆ **212/725-3866.** Subway: N, Q, R, B, D to 34th St.

Ophelia Lounge ♥♥♥ New York City rediscovered its verticality in recent years, with a slew of new bars and restaurants opened atop some of the city's most venerable skyscrapers. Set in a neo-Gothic tower built in 1928,

Sweeping city views from the terrace at Ophelia.

Ophelia Lounge is a high-ceilinged beaut, with ravishing cityscape views and, for decor, framed souvenirs from the time the building was a hotel for young women. The bartenders are jovial and very talented (try the Ophelia Ascending, a libation made with Jamaican pepper–rinsed mescal that comes out steaming, thanks to a dose of cedar smoke). ***A small warning:*** A DJ on Fridays and Saturdays keeps the place pretty loud, especially in the main bar room. To escape the sternum-shaking bass lines, reserve a table in one of the side rooms (they have the best views, too). 3 Mitchell Place (49th St. and First Ave.). opheliany.com. ✆ **212/980-4796.** Subway: E to Lexington Ave./53rd St.; 6 to 51st St.

Upper West Side

Dublin House ♥ NYC doesn't have many of this kind of old-fashioned, plain-as-porridge Irish pubs anymore. Started as an illegal speakeasy in 1921 (have the same bartenders been here all that time? It seems possible), this is a welcoming neighborhood bar where shots of whiskey are about as complicated as the mixology gets. And that's just fine. 229 W. 79th St. (near Broadway). dublinhousenyc.com. ✆ **212/874-9528.** Subway: 1 to 79th St.

Scarlet Lounge ♥♥ Michael Imperioli became famous for his role on *The Sopranos*, but bars are in his blood: he's the grandson of a bootlegger, and in the 1980s he and his wife Victoria ran a saloon in Chelsea. Their current venture is this Art Deco-esque bar, draped in red velvet (hence the name), with live music many nights of the week. The best drink on the menu? That would be the "White Lotus," a champagne punch named for one of the many TV shows Imperioli has starred in. 468 Amsterdam Ave. (at 83rd St.). scarletloungenyc.com. Subway: 1 to 79th St.

Live music and laid-back vibes at Scarlet Lounge.

Upper East Side

In addition to the drinkeries listed below, I *highly* recommend an evening visit in the warm weather months to the **Metropolitan Museum.** Beyond encountering fewer crowds in front of the art, you'll get to sip wine and cocktails on the roof, with Central Park at your feet. New York at its swellest.

Bemelmans Bar ♥♥♥ Put on the ritz at this iconic bar, decorated with murals by Ludwig Bemelman, the illustrator behind the famous *Madeline* children's books. How plush is it? The ceiling is covered by 24-karat gold leaf, and the bar is made of a rare black granite. Live jazz plays as you tipple, to account for a $10 to $35 cover charge on top of the already pricey drinks here (prices vary by where you sit, and who is playing). In the Carlyle Hotel, 35 E. 76th St. (on Madison Ave.). rosewoodhotels.com. ✆ **212/744-1600.** Subway: 6 to 77th St.

Keys and Heels ♥ The Upper East Side's version of a speakeasy is set behind a faux locksmith and shoe repair shop—it's a cute conceit. Inside it's a bit of a frat party with the DJ going full retro (lots of Madonna and Michael Jackson), and the drinks served, sadly, at room temperature. Still, the atmosphere is friendly, the disco ball makes it feel festive, and I'm sure at least one bar-goer will someday regale grandchildren with tales of meeting the love of their life in this hidden place. 1488 Second Ave. (btw. 77th & 78th sts.). keysandheels nyc.com. ✆ **917/557-0217.** Subway: 6 to 77th St.

Melody's Piano Bar ♥♥ A clubhouse for the 1%, Melody's has no dress code, but many of its well-heeled patrons show up in suits and heels nonetheless. You can feel the sizzle of million-dollar-deals being brokered as the jazz trio softly plays and expensive cocktails are ferried from the bar to the well-spaced tables. Palm-frond-adorned wallpaper and seashell-shaped sconces gives Melody's a Miami vibe. ***Warning:*** There are cover charges after 7pm ($10 Sun–Tues, $15 Wed–Sat). 1020 Lexington Ave. (btw. 72nd & 73rd sts.). melodys pianobar.com. ✆ **646/559-2808.** Subway: 6 to 77th St.

Harlem

The Honey Well ♥♥♥ The rec room in your parent's, or grandparent's, basement is playfully evoked at this sepia-toned bar, where the soundtrack is '70's funk, bar snacks are homey (like spinach dip with Ritz crackers and Chex mix), and a large poster of Tom Selleck leers down in the bathroom. My guess is few family members have the mad skills of the bartenders here, who whip up fab versions of classic cocktails, plus intriguing house drinks, all from artisanal liquors and fresh-squeezed juices. Before heading over, consider getting a reservation online: Standing is not allowed, so you'll have to wait to enter if there's no open seat at the bar or a table. Happy hour is daily until 8pm, with $11 cocktails, and $2 off dips and skewers. 3604 Broadway (btw. 148th & 149th sts.). thehoneywellnyc.com. No phone. Subway: 1 to 145th St.

Classic cocktails get a modern upgrade at The Honey Well.

Shrine ♥♥♥ Scruffy enough to feel real, but with high ceilings that keep divey-ness at bay, Shrine is just the type of place you'd hope to find in Harlem. There's live music most nights, the decor is funky (a mix of old LP covers on ceilings and walls, African statues in every nook), and people of all ages and backgrounds come here to chill. 2271 Adam Clayton Powell Jr. Blvd. (btw. 133rd & 134th sts.). shrinenyc.com. ✆ **212/690-7807.** Subway: 2, 3 to 135th St.

Brooklyn

It would take an entire book to list all of the spectacular Brooklyn haunts, but here's a small, subway-friendly sampling of the can't-miss variety.

The Golden Ratio ♥♥♥ Finally—a bar for both drinkers, and those who prefer life alcohol free! At this new watering hole, named for the ratios that go into a perfectly balanced cocktail, every drink on the menu has both a

party train: RIDE THE L FOR NIGHTLIFE

The neighborhoods of Williamsburg and Bushwick have more fun saloons per capita than any other part of the city. The L train knits these two areas together, and if you're on the train after 9pm most nights of the week, you'll see 20- and 30-somethings in their sexiest outfits, heading out to the following bars:

- **Bar Blondeau,** top floor of the Wythe Hotel, 80 Wythe Ave., Williamsburg (barblondeau.com; subway: L to Bedford Ave.). Stunning Manhattan skyline views recommend this fancy wine bar, along with its top-notch food.
- **Boobie Trap,** 308 Bleecker St., Bushwick (boobietrapbrooklyn.com; subway: L to Wyckoff Ave.). Dive-bar pricing with kitschy and, yes, breast-centric decor. All in good fun, though.
- **Brewer's Collective,** 381 Troutman St., Bushwick (kcbcbeer.com; subway: L to DeKalb Ave.). The taproom of this brewery is a, ahem, hopping place. Artisanal brews made here are found around the city, but the most esoteric ones are only served here. Go early; they close most nights by 11pm.
- **Carousel,** 36 Wyckoff Ave., Bushwick (subway: L to Jefferson St.) A multi-room ode to the 1970's, this may be the city's most egalitarian bar, where people of all backgrounds and ages are welcomed to shoot pool, hang out in the sunken living room, or dance under the disco ball. A really friendly scene.
- **Honey's,** 93 Scott Ave., Bushwick (honeysbrooklyn.com; subway: L to DeKalb Ave.). A specialist in fermented honey drinks, aka mead, produced on-site using foraged herbs, locally sourced fruits, and wild yeast.
- **Maison Premiere,** 298 Bedford Ave., Williamsburg (subway: L to Bedford Ave.). Channeling the spirit of New Orleans—Garden District, *not* Bourbon Street—this oyster/cocktail bar in Williamsburg is a wonderfully atmospheric place to while away an evening.
- **Radegast Hall and Bier Garden,** 113 N. 3rd St., Williamsburg (radegasthall.com; subway: L to Bedford Ave.). A surprisingly authentic Bavarian beer garden, complete with sausages, steins, and lots of bellow-singing to pop hits.
- **Skinny Dennis,** 152 Metropolitan Ave., Williamsburg (skinnydennisbar.com; subway: L to Bedford Ave.). Brooklyn's version of a honky-tonk, it has 18 beers on tap, a famed frozen boozy coffee, and live music many nights.

spirited and non-spirited counterpart. That's on top of a really fun "local drinking" concept which means that all alcoholic and non-alcoholic distillates and spirits are created in house, or very nearby. So you'll be tippling concoctions you can't replicate anywhere else in the United States (though you're going to really wish you could, as the drinks are delish). The food menu is tops, too, as is the chill but festive atmosphere. A great new addition to NYC's nightlife scene. 216 Greene Ave. at Grand Ave., Clinton Hill. goldenrationyc.com. Subway: G to Classon Ave.

Royal Palm Shuffleboard Club ♥♥ The kitsch quotient is high at this island-themed club at which, yes, shuffleboard is actually played. You'll pay $60 for your crew to rent a court for an hour; drinks from the bar—tropical cocktails, beer, or wine—are extra. Like bowling, shuffleboard lends itself quite nicely to an evening out on the town. 514 Union St., Gowanus. royalpalmsbrooklyn.com. ✆ **347/223-4410.** Subway: D, N, R, W to Union St.

Tatiana ♥♥ Acrobats! Showgirls! Crooners! Tatiana is a Las Vegas–meets–Vladivostok experience, a Russian supper club on the Brighton Beach boardwalk where vodka flows freely, the meal is an endless feast (of Russian and Continental foods), and expat Russians of all ages boogie until dawn. It's not cheap, but going here may well be your most memorable, if weird, night in Gotham. 3152 Brighton 6th St. (at the boardwalk), Brighton Beach. tatianarestaurantnyc.com. ✆ **718/891-5151.** Subway: B, Q to Brighton Beach.

Queens

See also our review for Bohemian Hall and Beer Gardens (p. 358).

Dutch Kills & Debbie's ♥♥♥ Venturing beyond the Manhattan and Brooklyn nightlife scene gets you two rewards: lower booze prices and far more room to spread out. That's the case at Dutch Kills out in Queens, where the masterful bartending is better than you'll find at most of the city's boîtes (just tell a staffer what flavors you like, and they'll create the perfect cocktail for you on the spot); there's loads of space at the bar, plus comfy British-style wooden snugs (booths), easily big enough for a party of six. Upstairs, the live music club Debbie's serves the same suave cocktails and hosts up-and-coming acts. 27-24 Jackson Ave. (at Dutch Kills St.), Long Island City. dutchkillsbar.com. Subway: E, M, R to Queens Plaza or N, Q, 7 to Queensboro Plaza.

Come out to Queens for a cocktail at Dutch Kills or catch a show at Debbie's upstairs.

Dance Clubs

No New York trends fluctuate quite as much as the club scene. We've listed some popular clubs here, but finding and going to the latest hot spot is not worth agonizing over. There are so many choices and no one club is the empirical best. Beyond the suggestions below, I suggest surfing to **timeout.com/newyork**, which lists the top club parties for the month. Many clubs offer guest-list sign-up services directly on their websites, and they are a smart buy, as the wait to get into a popular club can be hours. The **Dice** app (p. 346) is another good resource for learning about hot dance clubs. ***Note:*** New York nightlife starts late. With the exception of places that have scheduled performances, dance floors stay almost empty until midnight.

MANHATTAN

The Box ♥ New York nightlife at its raunchiest, the Box is a Belle Epoque–styled bar/theater, with a stage show that pushes many boundaries (I once saw a show here that involved urination). Guests arrive around midnight for drinking, dancing, and mingling; the burlesque show starts at 1am, always featuring topless dancers and usually some kind of oddball magician, acrobat, comedian, or contortionist. It can be a lot of fun, though it's definitely not for everyone. 189 Chrystie St. (btw. Stanton & Rivington sts.). theboxnyc.com. ✆ **212/982-9301.** Subway: F to Second Ave.

Nebula ♥♥ This dance behemoth, built at a cost of $12 million, brings in some of the world's most famous DJs each weekend to pump the bass in a high-ceilinged 10,000-sq.-ft. space spread over three levels. The main dance floor (5,000 sq. ft.) features six LED projection screens that descend just above the dancers, and visually mimic the music. 135 W. 41st St. (btw. Broadway & Sixth Ave.). nebulanewyork.com. No phone. Subway: 1, 2, 3, S to Times Square.

BROOKLYN

All Night Skate ♥♥ First things first: There's no skating here (for that, see Xanadu below). But there is a ton of nostalgia for the era when folks did go "skate dancing" at this diner-themed club, complete with a black-light mural, disco ball, and juke box (though most end up dancing to the tunes the DJ spins). If you get peckish from shaking your groove thing, they serve pretty good food here, too. Excellent drag shows on some nights (check the website). 54 Rockaway Ave. (at Marion St.), Bedford-Stuyvesant. allnightskate.com. ✆ **347/240-6263.** Subway: A, C to Rockaway Ave.; J, Z to Chauncey St.

Bembe ♥♥ A whole lot of shaking is going on under the Williamsburg Bridge at Bembe, though the style varies nightly from Arabic dance music to salsa to Afrobeats, merengue, soca, kompa, reggaeton, and more. Mostly it's DJs setting these international beats, but sometimes live musicians fuel the dancing. Check the website before heading over to see what type of scene you'll be stepping into. ***Note:*** The bar is cash only. 81 S. 6th St. (at Berry St.), Williamsburg. bembe.us. No phone. Subway: L to Bedford Ave.

GETTING beyond THE VELVET ROPE

Nothing will transport you back to the worst day of high school quicker than facing the gatekeeper at the door of a New York dance club. It's a humbling, depressing experience (especially if you don't get in), but there are ways to increase your odds of spending more time in the club than on the sidewalk.

1. **Go online for a reservation.** Most clubs offer priority entry, especially for folks who show up well before the action starts (say 10:30pm) or after the peak has passed (1:30am or so). It's a good way to avoid the "choosing" process at the door. At dance clubs with restaurants attached, those who dine get automatic entry, later in the evening. You can also reserve a table at a club in advance, but be careful: You'll be required to take "bottle service," which means you buy a bottle of liquor for you and your companions that can easily cost upward of $500, plus a 20% tip on that amount.
2. **Choose your companions carefully.** Large groups of men have little chance of getting into a club together. If you're traveling in a pack of guys, split up until you get inside. Women have a better chance of getting in, as do couples.
3. **Dress the part.** Look at the celebrity magazines and see what they're wearing when they sashay past the ropes. Usually it's an upscale casual look, but that will change season to season. Avoid suits at all costs, the same for "business casual," and if you plan to wear sneakers, make sure they're designer kicks.
4. **Make nice.** The "chooser" at the door has been entrusted by the owner to create a cool "mix" of people inside the club, so though you may not get in right away, you could be picked in 15 minutes, especially at a larger club, when they need more redheads, or tall women, or perhaps when the moon goes into Jupiter (I don't think even the gatekeepers have a clear idea of what they're looking for). You'll blow your chances, however, if you give the all-powerful guy at the door any argument or attitude.
5. **Never admit to being a tourist.** Clubs are where the worst New York snobbery comes to the fore. It's sad but true: They really don't want tourists. That doesn't mean you shouldn't go; just don't try to get in by telling them it's your "last night before you go back to Alabama."
6. **Say you're there to meet the DJ.** This is my sneakiest tip, but it actually works. Go to the club's website in advance, find out who the DJ will be that night, and say you're meeting them inside.

House of Yes ♥♥ Originally an artistic commune that threw house parties, this wildly creative, often psychedelic "temple of expression" (their apt term) is now devoted almost exclusively to events. Nights here are fueled by DJs, dancing, and performances (circus skills, burlesque, drag, and dance), and most parties have a theme, which they try to make all-encompassing by rewarding those who show up in the most appropriate costumes with free drink tickets. You can upgrade your look at the "Beauty Bar" in a room adjacent to the dance floor where a makeup artist patiently applies glitter, temporary tattoos, and more, for an extra fee. It all feels like an East Coast version of Burning Man. ***Note:*** Those who purchase tickets well in advance usually get in at the lowest price (you'll pay the most if you simply pay at the door). 2 Wyckoff Ave. (at Jefferson St.), Bushwick. houseofyes.org. No phone. Subway: L to Jefferson St.

Xanadu Roller Arts ♥♥♥ Roller disco is back, baby! This Retro-80's style club features a 5,000-sq.-ft. perfectly smooth Canadian Maple floor, sandwiched between a stage and a diner-like bar area (solid food and drinks of all sorts). Skaters of all skill levels boogie well into the night at themed parties (the music can change drastically from night to night, with occasional live bands) and at weekend afternoon skate parties that are open to kids. ***Tip:*** Look for a skate emblem on the calendar next to the event you're hoping to attend—a few events each month don't involve skating. Skate rental is available, but not included in admission. 262 Starr St. (near Wyckoff Ave.), Bushwick. xanadu.nyc. Subway: L to Jefferson St.

Rent skates to join in the roller disco revival at Xanadu Roller Arts.

QUEENS

Basement ♥♥♥ Set in, yes, the subterranean space below a century-old glass-and-steel-frame-door factory, Basement is massive—50,000 sq. ft.—and can host different types of dance parties on the same night. One section is always devoted to Techno, and the club gets some of the biggest DJs in the biz; what's going on in the second room (Studio) will vary, giving a night at this club more texture. Taking photos or videos here is strictly forbidden, and that rule is enforced, meaning this is one of the few nightlife venues where people actually unplug. ***Warning:*** For themed parties, even those with tickets are turned away if they're not wearing an appropriate outfit, so check the website when packing for your trip. 52-19 Flushing Ave. (at 54th St.), Ridgewood. basementny.net. No phone. Subway: L to Jefferson, then a looong walk (consider taking an Uber or taxi from the station).

Nowadays ♥♥ Should be called: "nights and days." This dance club complex often sponsors parties that start on Saturday night, and don't finish until 10pm on Sunday. But the club's backyard has hammocks for disco naps, and booths selling enough food dancers can make a weekend of it. Top techno, electro, Afro-house, club, and soul DJ's from around the world spin tunes here. 50-06 Cooper Ave., Ridgewood. nowadays.nyc. No phone. Subway: L to Halsey St.

THE LGBTQ+ SCENE

Though the stats are shaky, most experts estimate that New York City is home to the largest LGBTQ+ population in North America, if not the world. All in all, there are about 70 major bars and nightclubs to suit every taste, wardrobe, identity, and fetish, but the party only starts there. I'd recommend that you check out such publications as **GetOutMag.com,** the lesbian-centric ***GO*** (gomag.com), and the more mainstream ***Time Out New York*** magazine (timeout.com/newyork) for listings of these clubs as well as the innumerable dance parties, go-go and drag shows, karaoke, underwear nights, gay knitting circles (yes, really), and other happenings. There are more events than ever before at clubs and bars, a way for these venues to prove their relevance to gay life in the age of dating apps. Of course, many New York bars, clubs, and cabarets are mixed with both gay and straight clientele (especially in 'hoods like the Village, Chelsea, and Hell's Kitchen).

Boxers ♥ Yes, that's the outfit the bartender was wearing the night I visited, but the name of the joint also refers to the fact that this is a sports bar, with massive TVs lining the walls along with huge photos of ripped men engaged in all sorts of games. 37 W. 20th St. (btw. Fifth & Sixth aves.). boxersnyc.com. ✆ **212/942-1518.** Subway: C, E to 50th St. Also at 735 Ninth Ave.

Club Cumming ♥ Named for owner actor Alan Cumming—really!—the club first started in his dressing room during a Broadway revival of the musical *Cabaret.* Cumming would give his Tony Award–winning performance and

sing out louise **(OR LOU)**

The "Church of Show Tunes" is in joyous session 7 nights a week at **Marie's Crisis,** a basement piano bar that has a pedigree and an atmosphere like no other. In a low-ceilinged room, covered with Christmas lights, dozens of men (and some women) gather each evening to belt out Sondheim, Porter, Loesser, and Rodgers and Hammerstein. A few times an evening the roving bartenders will take a solo, but for the most part the crowd sings in a booming chorus, usually while grinning ear to ear. The drinks are cheap, the crowd friendly, and the voices darn good.

Marie's Crisis has been in business a good 40 years now, but the history of the building goes back to the 1800s (legend has it the ceiling beams were taken from old ships). Thomas Paine, author of *Common Sense* and *The American Crisis,* lived and died in this house, which explains the "crisis" part of the name. And after serving as a brothel from the 1850s to the late 1880s, it became a "boy bar" in the 1890s called "Marie's." The mural behind the piano was created by the Works Progress Administration, under President Franklin Delano Roosevelt (lord knows why it's here!); it portrays both the French and the American revolutions. 59 Grove St. (at Seventh Ave.). mariescrisiscafe.com. ✆ **212/243-9323.** Subway: 1 to Christopher St.

then host guests at the theater for salons and dance parties until the wee hours. Following that model, early in the evening this East Village club has sketching nights with nude models, drag king bingo, burlesque evenings, and more, usually followed by a raucous dance party to, sadly, not great pop music. Still, it's a fun place, with a *Cabaret*-inspired Weimar Germany decor. 505 E. 6th St. (off Ave. A). clubcummingnyc.com. ✆ **917/265-8006.** Subway: 6 to Astor Place.

Cubby Hole ♥♥ Early in the evening, the Cubby Hole gets a mixed neighborhood crowd of men and even straight women, but by 11pm it's strictly "lipstick lesbians" and club girls rocking out to the jukebox. It's a fun scene and the decor is hilarious, with hundreds of paper animals and fish, Chinese lanterns, and plastic flying pigs dangling from the ceiling. 281 W. 12th St. (at W. 4th St.). cubbyholebar.com. ✆ **212/243-9041.** Subway: A, C, E, L to 14th St.

The Eagle ♥♥ For "bears," "cubs," and the boys who love them, this dungeon-like club is the epicenter of the leather scene in New York. Forgot your chaps? Not a problem—the Eagle has a tiny "leather goods" store in the elevator for all your codpiece and whipping needs. 554 W. 28th St. (btw. Tenth & Eleventh aves.). eagle-ny.com. ✆ **646/473-1866.** Subway: C, E to 28th St.

Flaming Saddles Saloon ♥♥♥ Yeehaw! Welcome to "Coyote Ugly" for gay men (and the many women who show up to watch hot, shirtless bartenders hoof it on top of the bar every 40 minutes or so). The soundtrack is country-western and the mood exuberant. 739 Ninth Ave. (btw. 52nd & 53rd sts.). flamingsaddles.com. ✆ **212/713-0481.** Subway: B, D, E to 7th Ave.

Henrietta Hudson ♥ Dominated by a large pool table (always in use) in the center room, this divey bar hosts dancing many nights and seems especially popular among Latina and African-American women. Cocktails are a good $5 less here than elsewhere, which we applaud. 438-444 Hudson St. (at Morton St.). henriettahudson.com. ✆ **212/924-3347.** Subway: 1 to Houston St.

Hush ♥♥ A two-floor party that's proudly "sex positive," meaning there are often hardcore films on the screens here. Downstairs is a bar with a busy after-work scene. Upstairs is for dancing, and lots of shows from drag contests to watch parties to comedy shows. Every Thursday is a "Papi Party" for Latinos. 348 W. 52nd St. (btw. Eighth & Ninth aves.). hushhk.com. ✆ **646/833-7174.** Subway: C, E to 50th St.

The Monster ♥♥♥ A fabulous Art Deco space, once home to El Chico (a former flamenco cabaret whose murals still adorn the walls), the Monster has two faces. Upstairs is a piano bar with a crowd of show-tune-crazy regulars; downstairs a groovy discothèque with go-go boys, weekend tea dances, and the most popular Latin Night in the city. 80 Grove St. at Sheridan Square. monsterbarnyc.com. ✆ **212/924-3558.** Subway: 1 to Christopher St.

Plaques outside the Stonewall Inn explain its iconic place in gay history (p. 183), but inside it's no fusty museum piece, just a welcoming bar and community hub.

Stonewall Inn ♥♥♥ This is the OG. In the early hours of June 28, 1969, a police raid here sparked riots, which in turn fueled the burgeoning gay rights movement. That history is celebrated in the small national park across the street and a visitor center next to the bar (p. 183), but don't assume the Stonewall itself is just a historic relic or a mothballed scene. Head inside for drag shows, sing-alongs at the piano, pick-ups, and camaraderie. It's a genuinely fun place to hang out. 53 Christopher St. (near Seventh Ave.). thestonewallinnnyc.com. ✆ **212/488-2705.** Subway: 1 to Christopher St.

SPECTATOR SPORTS

For details on the New York City Marathon and the U.S. Open tennis championships, see the "New York City Calendar of Events" in chapter 9.

BASEBALL With two baseball teams in town—three if you count the minor league **Brooklyn Cyclones** (milb.com/brooklyn)—you can catch a game almost any day from Opening Day in April to the beginning of the playoffs in October (though prime Yankees tickets can be hard to come by). For info on pricing and availability of tickets for the **New York Mets,** based at Citi Field in Queens, visit mlb.com/mets or call the Mets ticket office at ✆ **718/507-TIXX** (507-8499). The **New York Yankees** play in the Bronx at famed Yankee Stadium; for single-game tickets, go to mlb.com/yankees or call the stadium ticket office at ✆ **718/293-4300.** You can also buy Mets and Yankees tickets by contacting **Ticketmaster** (ticketmaster.com; ✆ **800/745-3000**), visiting the stadium on the day of the game, or trying online resale sites such as **StubHub.com** or **SeatGeek.com.**

BASKETBALL Frankly, the women usually best the men when it comes to high powered b-ball in NYC, with the **New York Liberty** taking home the WNBA championship in 2024. Home games are at Brooklyn's Barclay's Center (620 Atlantic Ave.) between May and early September. For info on tickets, game dates and more, go to liberty.wnba.com.

Two NBA hoops teams play from late October through mid-April in New York City. At Madison Square Garden, Seventh Avenue between 31st and 33rd streets (msg.com or ticketmaster.com; ✆ **212/465-6741** or 800/745-3000 for tickets; subway: A, C, E, 1, 2, 3 to 34th St.), fans watch the **New York Knicks** play (nba.com/knicks; ✆ **877/NYK-DUNK** [695-3865] or 212/465-JUMP [5867]). Out in Brooklyn, the **Brooklyn Nets** play at Barclays Center, 620 Atlantic Ave. at Flatbush Ave. (nba.com/nets; ✆ **917/618-6100;** subway: 2, 3, 4, 5, B, D, N, Q, R to Atlantic Ave./Barclays Center).

FOOTBALL Both the **New York Giants** (giants.com) and the **New York Jets** (newyorkjets.com) play in the Meadowlands Stadium. It's located not in New York City, but in East Rutherford, New Jersey, and tickets are VERY difficult to get. Tickets are available from Ticketmaster.com and, if price is no object, StubHub.com or SeatGeek.com.

ICE HOCKEY NHL hockey is represented in Manhattan by the **New York Rangers,** who play at Madison Square Garden (nhl.com/rangers or msg.com; ✆ **212/465-6741;** subway: A, C, E, 1, 2, 3 to 34th St.); and the **New York Islanders,** who play at Barclays Center in Brooklyn, 620 Atlantic Ave. at Flatbush Ave. (nhl.com/islanders; ✆ **917/618-6100;** subway: 2, 3, 4, 5, B, D, N, Q, R to Atlantic Ave./Barclays Center). Rangers' tickets are particularly hard to get, so plan well ahead; visit **ticketmaster.com** for online orders or call ✆ **800/745-3000.**

PLANNING YOUR VISIT

9

Much has changed in the city in the last decade, so even if you've visited the Big Apple before, know that it's more important than ever to do some advance planning to ensure a successful visit. This chapter provides a variety of planning tools, including info on how to get there, how to get around within the city, and when to visit. And then, in an alphabetical listing, I deal with the dozens of miscellaneous resources and organizations that you can turn to for help.

GETTING THERE

By Plane

Three major airports serve New York City: **John F. Kennedy International Airport** (JFK; jfkairport.com; ✆ **718/244-4444**) in Queens, about 15 miles from midtown Manhattan; **LaGuardia Airport** (LGA; laguardiaairport.com; ✆ **718/533-3400**), also in Queens, about 10 miles from midtown; and **Newark Liberty International Airport** (EWR; newarkairport.com; ✆ **973/961-6000**) in nearby New Jersey, about 17 miles from midtown Manhattan. Almost every major domestic airline serves at least one of the New York–area airports; most serve two or all three.

GETTING INTO TOWN FROM THE AIRPORT

Generally, travel time between the airports and midtown by taxi or car is 60 minutes for JFK or Newark, and 45 minutes for LaGuardia. That said, a $19 billion renovation at JFK is curtailing some AirTrain service as we go to press (see below) and snarling already-sluggish traffic. The work is expected to be completed sometime in 2028. Always allow extra time, especially during rush hour or peak holiday travel times, especially if you're taking public transportation.

SUBWAYS & PUBLIC BUSES For a major international city, New York's public transit options to and from our airports are pretty crummy, but not impossible to navigate. The subway *can* be more reliable than taking a car or taxi at the height of rush hour, but ***a few words of warning:*** This isn't the right option for you if you're bringing more than a single piece of luggage or if you have young children in tow, since there's a good amount of walking, including

FINDING A GOOD airfare INTO NYC

Book at the right time. It sounds odd, but you can often save a good amount by booking domestic airfare 28 days in advance of departure. That figure comes from a 2025 study of over 40 million airfare transactions by Expedia and an industry group called the Airlines Reporting Corporation. Book earlier than that, and you won't have access to the lowest-priced seats, as the airlines only release them when they have an idea of how the plane is selling. Book too close to departure, and the airline knows they've "got you" and will charge more. That same study found that those who purchased their tickets on a Sunday spent 6% less statistically (the savings are higher for international fares).

Fly when others don't. Those who fly Friday, Tuesday, or Wednesday, and who stay over a Saturday night, generally pay less than those who fly at more popular times, according to the study cited above.

Do a smart online search. Frommers.com did an extensive study on airline pricing and found that Momondo.com and Skyscanner.com find the lowest airfares most consistently, delivering a broad and impartial search, with filters that allow users to search by ticket class, type of plane, and much more. Southwest Airlines now regularly appears in searches, so you no longer have to do separate searches for its fares.

Don't be particular about airports. Go to whichever airport is offering the cheapest fares. None of the three New York City airports are any more or less convenient to the city than the others (although LaGuardia is somewhat closer). JFK currently has a slightly better record than the other two in terms of delays and lost luggage, but it's not enough to influence your buying decision.

We should note that **MacArthur Airport** on Long Island and **Stewart Airport** in the Hudson Valley are now hubs for such low-cost carriers as Allegiant, Avelo, Frontier, and Breeze. You *might* be able to save by flying one of those carriers into these airports but, before buying, you MUST factor in the cost of transportation to the city. Both airports are much farther away than LaGuardia, JFK, or Newark, and the cost of a car or taxi into the city could wipe out any savings on the flight (public transportation would be *very* complicated).

Be anonymous in your search. Clear your cookies and engage the privacy setting on your browser, or better yet, subscribe to a virtual private network (VPN) and try your search from different cities and countries. The airlines and airfare booking sites do track users (though they deny it) and are getting increasingly expert in serving up fares tailored to customers' past buying history, and/or where they are based. To see the actual lowest rates, you may have to cloak your identity.

stairs, and usually a subway car that's too crowded for excess baggage. Also note that, depending on where in the city you're staying, public transport may double the time a car will. That's particularly true during off-peak travel times.

- **LaGuardia Airport:** Know in advance which subway you need to connect to, as that will determine which bus you take from the airport and where you get on or off the bus. The free **Q70 bus,** which is outfitted with luggage racks for tourists, zips in about 15 minutes between LaGuardia and the Jackson Heights–Roosevelt Ave/74th Street subway station, which connects to the E, F, M, R, and 7 trains, all of which go to Manhattan. The **M60**

bus will also take you to or from the city; it isn't reliable (I've waited 45 minutes), but it offers a lot of connections. It makes several stops along 125th Street in Manhattan, linking to the 1, 2, 3, 4, 5, 6 and A, B, C, and D subway lines, and also links to the N or W train at Astoria Boulevard station in Queens. Total cost for either of these two routes will be a $3 subway fare.

- **JFK Airport:** The commute from Manhattan to JFK Airport was vastly improved in 2023 with the opening of the Grand Central Madison station below historic Grand Central Terminal. Take the free **AirTrain** from the airport to Jamaica Station and switch to the Long Island Railroad, which will whisk you to either Grand Central Madison or Penn Station in NYC (total fare $13.75–$15.75, depending on time of day). Head to Grand Central if you're staying on the east side, to Penn Station if you're staying on the west side of Manhattan. Air Train runs every 3 to 5 minutes in both directions on weekdays, every 8 to 12 minutes on weekends and in the evenings. There's also a $2 cheaper, but slower, method, which is to connect with either the A, E, J, or Z subway at Jamaica Station and the Sutphin Blvd.-Archer Ave. Station; or the A subway at Howard Beach; either way, it's $11.75 total fare. Complete info on the subway/AirTrain link can be found at mta.info/guides/airports.
- **Newark Airport:** Passengers first take the **AirTrain** (panynj.gov; ✆ **888/EWR-INFO** [397-4636]) from their terminal to the Newark Airport train station, where they transfer to a **NJ Transit train** (njtransit.com; ✆ **973/275-5555**) heading to New York Penn Station at 33rd Street and Seventh Avenue. (***Note:*** DON'T accidentally board a train to Penn Station Newark, a common mistake. If you do end up in Penn Station Newark, you'll have to buy another ticket and change trains to continue on to NYC.) **Amtrak** (amtrak.com; ✆ **800/USA-RAIL** [872-7245]) will also connect to this station, but it is far more expensive than New Jersey Transit, so I don't recommend it. From New York Penn Station, catch either a cab, an Uber, subway, or a bus to your hotel. A one-way trip costs $19.80 at minimum for most passengers: $16.80 for the New Jersey train and then another $3 for the bus or subway in Manhattan to your hotel. Unlike the M60 bus to LaGuardia, service on NJ Transit is relatively frequent, with trains running at least six times an hour from 6am to 9pm and four times an hour from 9pm to midnight (there's no service 2–5am). NJ Transit tickets can be purchased from vending machines at both the air terminal and the train station. There are discounts for children and seniors. ***One warning:*** AirTrain does not go directly to Terminal A, just B and C. So, you'll need to allot an extra 10 to 15 minutes to get to and from A, either to take the shuttle bus, or to walk from Terminal B.

TAXIS & UBER/LYFT Both taxis and such ride-sharing services as Uber and Lyft are quick and convenient ways to travel to and from the airports—though they ain't cheap.

If you go the **taxi** route, they're available at designated taxi stands outside the terminals, with uniformed dispatchers at all three airports. Follow the

GROUND TRANSPORTATION or TAXI signs; at JFK, depending on the terminal, this could entail a 10-minute walk. There also may be a long line, but generally those lines move quickly. Fares, whether fixed or metered, do not include bridge and tunnel tolls ($5.76–$8.50, if applicable), a congestion pricing fee ($2.50), and a tip for the cabbie (20% is customary). They do include all passengers in the cab and luggage—never pay more than the metered or flat rate, except for tolls and a tip (8pm–6am, a 50¢ surcharge also applies on New York yellow cabs). **Taxis have a limit of four passengers,** so if there are more in your group, you'll have to take more than one cab or try to get a minivan taxi. For more, see p. 385.

- **From LaGuardia:** There's no set fare, but you can expect the meter to run about $45, plus tolls, tip, and a $5 state tax surcharge. Congestion surcharges (see above) also apply to trips to and from LaGuardia.
- **From JFK:** A flat rate of $70 to Manhattan (plus tolls, fees detailed above, tip, a $2.50 airport access charge, $4.05 in NY state fees) is charged. The meter will not be ticking up as you go but will start and end at that price (plus the surcharges listed above). If you are traveling between 4 and 8pm Monday to Friday, a $5 rush hour surcharge will also be added. Those going below 96th Street in Manhattan will also be charged a $2.50 surcharge.
- **From Newark:** The dispatcher for New Jersey taxis gives you a slip of paper with a flat rate ranging from $50 to $75 (toll and tip extra), depending on where you're going in New York City, so be precise about your destination. New York yellow cabs aren't permitted to pick up passengers at Newark. The yellow-cab fare from Manhattan to Newark is the meter amount plus $20 and tolls (totaling $75–$95). New Jersey taxis aren't permitted to take passengers from Manhattan to Newark.

If you decide to use one of the **ride-sharing services,** arrange your ride as you're getting off the plane (it will usually take a good 10 minutes, if not more, for drivers to make it to the airport). Then exit at the arrivals area, NOT departures, as that's where these cars liaison with passengers. The cost of getting into Manhattan is **usually $15 or so more than by taxi,** though how much more will depend on where in the city you are going, and what time of day it is.

PRIVATE CAR & LIMOUSINE SERVICES Private (or "livery") car and limousine companies range from sedans and vans to limousines and provide 24-hour door-to-door airport transfers for roughly the same cost as a taxi. Or at least that's the case for those who choose curbside pickup at the airport. Being greeted by a driver holding a sign with your name on it as you exit the baggage area is a service that comes at a premium. The advantage of indoor pickup is that you'll avoid the hassles of taxi lines. Frankly, I don't see much advantage to arranging for curbside pickup from the airport, because the wait can be up to 30 minutes (you'll call the dispatcher when you arrive) and the taxi line is rarely that long. **My advice:** Use car services to get *to* the airport, but simply hop a cab when coming from the airport into the city. ***Note:*** Ubers can now be reserved well in advance, but they tend to be pricier than the car services below.

Private car companies with the best reputations are **Carmel** (carmellimo.com; ✆ **212/666-6666**), **Allstate** (allstatelimo.com; ✆ **800/453-4099** or 212/333-3333), and **Dial 7** (dial7.com; ✆ **212/777-7777**). (Keep in mind, though, that these services are only as good as the individual drivers. If you have a problem, report it immediately to the main office.) Ask when booking what the fare will be. There may be waiting charges tacked on if the driver has to wait an excessive amount of time due to flight delays, but the car companies will usually check on your flight to get an accurate landing time.

Warning: When you leave the terminal, you may be approached by a private car driver trying to get a fare back to Manhattan, or a driver without a taxi/livery license looking to make extra money. It's illegal, as well as more expensive than doing Uber, taking a taxi, or using one of the services listed above. And you may be taken advantage of if the driver thinks you're a NYC newbie. Don't negotiate with them. Grab a cab, order a car, or take a bus or shuttle.

SHUTTLES Buses and shuttle services provide a comfortable and less expensive (but usually more time-consuming) option for airport transfers than do taxis and car services. **Uber Shuttle,** available through that app, has daily runs from central points in Manhattan, like Times Square, Grand Central Terminal or Union Square, and Grand Army Plaza in Brooklyn, to LaGuardia ($20), Newark ($20), and JFK ($24); return trips are the same price. The vans are new and quite comfortable. Uber's shuttles run roughly every 15 minutes from 5am until 9:45pm. More traditional services to Newark Airport include **Coach USA** (coachusa.com; ✆ **877/894-9155**) which provides service every 15 to 20 minutes between 7am and 11pm (every 30 min. 4am–2am) from Newark to Bryant Park (42nd St. and Fifth Ave.), the Port Authority Bus Terminal (42nd St., btw. Eighth and Ninth aves.), and Grand Central Terminal (41st St., btw. Park and Lexington aves.). Call for the exact schedule for your return trip to the airport. The one-way fare runs $23.50; $39.50 round-trip; $12.50 one-way for seniors 62 and over, and those with special needs. For JFK or LGA the top door-to-door shuttle operator is **GoAirLink** (goairlinkshuttle.com). It offers pick-up and drop-off at hotels in Manhattan and Brooklyn, starting at $35/person one-way to each. So, it's cheaper than a taxi if you're traveling solo, but the savings are minimal-to-nil for couples or larger groups. GoAirLink's one-way fare between Grand Central Terminal and LGA is $27.85 ($29.50 for JFK), a good option for those staying in east midtown.

By Bus

Busing to and from New York City from major East Coast cities has become the single most cost-effective way to get to the city. A number of companies offer frequent, regular service between most of the major cities in the east for a fraction of what you'd pay by train or plane. From Philadelphia, the average ride might range from $10 to $20; for Boston or Washington, D.C., you'll pay

$15 to $35, but occasional specials reduce the fares. The website GoToBus.com provides a comprehensive list of options, but I've found that **OurBus** (ourbus.com) tends to have the most consistency, in terms of low prices and good service. Check the website for listings of pick-up and drop-off locations throughout New York City.

By Train

Amtrak (amtrak.com; ✆ **800/USA-RAIL** [872-7245]) runs frequent service to New York City through Penn Station's beautiful, recently converted Moynihan Train Hall on Eighth Avenue between 33rd and 31st streets. The **Long Island Railroad** (mta.info; ✆ **877/690-5116**) also uses the Moynihan Train Hall, and underground corridors connect to the main Penn Station (Seventh Ave., btw. 31st and 33rd sts.), served by **NJ Transit** (njtransit.com; ✆ **973/275-5555**). You can get a taxi, subway, or bus to your hotel from the Penn Station complex. If you're traveling to New York from a city along Amtrak's Northeast Corridor—such as Boston, Philadelphia, Baltimore, or Washington, D.C.—Amtrak may end up being faster than flying (when you factor in time getting to the airport and getting through security), especially on the high-speed, newly upgraded Next Gen Acela trains. Acela Express trains cut travel time from D.C. down to a bit less than 3 hours, and travel time from Boston to a lightning-quick 3.5 hours.

GETTING AROUND THE CITY

Because most travelers confine themselves to Manhattan, I will as well in this section. Those traveling to the outer boroughs can be confident, however, that public transportation—subways, buses, ferries, or some combination of the three—can get you anywhere you wish to go in the city proper, whether it be the sandy shores of Brighton Beach, Brooklyn, or Yankee Stadium in the Bronx. The city's transportation network is run by the Metropolitan Transportation Authority (aka the MTA); maps and schedules for NYC's myriad transportation options can be found at mta.info.

Subway

I wish I could confine my transportation advice to just three words—**"take the subway"**—and be done with it. To my mind, the NYC subways, 123 years young in 2027, are the single most efficient, rapid, easy, and affordable way to get just about anywhere you'd want to go in Manhattan, with the exception of crosstown journeys above 59th Street. They run 24 hours a day, 7 days a week, and, yes, they can get crowded at rush hour (roughly Mon–Fri 8–9:30am and 5–6:30pm) and have had issues in the past few years with aging infrastructure. But even with these caveats they're still the fastest way to get from point A to point B.

You may have read that the subways are unsafe, and there were certainly problems in 2022. But serious safety initiatives were put in place in 2023—foremost among them a massive increase in the number of police officers patrolling subway stations and trains—and as we went to press, the number of incidents in the system were back down to their low 2019 numbers. In fact, the subway is so beloved that we've seen a rash of people deciding to stage pop-up weddings on the subway (no joke!). Of course, pickpockets remain a problem, as they are in Paris, London, and every other big city. So, remember to move your wallet to a place where you can keep track of it before boarding the train (if you're wearing pants, the front pocket is usually best).

And one last caveat: Though the cars are heated in winter and air-conditioned in summer, the platforms are not, and they often feel 10 degrees colder than the city streets in winter, and 10 degrees hotter in summer. Be prepared to shiver or swelter until the next train comes.

PAYING YOUR WAY

The relatively new **OMNY** system allows you to scan your contactless credit or debit card (one with the sound wave symbol on it) or a digital wallet on your smartphone or smartwatch at the turnstile. OMNY can be used to travel on both buses and subways. The key is to stick to one credit card or digital wallet, so that the OMNY system recognizes you each time you ride. OMNY will never charge you more than $35 in a week, which covers 12 rides. After that, you ride for free.

In 2024, the city introduced OMNY cards, which are like credit cards but only for public transportation in NYC. These were targeted to workers whose companies pay for their rides to and from work, but can be purchased by anyone at vending machines throughout the subway system, as well as at city drugstores, 7-11's, and other convenient locations. Frankly, I don't think buying an OMNY card makes sense for most visitors, since it's so easy to simply use your own credit card or Apple Pay.

Subway and bus rides cost $3 per ride. Children under 44 inches tall ride free (up to three per adult). There are also reduced-price tickets available for those 65 and over and persons with disabilities; you can apply for them online at reducedfare.mta.info.

Once you're in the subway system, you can transfer free of charge to any subway line that you can reach without exiting your station. You'll also get **free transfers** between bus and subway within a 2-hour period.

Mass Transit Fares in New York City

SUBWAYS, MTA BUS		
Fare Type	Full	Reduced*
Base Fare Per Ride	$3	$1.50
Express Bus	$7.25	$3.60
UNLIMITED-RIDE DEALS		
7-day	$35	$17.50

* Reduced fares are available to those 65 and over and persons with qualifying disabilities. Both groups must apply in advance for the discount at reducedfare.mta.info.

USING THE SUBWAY SYSTEM

As you can see from the subway map on the inside back cover of this book, the subway system basically mimics the lay of the land above ground, with most lines in Manhattan running north and south, like the avenues, and a few lines east and west, like the streets.

To **go up and down the east side of Manhattan** (and to the Bronx and Brooklyn), take the 4, 5, or 6 train. The **Q train** also zips down Second Avenue from 96th Street to 72nd Street before veering west to Lexington and 63rd, and then going further west to double the N and R lines (see below) in Manhattan.

To travel **up and down the West Side** (and also to the Bronx and Brooklyn), take the 1, 2, or 3 line; the A, C, E, or F line; or the B or D line. The E and F trains, however, veer east in midtown and head out to Queens.

The N and R lines first **cut diagonally across town** from east to west and then snake under Seventh Avenue before shooting out to Queens.

The **crosstown** S line, called the Shuttle, runs back and forth between Times Square and Grand Central Terminal. It's doubled by the 7 train for part of that route, but the 7 goes further west (to Tenth Ave. and 34th St.) and east into Queens (see box, p. 241). Farther downtown, across 14th Street, the L line works its own crosstown magic and goes on to Brooklyn.

Express trains often skip about three stops for each one they make; express stops are indicated on subway maps with a white (rather than solid) circle. Local stops are usually about 9 blocks apart.

Directions are almost always indicated using "uptown" (northbound) and "downtown" (southbound), so be sure to know what direction you want to head. The outsides of some subway entrances are marked UPTOWN ONLY or DOWNTOWN ONLY; read carefully, as it's easy to head in the wrong direction or get stuck on the wrong platform. When that happens, you'll have to exit and pay again to get to the right platform.

By Bus

Since buses can get stuck in traffic and stop every couple of blocks, rather than the 8 or 9 blocks that local subways traverse between stops (unless you catch a "Limited" bus), they're much less useful than the subway. I recommend using them only if you have to travel east to west. Note that you can combine a bus ride with a subway ride at no additional cost (the transfer has to take place within 2 hours of the time you first boarded either the subway or the train).

PAYING YOUR WAY

Like the subway fare (see above), a **bus fare** is $3, half-price for seniors and riders with disabilities, and free for children under 44 inches (up to three per adult). The fare is payable by tapping your contactless credit card on a screen right to the side of the driver (or using a digital wallet via your smartphone or smartwatch). Customers can also pay with **exact change,** but if you go that route, know that they do mean *change:* Bus drivers don't make change, and fare boxes don't accept dollar bills or pennies.

USING THE BUS SYSTEM

You can't flag down a city bus—you have to meet it at a bus stop. **Bus stops** are located every 2 or 3 blocks on the right-side corner of the street (facing the direction of traffic flow). They're marked by a curb painted yellow and a blue-and-white sign with a bus emblem and the route number or numbers, and usually an ad-bedecked bus shelter.

Almost every major avenue has its own **bus route.** They run either north or south: downtown on Fifth, uptown on Madison, downtown on Lexington, uptown on Third, and so on. There are **crosstown buses** at strategic locations all around town, generally at the wider numbered streets (14th, 23rd, 34th, and 42nd sts., to name a few). You'll usually find a crosstown bus route every 8 to 10 blocks, except in the area below 8th street. Some bus routes, however, are erratic: The M104, for example, turns at Eighth Avenue and 41st Street and goes up Broadway to West 129th Street.

Most routes operate 24 hours a day, but service is infrequent at night. There is one perk for rides between 10pm and 5am, however: Bus drivers will let passengers off between official stops if they so request. During rush hour, main routes have "Limited" buses, identifiable by the red card in the front window; they stop only at major cross streets.

Most city buses are equipped with wheelchair lifts, making buses the city's most accessible mode of public transportation. Buses also "kneel," lowering down to the curb to make boarding easier. Note that newer buses (they're dark blue with a yellow stripe on the side) offer Wi-Fi and have power outlets so that you can charge your phone.

By Taxi

Cabs can be hailed on any street, provided you find an empty one—and with so many cab drivers having left the biz during the pandemic, that's far more difficult than it used to be. However, if you don't see one, know that you can get one via the **Curb** app, which, unlike the Uber app, does not charge surge rates during rush hours. Taxicabs are pricey but can be convenient if you're tired or are not sure how to find an address. Don't assume they'll be quicker than the subway or walking, though. In traffic-clogged midtown at midday, you can often walk to where you're going more quickly.

Most **official New York City taxis,** licensed by the Taxi and Limousine Commission (TLC), are yellow, with the rates printed on the door and a light with a medallion number on the roof. Others, which operate primarily in the outer boroughs and upper Manhattan, are apple-green and are governed by slightly different rules. Like yellow cabs, they're hailable, but unlike the yellow ones they are not allowed to pick up passengers in Manhattan below West 110th Street or East 96th Street (though they are allowed to drop off passengers there).

The **base fare** on entering the cab is $3, plus a $2.50 congestion charge if you're driving below 96th street in Manhattan, a $0.75 fee for going below 60th street, and $1.50 in state fees. The **cost** is 70¢ for every ⅕ mile and for every 60 seconds in stopped or slow-moving traffic (or for waiting time). There's no extra charge for each passenger or for luggage. However, you must pay **bridge or tunnel tolls.** You'll also pay a **$2.50 surcharge** between 4 and 8pm, and a **$1 surcharge** between 8pm and 6am. A 15% to 20% tip is customary. All taxis are now equipped with a device that allows you to pay by credit card. (You can also pay automatically with the Curb app by entering the cab's pairing code.)

Drivers are required by law to take you anywhere in the five boroughs, to Nassau or Westchester counties, and to the major airports. They are supposed to know how to get to any address in the city. They are also required to provide A/C and turn off the radio on demand. Smoking in the cab is not allowed. Standard taxis cannot, by law, take more than 4 passengers, so don't even try it.

You are allowed to dictate the route that is taken. It's a good idea to look at a map before you get in a taxi. Taxi drivers have been known to jack up the fare on visitors who don't know better by taking a circuitous route between points A and B. Don't be afraid to speak up.

On the other hand, listen to drivers who propose an alternate route. These folks spend 8 or 10 hours a day on these streets, and they know where the worst traffic is, or where construction has dug up an intersection that should be avoided.

Another important tip: **Always make sure the meter is turned on at the start of the ride.** You'll see the red LED readout register the initial $3 and start calculating the fare as you go. I've seen unscrupulous drivers buzz visitors around the city with the meter off, then overcharge them at drop-off.

Taxi-Hailing Tips

When you're waiting on the street for an available taxi, look at the **medallion light** on the top of the coming cabs. If the light is out, the taxi is in use. When the center part (the number) is lit, the taxi is available—this is when you raise your hand to flag the cab. If all the lights are on, the driver is off-duty. Taxi regulations limit the number of cab passengers to four, so split up if your group is larger. Don't see any cabs? Use the Curb or Uber app to summon a nearby ride.

For all driver complaints, including the one above, and to report lost property, call ✆ **311** (or ✆ **212/NEW-YORK** [639-9675] outside the metro area).

By Uber & Lyft

These services have become so ubiquitous that the value of a taxi medallion (the official license necessary to own a yellow cab) plummeted from several hundred thousand dollars to well under half that amount in recent years. Both are accessible through apps you can download to a smartphone; the credit card you register when you get the app is automatically charged for the ride. (Tipping is optional but recommended.) You key in your pick-up and drop-off locations and receive a price for the ride. While these rides are sometimes cheaper than a taxi, rates can increase threefold when "surge pricing" takes effect. Both Uber and Lyft also have cheaper ride-sharing options, but often the wait times quoted for a share are unrealistically long. I recommend using Uber or Lyft only when they give you a wait time of 4 minutes or less. When the wait is longer, except in the most deserted areas of town, it will likely be more convenient to simply hail a taxi.

By Ferry

NYC Ferry is a wonderful, and much expanded, way to get around the city. It runs six routes that connect Wall Street, several stops along the east side of Manhattan (20th, 34th, and 90th sts.), Battery Park City, and West 39th Street to a number of stops in the Bronx, Brooklyn, Queens, Staten Island, and Roosevelt Island. It also runs a shuttle to and from Governor's Island. The cost is the same as the subway ($3). For those traveling to the very edges of the city, this method of travel is convenient, fast, and very scenic, though you will have to walk inland (or take a bus, bike, or taxi) from the shores of Manhattan and Brooklyn to reach most sights and hotels. For more information go to **ferry.nyc**.

By Bicycle

Believe it or not, New York is becoming a great cycling city. It boasts a number of designated bike routes and lanes, including some protected bike lanes painted green and with their own traffic signals.

And you don't have to bring your own wheels to ride, thanks to the **Citi Bike** bike-share system (citibikenyc.com), which charges $25 a day for an unlimited number of 30-minute-long rides (if your ride lasts longer, you pay 30¢ for every additional minute). E-bikes, which give you additional power and speed, cost an additional 37¢ per minute, although I don't recommend paying extra for an e-bike—the city is so flat you don't need it, and the oomph of electricity can make riders go faster than they intend to. Single rides are pricey at $4.99 a pop. Freestanding solar-powered racks dot many streets across the five boroughs, each holding around a dozen sturdy bikes outfitted with lights and tough tires. Download the Citi Bike app to find the rack nearest to you. For a current map of the ever-expanding city bike-lane network, visit the NYC DOT webpage at **nyc.gov** or

Beware: Pedi-Cabs & Horse-Drawn Carriages

They're cute and they make for great Instagram snaps—but there's no form of NYC transportation pricier than these two. Just go on any online bulletin board about travel, and you'll find horror stories about $800 half-hour pedicab rides (they charge by the minute). Central Park's horse-and-carriage rides have an even darker reason for a skip: They too are expensive, but more importantly there have been credible reports of mistreatment of the horses. There will be other photo ops, we promise.

nycbikemaps.com. Alas, helmets are not provided at these stands; it's a smart idea to bring your own.

By Car

Forget driving yourself around the city. It's not worth the headache or the expense. Traffic is horrendous, parking even more problematic, and congestion pricing adds $9 to the cost of driving in Manhattan every time you go below 60th street. If you do arrive in New York City by car, park it in a garage (expect to pay at least $40–$75 per day) and leave it there for the duration of your stay. If you drive a rental car in, return it as soon as you arrive and rent another when you leave. All the major car rental companies have multiple Manhattan locations.

Traveling from the City to the Suburbs

The **PATH system** (panynj.gov/path; ✆ **800/234-7284**) connects Manhattan with cities in New Jersey, including Hoboken and Newark, by subway-style trains. Stops in Manhattan are at the World Trade Center, Christopher and 9th streets, and along Sixth Avenue at 14th, 23rd, and 33rd streets. The fare is $3.

New Jersey Transit (njtransit.com; ✆ **973/275-5555**) operates commuter trains from Penn Station, and buses from the Port Authority at Eighth Avenue and 42nd Street, to points throughout New Jersey.

The **Long Island Rail Road** (mta.info/lirr; ✆ **511**) runs from both Penn Station's Moynihan Train Hall, at Eighth Avenue between 31st and 33rd streets, and Grand Central Madison (42nd St. and Vanderbilt Ave.) to Queens (ocean beaches, Citi Field [home of the New York Mets], Belmont Park) and points beyond on Long Island, to even better beaches and summer hot spots such as the Hamptons. You can also connect to the Fire Island ferry from the LIRR.

Metro-North Railroad (mta.info/mnr; ✆ **212/532-4900**) departs from Grand Central, at 42nd Street and Lexington Avenue, for areas north of the city, including Westchester County, the Hudson Valley, and Connecticut.

WHEN TO GO

"Anytime you like" is the short answer. New York is a 12-month, 24-hour destination, and there's always something exciting going on here.

Significantly, New York does not experience the real extremes of temperature of a Minneapolis or Phoenix. Yes, we sometimes get snowstorms and 10° weather, but rarely for more than a day or two, with the snow usually scooped into graying piles overnight. We also have heat waves, but it's unusual for the temperature to break 100°F (38°C) for more than 4 or 5 days each summer, though it will be a sticky heat when it hits and none too pleasant. In general, this type of extreme heat occurs only in July and August, with the blustery and bitterly cold days falling in January and February, and occasionally December. (Of course, in this age of climate change, you never know what will happen.) If you want to know what to pack just before you go, check the Weather Channel's online 10-day forecast at **weather.com**.

Culture, too, is a year-round exercise. Most of the major plays, musicals, and art shows debut between September and May, but in the summer months NYC still teems with arts events, as the city transforms itself into an outdoor theater/concert hall, with dozens of free shows from Shakespeare in the Park to Shakespeare in the Parking Lot. All the major art institutions participate in this summer free-for-all, with the Museum of Modern Art sponsoring concerts in its sculpture garden, the Metropolitan Opera bringing music to the parks, Lincoln Center staging a festival in its plaza, and dozens of other institutions, large and small, established and unknown, jumping on the alfresco bandwagon.

So, what it all comes down to, in my mind, is cost, and here there is a *major* difference between seasons. People who visit in the slower months pay the right amount for their lodging, and those who come when the city is crowded—and here I'm going to sound like the clichéd New Yorker—get screwed.

So, when are prices the most moderate? Deep winter, in the months of January (after the 4th) and February, it's not at all unusual to find a lovely room for as little as $129 a night. Visit in the fall, especially October and November, or around the December holidays, and that same room, in the same hotel, could cost upward of $599 a night. Spring is also pricey, albeit slightly less so than the fall, and prices drop into a middle range in the summer. Room rates over Christmas, New Year's, the New York Marathon, and Thanksgiving reach their pinnacles for the year. If you must visit at those times, get ready to pay a good $100 more than even the pricey fall rates.

New York's Average Temperature & Rainfall

	JAN	FEB	MAR	APR	MAY	JUNE	JULY	AUG	SEPT	OCT	NOV	DEC
Daily Temp. (°F)	39	40	48	61	71	81	85	83	77	67	54	41
Daily Temp. (°C)	4	5	8	16	21	27	29	28	25	19	12	5
Days of Precipitation	11	10	11	11	11	10	11	10	8	8	9	10

New York City Calendar of Events

I've included below a very limited sampling of what I consider "visit-worthy" events. As I can make no claims to psychic abilities, I can't include all of the nifty happenings that haven't yet been announced. To get a complete picture, look at ***TimeOut.com/NewYork***. The "Around Town" section will leave you dizzy—usually there are upward of 150 interesting events happening any week. For a more selective listing, buy the current ***New Yorker*** magazine, which devotes the first tenth of its pages to its picks for the most intellectually stimulating or artistically important events. **NYmag.com,** the website of *New York Magazine,* is another swell resource. For the most complete listings, go to the NYC Convention & Visitors Bureau's site: **nycgo.com**.

JANUARY

Winter Restaurant Week. A misnomer, because this gourmet shindig actually lasts 2 weeks. This is the time of year when foodies can get a 2-course lunch/3-course dinner for $30/$45/$60, depending on the restaurant (some of the best in the city participate). Visit **nyctourism.com** for the 2027 dates. You can make reservations starting 2 weeks in advance. Late January/early February.

FEBRUARY

Lunar New Year. Two weeks of parades, festive meals, and special performances staged throughout Chinatown's streets, and along East Broadway. Visit **explore chinatown.com**. Lunar New Year falls on February 6 in 2027.

Fashion Week. Early February is when American designers parade their new lines for the press and big department store buyers. It's impossible to get tickets to the runway shows (they go to the likes of Kim Kardashian and Zendaya). I only mention Fashion Week here because the event can tie up rooms at the midtown hotels (and at the more fashionable ones uptown and down).

Westminster Kennel Club Dog Show. I've always found it funny that Fashion Week—that parade of "Best in Breed" women—should be followed directly by a dog show. At least at the dog show, they're upfront about the purpose of the spectacle. The winnowing from just cute to anatomically awesome takes place at **Madison Square Garden,** with over 2,500 pooches appearing. Check **westminsterkennelclub.org** for further info. Tickets are available starting in mid-October via **Ticketmaster** (ticketmaster.com). Mid-February.

MARCH

Affordable Art Fair. Prices are capped at $12,000 (yes, that's considered "affordable" in NYC) and art galleries come from across the globe to sell their wares, many of which will undoubtedly increase in value. Frankly, I don't see much difference between this and the city's more celebrated art fairs, except that you might actually come home with an artwork from this one (I have!). See **affordableartfair.com** for location. Mid-March.

Easter Parade. No floats, no marching bands—just ordinary people strolling in extraordinary hats, making Easter one of the city's most low-key but charming celebrations. Fifth Avenue from 57th Street all the way down to 45th is closed to traffic 11am to 4pm, with the greatest number of chapeaus in evidence around noon. Easter is March 28 in 2027.

St. Patrick's Day Parade. Thanks to one of the largest Irish-American populations in the United States, St. Paddy's is an enormous event in NYC, rivaling only New Year's Eve for its displays of public inebriation. Every pub in town throws a party and all of 150,000 marchers parade up Fifth Avenue from 44th to 86th streets, starting at 11am. For more info: **nycstpatricksparade.org**. March 17.

APRIL

New York International Auto Show. Here's the irony: You don't need a car in New York, yet the largest car show in the U.S. is held at the Javits Center. Many concept cars show up that will never roll off the assembly line but are fun to dream about. More: **autoshowny.com**. Early April.

MAY

Dance Parade. On Saturday May 16, 2027, people from across the globe come to dance their way through the streets of Greenwich Village. It's a joyous display, featuring folk dancers from all cultures, hip hoppers, tap dancers, and more. The parade ends in Tompkins Square Park, where all the troupes dance and party together. For dates go to **danceparade.org**.

TD 5 Boro Bike Tour. For 1 day a year, an interconnecting chain of streets in all five boroughs is cleared of cars, and thousands of bikers tackle the entire route. A festival is held in Staten Island, the final stop. Registration and info at **bike.nyc**. First Sunday in May.

TEFAF. The world's leading arts and antique show (the European Fine Art Fair, long held only in Maastricht, Holland) brings exquisite pieces from the Stone Age through today to New York's **Park Avenue Armory.** The items are so rare they often make the news—in recent years treasures have included Persian drinking vessels from 1000 B.C., and a painting by 17th-century Spanish master Jusepe de Ribera. Contemporary art and design are shown, too. Go to **tefaf.com**. Mid-May.

Frieze New York. An offshoot of the London original, this artapalooza brings hundreds of international galleries to Hudson Yard's **The Shed.** Big money is spent and made here, but even if you're not a buyer, the chance to see art this cutting edge is exciting. **frieze.com/fairs**. Mid-May.

Fleet Week. About 10,000 Navy and Coast Guard personnel are "at liberty" in New York for the annual Fleet Week at the end of May. Usually from 1 to 4pm daily, you can watch the ships and aircraft carriers as they dock at the piers on the west side of Manhattan, tour them with on-duty personnel, and watch dramatic exhibitions by the U.S. Marines.

Even if you don't take in any of the events, you'll know it's Fleet Week because those 10,000 sailors invade NYC in their starched white uniforms. It's wonderful—just like *On the Town* come to life. Late May.

JUNE

Starting in June and through the summer, outdoor films are screened at a number of venues throughout the city. Check local listings.

Belmont Stakes. The final event in horse racing's grand trifecta (the Kentucky Derby and the Preakness are the first two). Any horse able to win all three instantly enters the record books and the owner becomes a multi-millionaire, thanks to the breeding fees they'll be able to collect for the rest of that horse's life. For information, visit **nyra.com**. Early June.

Mermaid Parade. A smaller, nautically themed, daytime version of Greenwich Village's Halloween Parade, the Mermaid Parade takes place in Coney Island. Founded in 1983, the parade has the same kind of home-grown ambience and raunch as its Greenwich Village counterpart. Along with the ball that follows, featuring performances by local burlesque acts, the event is a heck-uva lot of fun. Get details at **coneyisland.com**. Mid-June.

Gay Pride Weekend. More than just a parade (though the naughty, outrageous, rambunctious parade is still at the heart of the festivities), NY's pride weekend draws celebrants from across the U.S. for a weekend of lectures, dances, and rallies. Learn more at **nycpride.org**. Late June.

Tribeca Festival. Founded by Robert DeNiro and Jane Rosenthal in 2002, this film festival has quickly grown into one of the most influential in the nation—and broadened its scope to include tapings of top podcasts and live music performances. You'll see films from all over the world, from big studio pictures to tiny independent productions. And unlike other film fests, this one is truly for all ages, with a nifty street fair (usually featuring a zoo and rides), as well as children's films. To learn more, visit **tribecafilm.com/festival**. Mid-June.

JULY

Macy's Fourth of July Fireworks. Catch Macy's fireworks extravaganza over New York Harbor. It's the country's largest pyrotechnic show on Independence Day. **macys.com/fireworks**. July 4.

Summer Restaurant Week. Mid-July to early August (see "January," above).

Summer Concerts at Lincoln Center. Lincoln Center is known for bringing in performing artists from all over the world for both indoor and outdoor events, many of them free, including dance parties and kids' programs. More info at **lincolncenter.org**. July–August.

AUGUST

U.S. Open Tennis Championships. For one brief, bright-tennis-whites moment each year at the end of August (and into Sept), the city becomes a center for international sport with the start of the U.S. Open, one of pro tennis's four Grand Slam events. For full info, visit **usopen.org** or **usta.com**. Two weeks around Labor Day.

SEPTEMBER

Fashion Week. Part two of the event mentioned above (see "February"), and yes, it sends hotel rates soaring. See details on dates at **nyfw.com**.

New York Film Festival. Film at Lincoln Center's 2-week festival is a major stop on the film-fest circuit. Screenings are held in various Lincoln Center venues; advance tickets are always a good bet, and a necessity for certain events (especially evening and weekend screenings). Check out **filmlinc.com/nyff**. Two weeks from late September to early October.

OCTOBER

New Yorker Festival. The esteemed magazine presents a weekend's worth of lectures, events, and panels with the world's most intriguing thinkers (movie stars, chefs, politicians, professors, and more). Full info at **festival.newyorker.com**. Usually second weekend in October.

Open House New York. The doors are thrown open at dozens of homes and buildings around the city, all of which are usually off limits to the public and feature notable architecture. Mid-October. Exact dates at **ohny.org**.

Greenwich Village Halloween Parade. This is New York's most outrageous event and the world's largest Halloween parade. Some New Yorkers spend all year working on their costumes; if you dress up, you can march, too. For info on how to do that, and for the parade routing (which changes), visit **halloween-nyc.com**. To snag a viewing spot in Greenwich Village along the parade route, you'll need to show up at about 5pm (2 hr. before the parade starts) . . . or have a nice dinner and show up at 9pm to view the second half. The crowd will have thinned by then, though the event doesn't end until close to 11pm. October 31.

NOVEMBER

New York City Marathon. Some 30,000 runners from around the world participate in the largest U.S. marathon, and more than a million fans cheer them on as they follow a route that touches all five New York boroughs and finishes at Central Park. Go to **nyrr.org** for applications. First Sunday in November, the priciest week of the year to visit New York City.

Macy's Thanksgiving Day Parade. The procession of this much-beloved national tradition starts at Central Park West and 77th Street and finishes at Herald Square at 34th Street. Huge hot-air balloons in the forms of Minions, Snoopy, and other cartoon favorites are the best part. The night before, you can see the big blow-up on Columbus Avenue at West 77th and 81st streets. Thanksgiving Day.

Radio City Christmas Spectacular. This New York tradition now starts well before Thanksgiving, and it's still as extravagantly kitschy as ever, with laser-light shows, onstage ice-skating, horses, camels, and, of course, the fabulous Rockettes executing their 300-plus kicks per show. Shows run approximately 7 days a week, with six daily performances (on many dates) starting at 9am and going until 10pm. For info, go to **rockettes.com/christmas**; you can also buy tickets at the box office or via Ticketmaster at **ticketmaster.com**. Throughout November and December.

The Nutcracker. Ballet impresario George Balanchine's masterpiece. The music is by Tchaikovsky, and half the cast is under 15, selected from New York City Ballet's famous dance school at Juilliard. Your children will love it, though it's an expensive treat. The show sells out early, so make your reservations in October if you can, when the seats first go on sale. Go online to **nycballet.com**. Late November through early January.

DECEMBER

For a rundown on NYC's host of Christmas and Chanukah events, see **"Holiday Traditions,"** p. 198

New Year's Eve. The biggest party of all is in Times Square, where raucous revelers count down the year's final seconds until the ball drops at midnight at 1 Times Square. Standing in the cold, surrounded by thousands of revelers, all penned in by NYPD barricades, is a masochist's delight. Use the restroom before you wedge yourself in. More info at **timessquarenyc.org**. December 31.

Runner's World Midnight Run. Enjoy fireworks followed by the New York Road Runners Club's annual run in **Central Park,** which is fun for runners and spectators alike; go to **nyrr.org**. December 31.

Brooklyn's Fireworks Celebration. Head to Brooklyn for the city's largest New Year's Eve **fireworks** celebration inside Prospect Park. Visit **prospectpark.org**. December 31.

Public Holidays

Banks, government offices, post offices, and many stores, restaurants, and museums are closed on the following legal national holidays: January 1 (New Year's Day), the third Monday in January (Martin Luther King, Jr. Day), the third Monday in February (Presidents' Day), the last Monday in May (Memorial Day), June 19 (Juneteenth), July 4 (Independence Day), the first Monday in September (Labor Day), the second Monday in October (Columbus Day), November 11 (Veterans Day/Armistice Day), the fourth Thursday in November (Thanksgiving Day), and December 25 (Christmas). The Tuesday after the first Monday in November is Election Day, but all businesses remain open.

[FastFACTS] NEW YORK CITY

Area Codes NYC has six area codes: three in Manhattan, the original **212** plus **646** and **332;** and three in the outer boroughs, the original **718,** plus **929** and **347.** Also common is the **917** area code for cellphones. All calls between these area codes are local calls, but you'll have to dial 1 + the area code + the seven digits, even for calls within your area code.

Business Hours In general, **retail stores** are open Monday through Saturday from 10am to 6 or 7pm, and Sunday 11am to 5pm; for more on shopping hours, see p. 311. **Banks** tend to be open Monday through Friday 9am to 5pm, with many open Saturday mornings and some on Sundays.

Doctors Walk-in medical centers include **City MD** (citymd.com), with 29 clinics in Manhattan and dozens in the other boroughs. Hours vary widely. Their midtown office is at 952 Second Ave. (at 51st St.).

New York Presbyterian Hospital offers physician referrals at ✆ **877/697-9355.** Because of a shortage of hospitals in New York City, I don't recommend emergency room visits except in, well, dire emergencies. For a list of ERs, see p. 394.

Pack **prescription medications** in their original containers in your carry-on luggage. Also bring along copies of your prescriptions in case you lose your pills or run out.

If you have dental problems on the road, a service known as **1-800-DENTIST [336-8422]** will provide the name of a local dentist.

Drinking Laws The legal age for purchase and consumption of alcoholic beverages is 21; proof of age can be requested at bars, nightclubs, and restaurants. Liquor and wine are sold only in licensed stores, most of which are open 7 days a week. Beer can be purchased in grocery stores and delis 24 hours a day. Last call in bars is at 4am, though many close earlier. You can order cocktails on a carryout basis, so long as you are also buying food (to take back to your hotel room, for example), but it's illegal to carry open containers of alcohol in public—police can fine you on the spot.

Electricity Like Canada, the United States uses 110 to 120 volts AC (60 cycles), compared to 220 to 240 volts AC (50 cycles) in most of Europe, Australia, and New Zealand.

Emergencies For all emergencies—a fire, police, or health emergency—call ✆ **911.**

Family Travel The website newyorkfamily.com has timely info on what the city's top kid-friendly events are

Weed Whacked: New York Gets Legal Marijuana

In 2022, recreational marijuana was legalized in New York state, and the city has seen a boom in dispensaries. But you need to be careful about where you smoke, as anti-smoking regulations created for tobacco are still in effect in most public spaces. It's illegal to smoke weed at restaurants (indoor or outdoor), in parks, at beaches, in cars, or in public plazas. Most hotels, also, do not allow smoking in their guest rooms. As well, those under 21 cannot legally purchase or use marijuana.

each week, plus info on resources for children with special needs, free activities, and more.

The first place to look for babysitting is in your hotel (better yet, ask about babysitting when you reserve). Many hotels have babysitting services or will provide you with lists of reliable sitters. If this doesn't pan out, call the **Baby Sitters' Guild** (babysittersguild.com; ✆ **212/682-0227**). The sitters are licensed, insured, and bonded, and can even take your child on outings.

Hospitals The following hospitals have 24-hour emergency rooms. Don't forget your insurance card. **Downtown: New York Presbyterian Hospital,** 170 William St. between Beekman and Spruce streets (✆ **212/312-5000**). **Midtown: Bellevue Hospital Center,** 462 First Ave. at 27th Street (✆ **212/562-4141**); **New York University Langone Medical Center,** 570 First Ave. at 33rd Street (✆ **212/263-5550**); and **Mount Sinai West,** 1000 Tenth Ave. (✆ **212/523-4000**). **Upper West Side: Mount Sinai St. Luke's,** 419 W. 114th St. at Amsterdam Ave. (✆ **212/523-4000**); and **Columbia Presbyterian Medical Center,** 630 W. 168th St., between Broadway and Fort Washington Ave. (✆ **212/305-2500**). **Upper East Side: New York Presbyterian / Weill Cornell Medical Center** and **Komansky Center for Children's Health,** 525 E. 68th St. at York Ave. (✆ **212/746-5454**); **Lenox Hill Hospital,** 100 E. 77th St. between Park and Lexington aves. (✆ **212/434-3030**); and **Mount Sinai Medical Center,** Madison Ave. and E. 101st St. (✆ **212/241-6639**).

Internet & Wi-Fi New York is becoming one big "hotspot" thanks to some 7,500 LinkNYC kiosks in all five boroughs (you'll see monolithic slabs all over Manhattan). The free Wi-Fi they provide is 100 times stronger than found in other U.S. metropolitan areas. The large panels also have outlets for charging devices. You can see current LinkNYC spots at link.nyc/find-a-link.html. You can also get connected in almost all NYC subway stations, all Starbucks, and all public libraries. Your hotel will also provide free Wi-Fi.

Legal Aid If accused of a serious offense, say and do nothing before consulting a lawyer. In the U.S., the burden is on the state to prove a person's guilt beyond a reasonable doubt, and everyone has the right to remain silent, whether they are suspected of a crime or actually arrested. Once arrested, a person can make one telephone call to a party of his or her choice. The international visitor should call his or her embassy or consulate.

LGBTQ+ Travelers Gay and lesbian travelers need very little special advice when it comes to New York City. With one of the largest and most politically active gay populations in the world, and dozens of gay bars and clubs (see chapter 8), you should feel welcomed and accepted in the Big Apple. After all, this is where the Broadway musical was born, right?

Traditionally, the gay community of New York has been centered around Christopher Street in the West Village, but in recent decades it has expanded to Chelsea and Hell's Kitchen. If you're a bar-hopper, these are the three areas you'll want to explore, though gay bars are in every neighborhood of the city, just as there are gay people in every neighborhood.

Mail At press time, domestic postage rates were 78¢ for a 1 ounce letter. For more information go to **usps.com**.

Money & Costs In terms of how much to bring: not that much in cash. You never have to carry too much cash in New York, and while the city's pretty safe, it's best not to overstuff your wallet (although always make sure you have at least $20 in cash for small purchases).

In most Manhattan neighborhoods, there's a bank with **ATMs** (automated teller machines) every few blocks. Most delis have an ATM on the premises, so if you need cash quickly, you're probably never more than about 100 ft. away from one.

Packing The most important item in your

WHAT THINGS COST IN NEW YORK CITY	US$
Cab from JFK Airport to Manhattan (plus tolls, fees, and tip)	70.00
Single full-fare subway or bus ride	3.00
Standard ticket to a NY Yankees game	60.00
Pint of beer (draft pilsner or lager)	10.00
Cup of coffee in a cafe or bar	5.00
Coca-Cola in a cafe or bar	4.00
Cocktail in a bar	18.00
Bottle of water	2.00
Admission to Museum of Modern Art	30.00
Movie ticket	17.00
Walking tour	40.00
Discount ticket to a Broadway show	45.00–85.00
Full-price ticket to a Broadway show (orchestra)	145.00+

suitcase will be a pair of very comfortable shoes, because your dogs are gonna be barking! This is a walking city, and what with getting from place to place and trudging through the marble museum halls, a springy, supportive pair of shoes is essential (you may want to bring two pairs to increase your ease). Other than that, fill your suitcase with what pleases you most at home: Very few New Yorkers have the budget or time to dress like Sarah Jessica Parker. Unless you plan on going to the opera or a fancy restaurant, smart casual clothes should suffice.

Dressing appropriately for the weather is also key, so be sure to check the chart on p. 389 for the average temperatures at various times of the year. If you're visiting in fall or spring (mid-Sept to mid-Nov and mid-Mar to mid-May), bring clothes you can layer, as a balmy afternoon can turn chilly once the sun goes down.

Police Dial ✆ **911** in an emergency; otherwise, call ✆ **646/610-5000** (NYPD Switchboard) for the number of the nearest precinct. For non-emergency matters, call ✆ **311.**

Safety The most recent FBI report rated New York City as one of the safest large cities in the United States, with a crime rate well below the national average. Some 80% of the crimes were concentrated in outer borough precincts that tourists rarely visit. But it's best to err on the side of safety. So, trust your instincts and take the same precautions you'd take in any large city: Don't flash your money or carry too much of it at one time; stay in well-lit, crowded areas.

In general, the subways are safe (in fact, as we go to press, incident rates are back to their low 2019 levels). Still, always keep a hand on your belongings. When using the subway, **don't wait for trains near the edge of the platform** or on extreme ends of a station. During non-rush hours, wait for the train in view of the token-booth clerk or under the yellow DURING OFF HOURS TRAINS STOP HERE signs, and ride in the train conductor's car (usually in the center of the train; you'll see their heads stick out of the window when the doors open). Choose crowded cars over empty ones—there's safety in numbers.

Senior Travel New York subway and bus fares are half-price ($1.50) for people 65 and older. Many museums and sights (and some theaters and performance halls) offer discounted admittance and tickets to seniors; ask!

Many hotels offer senior discounts, but they may not be as good as the regular discounts one gets through bargain websites, so always check before pulling out your AARP card.

Smoking Smoking is prohibited on all public transportation; in the lobbies of hotels and office buildings; in taxis, bars, parks, beaches, and restaurants; and in most shops.

Student Travel Almost every museum in New York has student discounts, so student travelers should bring their school IDs with them.

Taxes **Sales tax** is 8.875% on meals, most goods, and some services. **Hotel tax** is 5.875%. **Parking garage tax** is 18.375%. The United States has no value-added tax (VAT) or other indirect tax at the national level.

Telephones Generally, hotel surcharges on long-distance and local calls are astronomical—when your room even has a phone!—so you're better off using your **cellphone.**

To make a **local call** in one of the five boroughs, **dial 1,** followed by the area code and the seven-digit number. **To make calls within the United States and to Canada,** dial 1. **For other international calls,** dial 011, followed by the country code, city code, and the number you are calling.

Calls to area codes **800, 888, 855, 877,** and **866** are toll-free. For directory assistance, dial ✆ **411** for numbers across the U.S. and Canada.

Mobile Phones: It's a good bet that your phone will work in New York City, but take a look at your wireless company's coverage map on its website before heading out. There's also the savvy option of using messaging apps like WhatsApp and Signal at Wi-Fi hotspots for free and very cheap calling.

Time The continental United States is divided into **four time zones:** Eastern Standard Time (EST), Central Standard Time (CST), Mountain Standard Time (MST), and Pacific Standard Time (PST). Alaska and Hawaii have their own zones. For example, when it's noon in New York City (EST), it's 5pm in London (GMT), 11am in Chicago (CST), 10am in Denver (MST), 9am in Los Angeles (PST), 7am in Honolulu (HST), and 2am the next day in Sydney.

Daylight saving time (summer time) is in effect from 2am on the second Sunday in March to 2am on the first Sunday in November. Daylight saving time moves the clock 1 hour ahead of standard time.

Tipping In hotels, tip **bellhops** at least $2 per bag and tip the **chamber staff** $2 to $4 per day (more if you've left a big mess). Tip the **doorman** or **concierge** only if they have provided you with some specific service (for example, calling a cab for you or obtaining difficult-to-get theater tickets). Tip the **valet-parking attendant** $5 every time you get your car.

In restaurants, bars, and nightclubs, tip **service staff** and **bartenders** 18% to 20% of the check (or you can double the tax on the check, which is 16%, and add a hair more). Tip **checkroom attendants** $2 per garment and tip **valet-parking attendants** $5 per vehicle.

As for other service personnel, tip **cab drivers** 15% to 20% of the fare; tip **skycaps** at airports at least $2 per bag ($3–$4 if you have heavy luggage); and tip **hairdressers, barbers,** and **massage therapists** 18% to 20%.

Toilets You won't find many public toilets on the streets in New York City, but they can be found in hotel lobbies, bars, restaurants, museums, parks, department stores, and railway and bus stations. Large hotels and fast-food restaurants are often the best bet for clean facilities.

You can find relief at the New York Public Library's main building on Fifth Avenue just south of 42nd St., or at Grand Central Terminal, at 42nd Street between Park and Lexington aves. In Times Square, head to 1 Times Square and use the very nice bathrooms upstairs for $2. Your best bet in other areas is Starbucks or another city java chain—you can't go more than a few blocks without seeing one.

Travelers with Disabilities New York is more accessible than ever to travelers with disabilities. Curb cuts in all sidewalks allow wheelchairs to go from street to sidewalk. The city's bus system is more wheelchair-friendly than the subways (only a third of subway stations are accessible). If you're looking for a ride, use the Uber app to order an UberWAV (wheelchair-accessible vehicle), or call ✆ **311** to get a hold of Accessible Dispatch—the 24/7 line that can help you hail a ride that fits your accessibility needs.

Most major sightseeing attractions are accessible. Even so, call first to be sure that the places you want to go to are fully accessible and lifts are operational.

Most hotels are ADA-compliant, but before you book, **ask lots of questions based on your needs.** Many city hotels are in older buildings that have been modified to meet requirements; elevators and bathrooms can be on the small side, and other impediments may exist. If you have mobility issues, you'll probably do best to book one of the city's newer hotels, which tend to be more accommodating. All **Broadway theaters** and many other performance venues provide total wheelchair accessibility; others provide partial accessibility. Many also offer lower-priced tickets for theatergoers with disabilities and their companions, though you'll need to reserve in advance.

Museums: In New York, the general rule is: the larger the museum, the more extensive its facilities for persons with disabilities. For example, the Metropolitan Museum of Art offers free rental of standard and extra-wide wheelchairs at all of its coat-check stands, regular sign-language and touch tours for the deaf and blind, attended elevators, and accessible bathrooms and water fountains. In smaller museums you'll find fewer such amenities, so call first for information.

Visitor Information

NYC & Company is the city's megaphone and its website, **nyctourism.com**, holds a wealth of free and ever-changing information.

Index

See also Accommodations and Restaurant indexes, below.

General Index

Accommodations

Restaurants

Photo Credits

Front cover: © Francois Roux / Shutterstock.com; p. i: CK Foto / Shutterstock; p. iii: Pandora Pictures / Shutterstock; p. 2: Courtesy of Edge NYC; p. 3: littleny / Shutterstock.com; p. 4: Pauline Frommer; p. 5: NEWAKP09/Shutterstock.com; p. 6: T photography /Shutterstock; p. 7: andersphoto/Shutterstock.com; p. 8: Ben Bryant / Shutterstock; p. 9: Popova Valeriya / Shutterstock; p. 10: Pauline Frommer; p. 11: Courtesy of The Museum of the City of New York / Filip Wolak; p. 12: HE Photography/Shutterstock.com; p. 13: Pauline Frommer; p. 14: T photography / Shutterstock; p. 16, top: Courtesy of Shabu Tatsu; p. 16, bottom: lev radin/Shutterstock.com; p. 17: Pauline Frommer; p. 18, top: Ron Adar/Shutterstock.com; p. 18, bottom: Courtesy of The Carlyle Hotel/ Andrew Moore; p. 20: Courtesy of The Statue of Liberty-Ellis Island Foundation / Paul Seibert; p. 22: Little Vignettes Photo/Shutterstock.com; p. 25: Murat Kucukkarakasli/Shutterstock.com; p. 26: Sean Pavone/ Shutterstock; p. 27: © Brooklyn Botanic Garden / Michael Stewart; p. 29: Brian Logan Photography/Shutterstock.com; p. 30: Mercedes Ponte/Shutterstock.com; p. 31: Topaz Le Tourneau; p. 32: Songquan Deng / Shutterstock; p. 34: Syndi Pilar/Shutterstock.com; p. 37: MNAphotography/Shutterstock; p. 39: Here Now/Shutterstock.com; p. 41: Pauline Frommer; p. 44: Courtesy of Hosteling International; p. 48: Courtesy of The Beekman; p. 50: Courtesy of Wall Street Hotel / Greg Powers Photography; p. 51, top & bottom: Pauline Frommer; p. 53: Pauline Frommer; p. 56: Pauline Frommer; p. 58: Pauline Frommer; p. 59: Nikolas Koenig/Courtesy of Faena Hotel; p. 64, top: Courtesy MADE Hotel; p. 64, bottom: Pauline Frommer; p. 65: Pauline Frommer; p. 66: Courtesy of 1 Hotel Central Park; p. 68: Courtesy of The Whitby Hotel / Simon Brown; p. 69: Courtesy of Casablanca Hotel / Stefano Pinci; p. 70: Courtesy of Civilian Hotel / Jason Greenspan photography; p. 71: Pauline Frommer; p. 72: Courtesy of The Pestana; p. 73: Courtesy of The Langham Hotel / Michael Weber Photography; p. 75: Courtesy of the Waldorf Hotel/Joe Thomas; p. 77: Courtesy of Hotel Beacon / Peter Vidor; p. 78: Pauline Frommer; p. 80: Courtesy of The Surrey Hotel; p. 81: Pauline Frommer; p. 82: Courtesy of The Hoxton / Emily Andrews; p. 84: Courtesy of Element Harrison—Newark; p. 87: Courtesy of BORO Hotel; p. 89: Courtesy of Frenchette / Melanie Dunea; p. 93: Courtesy of Xi'an Famous Foods / SIMIVIJAY; p. 94: Courtesy of Great New York Noodletown; p. 97: Pauline Frommer; p. 98: Courtesy of Russ & Daughters Café; p. 101: Alyssa Mattei; p. 102: Andrew Bezek/Courtesy Kabawa; p. 104: Bex Walton/Flickr; p. 105: The Institute of Culinary Education; p. 106: Pauline Frommer; p. 107, top: Justin Sisson/Courtesy of Smithereens; p. 107, bottom: Courtesy of Carnitas Ramirez / Stacie Joy; p. 109: Courtesy of Superiority Burger / Sunny Shokrae; p. 110: Pauline Frommer; p. 111: Pauline Frommer; p. 114: all Martien Mulder/Courtesy of Borgo; p. 115: Courtesy of Cote; p. 117: Pauline Frommer; p. 118: Pauline Frommer; p. 119: Pauline Frommer; p. 122: Courtesy of Shukette; p. 124: Courtesy Keens Steakhouse; p. 126: Serafina Marketing; p. 127: Pauline Frommer; p. 128, top: Pauline Frommer; p. 128, bottom: vsmusing/Shutterstock.com; p. 131: Pauline Frommer; p. 132: Pauline Frommer; p. 134: Courtesy of Tatiana; p. 136: Courtesy of Jacob's Pickles; p. 138: Pauline Frommer; p. 139: Pauline Frommer; p. 141: Rblfmr/Shutterstock; p. 142: Courtesy of Melba's / Amy Roth; p. 144: Courtesy of Aska; p. 146: Courtesy of Gage & Tollner / Lizzie Munro; p. 148: Michael Persico/Courtesy of Lasor Wolf; p. 150: Courtesy of Lilia Restaurant; p. 151: Pauline Frommer; p. 152: Courtesy of Strange Delight / Laura Murray; p. 155: Pauline Frommer; p. 156: Courtesy of Casa Enrique / Mariana Pelaez; p. 159: ventdusud/Shutterstock.com; p. 161, top: Pit Stock / Shutterstock; p. 161, bottom: Christopher Penler / Shutterstock; p. 164: Courtesy of Big Onion Tours / Dirk Vanderwalker; p. 166, top, right: Mohannad Khatib/Shutterstock.com; p. 164, bottom: David Thompson / Shutterstock; p. 168: Pauline Frommer; p. 169: John Westcott; p. 172: Courtesy of The Statue of Liberty-Ellis Island Foundation / National Park Service; p. 175: Serge Yatunin / Shutterstock; p. 177: Courtesy of International Center of Photography / Scott Rudd; p. 179: Photo by PRESS/Courtesy of the Museum at Eldridge Street; p. 180: Courtesy of The Tenement Musuem / Ryan Lahiff; p. 182: Courtesy Merchant's House Museum / Denis Vlasov; p. 184: Courtesy of The Whitney; p. 185: Apostolis Giontzis / Shutterstock; p. 188: Courtesy of Vessel /Max Loewenstein; p. 190: Courtesy of The Edge; p. 191: Kusska /Shutterstock; p. 192: EQRoy / Shutterstock; p. 194: Pauline Frommer; p. 196: bluestork/Shutterstock.com; p. 199: Cynthia Shirk / Shutterstock; p. 200: Courtesy of MSG Entertainment

Rana Faure; p. 201: KarlosWest / Shutterstock; p. 202: Maurizio De Mattei / Shutterstock; p. 204: AR Pictures / Shutterstock; p. 205: Pisaphotography / Shutterstock.com; p. 207: marcobrivio.photography / Shutterstock; p. 209: MACH Photos / Shutterstock.com; p. 210: 365 Focus Photography/Shutterstock.com; p. 211: Viktor_IS / Shutterstock.com; p. 213: Courtesy Cooper Hewitt; p. 216: Courtesy of The Frick Collection; p. 217: Tada Images/Shutterstock.com; p. 218: Brester Irina / Shutterstock; p. 219: Topaz Le Tourneau; p. 222: Topaz Le Tourneau; p. 223: Courtesy of American Folk Art Museum / Olya Vysotskaya; p. 224: mirigifford / Shutterstock.com; p. 226: STUDIO MELANGE / Shutterstock; p. 227: Jenna Bascom; courtesy of Museum of Arts and Design; p. 229: Topaz Le Tourneau; p. 230: Mark B. Schlemmer / Flickr; p. 232: Courtesy of The Bronx Zoo / Julie Larsen Maher; p. 233: Courtesy of New York Botanical Garden / Marlon Co; p. 234: Kolin Mendez Photography/Courtesy of The Brooklyn Musuem; p. 237: Christian Mueller / Shutterstock; p. 238: Inna_liapko/Shutterstock.com; p. 239: Courtesy of Industry City; p. 240: mirigifford/Shutterstock.com; p. 241: Pauline Frommer; p. 242: Courtesy of The Museum of the Moving Image / Thanassi Karageorgiou; p. 243: Courtesy of MoMA PS1 / Steven Paneccasio; p. 245: Courtesy of The Brooklyn Children's Museum / Winston Williams; p. 246: Courtesy of New York Hall of Science / Andrew Kelly; p. 247: Frank Roux/Shutterstock.com; p. 250: Lewis Tse / Shutterstock; p. 253: Courtesy of City Fit Tours; p. 254: Courtesy of Bryant Park / Colin Miller; p. 255: solepsizm/Shutterstock.com; p. 256: Courtesy of Governors Island / Julienne Schaer; p. 258: Hudson River Park; p. 259: Elzbieta Sekowska / Shutterstock; p. 261: Pauline Frommer; p. 263: Courtesy of Circle Line Sightseeing Cruises; p. 265: Courtesy of On Location Tours; p. 267: Francois Roux/Shutterstock.com; p. 270: Ttstudio / Shutterstock; p. 272: Oscity / Shutterstock; p. 273: Mariusz Lopusiewicz/Shutterstock.com; p. 274: Courtesy of South Street Seaport Museum / Richard Bowditch; p. 277: Angel L / Shutterstock; p. 278: Felix Lipov / Shutterstock; p. 279: Sean Pavone / Shutterstock; p. 281: Here Now / Shutterstock; p. 284: Rblfmr / Shutterstock; p. 286: Alerii Lavtushenko / Shutterstock.com; p. 288: MisterStock / Shutterstock; p. 290: Rolf_52 / Shutterstock.com; p. 294: Popova Valeriya / Shutterstock; p. 295: Alan Kolnick/Shutterstock.com; p. 296: Ryan DeBerardinis/Shutterstock.com; p. 298: littlenySTOCK / Shutterstock.com; p. 300: xbrchx/Shutterstock.com; p. 301: Pauline Frommer; p. 303: raw18/Shutterstock.com; p. 304: Becauz Gao/ Shutterstock; p. 306: Cindy Trinh/Courtesy Pearl River; p. 307: Courtesy of Dienst + Dotter Antikviteter / Weston Wells; p. 308: Courtesy of C.O. Bigelow; p. 309: Pauline Frommer; p. 310: Courtesy of Books Are Magic; p. 312: Emily Geraghty/Shutterstock.com; p. 313: EQRoy / Shutterstock; p. 315, top and bottom: Pauline Frommer; p. 318, top right: Dutch_Photos/Shutterstock.com; p. 318, bottom: Courtesy of E.A.T. Gift Shop / Romy Macari; p. 319: Courtesy of John Derian; p. 320: Pauline Frommer; p. 321: J T Tucker/ Shutterstock.com; p. 323: Courtesy of Fish's Eddy; p. 324, top right: Courtesy of Whisk; p. 324, bottom: Pauline Frommer; p. 325: Pauline Frommer; p. 327: Alan Kolnik/Shutterstock.com; p. 328: Pauline Frommer; p. 329: Pauline Frommer; p. 331: Jerome LABOUYRIE / Shutterstock; p. 333: Courtesy of TDF; p. 337, top: Courtesy of St. Ann's Warehouse / Richard Termine; p. 337, bottom: Courtesy of The New Victory Theater/ Hans-Juergen Herrmann; p. 338: Pauline Frommer; p. 341: Courtesy of American Ballet Theatre / Gene Schiavone; p. 343: lev radin / Shutterstock; p. 345: Courtesy of The Shed / Brett Beyer; p. 347: Pauline Frommer; p. 349, top left: Courtesy of Big Apple Jazz Tours / Stacy Taru; p. 349, bottom: Courtesy of The Jazz Gallery; p. 351: Courtesy of Caveat / Arin Sangurai; p. 353: Debby Wong / Shutterstock; p. 355: Bex Walton/Flickr; p. 356: Pauline Frommer; p. 359: Brian Logan/Shutterstock.com; p. 361, top: Courtesy of Mace / John Shyloski; p. 361, bottom: Courtesy of Flatiron Room; p. 363: Courtesy of Dear Irving on Hudson / Eric Medsker; p. 365, top: MJ; p. 365, bottom: Courtesy of Ophelia Lounge; p. 366: Pauline Frommer; p. 367: Courtesy of The Honey Well; p. 369: Courtesy Dutch Kills & Debbies; p. 372: Courtesy of Xanadu Roller Arts; p. 375: Pauline Frommer; back cover: © Mulevich / shutterstock.com.